Looking Out the Window,
Talking to the Person Next to Me

My Life in Airplanes

Eric Rush

Text and Cover Copyright © 2014 by Eric Eugene Rush

First Edition

ISBN 978-0-9960127-0-6

Also by Eric Rush
Light & Dark

Published by
Eric Eugene Rush
www.ericrush.com

When I was a kid in school, teachers complained that all I wanted to do was look out the window and talk to the person next to me.

So when I grew up, I got this great job where all I do is look out the window and talk to the person next to me.

— Anonymous pilot

For those who paid for this
And for those who benefited

Memory is a tricky thing — subjective, malleable to the needs of narrative or the fog of time. Some linguists believe that preliterate societies used myths to preserve their collective memories, and it seems possible, or at least poetic, that the style of memory is toward constructive storymaking, not simple retention. We remember the stories we tell about our lives; we invent our lives in the remembering.

—John Leland

Author's note:

I began keeping a record of my flying career thinking that perhaps my then unborn grandchildren might like to know what Grandpa did for a living at the end of the 20th century.

I don't want to intrude on anyone's privacy or embarrass anyone except perhaps myself. Where I've changed names, I've said so.

All pilots are certain they know how to run an airline better than management does. Commentary on corporate and decision making is neither comprehensive nor necessarily accurate. It is perception only.

There is a hand-tinted, framed photo of my mother and me taken by my father in Granville, Ohio, in 1944 when I was not yet two. I am standing atop a sundial at Denison College in maroon corduroy overalls. My mother is standing beside the sundial, holding me at the waist to keep me from falling, looking up at me and smiling. I am looking up, pointing at the sky, and yelling, P'ane! P'ane!

Student Pilot

One thing I did not want to do on my first solo flight was lose count of landings. A white-haired grandmother had lost count when she soloed a few days before my instructor signed my logbook and kicked me out of the nest. After the last of her traditional three landings, she called in on the radio to ask how many she'd made, and those of us watching chuckled and wondered aloud how anyone, on such a momentous occasion, could lose track.

I did not want to lose count of landings.

The first thing I did wrong on my first lesson was try to talk into the back side of the microphone. That was not a good sign, as I was a radio announcer at the time. The man in the control tower said I was unreadable. My instructor, a friend since childhood, laughed. My three-year-old daughter, riding illegally in the small baggage area behind the little Cessna's two seats, didn't get the joke.

Neither that first lesson on a wet and windy day in March of 1975 nor the next two lessons were part of a government-approved syllabus. I could not afford flying lessons. Forrest was going to teach me in his own airplane for the cost of fuel. The old Stinson 10-A, a wood and steel and fabric airplane, was having its rotted horizontal stabilizer rebuilt, so I'd rented the high-winged Cessna 150 for an hour at Forrest's employee rate in Renton, Washington, and he gave me my first lesson.

Katrina watched from her perch behind the seats as I followed Forrest around the airplane, squinting into blowing rain as he unhooked tiedown chains, looked for damage and defects, checked oil, and drained a little fuel from tanks in each wing into a clear plastic cup to look for water.

If Forrest had been a swimming instructor, he would have first thrown a new student into deep water to see how much he knew. I remember little of that first hour, but I do remember my first attempt to get the airplane back on the ground.

I did not realize the precision and authority with which a metal wing cleaves invisible air. As we turned over Lake Washington and descended toward the runway, I was afraid of driving nose first into the pavement. I thought—no, I *felt*—it was necessary to stop descending early, that the airplane's momentum would make it continue on its downward slant for a few seconds. I pulled the nose up and leveled off perhaps thirty feet above the runway, and, as the airplane ran out of flying speed, Forrest took over and finished landing. My log records three landings that day, but I don't remember the other two.

In the middle of April, Forrest flew the repaired Stinson to Port Angeles, where I lived, to give me my second lesson.

The red airplane, with its high wing and oversized vertical stabilizer, is cute in the way that Walt Disney's Dumbo is cute. The airplane's tail rested on a wheel that might have been scavenged from a grocery cart. Tailwheel airplanes at rest look jauntier than do tricycle-gear airplanes sitting sedately on even keel.

Katrina rode legally that time, belted into a small jump seat behind side-by-side pilots' seats. The old airplane was not as easy to fly or land as the Cessna. I flew basic maneuvers—climbs, turns, and descents—and Forrest made the landing.

He was a few miles east of Port Angeles that evening when he heard a loud *bang* overhead. The control yoke shuddered in his hands, and rudder pedals hammered the soles of his feet. Wind noise, loud in that airplane, became louder.

The nearest airport was almost directly below, a short, residential runway at Diamond Point. Forrest landed and got out to look at his airplane. The fabric skin had ripped loose just behind the top of the Plexiglas windshield and stripped back in the wind until what had been the forward end of the fabric fluttered like a flag against rudder and elevators. Most pilots would have called it a day and headed for the nearest bar. Forrest cut off the streamer of canvas with his knife and flew home.

The mechanic who had rebuilt the horizontal stabilizer inspected the Stinson the next day. Any one of half a dozen major defects should have grounded the airplane on its previous annual inspection. Repairs would take months.

Hey, Rush, you wanna go flyin'?

I was fresh out of high school with no idea what to do with my life. My enjoyment of flying was in books. I was a lineboy at the brand new Jefferson County Airport near Denver, driving fuel trucks, pumping gas, pushing small airplanes in and out of hangars, and sweeping floors. There was no control tower, and when there were two of us on duty and nothing was going on, we relieved boredom by drag racing the 80- and 100-octane fuel trucks on the runway.

Did I want to go flying? I didn't know my co-worker well and had no idea of his flying ability. I did know that people got killed in little airplanes.
No thanks, I said. Not today.

Forrest and I went up in another Cessna 150 at Renton early in July. I practiced flying turns and circles, and then we flew to the less busy airport at nearby Auburn. After a couple of tolerable landings, I began to think that maybe I'd get the hang of flying after all, but three lessons in four months was not going to get the job done. The Stinson was a long way from getting back into the air.

The handwriting in my logbook changed on the fourth line. I couldn't wait for the Stinson's resurrection. I was nervous on my first lesson with a new instructor and almost ran off the runway.

For a minimum-wage worker who changed jobs every few months, the expense of learning to fly was an obstacle so forbidding that I'd never allowed myself to consider it.

In the summer of 1974, Stu MacPherson, full-time dentist and part-time barnstormer, flew his 1929 Travelaire biplane to Port Angeles to join his friend Richard Bach in promoting the movie of Bach's book, *Nothing by Chance*. The ancient airplanes attracted crowds and Cap'n Mac stayed through the weekend, barnstorming in the old tradition, selling short hops in his open-cockpit biplane. My wife and daughter and I went for a ride, the three of us in the front cockpit, and Cap'n Mac flying from the rear.

I'd been up in small airplanes a few times by then, but never in an open cockpit behind a clattering radial engine. Riding in airplanes was okay, but it hadn't captured me the way books by Gann and Bach and Saint-Exupéry had.

Propeller blast over the Plexiglas windscreen in Cap'n Mac's biplane hit me just above the eyes, whipping my hair and making my scalp tingle. I looked out at steel wires sparkling between wings in the last golden light of day, watched fabric skin vibrate in the air. Flying became magic then. When we landed and climbed out of the cockpit, onto the wing, and down to the ground, I could not stop grinning. Fourteen years after graduating from high school, I finally knew what I was going to do with my life.

Once flying became possible, it became necessary.

4

The Port Angeles airport had been a P-38 fighter base during World War II. The tall, white, wood-framed control tower stood empty and unused. The flight school was just one part of Earl Pearson's fixed base operation. The FBO included airplane sales, rentals, maintenance, a radio shop, fuel service, charters, and a small airline flying three trips a day to Seattle with a twin-engine Cessna 402. A small building next to the control tower contained office, ticket counter, and flight school and served as a lounge where passengers waited and where students, flight instructors, pilots, and airport bums sat around drinking coffee and telling stories. I asked about instructors. I wanted someone who would not allow me to carry over into flying the general sloppiness of my disorganized life.

The airplane cost eighteen dollars an hour, an instructor five dollars more. We borrowed eight hundred dollars against my wife's car.

My new instructor was a couple of years younger than I. Paul looked at the three entries in my log and took me outside to a row of airplanes tied down in grass beside the asphalt taxiway. He, in jeans and sport shirt, looked at me, in coat and tie, and said I didn't have to dress up for lessons.

I'd made a disparaging comment about dress codes when I was in high school and was surprised my father disagreed with me. "It's good for discipline," he said. "You don't see boys in coats and ties playing grab-ass in the halls."

"Clothes make the man," Mark Twain said in another context. If dressing sharp made my thinking sharper, I wanted that in my favor.

I thought moccasins would give me a better feel for rudder pedals.

"Hmph," Paul said. "I learned to fly in combat boots."

He followed me around a four-seat Cessna 172 as I unfastened chains from wing struts and tail. I checked for loose bolts and missing rivets, for frayed control cables where they attached to ailerons, elevator, and rudder. I checked oil, drained fuel into a clear plastic vial to check for water, and climbed onto the built-in steps on fuselage and wing struts to look into fuel tanks and check that caps were on tight. Once strapped into our seats—student on the left, instructor on the right—I read the checklist aloud, then turned the key to start the engine.

My instructor didn't say much beyond terse instructions of what to do next. Because the airport did not have traffic controllers, and because some airplanes do not have radios, we turned a full circle to search the sky for landing airplanes. I announced our departure on the radio and taxied onto the runway, steering the nosewheel with rudder pedals to line up on the centerline. My right hand pushed the throttle all the way in, and away we went. In trying to track the centerline, I increased pressure on the wrong pedal and almost ran us off the side of the runway before lifting free of earth and entering the sky.

My logbook says we reviewed climbs, descents, turns, and—the hard one—straight and level flight. We spent much of the hour flying slowly, the stall warning buzzing almost continuously.

After we'd parked and tied down the airplane, I said, "I thought for a minute I was going to run off the runway on that first takeoff."

My instructor looked at me with a small smile. "Yeah," he said. "I kinda thought so, too."

Newspapers and TV always get it wrong. Airplane engines don't stall. Airplane wings stall.

At high speed, water skis lie nearly flat on the surface. When the boat slows, skis point higher to maintain lift. There is a speed below which no increase in angle will keep skis and skier on the surface. That is stall speed. It's the same with wings. Skiers sink until they reach equilibrium and float, but airplanes sink to the ground.

Rudder pedals work backwards.

The controls for pitch and roll make intuitive sense. Push the control stick—or yoke, if the stick has a steering wheel on it—forward and the nose follows and pitches down. Push or turn it left or right, and the airplane banks in the same direction. The airplane rotates the same direction around an axis as the control does. Push a rudder pedal, though, and the airplane turns toward that pedal, the opposite of what a child's sled does in response to pressure on its steering bar.

When a tractor isn't turning tight enough, you push the brake pedal on the side you want to turn toward. I thought of rudder pedals as wheel brakes until their proper function wore a groove in my brain. That was made easier by the fact that Cessna rudder pedals, when tipped forward with toe pressure, *are* the brakes for their respective wheels.

6

I should have cancelled my lesson. I'd been up late and I was tired and a little hung over, but I was eager to continue. We practiced landings, touch-and-go landings to save time and money. After the airplane is on the ground but still at speed, you raise flaps, reset pitch trim, and advance the throttle to full power and take off again. There is plenty of time to do all that, even for a student.

The throttle is a black knob on the end of a metal shaft. The engine is at idle when the knob is pulled out from the panel as far as it will go, about four inches. When it's pushed all the way forward, the engine is at full throttle. It's difficult to adjust power precisely without extending your index finger along the throttle shaft and resting your fingertip on the instrument panel. Holding the throttle that way becomes automatic.

I was thinking more about the transition from landing to takeoff than on following through with the landing. I was getting ahead of the airplane the way a shortstop sometimes thinks about the throw before he makes the catch and drops the ball. Just because wheels are on the ground doesn't mean they're going to stay there. The main gear chirped and I immediately looked inside as I took my hand off the throttle to reach for the flap switch.

"Add power," my instructor said.

"Hunh?"

I looked out at the runway and my hand went back to the throttle, index finger extended to the panel. We were back in the air and running out of flying speed. I was slow to assess the situation and pushed in the throttle only a little.

"More power!" Paul commanded and, as the airplane began to fall out of the sky, he slammed the throttle all the way to the panel in time to salvage what would have been a damaging conclusion to my bounced landing.

My extended finger, having nowhere to go, curled up the wrong way, not in the direction knuckles are designed to bend. It turned purple and blue, and I wore an aluminum splint for weeks to protect it. My instructor almost felt bad, but better a bent finger than a bent airplane.

Perhaps Paul sensed my impatience when our lesson was canceled for lack of an airplane. He told me not to worry, that I'd solo before the week was out. I worried. I couldn't imagine ever being ready to fly alone.

Learning to cope with engine failure is fun. If I am paying attention, which I will learn to do eventually, I am constantly looking for places to land should the engine quit. My instructor pulls the throttle to idle and tells me my engine has failed. When the shimmering disk becomes a fluttering blade and the low roar of the engine becomes a puttering idle, eyes widen and heart rate rises.

Knowing this is an exercise, it's easy to overlook the airport while evaluating the best corn field or cow pasture or clearing in the forest. While evaluating terrain, I need to consider wind direction. Airplanes and birds land into the wind for the same reason. Meanwhile, the airplane is descending. If there is only one small clearing within gliding distance, that will be my runway. If the ground is flat and choices are many, it's difficult to pick one.

We don't go all the way to the ground in practice. As soon as we are low enough to tell whether my approach will be successful or not, low enough for me to get a sense of what an off-airport landing looks like, my instructor smoothly advances the throttle to full power and we climb back to our place in the sky.

Three lessons in three days. Landing practice, stall recovery, emergencies. More landing practice. My landings weren't consistently smooth. Five days went by before I flew again.

I thought it strange that my instructor had me taxi back toward the tiedowns after only half an hour. I thought I was doing pretty well. He was already writing in my logbook. Maybe he was in a hurry because he had to fly a charter, or maybe he was late for his next student. He told me to shut the engine down right there on the taxiway. I pulled the red mixture control knob and the engine starved and died. He handed me my logbook with his signoff for solo flight in a Cessna 172 and told me to make three takeoffs and three landings to a full stop, taxiing back to the end of the runway for each takeoff. Then he opened the door and got out and walked up the hill to the flight school.

I did not feel ready. I pulled the laminated checklist from its pocket in the door and started at the beginning. The airplane got off the ground more quickly with just me aboard.

My first landing was smooth. I turned off the runway and taxied back. The next landing was okay, but not as good as the first. As I taxied back again, I tried to figure how what I'd done differently. Instead of improving, each landing was worse than the one before. Perhaps I was thinking too much and trying too hard. I turned off the runway and couldn't remember if I'd made three landings or only two.

Earl Pearson answered the radio. "Go ahead and make another one," he said. "Can't hurt anything." He obviously hadn't seen that last one.

I took off and landed again. The fact that I'd flown an airplane alone did not sink in for hours.

A few days later, my instructor got out of the airplane and sent me off to the practice area several miles east of the airport, out of traffic lanes and over the fields and pastures of Dungeness. As I pointed the airplane east and climbed from the runway, the Cascade Mountains on the horizon rose into the sky. An urge to keep going and fly forever came over me, a sudden and thrilling sense of freedom. Flying alone that August afternoon, free in three dimensions and dependent entirely on my own meager skills to keep me alive, was the most liberating feeling I have ever known. But exhilaration was momentary. It wasn't my airplane, so I'd have to bring it back. Besides, I'd run out of fuel in four hours, and I'd need to pee sooner than that.

Learning to fly wasn't all fun. It's easy to know which way is up when the difference between sky and earth is obvious, but rudder pedals aren't the only things in airplanes that work backwards. Sitting at a desk and designing the attitude indicator—the artificial horizon—must have been easy.

An airplane changes pitch and bank, but the earth's horizon remains fixed. Logically, an instrument depicting the airplane's relationship to the horizon should have a representation of the horizon that stays parallel to the real horizon. The airplane symbol in the center of the instrument should remain fixed so it will do exactly what the airplane does. It looks good on paper, but most beginning pilots, when trying to keep the airplane's wings level solely by watching that instrument, bank the wrong way.

When the artificial horizon appears to tilt to the right, it's because the airplane has banked to the left. The brain perceives the horizon in the instrument tilting to the right, and the student turns the yoke left to try to return that line to horizontal. Immediately, he sees the response in the instrument is opposite what he wanted and turns the yoke back to the right.

The airplane levels by banking to the right while the artificial (and the real) horizon appears to rotate to the left. Every airplane in the sky has that logically correct but intuitively backward instrument, and every pilot learns to keep the airplane right side up with reference to it.

Student pilots today, raised on video games and skilled in manipulating images on screens, may wonder what this goofy old man is talking about, but I confess that, years later, when very tired in the dark of night, I occasionally had the impulse to level the wings of a Boeing 727 by turning the yoke the wrong direction.

Even student pilots needs to be able to fly on instruments well enough to control the airplane if they accidentally fly into clouds or become disoriented at night. To simulate flying in clouds, a student wears a plastic visor that blocks vision up and to both sides. Nothing is in view but the instrument panel.

Without reference to instruments, it is impossible to keep an airplane upright when you can't see where earth ends and sky begins. One wing drops a little, and the airplane begins a gentle turn, but you don't feel the subtle change. The nose drops a little in a turn, but you don't feel that, either, and the airplane speeds up as it begins to descend. You know it's going faster because you hear it. If you don't look at your instruments, or if you don't *believe* the instruments, you will pull back on the yoke to pull up the nose and reduce speed. But pulling back tightens the turn which drops the nose more which speeds up the airplane more which causes you to pull back more and, as the airplane spirals down faster and faster and the turn becomes tighter and tighter, you panic, and any hope of understanding the situation and recovering from it is gone.

It doesn't take much. On a moonless night far from cities, the line between stars in the sky and lights on the ground is uncertain. Sometimes being over dark water is enough, especially if clouds block part of the sky and create a false horizon where stars end and blackness begins. You turn your head to talk to the person next to you, or you drop your chart on the floor and bend down to retrieve it. Head movement puts fluid in your ears in motion, and your brain senses unbalance and creates a false horizon to match misperception.

If you can see the real horizon, that visual image overrides the false one, and you are not aware of conflict. But on a dark night, with no city lights to define earth, your brain will see some lights as stars and some stars as lights in its effort to reconcile the difference between what inner ears feel and what eyes see. You bank the airplane to level the wings with the false horizon and descent begins.

Not for nothing has this been called, from the days of Orville and Wilbur, the Graveyard Spiral. It is almost certainly what caused young John Kennedy to crash into the sea.

It's not enough to be able to maintain control without looking outside. I had to learn to stabilize the airplane with reference to instruments after it had gone out of control and I'd become disoriented. I have never had a problem with motion sickness. My instructor did his best to change that.

Right after takeoff, the visor came down and I flew on instruments, following my instructor's instructions as to heading and altitude. After we climbed to three thousand feet, he directed me through turns so he could search the sky for traffic. Then he told me to let go of the yoke and put my feet flat on the floor and close my eyes and point my head down. The airplane lurched this way and that in climbs and dives, steep turns and slips. After a few seconds, I had no idea which way was up. Then he said, "You have the airplane."

What I was supposed to do then was put hands and feet on the controls and look at the instruments to see what our situation was and restore the airplane to level flight and normal speed. I wouldn't have wanted to fly that lesson after eating a greasy cheeseburger and fries.

I looked forward to cross-country flying. After being confined to the back yard, I'd be allowed to play in the neighborhood.

First, paperwork—plotting courses, calculating times, looking up radio frequencies, checking weather, and filing a flight plan with the FAA Flight Service Station in Seattle by telephone. All that for a flight to airports I could almost see from Port Angeles if I stood on a chair.

Looking out the window to know where I was worked just fine on that bright, clear day with wisps of ground fog evaporating in the morning sun. Looking out the window was what I preferred anyway, enthralled with seeing the earth below as a detailed map in full color. Decades later, the allure of flying remains the same, looking down on the earth from the sky.

My instructor didn't think much of Flight Following, but it was in the course and he had to teach it. You call the air traffic controller in your area on the radio, give him your airplane type and number, and tell him your altitude and where you are and where you're going. He gives you a four-digit code you dial into the transponder, and then he can tell which blip on his radar screen is you. Then, as you sail through the sky, he tells you where other airplanes are to help you see and avoid them. Flight Following is a bad idea. Shared responsibility is too often shirked responsibility.

The controller's primary duty is to airplanes on instrument flight plans. Flight Following is provided only when the controller has time for it. Murphy's Law being what it is, the controller will tell you about all the airplanes that are no danger to you, but he will be too busy to tell you about the one you're about to run into.

As we flew east over Port Townsend and entered busy Puget Sound northwest of Seattle, I called ATC and got a transponder code. When the controller told us of traffic, we looked hard to find the glints in the sky. Even though the airplanes in question might be several miles away and going away, failing to see them felt like letting the controller down.

And so it was that my instructor and I were searching the sky for an airplane crossing our course a few miles distant when a fast Beechcraft Bonanza shot across in front of us at exactly our altitude, so close that the span of time between seeing it streak past and feeling the bump of its wake was less than one second—zip-whump.

I looked at Paul with eyes huge and wide. He looked at me and shrugged. Meanwhile, the controller was telling us about another airplane that didn't matter, and we flew on.

A few years later, flying my own small Cessna into the blinding glare of the setting sun dead ahead, I called ATC to request Flight Following. Minutes later, a faster Cessna 310, flying the same direction and at the same altitude as I, almost ran me down. The pilot probably saw me at the last split-second when his squinting eyes saw my wings emerge from the sun. I heard the roar of engines as the twin swept over a few feet above me in a climbing turn.

My heart pounded in fright. I snatched up the microphone and yelled without preamble to the radar controller, *"Did you see that red-and-white three-ten that almost ran me down?"*

A couple of back-and-forths over several seconds with the man in the dark room re-established my identity. I explained what had happened. The controller, knowing the conversation was being recorded, said nothing for maybe half a minute. I calmed down enough to laugh at myself for identifying another airplane by color to a man looking at numbers on a glass screen. Then the controller told me of some innocuous airplane somewhere which I forced myself to ignore.

Before my checkride—a flight test and oral exam for a private license—I had to review and practice all maneuvers I'd been taught. I had to brush up on regulations and procedures for questions I might be asked. I'd missed only two questions on my written exam, but that had been months earlier, plenty of time for me to forget what I'd studied but perhaps not learned. And I had to know all pertinent information about a Cessna 172, including allowable weights, minimum and maximum speeds for various configurations, and proper speeds for different takeoffs, glides, and landing approaches. I flew five times in four days. Just after my instructor and I entered the traffic pattern for the last landing of the last day, the engine quit.

There are procedures to be followed when the engine dies. Checking the fuel tank selector is not the first thing on the list, but it's the first thing I did. My instructor had turned it to Off. Meanwhile, I was still at cruise speed when I should have immediately hauled the yoke back to trade excess airspeed for altitude. I'd have made the runway anyway, but I hadn't followed procedure.

I was glum as I tied the airplane down and trudged up the hill to the flight school. My instructor had gone ahead to fill out paperwork and, I suppose, to leave me alone with my thoughts. When I entered the building, he grilled me on proper procedure for engine failures.

The next day, he yanked the fuel mixture knob immediately after takeoff when we were only a few feet in the air. The engine stopped instantly. There was no time for checklists and procedures, nothing to do but lower the nose and land on remaining runway. Paul must have looked at my face, because he cackled with glee. But I passed forced landings.

In the early days of aviation, landing approaches were made with engine at idle, the airplane gliding to the runway. Engines often quit during landing until carburetor ice was understood and carburetor heat was added to engines. Depending on power rather than planning was not a reliable way to get to the runway. Being able to glide to a specific touchdown spot hones flying skill in general, and even pilots of jet airliners sometimes have to improvise power-off landings in odd places such as the Hudson River.

The airplanes I learned to fly in had forty degrees of flaps. They also had a placard on the panel that read, without explanation: Avoid Slips With Flaps Extended.

I asked my instructor what would happen if I put the airplane into a slip with full flaps. He told me to try it and find out. I throttled back and put flaps down. I pushed the left rudder pedal to its limit and turned the yoke far enough right to keep the airplane from turning.

We came down at a steep angle from the combined effects of flaps and slip. The airplane shuddered as air roiled by flaps and the semi-sideways flight path tumbled over the tail. There was no loss of control, just a disconcerting shaking and bucking of the entire airplane. The placard didn't say the maneuver was prohibited, so I thought no more about it until the day it saved my life.

Paul signed my logbook recommending me for a checkride. I asked about my lack of night flying. He said we'd pick that up later.

The chief pilot for Pearson Air's commuter airline and charter department was also chief instructor of record for the flight school. He had FAA approval to conduct checkrides and issue licenses. I knew him only to say Hello to. I was nervous as he asked questions about the airplane and regulations, nervous as I planned the cross-country flight we would begin as part of my ride.

A succession of squall lines blew through a few hours apart with clear, cold air between them. I was nervous as we waited for a gap between heavy rain showers, but once in the airplane, tension flowed away. We flew my planned course for a few minutes, just long enough for my examiner to see that I knew what I was doing.

As I flew required maneuvers, we kept an eye on weather moving down the Strait of Juan de Fuca from the ocean. We returned to the airport flying lower than pattern altitude to stay under scudding clouds. Even with an unfamiliar landing approach from lower than I was used to, I got the airplane back on the ground upright and taxied to the parking area. I was almost giddy as it sank in that I'd just accomplished something so far beyond reach that, until only fourteen months earlier, I'd not dared to dream it.

After paying the examiner's fee and buying my instructor a bottle of Scotch, I had seventeen dollars left from the eight hundred I'd borrowed. I immediately enrolled in the Commercial Pilot With Instrument Rating course. The GI Bill would pay 90% of the rest of my training, and Earl Pearson carried my 10% without interest for years.

The first thing most new pilots do is take their friends and family up for rides. I didn't feel competent to take anyone flying, and, until three weeks later, I didn't.

Pearson acquired a helicopter, and my instructor became the helicopter department. He had little time on his schedule for students, so I flew with any instructor available when I was.

I'd quit my job as announcer and engineer at a Port Angeles radio station to work as a plumber trainee. For a few weeks that autumn, I installed pipes in a new apartment complex under the approach to Runway 26. Pearson Air's twin-engine Cessna arrived from Seattle at ten, noon, and two-thirty, their arrivals signaling coffee breaks and lunch hour. Airplane engines roared overhead, unseen by me as I worked on my back in cold mud in a cramped crawl space while fumes from plastic glue destroyed my brain a few cells at a time and molten solder dripped up my sleeves. As I crawled out from under the building at break times, I thought of Pearson's pilots up there in clean, dry clothes.

Sunday was bright and crisp, and the quarter-inch of frost on the airplanes glistened in cold morning sun. Airplanes will not fly with frost on the wings, we are told, and that's close enough to absolute truth that it contributes to longevity to believe it. Sunshine melted the frost while I waited for my instructor, a man I'd not yet flown with.

After an hour of ground reference maneuvers and stall recovery in the practice area, Jim had me fly back the ten miles to the airport over the water, just off the beach at a hundred feet, lower than the cliffs at water's edge. I followed the curves of the shoreline, ground-reference maneuvering with the possibility of consequences. It wasn't in the syllabus, but it was good experience, controlling the airplane without thinking about what my hands and feet were doing. It didn't occur to me to ask what happens if someone else is flying the beach at a hundred feet in the other direction and you meet on a blind curve.

After another week of putting pipes together and sniffing glue, I spent another weekend flying and learned a lovely climbing reversal of course called a chandelle. When done the way the book instructed, it was pleasant enough, but when I steepened the climb and tightened the turn, it was more interesting and, when done accurately and smoothly, immensely more satisfying.

Lazy 8s were boring the way the book taught them, a continuous series of climbs, turns, and descents. I could never see the horizontal 8 the maneuver is named for. My friend Forrest flew them a little differently.

He started his Lazy 8 with a dive and pulled up into a steep climb. When he turned, he banked to ninety degrees as he began the next dive and leveled the wings before pulling up to start the second half. The maneuver was basically the same as the one in the book, but I liked Forrest's way better. In time, I flew them steep enough that the airplane described a shoelace loop with each climbing turn, and I could visualize the figure 8 on its side.

Extending a murky concept to its extreme often brings clarity, and not just in aviation.

Much of the course was repetition, solo practice to acquire enough flight time to meet the minimum required for a commercial license. Endless practice was never exciting and seldom interesting, so I sometimes flew just to be flying.

When fronts move through Puget Sound, wind splits and goes around the Olympic Mountains the way water goes around a rock in a river. Where streams of air meet again is the convergence zone, a line of turbulence extending several miles downwind to the northeast. Bad weather is always worse, and low clouds are thicker and lower in the convergence zone.

Strong southwest winds tumbled over and around the Olympics on a day I was free to fly. I planned to fly east past the mountains, then turn toward south toward good weather, just to be going somewhere. The only available airplane had no radio.

I flew above a scattered layer of clouds hung up in treetops and below a gray overcast a few thousand feet above me. When I turned the corner past the mountains, clouds below became solid. Visibility between layers was still good, though, so I pressed on. I had not yet learned to stifle my natural optimism, had not yet learned to consider the worst that could happen rather than assume the best.

Cloud layers were not sharply defined. After a few minutes, I could not tell where clear air ended and clouds began. Then I realized I was in them, in unbroken cloud near crowded airspace with no instrument clearance, no instrument rating, and no radio.

Pilots sometimes do stupid things when they are beginners, and I may have done more than my share. Such experiences are excellent teachers, if they don't kill you.

I took a deep breath, visualized where I was and where mountains were, and, on instruments, made a 180-degree turn to the left. Then I flew straight and level and waited. It was not possible to tell if I was truly in cloud or merely surrounded by gray at some undefined distance. After only a minute or two, I could see the ground again.

A little learning is more dangerous than total ignorance. I knew enough about instrument charts to know I was below the altitudes of nearby airways, so I thought I had that part of the sky to myself. Maybe I did and maybe I didn't. I had no way of knowing if airplanes were being vectored for approaches and landings at nearby airports. Perhaps controllers were steering airplanes around the unidentified blip on their radar screens that was me. It's possible that, without a transponder, I didn't show on radar at all. I cringe even now when I think of that day.

That same afternoon, one of my instructors was flying practice instrument approaches at Bellingham with two students. One student flew and the other sat in back observing. Bellingham did not have radar control, so only one airplane at a time was allowed in the control zone on instruments. They had landed but could not get clearance to depart because someone else was on approach.

It's dark at five o'clock in the Pacific Northwest in December. Although weather was good enough at Bellingham to fly visually, it was not good enough to fly back to Port Angeles. The instructor elected to leave Bellingham and stay under the low clouds, and, when clear of the airport's control zone, get an instrument clearance directly from Navy controllers on Whidbey Island to return to Port Angeles. While he was doing that, the airplane smashed into the steep spine of Lummi Island. Tall trees stopped the airplane, and it fell upside down to the ground. The instructor smacked his head and was critically injured. Both students were not badly hurt. I did not admit then, even to myself, that I was less concerned with the instructor's damaged brain than I was with the fact that the airplane I needed for instrument training was gone.

On Christmas Eve, I went up to practice maneuvers for three repetitive hours. Scattered puffs of cloud were too small to hide another airplane, so I flew over and under and between them, flying like a playful bird rather than a commercial pilot student. I pretended my modern Cessna was a World War I Spad and fought dogfights with my shadow on cotton ball clouds.

I spent almost three hours in the air the last day of 1975, practicing the same old maneuvers over and over until Earl Pearson called on the radio and asked me to fly high enough to call one of his pilots flying a charter fifty miles west near Quillayute. I raised the pilot on the radio when I reached seven thousand feet and gave him the message. I'd never flown that high, and, as long as I was up there...

Airline pilots are required to breathe oxygen if the atmospheric pressure inside the airplane drops below what it is at ten thousand feet. I climbed over the Olympic Mountains, circling and sightseeing, increasing cabin heat and decreasing fuel mixture until I'd coaxed the airplane to sixteen thousand. I knew nothing of regulations governing flight at that altitude.

In blissful ignorance, with almost half the earth's atmosphere below me, I looked down on the mountains and noted my inability to correlate features on the ground to those on my chart. Interesting, I thought. Lack of oxygen really does mess up the mind.

I could see nearly all of Vancouver Island across the water to the north, the Cascade Mountains from Canada to Oregon, and all of Puget Sound. How much of my exhilaration was response to the view and how much to oxygen deprivation, I didn't know.

An instructor insisted I not use radio navigation on our night cross-country flight east to Paine Field and then on to Arlington. Navigating by looking out the window was not difficult with the familiar pattern of shorelines and islands visible even at night, but I was more conscious of the sounds of air brushing past aluminum and the engine's steady rumble. Perhaps increased awareness of engine sound was out of concern that it might quit and commit me to a night landing in trees. It was easy to see how, if he was not where he thought he was, a pilot could fly into a mountain at night before he knew it was there.

The winter moon was bright enough I could read instruments with panel lights off. Dark mountains on the right gave way to lights of Seattle to the southeast. I never turned toward Seattle until I had lights in sight, even when mountains were visible in moonlight. I could see low clouds between me and Bremerton, so I made a U-turn, toward lights and away from mountains.

Night air was smooth and the world was silver in moonlight. I lingered in the practice area near Sequim, reluctant to return to earth. The sky was mine alone. The radio was quiet. There were no red and green airplane lights anywhere I could see. So rather than fly a proper rectangular traffic pattern, I lined up with the runway ten miles out, and held speed and descent steady for the few minutes it took to reach the airport. I reminded myself to look around for airplanes and not be lulled by the sense that I was sitting still in the air, waiting for the runway to come to me.

Paul had me fly through the Olympic Mountains one windy afternoon much lower than would have been safe for me alone. Wind blowing upslope and down, swirling over ridges and around peaks, makes for a rough ride. We cinched seat belts tighter. A sharp downdraft jolted my spine as though I'd been dropped on my butt on a concrete floor. That was moderate turbulence? I didn't want an example of severe or extreme.

We flew parallel to ridges in the updraft, surfing with engine at idle. My instructor explained but did not demonstrate what it would be like on the lee side of the ridge where air twisted and tumbled like a river flowing over a weir. Wind never caused me serious trouble in mountain flying. All I had to do was watch the invisible air.

The commercial course required longer, more complicated solo cross-country flights. My planned route over Washington and Oregon would take most of the day. The airplane I'd scheduled got back late from what was supposed to be a short charter, and by the time I arrived at my planned lunch stop on the Oregon side of the Columbia River, it was early afternoon. My head ached from hunger.

I grew up where rivers flow east. Flying west down the Columbia, my skittery brain reverted. As I approached Troutdale, heading downstream, I called the tower and reported myself five miles west of the airport and received instructions for entering the pattern and landing. The instructions made no sense, but I couldn't pull over and stop to figure out what was wrong. I entered the pattern on the wrong side of the airport for the wrong runway and against traffic.

When I reported downwind, the controller couldn't see me. Controllers at busy airports frequented by students and amateurs are usually patient with idiots. By the time we got the situation sorted out, I'd used up that man's quota of patience for the day.

My inability to think clearly when hungry impressed me. I decided to make food part of my travel kit.

February isn't an ideal time for long trips in little airplanes. Even an instrument-rated pilot, which I was not, could get into trouble. My innate optimism could not always tell in advance the difference between adventure and danger.

A requisite for a commercial pilot's license was a long, solo cross-country flight of at least three legs. A large triangle will do, but a more ambitious journey suggested itself. My father lived in California that year.

Had I planned to fly down Interstate 5 and then home up the coast, I'd have had less headwind southbound and more tailwind on the return. But if I flew down the coast, the shoreline would be on the left side of the airplane and I'd have a better view. I chose scenery over economy.

My title for the article I wrote for *Private Pilot* magazine five years later was "Into the Valley" from Tennyson's ode to the ill-fated Light Brigade. The magazine preferred a title more to the point. I've changed only a few words from the published version.

Scud-running on Empty

> In seconds, my universe becomes soft, white, and still. My little airplane's engine seems hushed. The altimeter needle still points to 100 feet. Nothing is different from what it was a moment ago except that the Pacific surf can no longer be seen crashing onto the rocks below me and the cliffs and ridges of the California coast on my left have disappeared into whiteness. This nearness to death has come quietly and without violence....

A 3,000-mile solo cross-country flight isn't required for a commercial license, but what fledgling isn't eager to Go Somewhere? Why not fly all the way down the coast and visit Dad in Santa Barbara?

Ragged chunks of cumulus tumble across the February sky, spewing snow flurries into the mountains and forests of western Washington. I pace the flight school floor, eager to leave before the day is gone, but not eager to fly into snow.

The Cessna 172 gives no sign of impatience as it sits on the ramp. In it are charts and pencils, a sleeping bag and a suitcase, sandwiches and a water jug. The sun breaks through at noon and evaporates the trace of melting snow as I phone in my flight plan for the first leg, to North Bend on the Oregon coast.

I stand under the wing and rock it gently as my fuel tanks are filled at North Bend to ensure no air is trapped inside. I want every drop they will hold. The wind increases from the southwest and blows an overcast of stratocumulus in from the ocean. It takes forty-five minutes to fly the sixty miles to Gold Beach, and the thickening layer of cloud is bringing darkness early. In another half hour, though, I'll be in California.

Rain begins and wisps of cloud form below me. The deepening gloom has a substance apart from the onset of night. I turn back toward Gold Beach and immediately feel relief from a building anxiety of which I've not been aware until now.

I sleep in the airplane and by morning the rain has stopped. Southwest wind is gusting to thirty knots and sun is shining through breaks in the cloud. I should refuel, but my credit card isn't acceptable at Gold Beach. There's plenty of fuel left to fly to Half Moon Bay, maybe even to Salinas. And if I run low, there are plenty of airports along the way.

With the continuing headwind, Half Moon Bay becomes a more realistic fuel stop than Salinas. Crescent City Radio tells of scattered clouds and unlimited visibilities in the San Francisco Bay area, so even if wind increases or my calculations are off, I can easily make Santa Rosa.

A hundred miles south of Crescent City, the sky becomes overcast. I fly past Cape Mendocino just under the ragged ceiling at 500 feet. Visibility is easily five miles.

My sectional chart is upside down on my kneeboard so that looking at it is the same as looking straight ahead through the windscreen. Every time I pass and identify a village, a stream, a headland, or a tower, I make a pencil mark beside it and write the time to the nearest half minute so I always know exactly where I am.

Fort Bragg creeps past the wing and again I think of fuel. Weather is not improving, but the chart says Fort Bragg is a private airport. So is the Georgia-Pacific Corporation airport just across the river, so I do not stop.

The ceiling and I are keeping company at 200 feet as I round Point Arena and its 300-foot tower.

There are no obstructions to radio waves from Point Reyes VORTAC after Point Arena. The recorded weather broadcast from Point Reyes tells of scattered clouds and good visibilities in the San Francisco Bay area just ninety miles away. Weather is the same at Ukiah, only thirty miles distant, but inland, on the other side of the coastal ridge that lies hidden in fog.

My fuel gauges are dancing around the one-quarter marks. With little more than an hour's fuel remaining, Half Moon Bay is beyond reach, but that's no problem. As soon as I get to all that good weather in another half hour or so, I'll turn left and go to Santa Rosa or Petaluma.

The ceiling is lower than 200 feet. The cloud base is no longer sharply defined, so I can't tell exactly how high it is. I descend over the surf to 100 feet and carefully trim the airplane for level flight, then crank in just is touch of nose-up so that if I become distracted, the airplane will not descend.

The visibility... well, it's hard to tell. I really can't see very far, but the murk looks brighter ahead. It must be glare from sunlight breaking through. In just a few miles, I'll be in the clear.

A small swatch of orange flashes by on my left. A windsock! An airport? It can't be Ocean Ridge. Ocean Ridge is along here somewhere, but it's at 940 feet. This weed-studded little gravel strip is on a promontory just 100 feet above sea level with a line of trees across the north end and a sheer drop to the water on the south. Except for that bright, new-looking windsock, I'd not have noticed it at all. It is not shown on my chart, but I mark its location and the time.

Sea Ranch, the last coastal airport before San Francisco Bay, is high in the clouds. My fuel gauges read less than one quarter. Several scattered new houses with long, straight driveways appear on my left. Paved driveways. Runways. I mark the time.

I must be exceptionally careful along here. The Russian River flows northwestward where it enters the ocean, nearly parallel to the coast. I must keep flying over the sea and not accidentally fly up the narrow river valley. The next obstacle is Bodega Head, and three or four miles beyond that is the edge of my chart.

It takes only a few seconds to remove the folded chart from my kneeboard, unfold it just enough to check the first few inches on the other side to note there are no sharp turns or towers, and return it refolded to the side on which I still am flying. It takes only a few seconds, but when I look out the window again, my universe is soft, white, and still.

The dark stone cliff lumbers out of the fog close to my left wing and I bank gently right. Towering rock materializes at my right wingtip! I level the wings and the rocks on my right and on my left recede into the fog behind me. All outside is white once more.

My heart pounds and my muscles tighten. Although my mind is functioning rapidly, it is calm and clear. And sad. I do not want to die.

Not for nothing have I practiced chandelles, the aviators climbing U-turn. But I've never done them in the blind.

Full power! Nose up to the second bar on the attitude indicator and thirty degrees right bank. *More right rudder!* Echoes of my instructor's command. The altimeter reads higher and the airspeed lower. Watch the airspeed! Keep climbing. Keep turning, but only 160 degrees. Completing the U-turn will put me back in the rocks.

The white outside is brighter. I'm at 600 feet and level, regaining speed lost in the climbing turn. The temptation to climb higher into the brightness, to get on top of the fog, is almost irresistible. But I dare not.

Perhaps the weather over the ridge has gone bad. Perhaps the recorded weather from Point Reyes is outdated, a siren song of scattered clouds and sunshine. And perhaps there are others up there in the fog who have a legal right to be there. My life is mine to risk, but I cannot risk the lives of others.

I reduce power and the airplane lowers its nose. The bright promise of sunshine fades as I descend. The cabin of my airplane becomes darker and the altimeter says I am going down, but outside there is no up or down. My world is in the instruments in front of me. There are only ten hours of dual instrument time in my logbook. I wish there were more.

The altimeter reads 100 feet again, but outside there is nothing. Seventy-five feet. Still nothing. Can it be that my wheels will hit the water before I can see it? Fifty feet, and there is the ocean, a small circle of gray, wrinkled water below me.

Now I must fly on instruments fifty feet above the waves and watch for the rocks standing vertical in the sea to my right.

Slowly and carefully I turn right. Fifty feet. So little room. Forty degrees of turn—twenty to complete the chandelle and twenty more to close the coast at a shallow angle.

What went wrong? What happened during the few seconds I spent looking at the chart? Maybe I should try it again, lower this time. I'm so very close to getting through. The fuel gauges are closer to empty than to one-quarter. I can either try again or go back up the coast until I find a place to land. There is not enough fuel to try again and fail and to return to a place to land.

Breakers appear beneath me. I glance at the fuel gauges once more and my decision is made. Enough. I've had enough.

A slight left turn puts me parallel to the shore heading northwest. The ceiling is higher and the visibility better, so I climb to 100 feet. As low as that is, it seems high to me now. I reduce power and lean the mixture to conserve fuel.

Back up the coast I fly, back to the bright orange windsock if the fuel lasts, back to those long straight driveways if it does not. It's raining hard now.

Sea Ranch airport is right up there! Right up there in the clouds. Right up there on the moon.

The rain is heavier but the ceiling is higher. I climb another fifty feet. Breathing room. There are the long driveways. Five miles more. Fuel gauges read empty, but when I push rudder pedals left and right, needles rise as from a deathbed and fall back.

There it is. The windsock, bright as a poppy, points away from me and straight down the narrow runway. The tailwind is too strong for landing straight in, so I'll fly a right downwind leg and turn base, then final, over the row of trees across the far end. But I can't turn base and final from downwind. I'm too close to the runway and only fifty feet above it. If I misjudge the turn and swing wide, I'll crash into the hills in the fog. If I turn too tight and lose altitude, I'll hit trees. I'll have to turn left, not right, away from the runway and out to sea, a minute and a half on instruments to turn 270 degrees. If the engine quits, I will drown.

There is no time to weigh alternatives. It must be done. The ninety seconds take hours, but when the turn is completed, trees and windsock are before me.

When I pull the carburetor heat knob and throttle back, the slowing propeller no longer blows rain off the windscreen and water obscures my forward view. I can no longer see the row of trees.

When the trees disappear just ahead, I pull back on the yoke and gain fifty feet while lowering flaps and trimming nose up. Turbulence rocks the airplane as it crosses the cliff edge on base leg. The runway comes into view out the right side window. I must have missed the trees. I can't see them out either side, so I must be right on top of them.

I bank steeply right turning final and can see the trees below me out the side window, pale undersides of their leaves shimmering in the wind. I've cleared them with plenty of room to spare. Too much room. The runway looks shorter and narrower than I'd thought and I am too high. There is not enough fuel for a go-around and another approach. In seconds I will be down, alive or dead.

Flaps full down and nose high to steepen the angle of descent. It isn't enough.

To hell with technique! To hell with approach speed! To hell with that little placard that says Avoid Slips With Flaps Extended! The only thing in the world that matters is, if I don't get this airplane onto the ground *right now*, I'm going to run off the cliff into the sea and I will die.

Nose down, control yoke left and full right rudder. The airplane shudders and the yoke bucks in my hand. The ground comes up sideways, zoom-lens fast. Kick it straight *now!*

The stall horn screams as I pull the control yoke back and all three wheels slam down hard in water and gravel. Empty wings rattle like kettle drums and the airplane skips back into the air. I drop the nose and haul back again to touch down on the main gear, brakes on. The wheels lock and slide. I ease up on the pedals for a moment, then push the brakes again. The control yoke is all the way back, levering weight onto the wheels.

We're slowing at last, this little airplane and I, but the end of the strip and the edge of the cliff are coming up too fast. I can stomp left brake and rudder pedal and groundloop into the mud and rocks if I absolutely have to, but it will break the airplane and my heart.

But it's slowing. Straight ahead and it's slowing. Slowing and stopping... stopped, sixty paces from the drop into the sea, the airplane is stopped. My sweat is cold and my hand is shaking as I reach to shut down the engine.

The little airplane is stopped, idling without care, rocking gently in the wind and rain.

What I left out of the magazine story was, after turning back in the fog bank and letting down over the ocean, I tried again. I thought that perhaps the airplane had climbed a few feet into the cloud while I was looking at the chart. I turned south at the shoreline and, with eyes wide open, I flew into whiteness just as I had before, and rocks emerged from the fog just as they had before.

And I did another chandelle, descended almost to the waves again before I could see, and then turned toward land and flew north to the gravel strip with the bright orange windsock. After landing, I got out and paced off the few yards of runway remaining and looked over the edge of the cliff at breakers crashing onto the rocks.

I walked through the rain-soaked grassy field in leather moccasins, across Highway 1 and up the hill to a house, still trying to figure out what kind of fog I'd flown into that I couldn't see until I was in it.

Blanche Wilson said Ole had never been in an airplane, but he kept a windsock on his pasture for the occasional flyer who was out of fuel and out of ideas. Until a few days earlier, the field had been crowded with sheep.

I used the Wilson's phone to call Ukiah Flight Service to close my flight plan and ask about weather. It was good everywhere except where I was. It was the first rain in a long time, and everyone in Gualala was happy but me.

I walked toward town and a man gave me a ride. Word of my landing in Wilson's sheep pasture had spread. I asked about fuel, but there was none for sale at the airport up on the ridge in the clouds. I called my father to tell him I wouldn't arrive that day after all. I asked him to call my wife in the evening when she'd be home from work, as I'd not be near a phone. I bought groceries for sandwiches and the man drove me back to my airplane. He suggested I move it off the runway in case someone else needed to land.

As I chocked wheels with large rocks, Ole Wilson came down from the house to chat, to learn who I was and to get some idea of what I was doing there. He walked back home, satisfied, I suppose, that I wasn't a drug runner or otherwise up to no good. I climbed into the airplane and settled into the back seats and slept twelve hours.

Overcast lifted to 500 feet and became lighter as the sun climbed unseen east of the cloud-shrouded ridge. Ole walked down from his house and invited me to go to town for breakfast with him and Blanche. After we ate, they drove me to visit a pilot friend of theirs. Jack Tibbets had an airplane at Sea Ranch, the airport on the ridge. We all drank coffee and I told my story. Jack wasn't an instructor, but he added to my education.

When weather conditions and temperatures are just right and the shore near the mouth of the Russian River is foggy, fog is thicker and denser where the river meets the sea. Local knowledge isn't on charts.

Jack said he'd give me fuel and drove us to the airport. Halfway there, we broke through the top of the cloud layer like a surfacing submarine and drove the rest of the way in bright sunshine. Jack drained five gallons from his airplane into a can and gave me the instrument approach plate for Ukiah—I do not know even now why that sheet of paper is called a plate—just in case weather turned bad before I got there. He wouldn't let me pay him.

There was an inch of gasoline in one tank and a little more in the other. I poured all the gasoline into the tank with one inch. I estimated I'd burn exactly five gallons on the short hop to

Ukiah, including first flying west over the ocean and climbing through clouds before turning back toward land. Cloud tops were below where anyone might be flying on an instrument flight plan.

An immediate climbing right turn took me into the cloud base. I headed toward Hawaii and watched the altimeter rise. I broke out at 1500 feet and, squinting in the bright light, turned east for Ukiah and a real airport with fuel for sale.

I called my father to give him a new estimate of my arrival. What was planned as a two-day trip was already in its third day. Dad suggested I call home. My wife was not happy that I'd left firewood for only two days. I'd taken all our spare cash with me, and she needed groceries.

I caught up with bad weather near Redding and landed. The man on the phone at Montague Flight Service would not advise flying over the Siskiyou Mountains, as they are high and clouds were low. Weather would be the same for the next two days. But, if I could get over the pass...

There is a dormant cinder cone next to the northbound lanes of I-5 between Dunsmuir and Weed. Black Butte is a mere bump on the landscape compared to Mount Shasta a few miles east, and on my chart, it was a black dot within a single circle of contour line. That dot represented a mountain more than two thousand feet higher than the highway beside it. The volcanic rock that formed the steep slopes of Black Butte is the color of its name, the color of the night sky.

Unseen clouds lay close above. I flew just to the right of the highway looking almost straight down on taillights a few hundred feet below. I didn't want to lose sight of those lights in dense rain, so I flew almost on top of the highway, which is why I didn't crash into Black Butte.

I called Montague Flight Service on the radio. Weather had not improved. I thought it wouldn't hurt to look.

While it's true that, even in mountains, Interstate highways don't turn sharper than a slow airplane can, drivers on the ground have yellow signs alerting them to what's ahead. Rain turned to snow as I flew just above the rising highway and climbed into the mountains. I was looking down at lights of traffic, so I didn't see the highway make a sharp left turn until I was overshooting it. Mountain highways turn because they have to go around something.

I yanked the airplane into a steep left bank and pulled hard on the yoke. My wingtip was pointed almost straight down at the highway and centrifugal force made me heavy in my seat. Aligned with the highway again and level, I looked to my right at snow on ledges of rock like white frosting between layers of a tall chocolate cake.

My hammering heart broke through my single-minded drive to get where I was going. I'd just missed Black Butte, and I'd come even closer to becoming one with the Siskiyous. I was climbing into ragged wisps of cloud that would become dense before I reached the pass. I could see across the valley to my left, see a few lights in scattered ranch houses through horizontal snow. Turning back at that moment was probably the only intelligent thing I did that week.

I went into the Montague Flight Service Station and told the man what the weather was like up the road. I told him about my close encounter with Black Butte. He said an airplane had hit it a few months earlier and killed all aboard, a light twin scud running at night just as I had been.

I slept sitting on a wooden bench. It was not warm, and I was no longer having fun. Weather moved east in the night and I flew home.

My commercial course was complete except for training in the new instrument airplane we didn't yet have. I also needed time in a complex airplane, one with an adjustable-pitch propeller and retractable landing gear. We didn't have one of those, either. I endured three weeks on the ground.

Tailspins killed a lot of early aviators before aerodynamics were well understood. A spin begins when one wing stalls while the other keeps flying. The airplane drops off on the stalled side, the nose falls, and the flying wing turns the airplane in tight circles around the stalled wing. The pilot panics and pulls back on the stick to raise the nose, which doesn't work because the stalled wing can't provide lift. At the same time, he tries to lift the fallen wing with aileron. That doesn't work for the same reason.

Spins still kill people, but when I learned to fly, spin training was no longer required. Training emphasized recognition of the onset of stalls and prompt recovery. If an airplane never stalls, it will never spin. My instructors taught spins anyway. I enjoyed them, once I realized how easy it is to resume flying, and I often practiced spin recovery on my own. A Cessna 172 with no weight in the back had to be forced into a spin. Relaxing back pressure on the yoke was all it took to resume flying.

One rule of single-engine flying is, if you lose your engine on takeoff, land straight ahead, regardless of what is in front of you, unless you have gained enough altitude to turn and glide back to the airport. Pilots trying to return with a dead engine often end up in the same condition. I wanted to know how high was high enough, and what was the best way to make the turn back to the runway.

Students, private pilots, and instructors gave me different answers. My instructor told me to go up and find out. I took off to play test pilot with a small clipboard strapped to my knee. Our practice area was flat land with straight roads and fences. I decided my runway was two thousand feet on the altimeter. I slowed to takeoff speed over a straight road, then applied full power and began to climb straight ahead as if I had just left the runway. When I'd climbed a thousand feet, I pulled the throttle to idle.

Turning at standard rate with no power took forever and a thousand feet or more to get turned and lined up in position for landing. Tighter turns took less time and lost less altitude. My clipboard filled with numbers

Climbing at best-rate-of-climb speed when I chopped power, I pulled the nose up firmly to what felt like nearly straight up, trading speed for altitude. I kept the stall horn screaming until just before the airplane stopped, then relaxed back pressure and pushed full left rudder and held it there until the airplane pointed down. As it accelerated, I pulled the nose up to maintain landing speed, the stall horn screaming again as I pulled out of the dive until I was on a normal, power-off landing approach and pointed back down the "runway" I'd just left. I lost only a hundred and fifty feet. It had taken only ten seconds from simulated engine failure to simulated landing. The Cessna I flew that day had the old-style flap switch that had to be held down against a spring, and I was too busy to deploy flaps.

I practiced those power-off hammerhead turns for an hour, varying speed at engine failure until I was satisfied that I could, in a lightly loaded Cessna 172, consistently reverse course and be in position to land with loss of no more than a hundred feet if I was at best-rate-of-climb or faster after when the engine failed. It made little difference whether I stomped left rudder or right, but turning left was more comfortable, as I could see the ground throughout the maneuver. On the twentieth try, I lost only seventy feet. If I ever lost an engine on takeoff, surprise would cost a few seconds, so I mentally set my return-to-runway altitude at one hundred fifty feet above the ground if alone and three hundred feet if I had passengers.

A few years later, I was giving a private pilot his biennial refresher and the subject of turning back after engine failure came up. I told him of my experiment and results. He was skeptical.

I'd not tried my technique since that afternoon of experimenting in 1976 and never in a Cessna 152 with a flap switch that could be pushed down and forgotten. I told the young man he should pull the throttle back to catch me by surprise and note the altitude. I established a climb over a road and looked out the side window so I couldn't see what he was doing. He pulled the power to idle and I hauled the nose up, stomped the rudder, and slapped the flap switch all the way down. When I pulled out of the dive, directly over the road and headed the other way ready to land, we'd lost only a hundred feet.

A new, red-and-white, fully instrumented Cessna 172 finally arrived. The only instructor qualified to conduct the rest of my instrument training was busy with chief pilot duties, flying his airline schedule, and teaching other students.

Another summer with its long days began. Pearson's newest airline pilot was also an instrument instructor. At the end of my first lesson with Larry, I said I'd do a power-off landing and touch down on the 8. I flew too far on downwind to complete a rectangular pattern, so I turned toward the end of the runway and said I'd extend flaps to balloon over the trees and add power only if necessary to miss the cows. My new instructor wasn't happy with that plan, so I added power and made a normal landing.

I didn't like instrument flying and wasn't good at it. It takes an organized mind to handle flying, navigating, reading charts, and talking on the radio, and I'd never learned to juggle. Although never a master of precision flying, I always knew where I was and what was going on around me. I figured that was more important than being able to fly precisely on heading, on altitude, and on speed into the side of a mountain.

Earl Pearson bought me an airline ticket to Oakland, California, so I could pick up a new Cessna 172 parked there and fly it to Port Angeles. There was not a cloud to be seen as the Boeing 737 cruised south in smooth air through western Oregon and northern California. I considered the view out the window a sufficient weather briefing for my return.

After taking off from Oakland in the 172, I flew northwest to Point Reyes and up the Pacific Coast. Just north of the Russian River, I descended to one hundred fifty feet over the sea and took pictures of the place where I'd flown into fog earlier that year. I took a picture of Ole Wilson's landing strip and its bright windsock, sorry there were no sheep on the runway for my photos. I continued north in a clear sky following the same route of my February flight. The steep slope of Black Butte beside the highway gave me a chill, even in daylight.

I was hanging around the airport after a day of plumbing when Earl asked if could go to Wichita to pick up a new airplane and fly it to the Cessna distributor in Troutdale, Oregon. When? Right now. I drove home, bathed, packed, and was back at the airport within half an hour to ride the evening flight to Seattle. As I stood in line to clear security at SeaTac, I wondered if I'd be able to keep my folding knife. The blades were under the four-inch limit by a hair.

Machinery most likely to fail is that which is new and untried. If an engine or a tool or an airplane doesn't fail in the first few hours of operation, it will probably last until it begins to wear out. I inspected the 172 as thoroughly as I could without taking it apart.

I hadn't slept on the flight to Wichita, but I didn't have far to go the first day. I planned to spend the night with my parents in Boulder, Colorado. Though I could have flown farther, I made my first stop in Goodland, Kansas, for fuel and lunch. I calculated fuel consumption and checked oil level and looked for leaks and missing parts. The airplane was good, the airport restaurant was cheap, and the teenaged waitress was pretty and pleasant.

After spending a day visiting family and friends, I left early the next morning while air was cool and smooth. At twelve thousand feet over Wyoming and Idaho, I flew through canyons in the sky between towering cumulus clouds. On the last leg to Troutdale, after falling asleep the first of several times, I trimmed the airplane slightly nose up so that, unattended, it would climb, and the change in sound would wake me.

During a long three weeks in August, my free time did not coincide with instructor availability. I scheduled an airplane and went up to repeat a lesson number from much earlier in the course, just to practice and have fun. A friend went along for the ride. My chandelles and lazy 8s, after a month of not having practiced them, were neither smooth nor accurate. I also did stalls for the first time in several weeks. And spins.

We'd been up less than an hour in the early evening when Earl called on the radio to ask if I'd fly the bank run to Boeing Field. The regular pilot was sick and everyone else was home or flying.

Sure, I could do that. Could I take a friend along?

Lynn and I called our wives to say we'd be late for supper. I fueled the airplane, called Flight Service for a weather briefing, and we stuffed canvas bags full of checks into the airplane. We loaded some into the baggage compartment behind the rear seats and tied a cargo net over them. We seatbelted others into the two rear seats and wedged the last few bags behind the front seats. Weight distribution, though within limits, was not what I was used to. A four-seat airplane with no load behind the front seats is nose heavy and stable. The farther aft the center of gravity, the lighter the back pressure required on the yoke to raise the nose.

I was not a commercial pilot, and it was not legal for me to take that flight, so, for the article for *Private Pilot* magazine a few years later, I changed the bank bags to "some stuff" I was taking to Seattle as a favor to Pearson.

Weather in Seattle was good—scattered clouds at three thousand feet with excellent visibility. Scattered meant that between one- and five-tenths of the sky was covered as viewed from the weather station on the ground. Scattered doesn't tell you *which* five-tenths is covered. My mind saw puffs of cumulus in a bright blue sky.

The straight-line route from Port Angeles to Seattle goes through Bon Jon Pass, a V-notch in the foothills of the Olympic Mountains. It is possible to fly through that pass at just over three thousand feet in daylight and in good weather. At night, or if clouds are low or if fog shrouds the hills, a dogleg around the foothills is wiser, and it adds less than five minutes to flight time. But it was still daylight, and we had good weather. Lynn bought a bag of Cheetos and we took off for Seattle.

As we approached the notch in the mountains, we could see that clouds on the other side appeared to be a solid layer. I hadn't expected that, but it wasn't unusual for clouds to bunch up next to the hills. When we got closer, we could see that a thick layer of clouds beyond the pass extended down into treetops. Rather than ducking under, we would have to climb above those clouds and let down on the other side between those scattered puffs of cumulus I'd envisioned. Lynn munched Cheetos as I pushed in the throttle and began to climb toward blue.

The climb angle was shallow with our heavy load as we entered the pass and flew above the lowest layer of cloud. My eyes latched onto a blue hole ahead in the clouds above. With my eyes and brain focused on that patch of blue, and with control forces light because of the load in back, I was not aware that I was steadily increasing back pressure on the yoke, raising the nose toward that hole in the sky. We were not going to make it.

The pass was too narrow for a normal U-turn. It was time for one of those return-to-the-airport maneuvers I'd practiced months before, but with power. I pulled the nose up and pushed left rudder. The stall horn screamed and the airplane snapped into a spin and we fell upside down into clouds. The rest happened slowly in my mind, but clock time from beginning to end was no more than five seconds and perhaps only three. Cheetos swirled in the airplane like flakes in a Christmas snow globe. The pilot's universal response to unpleasant surprise sounded in my head if not from my lips: Oh shit.

What the airplane was doing was not unfamiliar. We'd been practicing spins only an hour earlier. If nothing else, a spin is a tight, quick turn, but it costs altitude fast. I yanked the throttle to idle. There was nothing to see outside but gray. After what felt like half a turn, I eased the yoke forward and pushed right rudder and the spin stopped instantly. I pulled back smoothly and we shot out the bottom of the cloud bank as we pulled out of the dive, centered in the bottom of the V of the pass with trees flashing by off both wings. I was surprised that the heading indicator had not tumbled in the wild gyration. I was amazed and smugly pleased to see that we'd turned precisely 180 degrees. It was only after my heart slowed and we were established on a new course around the end of the mountain ridge that it sunk in how very, very close I'd come to killing us both.

The weather report had been correct, technically. In Seattle, the entire eastern half of the sky was clear and the entire western half was covered with a solid layer of cloud with bases at three thousand feet. Not included in the report was height of cloud tops, which, at the eastern edge of the layer, right over Seattle, was six thousand feet.

We landed at Boeing Field and quickly unloaded bags for the waiting van driver. Cleaning Cheetos out of the airplane took longer.

The next afternoon, I flew to Quillayute to pick up a fisheries biologist employed by the Quileute tribe. We flew along the Pacific shore to check on several crab pots just off the beach south of La Push. The flight was as illegal as the bank charter, but I'd have accepted any free flying short of smuggling drugs.

With a young instructor new to the school, I flew to Victoria one morning to practice instrument approaches. The airport was not as busy as those in Puget Sound, and it was closer to Port Angeles. I forgot to call the tower at the outer marker and didn't remember until we were almost to the runway. I was surprised at the cheerful sarcasm when the controller said, "Thanks for calling." Canadian controllers almost always seemed more relaxed than their American counterparts. Maybe they had a better union.

My instructor thought I needed more practice. The next day, we flew to Paine Field and flew several approaches. Then he recommended me for a checkride, and I understood better his reluctance to sign me off earlier. I was his first recommendation for an instrument rating.

My checkride spanned six hours. My examiner was again Pearson's chief pilot. After he quizzed me on what I was supposed to have learned, we had to wait for the airplane to return from a charter. I screwed up one approach because I didn't allow for a strong tailwind when calculating time between radio beacon and the airport. I knew what I'd done wrong, though, and a second attempt went well. After an approach on the arrival to Port Angeles, I had an instrument rating, another step on the way to making my living in airplanes. The best part was, I wouldn't have to fly under that goddam plastic visor again, not for a while anyway.

I'd accumulated 260 hours total time, more than the minimum for a commercial license. All I needed was experience controlling the pitch of the propeller and operating retractable landing gear. There weren't enough Commercial students in the flight school to justify buying a complex airplane, so Pearson was looking for one to lease for a month or two.

My parents came out from Colorado to visit. I took my father up for an hour on a clear, calm October day. We were able to fly near glaciers on Mount Olympus in smooth air and see them in lovely light of late afternoon. Dad said it was the best flight he'd ever had. His expression of superlative enjoyment was, to me, indirect approval of the direction my life was taking.

My father was the first in his family to attend college, going from a small, Texas farm to university during the Great Depression and ultimately earning a doctorate in physics. It must have disappointed him that I had no interest in school, that I was a poor student despite a reasonable amount of brains, and that I'd spent less than a year in college before deciding formal education was not for me. My father recognized the futility of trying to force a child to take an unwanted path through life. If he was unhappy with me, he did not let it show.

When I decided on a flying career, my parents provided financial support. They had helped my brother and sister pay for their educations and wanted to help me, too. My father's delight at the best flight he ever had meant more to me than money. I sometimes wondered if he envied me, maybe just a little.

Pearson leased a Cessna Cardinal RG. The unfamiliar airplane was like waxed skis after training on snowshoes. It was little different from the 172 I'd been flying, but wheels didn't hang out in the breeze. Slowing down required thinking farther ahead of the airplane.

The main landing gear retracted into the fuselage much like a flying bird's legs swing back and up out of the slipstream. The control is a knob on the instrument panel shaped like a lollipop to represent a wheel and distinguish it from the flap lever near it. Pull it out of a detent and move it up and the gear comes up and green lights go out. Pull the knob out and push it down and wait for green lights signifying landing gear is down and locked. Airplanes have warnings to let you know the gear isn't down when the power is reduced for landing, but even with a gear horn blaring, sometimes pilots forget to put the wheels down.

Two of Pearson's mechanics had to go to Portland. The commuter flight they'd planned to ride to Seattle filled up with paying passengers. My instructor and I were elected to fly the mechanics to SeaTac to catch their airline flight. It was only my second flight in the Cardinal RG. We had only half an hour to get the airplane ready to go and file an instrument flight plan. My instructor was at home.

The mechanics preflighted the airplane in the rain. Clouds were high enough for a visual takeoff but too low for visual flying to Seattle. I filed an instrument flight plan by phone. Mike arrived, grabbed his charts, and we were on our way.

I wasn't entirely comfortable getting into an airplane I had not inspected myself, but our passengers would pay the same stiff price my instructor and I would if they missed something critical, and we were in a hurry.

Mike took the instructor's right seat. With two mechanics and their gear in the back, we were near maximum weight. And we were in a hurry.

Four of us breathing in the small airplane fogged all windows. Mike was on the radio calling Seattle for our clearance. I was running the unfamiliar checklist, moving my thumb down the laminated card line by line as I checked each item while peering out at the taxiway through a small clear area at the bottom of the windscreen above defogging vents.

Mike and I were separately involved in our tasks, and neither of us realized we hadn't announced our takeoff on the radio. I wasn't doing anything with radios and hadn't paid attention to what frequency the second radio was tuned to. We didn't hear a pilot announce his straight-in approach.

I had just pushed in the throttle when the other airplane passed over us. Its pilot didn't know we hadn't seen him and assumed we'd sit on the end of the runway until he had landed and cleared. We should not have been on the runway, but he should not have landed over us. We stopped easily, as we'd just begun to move. After the other airplane had turned off the runway, I again pushed in the throttle, rattled and wondering what else we had missed in our haste.

Turn the friction lock one way and the throttle moves easily. Turn it the other way and the throttle stays where you put it. Normally, the pilot not flying raises the landing gear, but, as a student, I was supposed to do everything. As we began to climb, I took my hand off the throttle to raise the handle. I hadn't tightened the friction lock enough in the unfamiliar airplane, but we didn't notice the throttle slowly creeping back. I assumed our climb was shallow because we were heavy. The controllable propeller did not change RPM as power decreased, and there was no immediately apparent change in engine sound. The only indication aside from the slow climb was a decrease in manifold pressure, a gauge not found on airplanes I had flown and one I was not yet in the habit of looking at. Mike pushed the throttle in again and tightened the friction lock and the airplane resumed climbing.

One evening, I rented a familiar 172 and flew with my wife and daughter to Paine Field to attend a friend's wedding. I rented the instrument trainer and filed an instrument flight plan, although weather was good. When we'd passed the mountains and had a clear view of city lights in all of Puget Sound, I canceled IFR and continued visually, enjoying the sight of cities by night and paying no attention to navigation radios I'd set up to show the way to Paine Field.

We were near Everett, but I couldn't see the airport. I called Paine Tower and advised I was five miles northwest. Tower said I was not in sight. Moments later, I realized I was looking at Edmonds, not Everett. A glance at the instrument panel showed needles and compasses silently screaming, *Turn left!*

We flew home in clear weather after midnight. We were not on an instrument flight plan, but I paid close attention to navigation radios anyway. Later that day, I took my Commercial Pilot checkride.

The line in my log reads 276.7 hours total time. The examiner's entry says, Commercial Flight Check Satisfactory. Perhaps it was satisfactory by FAA standards, but I wasn't happy with my performance. The examiner talked about my deficiencies and how to remedy them. The big one was, I'd been so thoroughly indoctrinated in the importance of making landing approaches at idle, I couldn't yet accept that using power to adjust a landing approach was not a sin.

In the beginning, a pilot pays to fly. It was expensive even when aviation gasoline was under a dollar. The immediate goal is to have someone else pay for the airplane and fuel. The lowest rung on the employment ladder is Flight Instructor, and most new pilots spend a few years teaching others. Some merely endure it. Others enjoy teaching, but most instructors eventually burn out.

The biggest difference between all the flying I'd done and what I was doing in my Certificated Flight Instructor course was that I moved from the left seat to the right. The instructor acted as student.

My left hand had to learn to do what my right hand had done before. It was easy enough to work throttle and mixture controls that move in and out regardless of which hand operates them. What I had trouble doing was tuning radios. My left hand insisted on turning the knobs the same direction relative to my thumb as my right hand had always done. If I wanted to turn a knob clockwise, my left hand turned it counter-clockwise.

I began teaching my instructor, writing lesson plans, outlining what we were going to do, explaining how to do it, then demonstrating in the airplane. I had to explain to my student what he was doing wrong and show him how to do it correctly. I enjoyed the process and looked forward to teaching.

The CFI course involved only twenty-four hours of flying, but they were spread out over three winter months. Meanwhile, I was flying for hire at last. I never saw the few dollars I earned because Pearson applied them to my perpetual training bill.

My first legal revenue flying was a two-hour scenic flight in late November. My passengers thanked me profusely for the lovely ride and perfect landing. A week later, I was hanging around the airport when the afternoon commuter flight was overbooked by three and everyone showed up. I flew a 172 to Seattle to pick them up. That was the first time I flew passengers on a scheduled flight. I was, if I cared to stretch a point, an airline pilot.

Just before Christmas, I flew to Boeing Field to take the written exam for flight instructor. I didn't feel completely ready, but the sooner I got the rating, the sooner I could fly full time.

I flew to Colorado for Christmas in the passenger seat in an airliner. It is perhaps indicative of my single-minded pursuit of licenses and ratings that I do not remember whether I went alone or with my wife and daughter. I worked forty hours a week plumbing and spent another forty at the airport. That didn't leave much time or energy for family. From Colorado, I went to Wichita to ferry a new airplane home.

A Cessna 150 is to a 172 as a go-kart is to the family sedan. Seats are on the floor and legs extend straight out to the pedals. Everything about it is lighter and perkier. I stopped first at Goodland to check the airplane, refuel, and eat a late lunch. Night falls early in December, and the sky was fully dark when I crossed into Colorado. Westerly winds flowing over the Rockies made air increasingly rough as I approached the mountains.

I navigated by radio and by watching lighted towns and cities drift slowly underneath. With fifty miles to go, with Denver ahead and to the left, right where it should be, I could see lights of Boulder, the town I grew up in, right where they should be. I relaxed as much as I could in the bouncing airplane, ignored radio navigation, and kept my eyes on the lights of Boulder. I could even make out the traditional lighted star on Flagstaff Mountain just above the city, although, from my angle, the small cluster of lights did not look like a star.

I began looking for the airport just east of town that I'd ridden my bike to as a ten-year-old to watch little airplanes and dream. Lights on the mountain still did not look like a star and I became uneasy. It seemed there were too many lights below for the empty plains east of Boulder. Maybe the wind had blown me south of course after I'd stopped paying attention. Maybe the lights on the mountain didn't look like a star because they weren't a star. All those lights below must be the northern fringes of Denver. Maybe I was in Stapleton airspace without a clearance. I turned hard right to get away from any unseen airliners. I stared hard at the cluster of lights on the mountain to my left and confirmed it was just a cluster of lights.

I found a frequency for Denver Approach on my jitterbugging chart and called to ask for flight following and vectors to Boulder. I dialed numbers into the transponder and waited. Meanwhile, I was flying north.

Approach couldn't find me on radar, and I'd flown off the edge of my chart. I saw a small airport ahead and told the controller the runway numbers. He didn't know of any airport near Denver with that runway. He offered to give me a frequency to contact the en route controller to see if he could find me. I declined. I said there was a perfectly good airport directly ahead and that I was going to land on it and find out where I was.

"When you do, will you call us and tell us? We're kinda curious, too." I wrote the phone number on my hand.

Fort Collins-Loveland? I was nearly fifty miles north of where I thought I was when I turned north. I'd not been over Denver's northern suburbs as I'd feared but exactly where I should have been. I'd never flown over my home town at night and had no idea there were so many lights in what I'd always thought of as empty landscape. I had plenty of fuel, but I topped the tanks anyway and called Denver Approach to tell them where I'd landed.

If the runway lights at Boulder had been on, perhaps I'd have recognized it, star on the mountain or not. The air near the ground was smooth, and I made a nice landing in darkness.

My parent's living room had a clear view of Flagstaff Mountain. The star I'd hitched my wagon to was the lights of a restaurant across the road from where the star had always been.

Air in mile-high Boulder is thin, and maximum power is not what it is at sea level. On the last morning of 1976, my brother and I climbed into the little airplane. With Jon and me and full fuel tanks, we were eighty-five pounds over the limit, and neither of us is fat. I'd flown a 172 with that much overload with no problem. The inch of dry powder snow on the long, sloping runway would not hinder takeoff.

Few airplane crashes result from one failure or one error. The eighty-five pounds by itself wasn't a big deal. Neither was high altitude's effect on performance, and neither was dry snow on the runway. But little things add up.

The airplane accelerated slowly downhill to the east. We approached flying speed at the same rate we approached the end of the runway. The good news was, the ground fell away in a gradual slope and there were no trees or power lines in the way. We did not so much take off as allow the earth to fall away. We slowly began to climb, and, after beginning to breathe again, I made a gentle, shallow-banked turn toward Wyoming.

We landed at Rawlins for fuel, higher even than Boulder and with less air to feed the engine and float the wings. We made a long, wide, shallow turn after takeoff to clear the rim of the almost imperceptible ridge to the west. We fueled again at Rock Springs.

I did not like the look of the sky farther west. We detoured south into Utah. After stopping at Ogden for fuel, we headed up the highway to Idaho. Jon flew and I looked out the window.

I'd hoped we'd make it all the way to Port Angeles for Pearson's year-end party, but Burley, Idaho, was as far as we went. Night, mountains, winter weather, and an airplane that could barely climb combined to suggest we stop and go to a motel. The more I flew, the less brave I became.

A week later, I picked up the fisheries biologist at Quillayute and took him across the Olympic Mountains to Shelton. It was too foggy for us to land there, so we diverted to nearby Bremerton.

I can't help but wonder if impending death is somehow visible. There was nothing in the man's appearance or demeanor to suggest any such thing, and surely a future death by accident can't hint of its coming. But I'm haunted even now by my brief association with him, wondering if I noted at the time or only remembered afterward that there had seemed an unnatural grayness under his eyes.

A few years later at a high school reunion, I saw a former classmate for the first time in twenty years. Gray shadows under his eyes reminded me of the biologist. I thought no more about it until a few months later when my classmate's heart failed and he died. Even now, on rare occasions, the pallor of someone's face reminds me of those two men and I wonder.

The accident that killed the fisheries biologist, his pilot, and one of two young men in the back seats was, as is so often the case, the result of a convergence of insignificant factors.

Fish patrols were sometimes as simple as flying along the coast a few hundred feet up while the observer counts crab pots.

The more common patrols were slow, treetop flights along winding rivers in a Cessna 172 with flaps partway down for more lift at low speed. The pilot concentrated on keeping the airplane in the air and next to the river so the observer in the right seat could see into the water and count the gravel nests in which salmon spawn.

Pearson had not renewed the contract to fly bank data to and from Seattle. The courier company hired a young man, building time like the rest of us, to fly bank paper from Seattle to Port Angeles in the morning, stay all day, and fly back with the evening load. Lew spent a good part of each day hanging around the airport, so Pearson added him to the roster and used him to fly charters when company pilots weren't available.

Quileute Fisheries called to schedule a patrol, the simple kind along the coast. Two young fisheries trainees would ride along. The survivor explained what happened.

After the coastal check, the biologist wanted to look at a river. His pilot didn't know that river patrols were never flown with four people aboard. Flying near stall speed near the ground leaves no room for error. Wind was turbulent in the treetops and the stall horn chirped in the bumps. The biologist asked his pilot to turn around so he could look again at something that had caught his eye. The airplane stalled in the turn and crashed nose down into water and rocks.

Pilots have argued the hazards and aerodynamics of The Downwind Turn for a hundred years and will no doubt continue to do so for at least a hundred more. When flying into a headwind near the ground, then turning 180 degrees to fly with the wind on the tail, airplanes sometimes stall and fall out of the sky. I will skip the myriad incorrect arguments about why that happens and tell you in one sentence the simple truth: The danger in the mystical Downwind Turn is the result of an optical illusion and has nothing to do with wind's effect on the airplane.

When flying into the wind at low altitude, the ground is going by more slowly than it would for the same airspeed and no wind. The eye takes this in and the brain gets used to it. Then, when the airplane turns and headwind becomes tailwind, the ground goes by much faster. The pilot unconsciously pulls back on the yoke to slow the airplane to what his brain recalls was the rate trees were going by seconds before. If the airplane is slow to begin with, as it is while climbing immediately after takeoff, that pilot-induced reduction in airspeed in the turn is sometimes enough to make the wing stall.

Proof that other theories are wrong is simple: That dangerous, involuntary reduction in airspeed in a downwind turn never occurs when the pilot cannot see the ground.

Lew was a helicopter pilot. Quick turns in a helicopter require pedal pressure to swing the tail boom around. Turns in an airplane are made with ailerons and just a little rudder pressure. When turning left at low speed, all the pilot needs to do is relax a little of the constant right rudder pressure low-speed flying requires. My airplane full of swirling Cheetos is graphic reminder of what too much rudder pedal pressure at slow speed in a heavy airplane does. Add bumpy air and a downwind turn near the ground...

The crumpled airplane was dragged out of the river and hauled back to Port Angeles on a flatbed truck. It lay on the ground between hangars for weeks. Someone covered the airplane with a tarp, and then one day it was gone.

All the flying I did the last half of January and the first week of February was to finish my training to become a flight instructor. When my instructor judged me worthy, I made an appointment with an examiner at Boeing Field. Instructors had told me a secret to getting along with FAA examiners: Let them fly the airplane. They spend most of their time behind desks and only occasionally get to fly.

My examiner's main complaint was that I didn't talk loud enough to be heard clearly over airplane noise.

Flight Instructor

My second logbook contains three thousand hours of flight time over two and a half years. More than half is instruction given. The spine is broken and pages are separated here and there by newspaper clippings, obituaries mostly. The inside cover and first page are covered with columns of solo endorsements, students' written test scores, checkride recommendations, and Biennial Flight Reviews conducted. Only a few names are underlined in red, those who failed tests or checkrides.

Until I began instructing, I kept an account of my flying in a spiral notebook, a diary of my flying life. Once I began teaching, I was too busy, and later, I barely had time to keep up with sketchy logbook notes and comments. Many of those notes are undecipherable after more than three decades, thirty-five years that seem like forever and like no time at all.

I barely knew what I was doing myself, yet I was supposed to impart my knowledge and skill to others and send them into the sky alone, knowing that if I'd misjudged their readiness or had overlooked some vital detail, they might die. But I didn't have to begin with a beginner. My first instruction given was a basic instrument lesson with my friend Cleon McClain. I tried to remember to talk loud as I put him through his paces as he sweated under the training visor for an hour and a half. That afternoon, we went up again, work for him and pleasure for me.

Instructing a friend who was already a pilot got me comfortable with my new role. My first two unlicensed students each had many hours scattered over several years but were serious about finishing the requirements for private licenses.

Five or ten dollars bought an introductory flying lesson, half an hour in the air with hands and feet on the controls. That was often all it took to enroll another student pilot. Intros were short and simple, and I took pleasure in the pleasure of those I took up.

I needed five hundred hours total time to meet insurance requirements for flying Pearson's twin-engine Cessnas. Ferry flights built time quickly. Pearson sold a lot of airplanes, and I flew more than a dozen new ones from Kansas to Washington.

Weather and wind made an indirect, southern route better than the usual straight shot to the northwest, so I stopped first in Dodge City and then flew across the panhandles of Oklahoma and Texas into New Mexico. Climbing out of Tucumcari, my Cessna 172 almost collided with an eagle. As I descended to land at Albuquerque for the night, I looked down the Sandia Crest and imagined Kirk Douglas and his horse down there, running from the police helicopter in *Lonely Are the Brave*.

I took pictures of the Painted Desert with the morning sun at my back and then, as I approached Grand Canyon, descended to just above tops of scruffy pines, bouncing in thermals rising from the rapidly heating desert. All I could see of the canyon was the higher north rim, a hazy dark line on the horizon. The airplane bounced and rocked as treetops and sand streaked under me, and then sensation of speed stopped as the earth fell away and the panorama of canyon suddenly filled my view and the air became instantly smooth and still. I wished, not for the first or last time, that I'd taken a movie camera with me.

It occurred to me that, if my engine failed, there was no place to land. I gave up the view reluctantly and climbed to safe altitude. When I stopped for the night in California, I'd seen the Painted Desert, Grand Canyon, Death Valley, and Yosemite, all in one day.

I did not then and do not now always resist impulses, although something in me blocks those with irrevocable consequences. So it was that I did not attempt a touch-and-go on Yosemite's granite Half Dome. I was concerned less with death than with explaining to Earl Pearson how I'd wrecked his airplane, if I misjudged and was unlucky enough to survive.

One of my two private pilot students had fine motor skills, honed driving trucks and heavy equipment. That made my job of reviewing what he'd learned over years of scattered lessons easy. My other experienced first student did not have exceptional aptitude, but I confidently renewed his expired solo endorsement after only a few sessions in the air. My time between day job and darkness was short, but I flew nearly every day with at least one of my students in the first two weeks after I became a flight instructor.

When I told Earl Pearson in March that I had quit my plumbing job and was working for him full time, he said I was nuts. He was paying instructors only five dollars an hour, and that was for hours billed to students or time logged on charters. I told him I was making only six bucks as a plumbing trainee anyway.

We did not have fuel trucks until later. Airplanes pulled up to two gas pumps and either the lineboy, when we had one, or a mechanic or whoever was around pumped gas, cleaned windscreens, checked oil, and took the money. Most of the time, Pearson's pilots and students refueled airplanes after a flight, but sometimes, someone would have to start one up, taxi to the fuel pit, and then back to the tiedown ramp. That usually put a tenth of an hour on the Hobbs meter, the clock that recorded time when the master switch was on. Time was time, and I needed time. I started logging the tenth of an hour that clicked over on the meter during refueling taxis.

I mentioned what I was doing to another instructor, and he pointed out that taxi time was not flight time unless it was for the purpose of flight. So, being a stickler for accuracy in my log, I ran a red line through each taxi-only entry and adjusted the total.

Many pilots, when not building time to required minimums, don't bother to log flights at all. Others log hundreds of hours in a few afternoons with a handful of pens and logbooks. Some exaggerate flight time to improve their stature. I overheard a student ask a bank courier pilot how much time he had. "Oh, I don't know. I've got so much time, I quit counting."

I'd seen his logbook. The total was not much over a thousand hours, and he'd been logging his daily 35-minute trips between Seattle and Port Angeles as an hour or more each way.

I invited a student to go along on a ferry flight from Wichita at his expense for free cross-country time. The long trip would broaden his experience in ways that a dozen flights close to home would not. Doug had relatives in Oregon, and he asked me if we could visit them and maybe spend the night. I said we could if we went that way. I didn't know he then told them when we'd arrive.

Weather dictated a route southwest through New Mexico and Arizona, then north through California and Oregon. Soon after we got off the ground, Doug needed to pee. He needed to pee almost every hour.

There are piss cans designed for use in small airplanes, but I'd never needed one. Fuel tanks would be empty before my tank was full. At the rate we were going, we'd wear out tires and brakes on the trip home, assuming we didn't die of old age first. I told Doug to drink no more coffee. We rounded up a plastic gallon jug with a screw top and pressed on. We spent the first night in Albuquerque.

Doug called his relatives from Las Vegas to say we'd be later than expected. I doubted we would get there that day. We stopped in late afternoon at Sacramento's Executive Airport for fuel. Doug was eager to keep going, but I didn't like the looks of weather ahead. Fog formed on the airport as we taxied to a parking spot. I wanted nothing more than a good meal, a hot shower, and a long sleep. Doug saw no reason we couldn't press on. After all, the airplane and I were qualified to fly on instruments. I hesitated. Perhaps I was being unfairly negative. We walked over to the Flight Service Station for a briefing.

A warm front was sliding in from the sea. Tops of embedded thunderstorms reached thirty thousand feet. Low clouds and fog meant that any more flying that night would be solid instruments from takeoff to landing. Freezing level ahead of the front was four thousand feet. That was the minimum IFR altitude north of Sacramento, and that minimum rose to ten thousand crossing the Siskiyou Mountains. Redding, farther north up the valley and still in California, was the farthest we could possibly go.

Doug was more optimistic. Who knows? By the time we get to Redding, it might be better farther north.

There was no way in hell I was going to fly out of Sacramento that night, but I wanted my student to understand why continuing would be unacceptably dangerous. The trip was supposed to be a learning experience.

The FSS man stood on his side of the briefing counter much as a bartender might while observing two patrons argue relative merits of baseball players. I took a flight plan form from a pad on the counter, turned it over, and drew a line down the middle of the blank page. I told Doug we'd list all the factors in our favor in one column and all the things working against us in the other. After a few minutes, we had this:

Go	No go:
1. New airplane with all instruments and systems working.	1. New airplane that hasn't been flown enough to give any gremlins time to make their mischief known.
2. Reasonably competent instrument pilot.	2. Fatigued crew.
3. Copilot with enough experience and knowledge to help with the workload.	3. Crew unfamiliar with area.
	4. Night.
	5. Solid IFR weather from surface to 30,000.
	6. Embedded thunderstorms
	7. Probability of icing.

The fact that we would save a motel bill if we got to Oregon was not an operational consideration, so I didn't let Doug add that to the Go column. If all went well, we stood to gain a few dozen miles. If much went wrong, we could die. Doug stared at the facts displayed in black and white.

"I guess you're right," he said.

A few years later, I became bored with my subscription to *Private Pilot* because I was no longer the entry-level aviator the magazine was oriented toward. It occurred to me that perhaps I'd gained enough experience and insight that I could write for such a publication. I thought the method I'd used to help Doug realize that flying that night was not wise might be just the sort of thing *Private Pilot* would print. I wrote a query letter to the editor summarizing my proposed article. I have on the wall above my computer a large, framed photograph of the check, the manuscript, and the cover of the October 1981 issue of the magazine.

I wrote the editor again, asking if he'd be interested in the story of my truncated trip to Santa Barbara as a commercial student. I wrote it up, rewrote and refined it, and sent it off. Later, *Private Pilot* printed a third article, one featuring swirling Cheetos.

The articles I'd sold had been easy to write because they'd required no research. To continue writing for flying magazines after I ran out of near-death experiences would have required actual work, so I lost interest.

I enrolled in the Instrument Flight Instructor course in mid-March. Only ten flight lessons were required, but because scheduling required that my instructor and the airplane and I be free simultaneously, completing the course took four months.

As afternoons lengthened and weather improved, more people dropped by the airport to look at airplanes and to ask about flying lessons. Trying to come up with three thousand dollars kept many people on the ground.

Toward the end of March, I took my daughter to Wichita to ferry another new airplane. Katrina was five years old and too small to see anything but sky out the windows. It wasn't until late the second day that I realized she was airsick because she couldn't see the ground. I had her sit on a rolled sleeping bag so she could see the horizon and nausea disappeared.

Charts for visual flying are much like highway maps, but they include railroad tracks, and power lines. They show airports, radio beacons, and other aids to navigation. And they show preferred routes to fly through mountains when weather is not good. Contour lines and colors depict terrain.

Snow showers varied in intensity as we flew up the Oregon Trail from Boise to Baker City for our last fuel stop. The Interstate and the railroad between Baker City and LaGrande follow a broad valley northwest but take different routes through mountains and down into the lower valley beyond. The chart indicates the railroad is the preferred route through those mountains, but the highway takes a more direct line.

We flew low along the Interstate and I noted where the chart showed transmission lines strung from tall steel towers across the concrete highway. The chart showed the twisted S-turn the highway made as it entered narrow Ladd Canyon and dropped steeply into the next wide valley on its way to LaGrande. I'd driven the highway more than once, so even with poor visibility, I knew where I was and what came next.

Flying through snow showers just under indefinite cloud bases five hundred feet above the ground, I watched intently for the first indication that the highway was beginning its sharp right turn and descent. What the chart did not make clear was that the power lines did not follow terrain down one side of Ladd Canyon and up the other. They crossed the canon in one span like cables of a suspension bridge.

My eyes were on the road below and the mountains on each side. We were just beginning the right turn to stay over the highway when I saw steel towers at my altitude left and right on the top of the ridge.

I yanked the yoke hard and slammed in the throttle as several hard black horizontal lines materialized from the snow impossibly near and impossibly fast. I tensed for whatever hitting power lines feels like but nothing happened. I let out breath and pushed the nose down and pulled back the throttle to drop out of cloud and regain sight of the ground. The highway was turning, and I turned hard to follow. Seconds later, we'd passed through the gap and were cruising toward LaGrande. As shock subsided, anger rose. *Those fucking wires almost killed my little girl!*

True, the chart suggested following the railroad, but that was only a suggestion. I thought it criminally negligent that there was no note on the chart about the unusual hazard of a power line hundreds of feet above an Interstate highway with no orange balls on the wires. I wrote a letter to the FAA describing the incident and urging that those power lines either be run down the canyon slopes to cross the highway at a normal height, or, at the very least, be marked with balls and noted on the chart.

I would see those wires again.

To build time, I flew freshly washed airplanes once around the traffic pattern to dry them off and flew test flights when airplanes came out of inspections or repairs. Not a tenth of an hour went unrecorded. At the end of March, I logged six-tenths of multi-engine time riding right seat in a Cessna 402 to Seattle on my way to Wichita to bring back another new airplane. The pilot signed the time off as familiarization.

I tried to be on time for students, but some delays were beyond my control. If an airplane came back from a charter late, or if bad weather delayed a lesson, I might not catch up for the rest of the day.

Delays in the morning ate up scheduled lunch breaks. After McDonald's came to Port Angeles, whoever had a half an hour free would drive to the other end of town with orders from pilots and mechanics. My standing order was five cheeseburgers. I'd gobble them down while filling out one student's logbook and training folder as my next student was preflighting an airplane.

My roster of students gradually increased, but it was mostly a hodge-podge of on-again, off-again students who might never complete the requirements for a license. Many did not finish because they ran out of money.

I urged new students to get a loan, sell their car, rob a bank, do whatever it took to pay for the entire course up front. If coming up with money every week was not an issue, students flew often and finished in minimum time. Having to take time off until payday meant spending time and money brushing off cobwebs. Many such students dropped out.

Most of the names in my logbook evoke memories of faces, but some do not. Many were introductory flights or rental checkouts sandwiched between regular students, people I saw once or twice and never again. Some stand out because they were either exceptionally good or exceptionally bad, or because of some unusual problem.

Ray flew radio-controlled airplanes as a hobby, and turns with his models were made with aileron only. An airplane will turn with no rudder input, but, when you turn the yoke left, the nose of the airplane yaws first to the right as the airplane begins to bank left. When rolling the wings level after the turn, the nose will first yaw further left. Just a little rudder pressure in the beginning and end of the turn overcomes adverse yaw.

I had Ray fly back from lunch at the Port Townsend airport following every turn of US 101 with his hands in his lap and making all turns with rudder only. I took care of the yoke, holding it dead level. Turning with rudder alone is as sloppy as with aileron alone, but the airplane turns. By the time we got back to Port Angeles, Ray had absorbed awareness of what those pedals did besides apply brakes.

Another student had the opposite problem. He knew that rudder contributed to the turn, but he had no feel for it. In a climbing left turn, all that's necessary is to ease off some of the pressure being held on the right rudder. He would, instead, remove all pressure from the right pedal and push the left. The airplane would bank more sharply into the turn than he wanted, and, in his sudden attempt to make things right, his left turn would become a right turn.

I had him make climbing turns with aileron alone. I held proper rudder pressure while he made smooth turns. Then I had him put his right foot on the pedal but leave his left foot flat on the floor. He could get all the left rudder he needed by easing off on the right. Within a few minutes, he was flying climbing turns correctly.

Another student had a bad habit of taking his hand off the throttle while landing. After making the turn to final, he'd rest his right hand on his knee. No amount of telling him to keep his hand on the throttle made an impression. I was not going to let him solo until he consistently kept his hand on the throttle throughout the landing, ready to adjust power immediately should he have to go around.

I knew he was conscious of cost. One day, as we began to land at the end of his lesson, his hand settled on his knee and I said, "Go around."

It wasn't unusual to tell students to abort a landing without warning as part of training. But, when we came around again, and again his hand came off the throttle, I again told him to go around. He looked puzzled, but he did it. On downwind I said, "Scott, it takes a tenth of an hour to fly once around the pattern. It costs you two dollars and thirty cents every time you go around. We are going to stay up here and never touch the runway until either you keep your hand on the throttle or we run out of gas."

That didn't work with another student with the same problem but with more money. Finally, exasperated beyond endurance, after a couple of successive go-arounds, I was silent throughout the approach until, while concentrating on the landing, his hand came off the throttle as he was looking to his left, beginning his turn toward the runway. I leaned close enough to kiss his ear and screamed, *"Keep your hand on the throttle!"*

Months later, after he'd earned his license, he saw me and laughed. "I'll never forget that time you screamed in my ear," He said. "Every time I turn final, I remember. And I keep my hand on the throttle."

Most students were men and boys, but women and girls were much easier to teach. Whether it's biology or culture or both, I don't know, but women more readily accepted instruction.

There is another advantage to teaching women, a perk for instructors who teach in high-wing airplanes that have built-in steps for climbing on the strut to look in the fuel tanks. Airplanes that don't have those steps require the pilot to drag a stepladder out to the airplane to verify tanks are full and caps are secure.

One step is a metal ledge low on the side of the fuselage in front of the wing, and the other is a footrest midway up the wing strut. When a pilot is standing on those steps checking fuel, one leg is fully extended to the lower step and the other is bent sharply at hip and knee. When a female student wearing jeans or slacks is on the steps, the instructor can readily evaluate shape and muscle tone, and, depending on the fabric, even tell what style of panties she is wearing. Some instructors swear they can read the label on the panties, but pilots lie about a lot of things.

One Saturday in April, I was in the office answering phones and doing paperwork when a man and his son walked in. Chris was 16. His father did most of the talking.

While not wanting to discourage another student from contributing to my income, I stressed that the boy would not be able to get his license for nearly a year. That would add to his cost, as he'd have to fly occasionally for several months between training and checkride.

Chris's father asked about the wisdom of the least experienced pilots teaching others to fly. I argued that someone recently trained still had conscious awareness of what he was doing and could more easily transfer that knowledge to a student than could someone who had been flying so long that most of what he did was subconscious. At the end of our talk, he signed his son up. I handed over the red plastic zipper bag of textbooks with the Cessna logo and explained how the course integrated ground school and book learning with flight training.

The first student I signed off for a checkride failed. He was a commercial student I'd flown with only a few times toward the end of his training. After taking him through review of all the maneuvers that might be asked of him by the examiner, I thought he was ready.

Not having a student from beginning to end of training leaves open the possibility that something may not have been covered thoroughly. Any pilot who gets a pink slip feels bad, but his instructor feels worse. I flew with the young man twice more in the following few days, signed him off again, and he passed his checkride.

I flew an intro flight with a quiet young man just out of high school. Brian was the first student I had from first ride to checkride. He learned fast and flew well. Weeks later, I waited tensely for his checkride to end. When Brian taxied to the fuel pumps and shut down, his examiner climbed out of the airplane and shook my hand. "That was the best private pilot checkride I've ever seen," he said,

I signed off twenty-five more students for private pilot rides over the next two years. My record of never having a private pilot student fail was a growing source of pride, and I did not realize I was putting pressure on each successive student not to break my streak.

While I was busy instructing, I was also a student. I had to finish my Instrument Instructor rating and then get multi-engine training. I wasn't the only one whose VA education benefits would expire in August. The flight school was swamped the summer of 1977 with veterans wanting to burn unused credits before deadline.

A new federal requirement for non-professional pilots provided instructors with more flight time and a break from instructing. The Biennial Flight Review forced pilots to demonstrate every two years that they were still competent. Before the BFR, once pilots had private licenses, they could fly their entire lives without ever receiving more training or another check. The BFR was pass/fail, but failures were not recorded. I did not like BFRs. I did not like having to tell a pilot twice my age who'd flown in combat and had amassed more flight time than perhaps I ever would that he needed refresher instruction.

The first person I conducted a flight review for was in his seventies and had been flying half a century, but he didn't fly often and it showed. After an hour in the air, I realized that it wasn't just a matter of dealing with cobwebs and rust. So many regulations had changed over the years, the man would have had to take a private pilot ground school to fill huge gaps. I was as gentle as I could be in explaining why I could not sign him off. I offered to schedule him for remedial instruction, but he said he'd have to think about it. I never saw him again.

I asked other instructors how they handled BFRs. Most said that no private pilot is as sharp and as knowledgeable as on the day he got his license. What they looked for was, can this pilot fly safely in the kind of flying he normally does?

My expectations were perhaps too high. On the other hand, I didn't want to read in the paper that someone I'd just signed off had crashed and died.

One gray-haired infrequent pilot showed lack of understanding of basic aerodynamics. I didn't see how I could pass him, and I hated the prospect of having to tell him. I asked him to make a short-field landing. He got us on the ground without breaking anything, but it was ugly. When we taxied in and shut down, he spoke first. "I guess I'm rustier than I thought," he said. "I'll have to think about whether I want to get more training or just hang it up."

After that day, as soon as I realized I wasn't going to sign someone off, I tried to put him in the position of realizing for himself how deficient he was.

A man my age or a little older enrolled in the Commercial Pilot course. The state of Alaska was going to pay for his training, rehabilitation from an on-the-job back injury. Such injuries are great for milking disability insurance because it's impossible to disprove back pain. My new student—I'll call him Clod—was not interested in following the training syllabus. He just wanted to fly without paying for it.

Most heavy equipment operators handle airplanes easily. Their manipulation of several controls at once translates to smooth, coordinated control of the airplane. Clod must have done nothing but knock down trees with a bulldozer. He slammed the airplane around both on the ground and in the air.

Alaska sent evaluation forms for me to return to confirm Clod's progress in the course. I filled out the first one and sent it back with a letter. Not long after, Clod came in to complain. He couldn't understand why I hadn't gone along, why I hadn't scratched his back as he was scratching ours. I told him I preferred to earn my money, not steal it.

I'd rather have instructed new students without radios in the airplane. Almost everyone recognizes the hazard of using a telephone while driving a car, but many people are surprised to learn it's legal to fly an airplane and *not* talk on the radio.

Too often, students, and some professionals, make talking on the radio a priority over flying the airplane. Radio procedure was part of the course, though, and necessary for most flying. Listening for a couple of minutes while approaching an uncontrolled airport usually provides everything a pilot needs—wind, altimeter setting, and active runway—as others call in for that information. I told students to pretend it cost fifty cents a word to talk but that listening was free.

Pearson had the bank contract again and I flew many evening round trips to Boeing Field. Sometimes I took Katrina along for the ride. Taking my daughter along on charters was almost the only time I got to spend with her.

From the time I began flying lessons, the amount of time and energy I spent at the airport caused stress at home. We'd been married six years when we took that biplane ride that changed the course of my life and changed me. Being married to an impulsive, disorganized man had to be rough to begin with, and my wife did not like the tunnel-visioned, single-minded person I'd become. I was paying for years of goofing off, of changing jobs every year or two out of boredom, struggling at low-pay jobs with no prospect of ever living differently. This new lifestyle would be only temporary, I promised. I'd begun my flying career late, but once I caught up, I'd be back to normal.

I wasn't the only one with a new direction. My wife was developing interests and associations of her own. I didn't share her life any more than she shared mine.

In addition to the large number of students that summer weather brings, we had the surge of veterans taking advantage of their last opportunity to use the GI Bill. Tourists wanted scenic flights. Charter demand was high, and we flew fire patrols for the Department of Natural Resources.

Whether fire patrols were fun or boring depended on the observer. The DNR specified precise routes, speed, and altitude. We were supposed to fly slower than normal to give the observer plenty of time to plot smokes on maps and call them in on her radio. We were not supposed to deviate from the route for a closer look.

Two and a half hours in the hot sun took forever, especially while droning along over the same track every day. Some observers insisted we fly by the DNR book, but others had more sense. With them, we flew at normal cruise speed, and that gave us time to go look at things off the prescribed track and still cover the ground in the allotted time. If the observer was really laid back, we'd fly low just offshore for a few minutes and open side windows to cool off in ocean air.

Once, on a boring, by-the-book fire patrol with a serious observer I'd not flown with, I demonstrated weightlessness. After explaining how it worked and asking her permission, I put the airplane in a shallow dive to build speed, then pulled up into a climb and pushed the nose over to fly a parabolic arc for a few seconds. If done right, objects in the airplane rise and hover before the airplane pulls out of the dive on the other side of the arc. To my surprise, the prim observer thought that was great sport, so we did it several more times. It didn't even bother her when the engine sputtered as gasoline floated in the carburetor and interrupted the flow to the cylinders.

My worst fear as a flight instructor was that someone I had taught might crash because I had not been thorough. There was no chance of overlooking something vital when I had a student from first lesson to last and followed the syllabus. Many students, like my first two, got flying lessons when and where they could, their training scattered over many years and different instructors

One such man ran into a mountain at night flying his Cessna 182 from Seattle to Port Angeles. He did not give mountains enough room, did not stay on a safe course over water and low ground until he could see the lights of Sequim and Port Angeles. He slammed into tall trees on a steep slope and his daughter died.

He was a busy man and had been an off-and-on student for years before receiving his license. I wondered if he'd not have crashed if he and I had flown a cross-country training trip at night rather than in daytime as we did the only time I flew with him. I'd have emphasized the greater safety margins night flight required, especially near mountains. Perhaps he would have remembered, and perhaps he would have given those mountains a wider berth.

Cleon McClain went with me to Kansas to ferry two new Cessnas for Pearson. At lunch in Boise the second day, I said I'd show him the power lines I'd nearly hit. There was no snowstorm that July day as we flew up the highway toward Ladd Canyon, but the wires had been moved. They followed the slopes down both sides of the canyon and crossed the highway between towers at a normal height, far below where any small airplane might fly. And they were marked with bright orange balls. I remembered the letter I'd written to the FAA and was impressed with the power of my pen.

A short time later, I saw an article in a Seattle newspaper about settlement of a lawsuit against a power company filed by relatives of people killed when a small airplane hit unmarked power lines in northeast Oregon months before my own close call. Maybe my pen wasn't so powerful after all.

* * *

None of my students got higher than 90% on a written exam, although I had high hopes for perfect scores from a few. We went over the three questions one perfectionist missed and discovered I'd been teaching the wrong answer to a weather-related question. As I'd been a weather observer in the Air Force, my embarrassment was deep. It was an error on a level of a radio announcer on his first flying lesson talking into the back side of the microphone.

Some students had difficulty with multiple-choice tests. I taught a backdoor approach to choosing correct answers on any exam that offers choices: Instead of looking for the right answer, read each answer and give yourself a good reason why it is not correct. If only one answer can't be eliminated, it's the correct one.

I advised not studying in the twenty-four hours before a test. Go to a movie, take a hike, do *anything* that day except open a textbook or review notes. It takes the brain about a day to organize and file information.

The first student I sent to Seattle to take a written exam was a retired man who had not been exposed to formal education in decades. I taught him my method of arriving at correct answers, and he did well enough on practice exams. I suggested he drive to Seattle the night before taking the test, get a room, have a good dinner, go to a movie, and get a good night's sleep.

The man was as sheepish as a five-year-old explaining an empty cookie jar when he brought in his test result several days later. He'd gotten up at three in the morning to drive to Seattle. He made a good ferry connection and arrived a couple of hours before FAA offices opened, so he sat in his car and studied. He scored an embarrassing 47%, and I was never able to persuade him to try again.

The last student I recommended for a private pilot checkride was young man who learned fast and flew well. In discussion, he showed solid understanding of what he was learning, but on practice exams, his scores were almost at the level of chance.

After one miserable performance on a practice test, I sat down with him to take however long it took to go over every question in the book of several hundred from which each student's FAA test was drawn. If he had to memorize the entire book, that's what I was going to have him do. After a few minutes, I realized he did not know how to read.

He could read slowly in the manner of a beginner, pointing at each word, sounding it out, and then saying it. A sentence to him was a collection of words, not a cohesive unit expressing a thought. By the time he'd deciphered the last word of a sentence, he had no clear idea of what he'd read.

I spent an afternoon with him, trying to find a way to overcome an unfathomable gap in his education. He'd graduated from high school and had never been held back to repeat a grade. At the end of the day he said, "You've just spent more time helping me learn to read than any of my teachers ever did." I had to turn away so he couldn't see my eyes. When he passed his written exam and private pilot checkride, no one could have been more proud of him than I was.

I tried to come up with ways for students to get more out of training than the minimum in the syllabus. It would be more fun for students and less monotonous for me if I filled the seats and made a cross-country flight long enough and far enough that each of three students could plan and fly a third of the trip. They'd fly a four-seat airplane with a full load for the only time in their training, and calculating weight and balance would be more than a formality.

Three of my students were ready for cross-country. All three thought the long flight would be fun. We got started late and landed at Port Orchard for our scheduled lunch break at the airport café, and that is when the day began to go to hell.

The first one of us served had finished eating before the second burger came off the grill. A substitute cook was incapable of frying more than one piece of meat at a time. Lunch, planned for less than an hour, took two.

We flew to Olympia and Toledo and refueled. The FAA man gave us a tour of the Flight Service Station and a weather briefing. We flew into Oregon and students swapped seats. After landing at two more Oregon airports, we re-crossed the Columbia River for a night landing at Yakima. I was beginning to think a long trip with students wasn't such a bright idea. It was late and we were tired.

The third student got cheated out of his planned route. Even flying straight back to Port Angeles, we'd arrive near midnight, and shallow fog often formed at night in August. I filed an instrument flight plan and we took off. Nobody talked much as we crossed the Cascades and Puget Sound. We could see Port Angeles, but airport lights were diffuse under a blanket of fog.

The Coast Guard base at Port Angeles is at the end of a long sand spit forming a natural breakwater for the harbor. Pearson had an agreement with the Coast Guard that allowed us to land there when weather wasn't good enough at the airport. The VOR approach was over open water and allowed descent to much lower altitudes than did the approach to Port Angeles with mountains just south and tall trees all around.

At five hundred feet, we were still above broken fog. By the time we saw the runway, we were too close to it to get down. Had it not been so late and had we not been so tired, I'd have probably done the intelligent thing and gone where weather was good, but the desire to land where the car is parked is strong, and fatigue weakens defenses against stupidity.

At one time, the minimum approach altitude for the coast guard base was lower than five hundred feet. Except for ships in the harbor, there was nothing nearby to hit. I explained all this to my students and said I was comfortable shooting the approach at three hundred feet, but if anyone had the slightest discomfort, we'd go somewhere else.

It was not a discussion among equals. It was unfair to ask students to agree to something they only marginally understood. It was unfair of me to break rules with students captive and at my mercy. But we were all tired and wanted to get on the ground. We took a taxi to the flight school and our cars.

Some people should not fly airplanes. Some don't have enough physical coordination or spatial awareness to park a car, but I considered bad attitude equally disqualifying.

A man with thinning gray hair and bib overalls came in one day. He'd taken lessons at an airport closer to home, but he said his instructors there didn't like him. I thought perhaps those he'd flown with lacked the patience required for teaching older students, but, after only a couple of flights with him, I understood the problem. He could not accept correction.

I always tried to temper criticism with praise. "Nice job on the bank and altitude, Al, but we lost a little speed. You need to add a little more power in the turn. Let's try it again."

Most students would nod and try again. Not Al.

It's good when a student can verbalize the reason something didn't work, but there is a difference between reason and excuse. Al's excuses were about anything but him: "You didn't say how much power to add," or, "This airplane is different from others I've flown." And he was a whiner. If we were booked solid on a day he wanted to fly, he implied we were lying because we didn't like him. He was the most negative student of any age I ever encountered, and I was not unhappy when he moved on to make some other instructor miserable.

A student I'll call Tom was more afraid of being in the air than any other student or passenger I ever encountered. Mild turbulence turned him ashen. In a moderate bump, he'd take his hands off the controls, grab the bottom of the seat with his right hand and brace his left against the post between windscreen and door. We couldn't get past Lesson 4. Stalls scared him to death. When air let go of the wing, Tom let go of the yoke and grabbed handholds.

One day, he came in for another attempt to get past stalls. Weather was lovely with blue sky and puffs of cumulus, but the air was not smooth. It was not rough enough to cause discomfort for other students, but I knew that I'd be wasting my time and his money to fly with Tom that day. I told him it was rougher than he'd be comfortable with and suggested we reschedule. Never had I seen such a chasm between spoken words and body language. "Gee that's too bad, and it's such a pretty day!" he said, but the relief in his face and posture could have been read from across the street.

I sat down with him after his next attempt to complete Lesson 4 and suggested he might want to fly once or twice with a different instructor, that perhaps it was chemistry between us that made him uncomfortable in the air. I scheduled him with a part-time instructor, a retired Air Force general liked by all his students. Perhaps Bill Georgi could get Tom over his hurdle, though I didn't have high hopes. A few days later, I noticed that Tom had canceled his lesson with Bill, and a few days after that, I heard his voice on the radio.

There was another flight school at the other end of the airport, a small operation with a couple of instructors and two or three airplanes. When I heard Tom announce his departure, I went outside to watch. The little Piper Tomahawk lifted into the air, and there was only one person in it. I asked his instructor later, "How did you get him to solo so fast? I couldn't get him through simple stalls and steep turns. We never even got to emergency landings. How did you do it?"

"Well, I saw he had ten or twelve hours in his log, and I went up with him and he made a couple of nice landings, so I signed him off and got out."

I was astounded that an instructor had soloed a student he'd flown with only once and who had not been introduced to important pre-solo procedures. But his first solo got Tom over his psychological hurdle, and he went on to earn his license.

I had a student too short to reach the pedals, even with the seat all the way forward and a pillow behind her back. I was afraid to sign her off for solo in a 172 for fear that she might not be able to control it if things went wrong. She was serious about learning to fly, was comfortable in the air, and flew often.

Our first two-seat Cessna 152 solved her size problem, and I soloed her the second time she flew it. Last I knew, she was an airline pilot.

One day, as a student and I finished a lesson over the practice area several miles east of the airport, another instructor was in the area with his student. We kept in radio contact with other airplanes in the practice area, and, on that day, we heard words you never want to hear in airplanes: *Watch this!*

A snap roll is a horizontal spin. You slow the airplane down in level flight to a speed at which the wing will stall before it breaks and yank the yoke back to the stop as you stomp a rudder pedal. One wing stalls and the horizon spins around the nose of the airplane. As the line between land and sky returns to level, you relax on the pedal and yoke and the airplane continues on its way as if nothing had happened. I'd never done one.

The airplane in front of us did a snap roll. I said to my student, "You wanna do that?"

"Sure!" she said.

Someone saw us. The chief pilot chewed out the other instructor and me, not so much for the illegal snap rolls as for the example we had set for our students.

Instructors weren't the only ones who did dumb things. Chris, my 16-year-old, had completed training and was killing time, waiting for his birthday and checkride. We got a call one Saturday afternoon from an irate city resident. Someone was buzzing her neighborhood in a blue-and-white Cessna. Moments later, Blackball called to say that someone was flying low over the *M.V. Coho*, the Port Angeles-to-Victoria ferry, in a blue-and-white Cessna. Chris was flying a blue-and-white Cessna. The chief pilot suggested I have a word with him.

Chris parked the airplane and came inside to turn in the key and log sheet. I said, "Just how low were you over the *Coho*, Chris?" His young face froze.

"Uh, five hundred feet."

"A full five hundred? You sure you weren't maybe a hundred or so lower?"

He was sure.

"Well, we got a call that you were pretty low, but I know people on the ground aren't usually good judges of altitude," I said. Chris's face relaxed.

"How about when you were circling over town?"

Wariness returned.

"A thousand over town," he said.

"AGL or MSL?"

The rule was, over towns and congested areas, a thousand feet minimum above ground level with an overriding requirement to be high enough to be safe. Port Angeles rises from sea level downtown to several hundred feet in outlying areas. Chris conceded he'd been going by the altimeter.

I tried to be properly stern without making a big deal out of it. He was a good kid, and I was pretty sure he'd not do that again.

Chris passed his checkride when he turned seventeen and served in the air force as a fighter pilot and flight instructor before becoming an airline pilot.

I learned not to rely on others when my life was on the line. A national park ranger chartered a survey right after Mark came to work one summer as a fire patrol pilot. Mark's brother Larry flew the airline schedule and instructed for Pearson. Mark went along for the ride with the ranger and me to see some of the country.

Ragged and broken clouds obscured mountain tops and high ridges. The park ranger, riding in the back seats so he could look out either side, directed me up the Dungeness River into the mountains. I followed his instructions as we climbed closer to cloud bases and visibility diminished. Steep sides of the valley rose into the clouds and the narrowing valley floor rose ahead. It was a good thing the ranger knew where we were, because I didn't. Then he leaned forward, his head between Mark's and mine, and muttered, "This doesn't look right."

I yanked the airplane into a tight diving turn and we retreated. The ranger got his bearings and redirected me up a different arm of the valley, but I refused. After that experience, I resolved that if I didn't know exactly where I was and where I was going, I wasn't going. The next day, Larry said to me with no more than a hint of a tight-jawed smile, "I hear you tried to kill my little brother yesterday."

Income depended solely on time spent in the air. Days began early and ended late. To take a day off or to go home early was money not earned and hours not logged. At the ends of such days, there wasn't much energy left for family. Too often, when I thought I'd be home in time for supper, a charter would pop up or a prospective student would walk in the door.

When I had a couple of hours free and there were empty seats both ways on Seattle flights, I'd take the right seat to log multi-engine time toward the five hundred hours in the airplane I needed to make the insurance company happy. I had my own lessons to fly, too, and time left on the GI Bill was short. In July, I passed my instrument instructor checkride. All that was left was the multi-engine course, and I had the busiest month of the year to get it done. The records show I made it in time, some of the records, anyway. I logged 140 hours in August, twenty-one of them as instruction received in a Cessna 402 that I hadn't set foot in.

I flew three national park rangers on a search for climbers marooned between glaciers on Mount Olympus. A fully loaded 172 near high mountains required all my attention. The ranger in the right seat spotted the climbers and opened the window to drop a message on a long, bright-colored streamer. The unexpected noise of the window snapping open and the loud rush of cold air when I was focused intently on nearby rocks and ice almost stopped my heart. My passengers thought it was funny.

While flying into Paine Field on charter in a 172, my radio failed. I would have entered the traffic pattern above normal altitude and waited for the tower to notice me and signal with the green light that I was cleared to land, but low clouds held me to pattern altitude. I was focused on the tower more than what was around me and came uncomfortably close to another small airplane. Then the radio started working.

Once on the ground and clear of the runway, I called Ground Control to check the radio. It worked fine. Another pilot, overhearing the conversation, made some remark about pilots who don't know how to use the radio and blame the equipment. I wanted to invite him to Port Angeles where I'd have the radio checked. I'd make him a deal. If there was nothing wrong with the radio, he could watch me eat it. If it was defective, I'd get to jam it up his ass. But I kept my mouth shut and left the microphone on its hook.

The radio worked again long enough for me to get taxi and takeoff clearances before dying again. Our radio man found the malfunctioning circuit. For a long time, I hoped that the pilot who had called me a liar would recognize my voice and say something to me, preferably in person.

As days became shorter, I continued flying the mix of students and charters and occasionally the scheduled commuter run to Seattle when loads or overloads were light enough for a single-engine airplane.

In early December, my schedule eased and I got to ferry another new 172. Storms and adverse wind dictated the southern route. I flew low through Monument Valley, lower than the tops of the massive red rocks, flying through gaps between them, slaloming between pinnacles.

After leaving the valley, I descended to less than a hundred feet and followed the slope of the empty desert land, up and down and around. When I zoomed up one hillside and pushed the nose over at the crest, I flew over a hogan, scattering chickens and startling horses in a corral. A Navajo family looked up as I blasted through their peaceful morning, and in an instant, I was gone.

That took all pleasure out of my day. I could imagine what I'd be thinking and feeling if some jerk like me had roared through my front yard.

Two days later, I went to the Cessna plant to ferry a two-seat 152. Bad weather in the west forced an early stop for the night in Laramie and a rare stay in a motel. Weather wasn't better the next morning, and I turned back when snow and low cloud reduced visibility to near zero. I waited two hours at Rawlins until snow showers had passed.

The cold front was still northwest of me and flowing my way like a wall of wet concrete. Cold air spilling out at the bottom pushed a roll of dust ahead of it. I turned left to parallel the front and edged close to it until my little airplane was surfing on rising air pushed up by cold air flooding the land below. I coasted on the updraft into Utah and landed at Vernal for the night, happy to be on the ground as storms roared through.

Ancient shorelines of Lake Bonneville are visible on the sides of mountains around Great Salt Lake. I climbed to the altitude of the highest bench mark and leveled off there, imagining I was sailing a boat on the surface of the former lake. So thoroughly was I engrossed in my boat movie as I sailed north, I had to remind myself to climb to avoid running aground at the shoreline.

Late in December, I was called in early on a day off to fly an extra section on the first flight of the day to Seattle. The windshield on the Cessna 207 was dirty, so I dragged a stepladder to the airplane and cleaned the Plexiglas, first the left side and then the right. I forgot about the ladder as I finished inspecting the airplane and couldn't see it from the left seat. I was in a hurry and ran into the ladder and dinged the fiberglass wheel cover. It was the first time I'd damaged an airplane.

Months later, again in a hurry, I taxied a 172 into its tiedown spot near the front of a large hangar. The accordion-style door was open and I sheared off a plastic wingtip.

An Air India 747 crashed on New Year's Day of 1978 and brought me several new students. Every time an airliner crashed, people came out to the airport for introductory lessons. Any publicity is better than no publicity.

Early in February, I completed one full year as a flight instructor. In that year, I logged more than twelve hundred hours in the air.

The two-place Cessna 152 was fun to fly and fun to teach in, but the little engine fouled spark plugs. The older Cessna 150 burned leaded gasoline not much different from automobile fuel. The new model's engine burned low-lead fuel, better for the environment but not good for peace of mind.

My student was practicing slow flight when the engine began running rough. I thought a magneto had gone bad, but switching between them made no difference. I found a power setting that kept us in the air without shaking the airplane too hard and flew us back to the airport. Mechanics discovered fouled plugs.

Old school thinking was, you ran the engines full rich below five thousand feet and leaned for better performance at higher altitudes where air was thinner. New manuals advised leaning above three thousand. Lean mixtures burned hotter and kept plugs clean.

The 152 needed to be leaned out anytime power was low, including taxiing, to keep spark plugs functioning. The hazard to leaning the mixture as soon as the engine started was forgetting to push the knob back in to full rich for takeoff to get maximum power and to prevent overheating.

I bought a new 152 later that year and leased it back to Pearson for instruction and rental as a way to pay for it. After several instances of fouled plugs, I adjusted the mixture cable at the carburetor so that when the knob was all the way forward, the mixture wasn't quite full rich. Every time my airplane was scheduled for maintenance, I'd put the mixture cable adjustment back where it belonged. After mechanics finished, I'd reset it to my satisfaction.

Meddling under the cowl was not legal, not smart, and not safe. It was one thing to alter an airplane no one flew but me, but mine was flown by students and renters who paid for the privilege. My thinking didn't go that far at the time. I'd discovered a way to keep plugs from fouling, and that was good enough for me.

One busy weekend in March, a young couple came in to ask about lessons. The young man enjoyed his intro flight, but his wife was bubbly with excitement after hers. She talked him into signing them both up for lessons. I suggested they have different instructors. If one progressed faster than the other, they could blame it on differences in instruction. They both wanted to fly with me. They lived some distance away and scheduled lessons for both days every weekend.

As first solo approached, both became nervous. The young woman's hour stretched to two. Apprehension interfered with her flying, and after several bad landings and her increasing despair, I told her we were wasting her time and money, that we'd try again another day. But I had a plan.

After they'd gone to town for lunch, it was her husband's turn. He was calm and flew well, so I signed him off and stood next to the flight school with his wife and watched him fly his three landings. She was miserable.

After he taxied to the fuel pumps and got out of the airplane with the customary huge grin, and after congratulations had been offered by me and a few students and instructors who'd been watching, I told his wife that I didn't want her go home with her bad day festering in her mind all week. I talked her into going back up for a couple of landings. Without the pressure of impending solo, she handled the airplane as well as she ever had. I signed her off and got out.

After she finished her landings, the young couple chattered with excitement at their accomplishments as I entered times in their logs and training folders. They'd each soloed after exactly the same amount of instruction. Both passed their checkrides on the same day in July.

Soon after I went to work for Pearson, we rented a new 172 to four men for a multi-day trip to Canada. When they returned, the airplane reeked of smoke so much that few of us could stand to be inside it. We left the doors open for days, but the stench persisted. Pearson made a rule prohibiting smoking in his airplanes.

The sinus problems that had plagued me all my life hadn't gone away when I quit smoking the day my daughter was born. Some of my students were smokers, and I didn't like having to sit shoulder to shoulder in a small airplane with the odor. But, with an air vent blasting in my face, I could tolerate it. A few smokers, though, didn't smell like smoke. Their breath suggested they ate dog shit and never brushed their teeth. One student, a real estate agent, was one of those. He was a good student and a likeable man, but he stank. Even with my air vent open full and blowing fresh air in my face, I could not escape. I had him make most of his turns to the left because I didn't want him to turn toward me to look out the right window. No one was happier than I when he passed his checkride.

Only once did I allow a passenger to smoke. The man was nearly blind and I knew he had only a short time to live. When I saw him fumbling a pack of cigarets out of his pocket, I opened my mouth to say something, but then, for once, I shut it. There were no other passengers on board, and I wasn't going to deny the man one of his few remaining pleasures.

A few years later, I had a full load on the scheduled evening flight from Seattle in the single-engine Cessna 207. As I led my six passengers across the ramp to the airplane, one young man asked if he could smoke. He'd obviously been killing time in the bar. I briefed everyone about seat belts and life jackets with emphasis on the smoking prohibition. The man who wanted to smoke sat directly behind me.

Golfers visualize their swing and the flight of the ball in hopes their muscles will mimic that model. Other athletes use similar mental movies. After takeoff and climb to cruising altitude, my mind wandered and I visualized the man behind me lighting a cigaret and me reaching back and snatching it out of his mouth. It was a fleeting image, and then I was back to flying the airplane.

Moments later, I smelled a wooden match and turned my head just as the man put fire to his cigaret. Encumbered by seatbelt and shoulder strap, I reached over my right shoulder with my left hand and ripped cigaret, match, and part of his scraggly mustache from his mouth.

"I said *No Smoking!*"

He said, "I asked the other people if they'd mind, and they said it was okay."

"They aren't in charge of this airplane. I am, and I said No Smoking."

The cigaret and match were both crushed out in my fist. I dropped them on the floor in front of my seat to clean up later. Then I began to worry about how he might phrase his complaint to my boss.

I helped passengers down from the airplane and thanked them for flying with us. The smoker was the last one out. We both began to apologize at the same time, and that was the end of it. Even if he'd complained of ill treatment, I'd not have been disciplined. I was not yet aware of how much authority an airplane's pilot-in-command, like a ship's captain, has.

Soon after that incident, another passenger didn't get the message. The young man was slightly drunk and wore a cheap suit. He came across like a mafia wannabe, a tough guy. He lit a cigaret in the airplane, and I turned and told him to put it out. He pretended not to hear. I yelled at him, and he said, Hunh? A big man across the aisle from him repeated the message, and the tough guy ground out his cigaret in the ash tray.

When we landed in Port Angeles, the same man lit up as soon as he stepped out of the airplane. I ordered him to put it out and not smoke until he was inside the terminal. The sullen punk dropped his cigaret on the ramp and ground it out, glaring at me from under droopy eyelids. When he walked into the terminal, sheriff's deputies, tipped off that the subject of outstanding warrants was on the passenger list, slapped handcuffs on him and led him away. One of my passengers nudged another and said, "Wow, they take this no-smoking business *seriously!*"

My ultimate goal of flying a twin-engine Cessna 402 back and forth to Seattle sometimes seemed like the carrot dangling from the stick, always one step beyond reach. When I began my quest, a commercial license with instrument rating was all I needed to fly for a scheduled commuter airline. With a new rule from the FAA, commuter pilots had to have an Airline Transport Pilot license, the same license United and Delta pilots have. And Pearson's insurance company required five hundred hours in the multi-engine airplanes Pearson flew, not the five hundred hours total time we'd understood the rule to be.

I didn't yet have a multi-engine rating. We'd filled out my training folder and logbook with twenty hours of instruction spread over the last days of August prior to expiration of my GI Bill benefits. I rationalized that it was only cheating a little bit, a matter of incorrect dates in my log. Pearson promised I'd get the training when things slowed down, probably after Christmas. In early 1978, I flew the time I'd fraudulently logged the previous summer.

I was slow to make allowances for the faster speed of the Cessna 402 when flying traffic patterns for landing practice. After overshooting the turn to final several times, I said, as much to myself as to my instructor, "You'd think I'd quit doing that." He said, "Yeah, you'd think so." I widened my pattern and stopped overshooting.

In the simple airplane operation manuals of the time, critical speeds were predicated on a fully loaded airplane. In training with the airplane empty, using book numbers didn't work, so my instructor and I had come up with climb- and engine-out speeds for the lighter weight.

I worried that the examiner would question the long gap in my log between completion of training and checkride. My instructor told me how to handle that. One of Pearson's pilots went with me when I flew a Cessna 402 to Boeing Field for my checkride.

The examiner paged through the airplane manual and asked questions until he was satisfied I knew the airplane. Then he opened my logbook.

"Before I forget, I have something my instructor and I want to ask you about," I said.

I pulled out a sheet of paper on which we'd printed the lower speeds we'd used for training. I explained why and how we'd arrived at those numbers and asked if he thought our calculations were correct.

The examiner closed my logbook and pushed it aside. We spent several minutes talking about numbers. He thought our speeds looked pretty good. Then he noticed the time and said we needed to get going. He didn't look at my logbook again.

Pearson's operating certificate allowed single-pilot operation in instrument weather conditions with the autopilot working. Canadian rules required two pilots regardless. I slowly built multi-engine time flying as copilot when one was required, and going along for the ride on scheduled flights when a seat was available and I had time. Five hundred hours was going to take forever.

My wife's resentment of my single-minded focus on flying was compounded by my further emotional withdrawal from life at home as tension rose. The only thing that kept us together was our daughter. I could not envision life apart from my little girl. As discussion led toward divorce, agreement that Katrina should stay with me removed the last obstacle.

Juggling full-time parenthood and a more than full-time job wasn't easy. When I impulsively bought an airplane, economic stress became a greater factor in my life than it ever had been before. I rented two rooms to pilots and moved my bed to the living room.

The chief pilot lived nearby. His two children were near Katrina's age, and his home became Katrina's. She went there after school and I picked her up, often in her pajamas and asleep, when I got off work.

One of our students was taking instruction to become a flight instructor. When he reached the end of his course, his instructor left for a job overseas without signing a recommendation for checkride. I looked over the training records and the man's logbook and assumed his instructor had forgotten. I forged his name on the application and the student failed. The FAA examiner wanted to talk to the man's instructor. I explained he was en route to the Middle East. The examiner was not happy. I was scared.

We gave the man more training in areas in which he'd been weak, and on the next try, signed off by me with my own name, he passed.

The first twenty-four private pilot students I signed off passed checkrides on the first try. I was pleased with my record and bragged some. My twenty-fifth failed. Anyone who fails a checkride feels bad, but Bruce felt worse than most. He felt he'd let me down and ruined my record.

I told him I'd let him down by signing him off for his ride before I was certain he was ready. He took another checkride again the next day and passed.

A fierce storm early in 1979 sank half of the Hood Canal floating bridge and cut off direct road access between Seattle and the Olympic Peninsula. Demand for seats was immediately more than the airline could supply. Pearson expanded the schedule to seven trips a day with two airplanes on each flight, and he raised ticket prices.

Pearson was reluctant to add airplanes and hire pilots. Many people thought that, when the state rebuilt the bridge, air traffic would drop back to near what it was before the bridge sank. I didn't think so. Once people got used to the convenience of flying, they'd not go back to the long drive. When the bridge reopened, the drop in passenger loads was hardly noticeable.

A local man started an airline to tap into the demand for seats. Pearson acquired more airplanes and hired more pilots. The flight school manager moved up to flying the commuter schedule full time soon after the bridge sank, and I moved into that job. Pearson sent me to a two-day Cessna Pilot Center manager course to learn how to run a flight school properly. I paid attention, took notes, and returned to Port Angeles with enthusiasm.

The airport authority built a proper terminal building adjoining Pearson's maintenance hangar, complete with ticket counters and a small restaurant. When the control tower and Pearson's small building were taken down to make room for airplane parking, the flight school moved to an office and rooms in a large hanger next door to the new terminal. No longer was one person at one desk sufficient to answer a common phone for all departments.

To run properly, the flight school needed a full-time manager, and someone had to be in the office to answer the phone. I lobbied for a full-time secretary, receptionist, records keeper, and billing clerk. Earl said we couldn't afford it. Pearson's way was, if something didn't directly bring in money, we didn't do it. Either I or one of my instructors would have to be in the office all day.

Flight instructors were expected to fly charters if no one else was available. Having lessons cancelled with little or no notice infuriated students, but students could be rescheduled and charters made more money. When Earl's daughter called over from the main office one day to tell me we had a charter, I told her we had no one available to fly it. She asked what I was doing. I said I was on office duty.

Soon the boss was on the phone. I reminded him that he'd insisted the school phone and office be attended, and that I was the only one there to do it. Soon after that, I got full-time office help.

Flight instructors don't get paid for sitting around. As school manager, I wasn't earning enough to live on. I worked out graphs and tables showing how much the school was bringing in and how little I was being paid. I offered three different proposals for bringing my compensation up to what it had been when I was flying full time. My proposals ranged from high salary and low commission to low salary and high commission on money the flight school brought in from students and from single-engine charters. I hoped Pearson would not reject my proposal out of hand, but he did me one better, selecting the highest salary *and* the highest commission as my future compensation.

My incentive to sign up new students and make sure we didn't turn down charters was strong. I no longer needed ferry flights to build flight time, but they were welcome breaks and I enjoyed the freedom.

I was approaching Spokane to land for fuel in a new Cessna 172 when the controller told me of a Boeing 727 overtaking me. I asked for the airliner's altitude. He curtly responded and added that the Boeing had me in sight. Yeah, right, I thought. Maybe like in San Diego when the PSA jet had a little airplane in sight but not the one it hit.

* * *

Log pages filled fast that summer with charters, students, and fire patrols. I reached the end of my first big logbook in August 1979, the one I began with my first hour as flight instructor. It spans two and a half years with three thousand hours of flying time, more than half instruction given.

Charter Pilot

When I realized I was not giving complete attention and best effort to my students, it was time to quit. I was exhausted in general and burned out on teaching in particular. I handed off some students to other instructors and finished up those whose training was nearly complete. I'd enjoyed instructing, but I was happy to be done with it. The instructor phase of my nascent flying career ended the summer of 1979 when several things came together.

We were flying many more charters than before the Hood Canal bridge sank. I didn't have time to fly charters and instruct and manage the flight school. Because Earl had agreed to a pay structure that exceeded what I'd asked, by midsummer, I was the highest paid pilot in the company. I was making more money because the flight school and charters were making more money, but Earl had second thoughts about his generosity.

In September, we began flying to Victoria, British Columbia. I flew the route three times a day, except when a flight was cancelled because no one was booked or on rare occasions when a twin-engine airplane was required for passenger load or weather.

The city of Victoria is only twenty-two miles north of Port Angeles, but the airport is fifteen miles north of the city. The narrowest span of water between the Olympic Peninsula and Vancouver Island is eight miles, so I could fly as low as three thousand feet, high enough to glide half that distance if my engine failed over water.

I had an hour or more on the ground in Victoria between arrivals and departures, time to get to know Customs officers and the Air Canada agents who handled our ticketing and baggage, time to read *War and Peace*, and time to waste quarters playing Space Invaders when video games were a novelty. I enjoyed being able to relax away from the fast pace of the Port Angeles end of the business.

Clear weather held through October. I flew fire patrols and charters when I had time on my schedule. When I wasn't scheduled for anything, I continued to ride flights to Seattle to build time in Cessna 402s. At the rate those hours were adding up, it would take years to reach the insurance requirement, and then perhaps the minimum would go up again. In my log, I assigned the numbers of our several twin Cessnas to the single-engine airplanes I flew and kept track of which entries were really flown in single-engine airplanes.

An FAA regulation requires airlines to supply its pilots with charts. Pearson bought one Jeppesen subscription and made photocopies of instrument charts for the airports we commonly flew to. There was no system for making sure charts in each airplane were up to date.

The first time I flew an instrument approach in low cloud and fog to SeaTac in the large, single-engine Cessna 207, ILS needles did not come alive and the red flag remained in the instrument's window. I asked the tower if the localizer was on. It was, and the controller included the frequency in his reply. It wasn't the one on the chart. I clicked the radio knob over a couple of numbers. The flag disappeared and needles came to life. The identification signal was correct, and I turned to intercept the approach course only seconds before I would have flown through it.

Once on the ground, I had time to get mad. I bought my own Jeppesen manual and paid for my own subscription.

I was afraid of only two things in the air—fire and collision. Almost anything else could go wrong and leave a good chance of survival. In clear weather, coming back from Seattle with four passengers in the 207, I cancelled my instrument clearance and began descent with Port Angeles in sight.

Usually, conflict arises when a low-wing airplane above converges from with a high-wing airplane below, each hidden from the other pilot by wings. That time, the low-wing Piper was below me and overtaking from my right in level flight and converging with my descending airplane at a shallow angle. The Piper was in my blind spot, but why its pilot did not see me, ahead and a few degrees to his left and descending into his field of view, I do not know. I didn't know he was there until he appeared in front of my nose no more than fifty feet below me, slowly pulling away. Such incidents made me glad my normal blood pressure is low.

In the same airplane, I was returning from Seattle with a full load in marginal weather one afternoon in November. We were halfway to Port Angeles between an overcast and scattered clouds below when I smelled something burning. The passenger in the right seat smelled it, too, but neither of us said anything as we looked at the instrument panel for an indication of what was wrong. The alternator-off light in front of my right knee glowed bright, and as I reached to turn off alternator and battery switches, the red plastic cover of the light melted and slid down the instrument panel like candle wax.

With master switches off, I had no lights, radios, or flap motors. My last contact with Port Angeles had indicated visual weather, but just barely. I kept my eyes open for other airplanes and landed straight in, eager to get the airplane on the ground in case there was more to the problem than I was aware of. As passengers walked toward the terminal, the man in the copilot seat hung back and asked what the problem was. I said we'd had an electrical problem and I'd shut off the electrical system as a precaution.

A broken wire had caused a short circuit. Turning off the switches had been the right thing to do.

In March 1980, when Katrina was in third grade, I took vacation during her spring break and we flew to Maine in our Cessna 152. I wrote the trip off on income tax. I was a leasing company, leasing my airplane to Pearson Air. I called the flight to Maine business trip for the purpose of demonstrating my product to a prospective customer, a friend in Maine who owned a flight school and charter operation. Perhaps that reasoning wouldn't have stood up to an audit, but, compared to the shenanigans professional money changers pull every day in the temples of commerce, it was an overtime parking violation.

Spring break was only a week, but we took two. I thought Katrina would gain more education from seeing the country than she would lose from missing a few days of grade school. We took off on the 28th of March. Mount Saint Helens was beginning to smoke.

Not much was going on at the airport that sunny Sunday morning in May a few weeks after we got back from Maine. I was in the office chatting with the ticket counter agent when we felt and heard a heavy thud. I went outside to walk around the building but saw nothing unusual. When I went back inside, the agent was hanging up the telephone.

A Pearson flight had just taken off from SeaTac, and the pilot was looking right at Mount Saint Helens eighty-five miles south when it blew. It was amazing luck that the eruption occurred, not only in daytime, but on a clear day with unlimited visibility.

The phone rang. The local newspaper wanted to fly a photographer to the scene. It rang again. A geologist at the community college wanted a close look. The phone rang again as I headed out to preflight an airplane. Smoke and ash were still boiling into the sky and drifting northeast when we arrived in the slow, seven-seat, Cessna 207. I counted fourteen airplanes, including the governor's, circling the flood crest raging down the Toutle River. All were circling clockwise. My photographers were on the left side of the airplane, so I circled against traffic to give them a good view.

I wondered how many of the other pilots were paying more attention to the amazing sights than to where they were going. It was difficult to ignore the scene below and the billowing smoke and ash a few miles away. Our airplane was probably the slowest in the circling flock, and I was glad we had traffic coming at us from the front where I could see it rather than overtaking us and perhaps running us down. I snatched glimpses of the once clear stream, brown with mud and carrying hundreds of tumbling trees and slamming into houses and bridges.

      A few weeks later, I picked up three men in Olympia to fly over the crater and observe the new lava dome building within. We flew low over the rim and I banked left and right so my passengers could see straight down. One of them photographed the swelling, smoking, craggy mini-mountain growing at the bottom of the crater. The next day, the dome blew out like a shattered champagne cork.

I considered myself to be more rational than most, but I discovered I was not immune to allowing personal differences to interfere with safety.

One evening, when I was still an instructor and logging multi-engine hours as fast as I could, the last flight of the day to Seattle was empty and not quite full coming back. The pilot hadn't been with us long and I'd not flown with him before. I got to fly from the left seat when there were no passengers.

To start the engines in a Cessna 402, you first push the fuel mixture levers forward from cutoff to full rich. In my excitement at getting to fly from the captain's seat, I forgot the mixtures and continued the starting procedure. What Roger should have done was let me find my own mistake when the first engine didn't immediately start, but he clamped his hand over mine on the throttles and said, "Stop!" Then he gave me a lecture on how to start engines. That did not put me in a congenial frame of mind.

On the return, he didn't offer to let me fly. It was the captain's prerogative, but still...

So I was in a bit of a snit, in spite of the lovely, smooth, moonlit night. We'd flown out of Port Angeles under a low overcast that ended just east of town. When we returned and turned the corner of the mountains, the cloud layer had moved several miles east. To get under it and avoid flying a full instrument approach, we would have to begin descent immediately and perhaps swing wide on the turn to get below the clouds with a normal descent rate. I was surprised when the captain didn't descend, but I said nothing.

Moments later, he recognized our situation and started down. I saw that we'd fly through the edge of the cloud layer on the descent. Although illegal on a visual clearance, clipping the cloud for a few seconds wouldn't be a problem on the course we were on with mountains to the left and low flat land and open water ahead and to the right. We flew into the cloud, still descending, and my blood went cold as Roger began to turn left.

I checked my compass against his, checked my altimeter against his, checked to see that he really was turning toward mountains cloaked in cloud and darkness. My mind was just forming the command to my arms to take control and turn right and climb when the captain reached the same conclusion. He leveled off smoothly as he began a gentle climbing turn. We popped out of the cloud deck and flew northwest a little farther, then let down in clear air and turned toward Port Angeles, clearly visible in the west.

When the airplane was secured for the night and the passengers had gathered their luggage and left the terminal, I said, "We need to talk about flying into that cloud and turning toward the mountains." The captain turned away and walked out the door as though he hadn't heard me.

If he had talked to me, if he'd said something as simple as, "My mind was wandering, and when we went into the cloud, it took me a couple of seconds to realize exactly where we were," perhaps I'd have said, "Well, you got my attention when you turned the wrong way. I'm glad you figured it out as fast as you did," and that would have been the end of it.

I had trouble going to sleep that night. The next day, I called the chief pilot and told him exactly what had happened, but I also said to be sure to get the other side of the story. He called me back later. He'd been all set to fire the man on the spot, but Roger did not try to weasel out of the facts as I'd outlined them. He also pointed out that I, having much more familiarity with the area than he, should have said something when I saw the situation going bad. The chief pilot agreed with him, and, I had to admit, so did I.

I was working long hours with few days off and had little time and less money to prepare for an ATP checkride. I was eager to get that last hurdle out of the way before my high school reunion in Colorado. An FAA examiner flew over from Seattle on a clear day early in August. We flew a 402 to Paine Field and requested an ILS approach to Runway 16.

Flying small airplanes amongst large, fast airliners taught us to make accommodations for the traffic mix. The tower was busy and asked if I could accept a turn-on at the outer marker and keep my speed up. I said I could.

Close to the airport, the localizer needle is sensitive. In accepting a turn at the outer marker, by the time the needle began to move from the side of the instrument toward center, it would be too late to make the turn to final approach without overshooting. But Paine had a VOR on the field, so I tuned my second navigation radio to that VOR and set the inbound course to match the ILS. The VOR needle would give me an early indication that I was almost on course, plenty of time to make the turn without overshooting. But the VOR was not on that day. I overshot a little and got back on course immediately, but, on a checkride, immediately is not soon enough.

My examiner told me why he couldn't pass me on the botched ILS. He advised me to demand long final approaches and to refuse shortcuts on checkrides. He asked me if he made me nervous.

"No, *I* make me nervous. I know I'm not as prepared for this ride as I have been for all the others."

If I wanted to fly with him again, he'd call the checkride incomplete. We hadn't done holding patterns. If I wanted to fly with another examiner, he'd write me a pink slip and I could schedule with someone else. I told him I liked flying with him just fine.

A week later, I was home from my reunion, and again, the examiner came over from Seattle. We flew to Victoria, the nearest airport with an ILS. I flew approaches correctly and we headed home.

I was grinning under the training visor. All that was left was a holding pattern. He directed me to fly to the Port Angeles VOR, then located near the Coast Guard base, and hold as published.

You can enter the racetrack holding pattern in any manner you like as long as you stay within the boundary of protected airspace. For training and for checkrides, there are only three ways to enter a holding pattern based on the entry course as it relates to the holding course and on the direction of turns in the holding pattern. All three methods keep the airplane in safe airspace, but only one is considered correct for a given angle of entry.

I sailed along happily, glad my long trek was at an end, my goals finally achieved. I was still grinning as I crossed the holding fix and realized I'd given no thought whatsoever as to which of the three entry procedures was correct for my angle of approach.

I did know which was the safe side of the inbound course, though, so I turned sharply to avoid overshooting protected airspace and entered the holding pattern. After less than one full turn, the examiner told me to take off the visor and head for the airport. I wasn't grinning anymore.

After I'd gathered headset and charts, I walked into the office. My examiner was writing on a small form—white, not pink. He handed me my license and shook my hand. "Oh, by the way," he said. "I liked the way you entered the hold with a teardrop. I don't like those parallel outbound entries, either."

My ex-wife and I sold our house. I rented a small one four blocks from a grade school across town from the airport. After school, Katrina rode the city bus either to the airport or to her after-school baby sitter's if I had to work into the evening.

My biggest expense was the airplane payment. Even though it earned enough to pay for itself on lease back to the flight school, earnings and expenses were irregular. I had to write the check to the bank every month regardless. Rent and child care ate up most of the rest of my income.

The only passenger on my first revenue trip in a twin-engine airplane was a drunk woman who showed up early for her scheduled flight to Seattle. Earl sent her over alone with me, as I had to go anyway to bring overbooked passengers back.

Regulations prohibit allowing drunks on airplanes, but we took them anyway. I landed in Port Angeles with one man so sound asleep I couldn't wake him. We didn't need the airplane for a couple of hours, so I parked it where we could keep an eye on it. Twenty minutes later, the groggy passenger began moving around, and I went outside to help him out of the airplane and get him pointed toward the restroom.

Although I finally flew a regular schedule, I still flew all the charters I could to boost my income. One evening, I picked up two men and two young women in Seattle to take them to a small airport in the Cessna 207. Someone was waiting to pick them up, and, after they'd climbed out of the airplane and I'd unloaded their bags, one of the men handed me a fifty-dollar bill.

I said, "Sir, that's not necessary."

"I know it's not," he said.

I said the only thing I could say. "Thank you."

The man frequently booked charters between that small airport near his home and Seattle. I volunteered when I saw his name on the schedule, no matter what time of day or night. Tips were smaller when he was alone, larger when he was accompanied by a different young woman than on the trip before. He was not predictable. The last time I picked him up, he tipped me a hundred dollars on a hundred-dollar charter.

Line Pilot

When I began flying lessons, the early morning pilot was the first to arrive at the airport. Pearson pilots did not yet wear uniforms, although they weren't so casual that they flew in jeans and T-shirts. The pilot unlocked the door, plugged in the coffee maker, and went out to get an airplane ready for flight. In winter, the airplane would often be in a hangar and he'd have to push it outside by himself. He'd start the engines, warm them up, perform magneto checks, and cycle the propellers' pitch controls to circulate warm oil through the hubs. When he was satisfied with the airplane's condition, he'd taxi near the little wooden building that served as office, flight school, and terminal.

By then, passengers were being dropped off or parking their cars in the unlined, unfenced, lot. The pilot wrote tickets, tagged baggage, and trundled it out to the airplane.

The baggage compartment in a Cessna 402 is in the nose with doors on each side hinged at the top and held open by struts like hoods of ancient cars. Trailing ends of engine nacelles atop the wings are baggage compartments with space for briefcases and other small items. If there wasn't enough room for bags and freight in the nose and nacelles, it was stowed behind the last two seats and secured with a cargo net tied to rings in the floor.

At departure time, the pilot turned off the coffee maker, locked the building, and led his passengers down the hill to the airplane. The main entry door on the left side behind the wing is in two sections. The smaller, upper section contains a window and is hinged at the top. It opens first and closes last. The lower part is hinged at the bottom and held shut by spring-loaded deadbolts. When unlatched and let down, cables or chains on each side support it and double as handrails. Two steps in the door unfold when the door is down.

The pilot stowed unchecked carryon luggage in the wing locker as passengers boarded. He instructed them to fill forward seats first. If large people boarded first and sat in rear seats, the airplane tipped backward, nosewheel in the air and tail on the ground. That did not instill passenger confidence.

When all were aboard, the pilot closed and latched the wing locker and walked around the airplane to check that the locker on the right wing was latched and that the nose baggage compartment was not only closed but latched on both sides.

The pilot entered through the same door the passengers did. He'd pull the lower part of the entry door up with the chains and then pull the upper part down and latch it before making his way in a crouch up the narrow aisle to the left seat. In some airplanes, he could close the passenger entry door from outside, step onto the wing, and open a hatch next to his seat.

The passenger briefing was little more than, "Fasten your seat belts." Long before I went on the line, "No Smoking" was added. The pilot started engines, taxied to the runway, and, unless weather required an instrument clearance for departure, he took off and flew to Seattle.

Commuter flights at SeaTac all went to Concourse A. The pilot helped passengers down, handed them their carryons from the wing locker, and escorted them across the concrete ramp to a door and a stairway up to concourse level. Baggage handlers took checked bags inside to the carousel. Passengers continuing on other airlines had to claim bags and recheck them. Within a few years, commuter airlines entered into interline agreements with major carriers that allowed passengers to book a reservation from anywhere in their systems to anywhere in the world. No longer did travelers have to claim bags in Seattle and check them again at Delta or Continental.

When flights were on time, a pilot could take a short break in the employees' cafeteria. Then he went to the ticket counter belonging to a larger commuter airline that handled Pearson's ticketing and baggage. He gathered his passengers and escorted them to the concourse, down the stairs, and out to the airplane for the flight to Port Angeles.

Rule of thumb was, if the nosewheel stayed on the ground when the pilot put his weight on the step, the airplane was in balance. Normally when landing, the control yoke is pulled back as the airplane slows. On some occasions, *forward* pressure on the yoke was required to keep the tail from dropping, a sure sign that the airplane was tail heavy. We were acutely aware that, if it got too slow, the tail would stall sooner than the wing, and the airplane would fall out of the sky. But we didn't know how slow was too slow.

My log for the first several weeks of flying after I went on the line late in 1980 contains few notes to indicate anything other than routine half-hour flights to Seattle and back:

No heater. Came back at 2000 feet. Air 15 degrees warmer.

Seat back broke. Wheel chair at last minute. Forgot freight.

Rough. Right seat puked.

Got Wally Schirra's autograph today.

My scientist father laughed aloud when Schirra, one of the first seven astronauts, ruffled NASA feathers by smuggling a corned beef sandwich aboard Gemini 3. Schirra came to Port Angeles in 1980 in conjunction with Olympic National Park becoming designated a World Heritage Park. I introduced myself when he and local dignitaries arrived at the airport and asked him to sign my logbook.

A name on a manifest rang a bell from my disc jockey days. The name, coupled with the small musical instrument case he carried, was enough to prompt me to ask if he was the flutist. He seemed surprised that I'd recognized him. When we landed in Port Angles to drop off passengers before continuing to Victoria, I ran inside to get my logbook, and Paul Horn signed it for me.

One evening late, I flew a 182 to Seattle to pick up Betty Friedan who was to give a lecture at the local community college. The feminist author was my mother's hero, but I didn't think to ask for her signature.

Ernest K Gann lived in the San Juan Islands. The author of *The High and the Mighty* and *Fate is the Hunter* flew his Cessna 310 to Port Angeles now and then. Although he was a friendly and approachable man, I never introduced myself to ask for his autograph. I didn't want to appear a star-struck fan, which is what I was.

Other famous and infamous people came through our far-off corner of the country. If I hadn't quit instructing, I might have logged Instruction Given for Tony Lester when he enrolled in our private pilot course. None of us knew he wasn't just another young man learning to fly until the FBI arrested him at a local restaurant as Christopher Boyce, the escaped spy and real-life Falcon of *The Falcon and the Snowman*.

* * *

One dark evening in November, I was flying Katrina to Everett in our airplane to spend the weekend with her mother. On the radio, I heard a former student who had just taken off from Paine Field to fly home to Port Angeles. He told the controller he was returning to Paine because of weather.

I'd just flown through the weather he was turning back from, and I knew he'd have had no trouble with it, even at night, but I kept my mouth shut. If he didn't like the looks of the weather based on his limited experience, I was not going to encourage him to stick his neck out. Being too careful doesn't get you killed.

I'd heard another pilot turn back because of weather soon after I began instructing. His reputation and stature was such that my brain retained the message. The incident formed the conclusion of my first published article in *Private Pilot* magazine:

> There was little chatter on the Unicom that blustery afternoon. The wind from the North Pacific was accelerated eastward through the venturi called Strait of Juan de Fuca formed by the Olympic Mountains in Washington and the spine of Vancouver Island in Canada. The wind was in excess of 20 knots and gusting to 35 and more. I was killing time in the flight school drinking coffee and reading magazines.
>
> The main runway at Friday Harbor on San Juan Island lies roughly north and south. To say it's paved is almost an exaggeration. There is a grass strip some 1200 feet long for landing when the wind is strong from the west.
>
> Occasionally my mind was diverted from the magazine by pilots talking to Friday Harbor Unicom. Some landed on the cross strip and others fought the crosswind to land on the narrow main runway, but if anyone failed to land, I didn't notice. The radio was silent for a few minutes, and again I became absorbed in what I was reading.
>
> The next voice on the Unicom was solid and commanding, but with the slightly gravelly quality of a man no longer young. I put down my

magazine and moved closer to the receiver. The voice was only slightly familiar then, but the airplane's number already had a permanent place in my memory. Twin Cessna 58 Quebec was calling Friday Harbor for a wind check.

With the squelch turned all the way down, I could hear bits of Friday Harbor's reply: ...gusting...most...cross stri...okay....

The fast twin couldn't land on the short cross strip, of course. The Unicom operator included the information that others were landing on it to indicate the severity of the crosswind. Five-eight Quebec was not unknown there. The pilot announced his intention to land to the north, uphill. Then the radio was silent but for the unsquelched hiss and crackle.

I felt the dramatic tension inherent in the radio's near-silence, not as great as the tension I felt in reading *The High and the Mighty* or *Fate is the Hunter* perhaps, but essentially the same—a man and an airplane in contest with the gods.

But of course he'd make it. What's a little crosswind to a man who has probably seen the insides of more airplanes than I'd seen the outsides of?

"Friday Harbor, this is Five-eight Quebec. This is a little too rough. Will you call Dodie and tell her I'm going back to Boeing Field?"

Just like that. The voice was the same. There was no undertone of disappointment or frustration. It's a little too rough. I'm going back. That was all.

Whenever I hear the siren singing, "just a little farther," or, "give it another try," I remember the dispassionate voice on the radio that windy day, and I remind myself that if Ernest K Gann can turn around when it might be unwise to continue, then, by God, so can I.

Other commuter airline pilots wore uniforms. Pearson didn't like the idea, probably because of the expense, so he compromised on brown polyester suits over short-sleeve shirts.

The coat's lining irritated the skin of my bare arms, so I took it to a tailor to have the sleeves relined with cotton.

Before Port Angeles had a full Instrument Landing System, one of the few legal ways to land in bad weather was a VOR approach, one that guided you to a point over the airport but did not provide guidance to a specific runway and did not get you near the ground. Another way was a contact approach. If the airport reported one mile visibility or better, and if you believed you could see a mile and stay out of clouds, you could ask for a contact. We had an unofficial variation we called the Graveyard Arrival.

The airport at Port Angeles is officially 291 feet above sea level. The northwest end of Runway 13 is lower. An airplane landing to the southeast from over the Strait of Juan de Fuca crossed a cemetery on the bluff, the road to the city dump, and a fringe of trees before reaching the low end of the runway.

An arriving airplane on a contact approach could fly west over the water at 350 feet, turn left at the graveyard, and once past treetops, Runway 13 would rise to meet the descending airplane. Where it got tricky was when the runway wasn't visible from the cemetery and when visibility over the water wasn't good enough to allow us to see the shoreline from far enough away to be able to make a tight left turn to line up with the unseen runway. In that case, we could turn right, the long way around over water, to get from west to southeast.

I practiced that approach a few times in clear weather and memorized which tree to line up with a small building on cemetery grounds that gave me the course to the runway, and I counted the seconds from shoreline to touchdown.

Without radar control all the way to the ground, only one airplane at a time could get an instrument clearance to take off or land. Even if visibility was unlimited, if the cloud ceiling at the airport was lower than a thousand feet, a clearance was required. It was on just such a day that a single-engine airplane from an airport in Puget Sound took off to the east and climbed into the clouds. Normally, the departing airplane would be high enough for radar to see it within a minute or two, and the next in line could be cleared. Departure charts give specific instructions on how to leave an airport and join an assigned airway, but you have to read the chart.

In absence of radar contact, airplanes departing Port Angeles flew west a few miles toward a radio beacon, climbing all the while, until in radar contact. Then the controller assigned a heading to intercept the airway. If radar was down, the airplane climbed in a holding pattern at the radio beacon until reaching six thousand feet, the minimum instrument altitude on the airway at that time.

Six thousand feet is more than high enough for safety on the charted airways between Port Angeles and Seattle. If obstructions were the only criteria for establishing a minimum altitude, it could have been lower, but the VOR beacon on which the airway was predicated was many miles west of the airport. Six thousand feet is high enough to receive the signal on or near the airway, but it is not high enough if you take off and fly toward seven-thousand-foot mountains.

Whidbey Approach couldn't see the airplane on radar. The instructor and his instrument student reported level at six thousand. Then Whidbey couldn't talk to them.

This being America, families of the dead men filed suit contending that the airplane crashed because the VOR signal was unreliable. I got a call from a government attorney. Could I testify for the FAA? I could hardly wait. What I wanted to say was, if you bake a cake without reading the directions on the box, the result is not Betty Crocker's fault.

I didn't get to make my analogy. The FAA settled out of court and raised the minimum en route altitude for that airway to eight thousand feet. The airplane that crashed would have hit the mountains anyway before it got that high.

When high pressure parks itself over Western Washington, the sky is clear and wind is light. Sometimes, on return flights from Seattle, we'd fly over the Olympic Mountains and descend through the Elwha Valley. When air was smooth, passengers loved the scenic route, and flight time was about the same.

Wind makes air near the ground rough as it swirls over hills and ridges, but sometimes, when strong wind over mountains becomes chaotic and bounces little airplanes every which way, staying low and flying close to the mountains made for a smooth ride.

I always briefed my passengers before takeoff if I planned to do something they might find unusual. I'd explain what the wind was doing and why we were flying low for the first half of the flight. There was no way to avoid turbulence once out of the shelter of mountains, and I told them what to expect. Being a passenger in a small airplane was scary enough for some people. It was worse when they didn't know what was going on.

As Katrina grew older, I began thinking ahead to her teen years. Even if I'd been capable of being father and mother to her, my job would not allow enough time for proper involvement in my daughter's life. I evaluated women I dated as potential stepmothers.

I had a saying to fit each marriage after the first, the first being too short to earn a saying other than perhaps, "Uh-oh." Next came, "Once for practice, once for keeps." After I married again in 1982, "Third time's a charm."

Airline pilots can live anywhere and commute to work. A Braniff captain whose son had been my student rode our airplanes to Seattle to catch a ride to Dallas. One day, he invited me to look inside the cockpit of a Boeing 727 parked at the Braniff gate. The profusion of instruments and gauges on the pilots' panels, the thicket of switches overhead, and the flight engineer's panel with an unintelligible array of knobs, switches, and gauges overwhelmed me, but it didn't matter. I was ten years too old to be hired by a real airline. I wore contact lenses and had no college degree or military flying experience. I would never fly anything like that jet airliner.

Log entries for spring and early summer of 1981 are mostly unremarked round trips to Seattle. A note at the bottom of the last June page under the single- and multi-engine totals reads, "S & M correct now."

At the suggestion and urging from fellow pilots, I'd falsely logged single-engine flying as multi-engine time until I reached five hundred hours in Cessna 402s to meet the insurance requirement. "It's not how many hours you have, it's how you fly the airplane," they said. It would not have occurred to me to make false entries, and I'd not have done it to evade an FAA regulation. The alternative was to spend a few years riding empty seats on my own time to reach five hundred hours, and it would have been the same hour five hundred times.

I had assigned a different 402's number to each of several single-engine airplanes I flew. Once my log showed I'd reached the insurance minimum, I began undoing the inaccuracies, logging the single-engine airplane's number corresponding to the 402 I actually flew. Other pilots were amazed that I'd go to so much trouble. It makes no difference to the Universe, but it made me feel better. At the end of my career, times in my logs are accurate, except for one missing entry. I forgot to log flight time the day I took my multi-engine checkride.

Perhaps nothing is more traumatic in the life of an airline pilot than merger with another airline. Seniority is everything, but seniority does not carry over. A veteran captain starts over at the bottom of the list when he changes employers.

Pearson Air was a typical general aviation Fixed Base Operation with a small commuter airline. It wasn't a noticeable blip on an acquisitor's radar screen before the surge of growth following collapse of the Hood Canal Bridge.

San Juan Airlines, based in Friday Harbor, was the oldest commuter airline in the country in continuous operation. It flew charters and scheduled flights out of short strips on the many San Juan Islands and a commuter run from Friday Harbor to Seattle. When San Juan's owner cast his eye on Pearson's increasing traffic and his Canadian landing rights, Pearson sold the airline and moved the rest of his operation to Olympia.

In a simple merger, seniority lists are also merged, usually with some formula to protect senior pilots with recent dates of hire at a fast-growing airline from losing their jobs to junior members of the other airline who had been hired earlier. But we weren't being merged. We'd been bought outright, and San Juan could have stapled Pearson pilots to the bottom of its list. That would have put our most senior pilot one number below San Juan's most junior, and any layoffs that might occur as overlapping service was consolidated would come from the Pearson group.

We were relieved and delighted when our new owner merged seniority lists straight across by date of hire. That put the most senior San Juan pilots lower on the list than senior Pearson pilots. What prevented wailing and gnashing of teeth was that few, if any, island pilots wanted to be based on the mainland, and few, if any, of us wanted to move to the islands. Seniority within Friday Harbor and Port Angeles didn't change. My seniority with Pearson was based on my date of hire as a flight instructor, not the date I went on the line more than three years later. That put me high enough on the list to fly the schedule I wanted.

We flew Cessna 402s, supplemented by single-engine Cessnas. San Juan Airlines also flew single-engine Cessnas, but its twins were Britten-Norman Islanders, slow, noisy, high-wing twins ideal for short runways. We weren't qualified to fly their equipment, and they weren't qualified to fly ours.

The combined airline flew from Friday Harbor to Seattle and to nearly all San Juan Islands that had places to land. From Seattle, we flew through Bellingham to Vancouver, British Columbia. Spokes from Seattle extended to Olympia, Bremerton, Hoquiam, and Port Angeles, and through Port Angeles to Victoria. As schedules became more complex, pilots flew through stations they were not thoroughly familiar with, and we long-runway pilots got our share of challenging island flying. Dispatchers kept track of airplanes and passenger loads and sent extra airplanes where they were needed. San Juan moved its operations center to Port Angeles. We were all uniformed in dark blue with white shirts and silver stripes, just like real airline pilots. We didn't have uniform hats, though, a good thing, as our airplanes were too small to accommodate a tall pilot wearing a hat and there was no place to stow them.

The larger operation required our own counter at SeaTac and our own baggage handlers. At times, half a dozen airplanes might be crowded onto our ramp, so bag handlers doubled as marshalers, directing us with hand signals to parking spots.

Most pilots, accustomed to parking without direction, paid little attention to signals. That led to the marshalers' diminished interest in doing a proper job. I told them, "I will follow your instructions precisely, but if you run me into something, I'll get out of the airplane and kill you." We got along fine.

It was not uncommon to fly eight or ten legs in four hours of flying in a day. Island pilots sometimes logged more than a dozen landings a day, with some flights between islands so short, walking would have been faster except for water in the way. Ten legs in five flight hours were far more tiring than an eight-hour non-stop. Workload is high in transitions between earth and sky, but once aloft and level, pilots can relax a little.

I seldom used the autopilot. As long as my hands were controlling the airplane, I was paying attention. If a malfunctioning autopilot steered me into danger, I was afraid I might not notice. An L-1011 full of passengers crashed into the Everglades one night in 1972 because the entire flight crew was trying to fix a malfunctioning warning light. No one noticed the autopilot had disconnected until seconds before the jet hit the swamp.

When propellers were not turning at exactly the same speed, the continuous wah-wah-wah irritated most people and drove me nuts. Some of our airplanes had synchronizers, but they didn't always work. I always tried to adjust propellers to exactly the same speeds and to set them at the quieter phase between wah and wah.

More annoying than out-of-synch props, especially for people toward the rear of the airplane, is yaw. If air is not perfectly smooth, bumps cause the airplane to fishtail slightly. Many otherwise good pilots ignored that, either out of laziness or because, sitting near the center of rotation, they didn't notice the unsettling effects on weak stomachs. A usual excuse was, "This airplane doesn't have a yaw damper."

Pilots have two yaw dampers, one at the end of each leg. Walking the rudder pedals to counteract yaw became automatic with me. I couldn't *not* do it.

We all had favorite airplanes and airplanes we didn't like. One of our older 402s had the radio master switch in a different location from our other airplanes, and one night on approach to Port Angeles in fog, I accidentally turned off all radios and navigation equipment when my fingers flicked the out-of-place switch.

I hated changing airplanes during the day. To change between flights required building a new nest and adjusting to minor differences, differences such as where the damn radio master was in *that* particular airplane.

Some 402s had nine seats total and some had ten. Sometimes the extra seat was needed for another destination, so pilots had to gather their charts, headsets, and whatever else they had in the airplane, and move it to another one. Then we had a choice. We could trust the other pilot to have done a thorough preflight inspection when he began his day and say to ourselves, "If it flew in, it'll fly out." Or we could take the time to check everything as though it was the first flight of the day. Sometimes, taking that extra five or ten minutes would make the departure late. I took the time anyway.

Another problem with last-minute airplane swaps was baggage. I learned to check a couple of destination tags when I walked around checking locker latches. It was embarrassing to land in Port Angeles with Bellingham bags.

It doesn't take much ice in the wing to prevent an airplane from getting off the ground. Snow had to be cleaned off unless it was light and dry enough to blow off as the airplane accelerated down the runway. One morning, all airplanes were covered with an inch of fluffy snow. During preflight inspection of my 402 for that day, I checked a couple of places on the wing and tail, and I could blow snow off with my breath. I was going out empty, so there were no passengers to rightfully worry about snow on the wings. It was my bad luck that I'd tested snow only in small areas where it didn't stick.

The airplane, being empty, flew anyway, but it was not happy. Controls buffeted in my hand and the airplane did not climb well. Air was warmer a few hundred feet above the ground, and what snow remained after takeoff quickly melted and disappeared in the slipstream. When my heart slowed to near normal, I considered that perhaps I should exercise the same degree of caution when flying alone as I did with passengers in my care.

Pilots are supposed to fly landing approaches assuming they will have to go around. Being able to put the airplane on the ground should be a pleasant surprise. But, after hundreds of landings, it's the go-around that's a surprise.

Procedures vary among airplanes and company procedures, but, in general, the moment you decide not to land, you advance throttles to maximum allowable power, pull the nose up to the correct climb attitude, and reduce flaps. When the airplane is climbing, you raise the landing gear and, when speed and altitude allow, you raise flaps the rest of the way. It's easy to do it correctly when you're expecting it.

Pilots landing at Port Angeles who wanted lights at the end of the runway clicked the microphone button on a specified frequency a specified number of times to turn the array on. Approach lights are a standard, identifiable pattern, so when they appear out of the fog, a pilot knows where he is in relation to the runway.

Intensity is also controllable. Some pilots wanted lights as bright as possible to be sure to see them in dense fog. I preferred them dim so the less intense runway edge lights and centerline lights were easier to see. Landing at the end of my shift one foggy night, either I didn't click the correct number of times or something interfered with the radio signal. When I came out of the clouds two hundred feet above the ground, approach lights were blinding bright and, rather than try to land, I went around.

The heavier the airplane is, the greater the penalty for error. I had only a few people on board, so the airplane climbed with gear and flaps down. It took me several seconds to switch my brain to go-around mode and get the airplane cleaned up for another approach.

I considered myself a careful, conscientious pilot, yet I managed to scare myself now and then. It made me wonder what life must be like for those more casual in attitudes and practices.

Fog at Seattle was too dense for landing. I was holding with a full load of passengers at three thousand feet in bright sunshine just above the top of the fog a few miles north of SeaTac. All of Puget Sound was hidden under a white blanket. A huge balloon popped out of the fog just ahead and a bit to my left. I was past it before I could react.

Hitting the balloon might not have caused major problems beyond a few heart attacks, but had the box of instruments it carried come through the left windscreen, we would have crashed, and I wouldn't have been alive to know it. I told Approach that I'd just missed what appeared to be a large weather balloon with an instrument package. Controllers hadn't been notified of the launch and didn't know where it came from. The University of Washington was almost directly below. I considered that a clue.

The combining of San Juan Airlines and Pearson Air attracted scrutiny from the FAA and an audit of maintenance records and pilot training logs. Inspectors met us as we stepped off our airplanes to check licenses and flight paperwork. Nine pilots were deemed not qualified to fly because of records deficiencies, but the FAA wouldn't say which pilots.

Management guessed the nine were among the island pilots, so we Pearson pilots had to fly long days, riding right seats as copilots with San Juan pilots until they were surely legal again. We treated this route familiarization so long after the fact as the joke it was, and I got a lot of reading done. It was only after all boxes on that page had been checked that we learned that it was Pearson pilots whose records were incomplete, so island pilots rode around in our right seats for a few days.

On a typical day, I'd take off in Port Angeles for Seattle, return to Port Angeles and continue to Victoria BC, fly back through Port Angeles to Seattle, back to Port Angeles and through to Victoria again, then to Port Angeles and Seattle before the final leg home. The schedule was often complicated by weather delays, airplane changes, missing luggage, freight that wouldn't quite fit the baggage compartments, and passengers showing up at the last minute. After the last landing of the day, I was ready for a beer or three. It was by far the best job I'd ever had, and, at ten bucks an hour, the highest paying. We didn't have health insurance or retirement. What we did have was a job that was a hell of a lot of fun.

My first work day of 1983 was one of nine landings. I'd averaged more than a thousand hours a year for six years. The airline grew and schedules became too tight for rest breaks between flights, too tight for meals during some shifts. The schedule could be maintained if nothing went wrong, but a delay early meant late departures all day. Enough of us complained that schedules were adjusted to allow some slack and time for a meal. I spent breaks in Victoria eating lunch and finishing *War and Peace*.

When an extra section to Seattle wasn't needed on the return flight, airplane and pilot would sit for a couple of hours or more until needed. As we were paid for our hours at work, I was perfectly happy to sit in the employees' cafeteria drinking coffee and reading a book.

I should have recognized trouble at the gate in Seattle. The agent told me that a passenger had asked to sit in the right seat. The request was not unusual, but the man came up to the counter at that moment to introduce himself and ask for the seat. He said he had a commercial license and insisted on showing it to me. I told him we didn't reserve seats, that if he wanted to sit up front, he should be first in line.

I didn't normally think it necessary to tell right seat passengers not to touch controls or push buttons, but that guy seemed a little too eager to sit up front. Maybe he had heroic dreams of landing the airplane should I drop dead en route. I told him not to touch anything, but the son of a bitch just had to get his hand in.

After landing, pilots don't do anything during rollout until clear of the runway. Priority is to control the airplane, and diverting attention to raise the flaps is inviting the error of raising the landing gear by mistake. The instant tires chirped on the runway at Victoria, the hero reached forward and flipped up the flap switch. I said through gritted teeth, "I told you not to touch anything!"

When we taxied to a stop at the terminal and shut down, I told him to stay where he was. I said my usual piece, thanking passengers and saying I hoped they enjoyed the ride. Our ground handlers opened the door and escorted passengers to Customs and Immigration. When everyone else was off the airplane, I told the man I could have him arrested on charges of interfering with a flight crew—air piracy. He wasn't impressed. When I related the incident to the chief pilot, he said, "You should have broken his arm."

We'd begun doing part of our annual recurrent training in a no-motion flight simulator in Seattle. Simulators are cheaper than airplanes, and they don't kill people when they crash. I was scheduled for two hours of sim during a normal working day, so I turned the airplane over to someone else in Seattle and went to the nearby training center. Then I resumed my schedule, one last night flight home to Port Angeles. I was beat from the intensity of simulator work and angry at a belligerent drunk passenger, which is why I flew all the way home with the landing gear down. I wondered why the airplane wasn't going as fast as normal, but I wasn't sufficiently interested to investigate, not observant enough to notice three green lights in front of the right-seat passenger's knee. I didn't realize the wheels were not up until I reached over to put them down for landing.

In early October, after vacation and days off, I'd not flown an airplane for twenty-six days, my longest break from flying in eight years.

Because I had no passengers to Victoria, I spent a few extra minutes relaxing in Port Angeles. I planned to arrive just in time to clear Customs, complete paperwork, and depart on time, but I cut it too close and flew fast.

I kept an eye on airspeed after throttling back and lowered landing gear the moment the needle reached the upper speed limit and pushed the flap handle down to the first detent. The flap motor whirred and flaps started down. The flap indicator, attached by a follower to a flap pushrod, began to move. When the indicator reached the flap handle's position, it signaled the flap motor to stop. The moment speed decreased to the upper limit of full flaps, I pushed the handle the rest of the way down. I heard a loud metallic bang and the airplane rolled left.

A general rule is, when something goes wrong, undo what you just did. While turning the yoke right and pressing right rudder to counteract roll, I raised the flap handle and nothing changed. The airplane required two-thirds of the aileron's travel just to stay upright.

The Cessna 402 has split flaps. Rather than a complete section of the trailing edge of the wing moving down, only the bottom surface moves. Split flaps aren't visible from front seats.

I had already made my first call to Victoria Tower. I called again and declared an emergency. I said I had a control problem and would land. A go-around would not be possible.

What I didn't notice, being busy staying upright, was that the flap indicator showed full up. It was obvious that the right flap was down. I didn't know if the left one was still attached to the airplane. As the airplane slowed, more aileron was required to keep from rolling over. I would need even more aileron and rudder input to make the right turn to the runway.

I didn't notice immediately that the tower had not replied to my emergency call. A Cessna 172 was in position for takeoff on Runway 8 as I turned final.

Radios are not like telephones. My emergency call had been blocked by the tower's simultaneous call to the 172 clearing it for takeoff. My call and the tower's were exactly the same length, so neither he nor I realized we'd been blocked. The pilot of the 172 would have heard nothing but a loud squeal. It would have been nice if he'd said, "Blocked," but he didn't. The tower told me to pull up and go around as the 172 began to roll. I said I was unable and again declared an emergency.

Tower told the 172 to get off the runway, and the little airplane veered toward the grass. I didn't want the pilot to damage his airplane in rough ground on my account. I told Tower it would be okay if it just stopped.

Tower told the Cessna to stop, and it did.

During the confusion and distraction, I'd shallowed my descent. I was too high and running out of runway, and I didn't know how slow I could fly without losing control and cartwheeling across the airport in a ball of fire. The wheels touched asphalt just before the control yoke reached the limit of travel and I made the last turnoff.

There had not been time to roll fire trucks, normal procedure for an emergency landing. Tower asked if I needed assistance. I said I was okay. The flap handle was up, the flap indicator was up, and the man in the tower said both flaps appeared to be down. I taxied to my parking spot and got out. With one hand, I could lift the left flap all the way to the wing. I cleared Customs and got on the phone to Port Angeles.

I explained to the counter agent in Victoria that departure would be delayed half an hour while another airplane flew up from Port Angeles. A mechanic rode the rescue flight. I related the sequence of events as he looked the airplane over.

The cable that pulled the pushrod that drove the flaps down had snapped and airflow had slammed the flap up to the wing. The follower that drove the position indicator was on the left flap's pushrod. When air pushed the left flap up, the indicator moved up to its full-up stop. The flap motor kept running, waiting for the indicator to catch up with the down flap handle. When I flipped the handle up, it agreed with the indicator which cut off current to the flap motor.

The mechanic turned on the master switch and pushed the indicator down against its spring with his finger. The flap motor, seeing the indicator and flap handle did not agree, whirred and raised the right wing's flap. When it was up, the mechanic released the indicator and the motor stopped. Then he fastened the left flap up against the wing with a large sheet metal screw, and we flew home to a no-flap landing.

Victoria figured more than once in providing exciting breaks in routine. I was over the city at three thousand feet, northbound to the airport. The sky was clear, and I'd been squinting into the glare of hazy summer sun for days. I'd cancelled instruments with Whidbey Approach rather than be handed off to Vancouver and then to Victoria Tower. Vancouver's frequency was always busy and talking to them wasn't necessary in good weather. Victoria tower's frequency was busy, too, and I couldn't get a word in for several miles.

The compass in a Cessna 402 is in the same position high on the center of the windscreen as the rear view mirror is in a car. My compass sprouted wings and floats.

I pulled up hard in a left turn. The de Havilland Twin Otter turned left and dove under me. By less than a second, we'd avoided scattering torn aluminum and broken bodies on field and forest below. My passengers didn't say anything.

I talked to the Air BC captain by phone. He said I was hidden from his view by the post on the left side of his windscreen and from his copilot's view by the center post.

I said I was surprised that he was so high so near the Inner Harbor where they land. He said they like to stay above three thousand feet crossing the Victoria airport so they don't have to talk to the tower on its congested frequency. After clearing the airport, they descend and switch the radio to the air-to-air frequency floatplanes in the uncontrolled Inner Harbor used to keep track of each other.

In my company incident report, I suggested we monitor that frequency on the second radio when near Victoria. And I conceded that not talking to Vancouver Approach might not be as smart as it was expedient.

When I decided to learn to fly, my career goal had been to fly Cessna 402s back and forth to Seattle. I didn't foresee Pearson Air being bought by San Juan Airlines, didn't foresee the single-route schedule expanding to include more cities, the San Juan Islands and Canada. I also didn't foresee bigger airplanes. The era of commuter airlines packing six or eight people into little airplanes with piston engines was fading, and the new dawn included twin turboprops with two pilots.

We didn't fly high enough to need the expense and complexity of pressurization, and because a nineteenth passenger required a flight attendant on board, eighteen was an economical maximum. San Juan Airlines began to add Embraer Bandeirantes to the fleet early in 1984. Captains' seats would be filled by seniority, of course, and that included me.

When I achieved my goal of flying commuter flights to Seattle, self-imposed pressure was off, and I was back to being what I considered my normal, easy-going self. But there was always one more mountain to climb. Qualifying to fly the twin turbo-prop Bandeirante wasn't just a matter of reading the manual and getting checked out. It was back to school for the four of us whose seniority gave us first shot at the left seat in the new airplane.

Baggage and freight went into a compartment in the back of the airplane. The biggest mechanical difference between the Bandeirante and everything I'd flown was screaming turbines instead of clattering pistons. The other big difference was social.

Experience as a first officer—the copilot—is the usual route to the captain's seat. First officers pine for the day they can be the boss and take home larger paychecks.

My seniority allowed me to bypass the right seat. I'd have a person next to me in a role I had no experience in. I'd have to learn on my own how to be in command, not just of an airplane, but of a crew.

For most of aviation's first century, the captain was God and everyone else was along for the ride. The first officer's job too often was, "Gear up, flaps up, and shut up." Studies of accidents showed lack of cooperation contributed to crashes, so Crew Resource Management was developed to teach flight crews how to work together. Captains became managers.

After a week of classroom study of the airplane and its systems early in 1984, my first logged time in the Bandeirante was three hours over three days wedged into my work schedule. After flying five legs of my schedule on the morning of the fourth day, I spent a couple of hours in the afternoon flying instrument approaches at Paine Field in Everett and getting used to having someone in the right seat to do a share of the work, primarily, talking on the radio.

The fifth day was more of the same. On the sixth, three of us flew the airplane to Boeing Field to pick up an FAA examiner for checkrides and type ratings we'd need to fly the newer, heavier model of the Bandeirante we'd soon have. We played musical chairs in the air as each of us completed required maneuvers. I, being junior, went last. The air over Puget Sound became rough, and my ride was short. Our examiner retired to a passenger seat and said to the chief pilot, "That's enough. If he can get the airplane on the ground in one piece, he passes."

Top pay for Cessna 402 pilots was ten dollars an hour. The Bandeirante carried more than twice as many people, and a senior captain's hourly pay was fifteen dollars. We were still paid for time at work whether in the air or on the ground. My morning schedule included a Seattle layover of more than two hours. I ate lunch, drank coffee, and read books at Bandeirante captain's pay.

While I sat in my seat in front of a bulkhead separating cockpit from passenger cabin, my first officer stood on the ramp in the rain and assisted passengers up the airplane's stairs. The first officer, not I, argued with passengers who wanted to bring aboard bags too large to fit under seats. The first officer was the one who walked around the airplane to be sure all doors and hatches were buttoned up before climbing aboard and pulling up the stairs and latching the entry door. The first officer was the one who read the passenger briefing card over the PA system. Life was good for captains.

First officers do not need the same level of experience as captains do. Commuter airline copilots worked for almost nothing to log the hours to qualify them for the left seat. A few companies *charged* first officers for right-seat time until the government made them stop.

Traditionally, captains and first officers take turns flying unless bad weather or some legal consideration requires the captain to handle the controls. Before each takeoff, the pilot flying that leg briefs the other on how he will conduct the takeoff and departure. Then, toward the end of the flight, he briefs the other on the type of approach they'll fly and how they'll do it. Each briefing ends with, "Any questions?" Usually there are none.

Briefings were pretty much the same every leg in good weather when all flights were between the same two or three airports. Our briefing format was longer than it needed to be for the same crew flying together over the same route for days or weeks at a time. After a few months, when the airplane had become as comfortable as a 402, briefings became brief. Unless I was flying with someone I didn't know or a new-hire just learning the job, my departure briefing was, "I fly, you talk," or vice versa. "Any questions?"

Now and then, the chief pilot rode along to observe how we were doing. After a few weeks, we line pilots had far more experience in the airplane than trainers and the chief pilot, and they did not like shortcuts in procedure.

Reversible pitch propellers were new to all of us coming from piston engines. Pulling the prop levers into reverse after touching down slowed the airplane rapidly without wearing out brakes. It also made it possible to stop a lightly loaded airplane in a very short distance, a feature that got me into trouble.

When I was a student, the entire paved length of the main runway at Port Angeles was useable for takeoff and landing. A later evaluation of tree heights off the east end of the runway required that the landing threshold of Runway 26 be moved a few hundred feet west to allow plenty of clearance between treetops and airplanes making a normal descent to land.

The displaced threshold was a white line across the runway. A right-angle turnoff to the parking ramp was just beyond that painted threshold and right in front of the terminal. In small airplanes, many of us familiar with the airport ignored the displaced threshold and landed near the beginning of pavement so we could make that exit.

Landing the Bandeirante empty one day, I touched down early, reversed propellers, and easily made that turnoff. An FAA man in the terminal was gazing out the window. By the time I'd parked the airplane and gone inside, the Fed had had a chat with the chief pilot, so the chief pilot had a chat with me.

As business picked up in summer, schedules tightened and my long lunch break in Seattle disappeared. After a fifteen-landing day with no opportunity to eat in the first eight hours, I began packing sandwiches in the black steel lunch box I'd used when I was a plumber. If flying a Cessna, I'd put it on autopilot, pull the battered box from under my seat, and eat en route, a silent protest against not having time to eat on the ground. I made fulsome apologies to passengers and explained that our schedules allowed no meal breaks.

I carried a small 35mm camera in my jacket pocket. I tossed my jacket behind the back seats of the 402 I flew one warm day and my camera disappeared.

I'd flown only one trip with my jacket back there when I realized the camera was gone. The manifest gave me the name of a young man who had sat in the back seat nearest my jacket on a half-full flight from Bellingham to Seattle. I pulled up his reservation on the computer and saw he was going to Miami, round trip. I made a note of his return flight. Two weeks later on a day off, I rode to Seattle and explained the situation to our baggage crew.

I checked name tags as the automated rail cars dumped bags coming from other airlines. The one belonging to my suspect wasn't locked. My camera wasn't in it.

When the pilot led his passengers across the ramp to the 402, I stood by the wing to assist with hand luggage. If the thief recognized me from two weeks earlier, he didn't show it. I took his small bag from him and, instead of stowing it in the wing, took it to the front of the airplane where he couldn't see me and quickly checked through it before stowing it in the baggage compartment in the nose. If he had my camera with him, it was in his pocket. Just as likely, he'd left it at home. Or perhaps he'd pawned it.

I wrote to the Miami police department and explained how I'd lost my camera. I gave them the serial number and enclosed a self-addressed post card with several check boxes including, "Sorry, we don't have time for this." A detective sent the card back with a check in the box beside, "We'll keep our eyes open." I never saw my camera again.

I logged nearly a thousand hours in 1984. Schedules were less relaxed than I liked, but the variety of destinations and crewmembers kept things interesting.

We had Bandeirantes during all of 1985. For younger pilots, commuter airlines were time builders toward flying jets for real airlines. I had no career goal beyond doing exactly what I was doing. My income for that year, thanks to overtime, was a hair over $30,000. My wife had a good job, and I felt financially comfortable for the first time in my life. I bought a new pickup truck.

In those first years after deregulation in 1979, new airlines started up and old ones expanded. The traditional labor pool of former military pilots began to dry up. With discriminatory walls falling and airlines desperate to demonstrate dedication to diversity, times were good for women and for members of racial minorities. At 42, I was over the hill and headed down the other side.

In February, our most senior pilot, only a year younger than I, left to fly DC-9s for Sunworld, a new but short-lived airline out of Las Vegas. He was the first to leave for distant horizons and jet airplanes that year.

The beginning of March marked ten years since my first flying lesson. I'd logged more than eight thousand hours, almost one full year in the air. I'd averaged nearly two and a half hours a day every day for a decade.

A Bandeirante first officer left in May to fly for Republic Airlines. Soon, a couple of other pilots followed her. It helps to know someone to carry in your résumé and put in a good word for you. Often, pilots migrated from one airline to another in a cluster.

We had a Bandeirante first officer who couldn't judge when to begin a descent for landing. Approaching Port Angeles, he announced we were fifteen miles east of Morse Creek when the actual distance was two. Approaching Seattle, he reported us at a position many miles behind us. But he was a nice guy, and he and the chief pilot had been friends for years.

Another first officer was a roly-poly teddy bear of a man, an in-your-face friendly sort of fellow who loved to talk. More than anything else, he loved talking to passengers on the PA system, just like a real airline pilot. He had no sense of personal space. When we walked together from airplane to terminal, he'd walk backwards in front of me so near I'd step on his feet if he got out of step, his mouth running all the while. He seemed unsure of himself around airplanes, though he'd allegedly been flying for years. Procedure for landing gear retraction in the Bandeirante was to apply brakes gently after takeoff to stop wheel spin just before calling for gear up. One day, he stepped on the brakes and called for gear up before we'd left the ground.

Rambo was a new hire I was lucky enough never to fly with. He wore a baseball cap with gold braid on the visor when not in uniform and carried a large knife in his boot—his anti-hijacking tool, he said—until the chief pilot saw it one day. Rambo thought our nickname for him was a compliment. I heard one instructor tell another that the man was weak in everything. The second instructor asked if he'd passed him. The first one shrugged. "We need pilots, don't we?"

Rambo said he flew King Airs in the Army. We figured he must have been the cabin steward. One of our dispatchers overheard him on the phone telling a friend about the Bandeirante: "Boy, that eighteen-passenger airliner is some airplane. It's all I can do to keep 'er straight and level!"

In December, A friend left San Juan for some freight hauler nobody had heard of called DHL. Though a major player in the rest of the world, DHL was small and almost unknown in this country in the shadows of UPS and Federal Express. Its fleet comprised ten new Swearingen Metroliner twin turboprops, a couple of Lear jets and helicopters, three Boeing 727s, and a lone Cessna 402, but DHL had plans for domestic growth.

Another of our pilots was on his way to take Republic's physical exam the same day Robert left for DHL. I was beginning to feel left behind.

Early in 1986, San Juan Airlines decided it didn't need Bandeirantes. Reverting to Cessna pay would cut my income considerably. Airline pilots who flew with us on their commutes to Dallas and Denver encouraged me to apply in spite of my age. I sent résumés to several airlines.

I got up early to ride to Seattle and then to Bellingham to begin a day of fifteen landings in the 402, mostly in the San Juan Islands. Then I parked the airplane in Bellingham and flew a 172 home. The job was beginning to feel like work. Two more pilots left for Republic.

Passing the FAA's written exam for Turbojet Flight Engineer was requisite for getting hired by a jet airline. I'd been opposed to weekend ground schools that teach to the test, but misgivings were swept away when I learned that any airline I went to would teach the entire job, so it didn't matter much whether I fully understood what we learned in class. I went to a two-day ground school in Seattle.

Northwest Airlines bought Republic. A former San Juan pilot carried my résumé in the day Republic froze hiring.

I was perhaps too proud that I'd never put the tail of a Cessna 402 on the ground and that I had never taken off with a baggage door unlatched.

In Victoria one afternoon, I was in a hurry to get people aboard the airplane and out of wind and rain. Perhaps the first few to board didn't hear me when I told them to take forward seats. I was arranging carryon bags in a wing locker when the nose began to rise. I lifted on the bottom of the wing locker nacelle, but weight in the back seats overcame my effort. The tailskid touched concrete.

I don't remember what I yelled at the wide-eyed passengers visible through the open door in the rearmost seats, but it was neither tactful nor polite. I ordered them to move forward and stepped back to the horizontal stabilizer to keep the nosewheel from dropping hard when weight shifted forward. A memo months earlier said airplanes were not to be flown after tail strikes until they'd been inspected by a mechanic. That memo didn't apply to me, so I promptly forgot about it. My tail strike was more of a touch than a bump, and there was no way it could have caused internal damage. Even if I'd remembered the memo, I'd probably have ignored it. I grumbled about the incident within the chief pilot's hearing. He forcefully reminded me of the new procedure and put a letter of reprimand in my file.

I may have been the only one of our Cessna 402 pilots who had not taken off with a nose baggage door unlatched. When the airplane reaches flying speed, airflow raises an unlatched door. The embarrassed pilot pulls off the runway, shuts the engines down, and climbs out to latch the door he should have checked in the first place.

I argued strongly for a policy of never closing baggage doors unless they were also latched. I couldn't win that argument. In windy or rainy weather, baggage handlers and most pilots closed the doors but did not latch them if the airplane was to be loaded soon. I never climbed aboard until I had checked every latch, so I couldn't believe it when the door rose in front of my face.

With the long SeaTac runways, there was plenty of room to reject the takeoff. I cleared the runway and asked Ground Control for permission to stop on the taxiway. I shut down both engines, got out, closed and latched the door, and walked around the airplane again, wondering how I'd missed the unfastened latches on that door and wondering if I might have missed something else.

When something is checked over and over, the routine becomes too routine. I'd started my walk-around and was approaching the left side of the nose when something on the ramp by the tire caught my eye. I was looking down, not up at the latches, when I walked past the baggage compartment, so I missed the one thing that was not as it should be the one time I needed not to miss it.

With Bandeirantes gone, income was down and workload was up. Small incidents became large irritations. A man dropped a banana peel in the aisle when he left the airplane. I caught up with him clearing Customs and handed it back to him. Our director of operations heard me grousing about some insignificant irritant. He smiled like Mister Rogers and said, "It's tough being perfect in an imperfect world, isn't it, Eric."

Even today, when I'm disproportionately torqued at some petty problem, I remember that line and relax a little.

I had to fly a short test flight in Port Angeles because the airplane had a new propeller installed. That made me late to Seattle, arriving when I should have been leaving. I stepped into the baggage office to fill my coffee mug before heading upstairs to sign paperwork and escort my passengers to the airplane. The girl at the gate called down on the intercom to tell me what time it was. I said, "I've got a fucking watch."

She was new at the job, and I felt bad. When I went upstairs, I found a shop and bought flowers to accompany my apology. I didn't like losing my temper, especially around airplanes.

One evening, a former Pearson pilot who had gone to Sunworld rode home to Port Angeles with me on the last flight. We went out for a beer and talked. He said the only reason I didn't get an interview was, they'd raised the minimum turbine requirement to a thousand hours. I had a little over eight hundred in the Bandeirante.

Robert tried to persuade me to apply at DHL. He was based in Cincinnati, but his schedule was one week on, one week off, and he commuted from Port Angeles. DHL was hiring for the Metroliner, and new-hires just out of training as first officers had to retrain almost immediately for upgrade to captain.

Changing jobs is stressful under any circumstances, but to leave a known position for one far away and completely new was a fearsome hurdle to contemplate. I countered my friend's arguments as best I could. My last stand was, "I can't stand cigaret smoke, and San Juan doesn't allow smoking in the airplanes."

"Neither does DHL," he said.

DHL Worldwide Express began as a courier service carrying paperwork from the mainland to ships sitting idle in Hawaii awaiting orders. While never as large a presence in the United States as FedEx or UPS, it became huge in the rest of the world. The American piece of the company was DHL Airways, a privately held corporation. The cover story in *Professional Pilot* magazine of February 1986 was about DHL and its plans for growth. Pilot backgrounds they were looking for fit me so well, I'd not have been surprised to have seen my name in the article. I sent my résumé to San Francisco and got a call.

With DHL's hiring profile in mind, I thought that, as long as I didn't say something stupid, I was in. To avoid saying something stupid, I didn't say much at all. I flew home from my interview and resumed flying, but my mind was already leaving for my new job. A week later, I learned I didn't have a new job. I'd been turned down because interviewers got the feeling that I wasn't really interested. Three pilots I knew at DHL urged human resources to give me another shot, even though the company had never reconsidered rejected applicants.

I shook off hurt feelings and wrote thank-you notes to the pilot on my interview panel and to the director of human resources. I said I hoped I'd be considered the next time they hired.

A week later, I wrote another letter to the HR director:

> Dear Mr B——:
> Several times a week, I depart Seattle-Tacoma airport right behind DHL 404. This causes me a minor problem.
> Watching that 727 lift off into the golden light of early evening makes me drool, and the drool stains my neckties.
> The obvious solution is for me to fly DHL airplanes rather than just watch them.

"Ah, Mister Rush," the voice on the phone said. "Your name keeps coming up. We don't normally do this, and we've thrown away your file. Send us your résumé again and a copy of your flight engineer written."

On the last day of July, I flew to San Francisco for another interview. As soon as we sat down to talk, I asserted myself as I had not done the first time.

"I understand you didn't hire me because you thought I didn't really want the job." I opened my copy of *Professional Pilot* to the page where I'd highlighted qualifications and characteristics DHL was looking for. I said that, having never formally interviewed for a job before, I thought I was a shoo-in as long as I didn't say the wrong thing.

I put a positive spin on things they could perceive as negative. Most pilots bounced around from one flying job to another, always trying to gain more and better experience. My record showed I was not a job hopper. I said that, at age 43, I had only one job change in me. If they hired me, they'd have me for life.

I had no time in Metroliners, but that was to DHL's advantage, I said. They'd not have to unteach me another company's procedures.

They said a lot of pilots don't like flying at night. I said I preferred it, as there is less traffic and you can see other airplanes at great distance.

They asked how I'd feel flying as a junior crewman to a captain who was younger and with perhaps less experience. I said my experience was not broad. It was more like one hour, nine thousand times, and most of my flight time was within a hundred miles of where I learned to fly. I did not think I had the sort of ego that would resent not being in charge.

When the three men stood to signify the interview was over, I stayed in my chair and said, "Before I go, *have I convinced you guys I want this job?*"

They laughed and we shook hands all around. I floated out the door to catch the shuttle back to the terminal. A few days later, I got a call to go to Cincinnati for a physical exam and a simulator check.

A DHL instructor pilot picked up several of us at the airport and drove us to the company doctor's office. Others were there ahead of us in the waiting room. We were all active pilots with medical certificates, but the company conducted its own physicals and drug tests. Some doctors would sign off a medical if you could walk in the door. Others seemed to consider it a personal defeat if a pilot passed his exam. The company's doctor would at least evaluate everyone equally.

DHL put us up overnight in the Drawbridge Hotel, a sprawling complex with a castle theme not far from the airport. The next day, a van took us to Lunken Field, the original Cincinnati airport, where we demonstrated our instrument flying skills. The simulator was not a full-motion mockup of a real airplane but a desktop instrument panel with control yoke and rudder pedals almost identical to the one we used for annual training at San Juan Airlines.

Anyone can fly such a simulator with a little practice. Where pilots differ is in awareness and judgment. I never considered it likely that I'd fly into a mountain because some controller mistakenly turned me into high terrain, and I was not reluctant to refuse instructions I didn't like.

Once back at the Drawbridge, the ten of us who did not have immediate flights to catch gathered in a hotel bar to drink beer and get to know each other.

I flew home that evening. DHL called the next day. I gave San Juan two weeks' notice calculated how many landings I had left, how many Customs forms to fill out, how many more lunches in Seattle. The last few days zipped by. San Juan's owner wished me well. Ticket agents and baggage handlers in Victoria gave me a card covered with signatures. On my last day at work, off-duty pilots and friends and mentors who'd known me since I began flying lessons came to a going-away party in the airport restaurant.

Metroliner Pilot

Cincinnati's airport is across the Ohio River in Boone County, Kentucky. Classrooms near DHL's sort building at the north end of the airport were in a double-wide trailer on concrete blocks. We learned the company's operating procedures and systems of the Swearingen SA-227 Metroliner, a paper towel tube with wings and two turboprop engines nicknamed Lawn Dart.

Of my class of nine, I was oldest and senior with number 114. I shared a room at the Drawbridge with another new hire. We congregated at a pilot's apartment to study. One man seemed to think he needed to memorize every word in the books and in his notes. He put so much pressure on himself that, halfway through training, he quit. Another was fired when DHL learned what he'd claimed as recent flying experience was time spent driving a concrete mixer.

DHL contracted with Flight Safety in San Antonio for Metroliner simulator training. Our class was an experiment. Acquisition of more Boeing 727s made turnover high in the Metroliner. Rather than train new pilots for the right seat and put them through training again a few weeks later for upgrade to captain, DHL decided to save time and money by training new hires to captain standards capped with a type rating checkride. This would have been okay, except both pilots in the simulator were new hires, and we traded seats in the middle of each session. Rather than fly simulator checkrides with qualified Metroliner pilots, as would have been required in the airplane, our training partners served as right-seat support. Neither my training partner nor I had experience in the airplane.

I was senior to my partner because I was three months older. I elected to fly the left seat in the second half of each lesson so I could learn from Kurt's mistakes. We had one instructor for the entire twenty-four hours spread over six days with one day off after each three in the box.

After training for six weeks, we were all eager to finish and go home. Kurt and I were the scheduled for the first checkrides. A DHL pilot I'll call Queeg had just been designated an examiner by the FAA and would conduct our oral exams and checkrides in the simulator. Not only were Kurt and I the point men for the company's training experiment, we were also Captain Queeg's first victims.

After a few questions and answers, an examiner can tell if an applicant knows the airplane. If weak areas of knowledge show up, the exam becomes more involved. Checkrides themselves comprise a variety of instrument approaches, holding patterns, and inflight emergencies that must be performed within specified limits. Normally, a combined oral and ride should take two or three hours. Kurt's and mine together took nearly fourteen, and Kurt didn't have time to finish.

Misery began with a joint oral exam. Queeg questioned us together, with our acquiescence, to save time. Queeg, with his new examiner's authority, was like a kid with a new toy and determined to get the most out of it. Kurt and I were already tired when we broke for lunch.

Although I'd gone second each session, I volunteered to go first on the checkride. Kurt and I did not realize we would fly right seat for each other, and I thought that, by going first, I might finish early enough to go home that day. I remember only two elements of my checkride.

When an engine fails during takeoff on a piston-driven twin, a pilot has to quickly identify the failed engine and feather the propeller. In the Metroliner, we were supposed to do nothing until the airplane was four hundred feet above the ground. On my checkride, I reverted to original training and began the engine failure procedure well below four hundred feet. The other thing I remember doing wrong was the last item on my ride, an NDB approach. Kurt and I remember it differently.

A Non-Directional Beacon approach is a primitive, almost obsolete way of finding a runway in bad weather, a matter of keeping on course with a gyroscopic compass with a needle that points to a radio beacon. It's simple if the beacon is on the airport. If it isn't, you use speed and time to know how far you are past that beacon. If there is a crosswind, and there always is crosswind on checkrides, the airplane will drift off course without a heading correction.

Many pilots get confused about which way to turn the airplane to keep the Automatic Direction Finder needle on the correct course. Once past the beacon, the arrow on the ADF needle points toward the tail of the airplane, and the tail of the needle should then be on the course. I never had trouble visualizing the relationship between needle and course corrections, had never gotten lost on NDB approaches because I got confused and turned the wrong way. I found other ways to screw up approaches, but they did not involve course confusion.

So, almost brain dead from fatigue and angry at being subjected to such an arduous oral exam and checkride, I began the last element, an NDB approach.

Simulator partners work out a simple system of surreptitious signals. A tap on a rudder pedal means what you're doing is wrong. On the way inbound to the NDB, I had time to arrive at the correct heading to compensate for crosswind. We crossed the NDB and the needle reversed direction. I started the clock and reduced power to begin descent. Then I felt the tap on a pedal.

I checked my course and heading. I was off a little but making the correct change to get back on course. Kurt tapped again and muttered, "Other way." He was insistent and I was tired, so I believed him and turned the airplane the other way. Captain Queeg called an end to the ride.

Kurt and I argued about that approach during our break before his checkride. I'd have failed because of my premature clean-up after the engine failure, even if I'd successfully completed the NDB approach. My pink slip lists, by code number, six items that I'd be checked on in a re-test, but I didn't care enough to look them up. My plan was to get into an airplane big enough to stand up in as soon as possible.

After our break and debrief, we went back into the simulator. Kurt was in the captain's seat and I was his first officer, his support pilot. I was drained of energy and interest, disgusted over my failure, and was still blaming my partner for leading me astray on the NDB. I was angrier with myself for letting him do it.

Kurt flew much better than I did, and then he was assigned the same approach I'd failed. He briefed the approach, we set up our instruments, and, when he crossed the NBD and needed to make a small course correction, he began to turn the wrong way.

At that moment, a loud knock interrupted. Queeg pushed a button to freeze the simulator in time and space and opened the door, flooding the cockpit with light and destroying the illusion of flight. Time was up. Maintenance needed to work on the simulator. Kurt's checkride was an incomplete, not a failure.

I was convinced that Kurt had begun turning the wrong way, and he was adamant that he had not. We argue about that nearly thirty years later.

He and I wrote sharp critiques of the training process with emphasis on improperly supported checkrides. The rest of our class had instructor pilots in the right seats for their checkrides. Everyone passed.

Kurt didn't get to finish his captain's ride. He and I got ninety minutes each of retraining in the right seat of the simulator and a checkride with an instructor as captain to qualify us as first officers. We went back to Cincinnati for a short checkride in the airplane. A few hours later, at three o'clock in the morning, I signed in for my first revenue flight, still in civilian clothes, to Charlotte, North Carolina. I rode and observed the crew from the tiny, fold-down jumpseat behind the cockpit and watched the flow of the operation and paperwork.

DHL did not skimp on crew accommodations. We always had rooms or suites to ourselves. Per diem for time away from base began when we showed up for work the first day and continued uninterrupted until our week's duty ended.

A limousine picked the three of us up at the airport in Charlotte and took us to the Registry Inn. When I walked into my room and sank into the carpet, when I looked around at the big, fluffy bed and ornate furniture, when I checked out the bathroom with more thick towels that I'd use in a week, an elegant bar of soap in a brass dish on a marble countertop, I was reluctant to touch anything. I showered, used one towel, and wiped up water splatters when I finished. When I told a friend of my reaction to the sumptuous room, he said, "In a couple of weeks, you'll be bitching if everything's not perfect, same as the rest of us."

The captain flew the first leg that night from Charlotte to Greensboro. I was in the right seat and the first officer rode the jumpseat and watched me do paperwork. I flew us to Knoxville to pick up more cargo and do more paperwork. When we landed in Cincinnati, the first officer was satisfied I could manage on my own. I could finally go home.

Protocol demanded that riders request permission to ride a jumpseat, even if the captain was a friend and you rode his airplane every week. I'd heard stories about The Skipper, but I'd never met him.

Rod Scamahorn was a former US Marine pilot with a theatrical persona and many compulsive rituals. He insisted his crew lace their shoes left over right. In preparation for my first ride with The Skipper, as he preferred to be called, I re-laced my shoes before introducing myself and pulled up the cuffs of my slacks to show that my laces were correct. Damned if I hadn't laced them right over left.

The Skipper looked up at me with a Popeye-the-Sailor-Man squint. He was below average in height, so he got a lot of practice looking up at people. I suppressed a smile and said I'd correct my laces before departure.

There were three options for dealing with The Skipper. One was to go along with his rituals and games, and another was to ignore him. The worst was to fight. I didn't mind going along with his shoelace fetish, with blessing the flight, and with his other peculiarities. In time, we became friends, and I cried when he fell out of the sky and died.

Most of us did not live in or near Cincinnati. DHL's domestic airline had begun a few years earlier at Tacoma, Washington, and many senior pilots lived in the area. We commuters got from home to Cincinnati and back on jumpseats in our airplanes or on the few other airlines that allowed us to ride. Metroliners had one seat. Boeing 727s had two. We could reserve seats thirty days in advance, beginning at seven in the morning Eastern Time. Because many pilots lived in Washington and Oregon, and because most work weeks began on Wednesday morning, demand was high Tuesday nights inbound to Cincinnati and westbound the next morning.

Because of the time difference, we on the west coast had to reserve seats at four o'clock in the morning or risk missing out. I kept my alarm set for 3:57 and my watch accurate to the second. It took a minute to struggle into wakefulness and figure out why I was awake. It took another minute to figure out which flight I needed and get to the phone. I punched in all but the last digit of Crew Scheduling's number, and then, when the second hand of my watch approached twelve, I'd hit the last digit and cross my fingers.

An alternative to not having a jumpseat was to go in a day early and either stay in a hotel or take someone's last trip so he could go home a day early. With luck the other pilot might be able to return the favor someday.

Some commuters rolled out sleeping bags in the entryway behind the 727's cockpit door. A few strung hammocks in the narrow space between the cargo net and the first cargo container behind it. I could sleep well enough sitting up in the seat directly behind the captain, or, if I was lucky enough to get the seat behind that one, a rolled-up overcoat on a small side table made an acceptable pillow. Some of us had cars parked at the DHL building near the north end of SeaTac airport. Wives picked a few pilots up, and some of us walked or bummed rides to the passenger terminal to catch a free ride on whatever commuter flight was going our way. I rode home from Seattle on San Juan for a two-week stay. I flew my own airplane one day, just to play in the air.

The first day home after a week of working nights and sleeping days was, for me, a throwaway. Some pilots took naps when they got home and went to bed that night at a normal time. When I got tired past a certain point, settling down to sleep was difficult. With Katrina in school and Barb at work, I didn't have to interact with human beings. All I wanted to do was open a beer, read the week's mail, and perhaps do something that didn't require a functioning brain such as cutting firewood or mowing the lawn. I'd sleep ten or twelve hours the first night home and then be pretty much back to normal.

Crossing three time zones eastbound to start a work week wasn't a problem if the first trip was short. By the time we landed near the east coast to spend the day, it was only about four o'clock in the morning at home, and, if we'd slept an hour or two on the ride to Cincinnati, we began our week in good shape.

Where we landed Saturday morning, we stayed until Monday evening. We bid schedules every four weeks and bid weekends either near home or in places we liked to spend time.

My first night at work after two weeks off did not go well. I was sleepy and had forgotten how to fly a Metroliner. Being new and slow, I tried to stay ahead of things, getting paperwork done early and calling for clearance early so I could set up my radios and study charts of an unfamiliar part of the planet. My captain was a blond, disheveled Norwegian with a pronounced accent. He kept telling me to relax.

I always kept precise times in logbooks. Times in my first logs were in tenths of an hour taken from Hobbs meters. At DHL, we used clock times. My captain liked to round times off to the nearest five minutes because it made adding them easier. He grumbled constantly. I couldn't understand everything he muttered, but "morons" was frequent and recognizable.

* * *

Unless trip trades, vacations, or sick days interrupted, Crews flew together for the entire four weeks of the bid. Only two of those weeks were work, and each work week was five days of flying. Even if paired with someone I didn't like, ten days a month was tolerable. In my first full week, I flew with a different captain every night.

I wrote up each day's events in a small notebook. My handwriting is hard to read unless I write slowly, and I can't write slowly. I bought a small, electronic typewriter and carried it with me.

Document envelopes and packages went through a maze of conveyor belts and chutes in the DHL sort building in Cincinnati as inbound loads were sorted and reloaded into fuselage-fitting fiberglass or aluminum containers for our 727s and chartered DC-9s and DC-8s. Cargo for smaller airplanes went into canvas mail bags or was loaded loose. Dispatch and Crew Scheduling offices were upstairs and the crew lounge was a large room filled with reclining chairs on the ground floor. A scheduler came down to a desk in the lounge for the few hours pilots were there in the middle of the night between inbound and outbound flights. A large whiteboard showed what crews and airplanes were going where. When the last flights had left, reserves were free to go to home or to a hotel. They'd write the phone number of where they could be reached next to their names on the whiteboard with erasable felt pens.

Most pilots carried enough clothing to last all week. I traveled light and washed clothes in the hotel room. Shirt collars got dirty fast. Pressurized air comes from compressor stages of jet engines. Although that air was tapped ahead of fuel and fire, something black came into the cabin with it, and, after seeing what it did to shirts, I wondered what it was and what it was doing to my lungs.

Some pilots made the most of their weekends, renting cars, going to shows and visiting sights. Others went into their rooms and seldom come out until time to go back to the airport. I preferred to eat alone because I'd rather read than make small talk with people I hardly know. I spent layover time in my room reading or watching TV and writing. With my little typewriter, it was easy to keep a diary of my working life.

Each pilot, and even second officers—flight engineers—on the 727, carried a Jeppesen binder three inches thick full of charts for approaches to all the airports we normally flew to. In addition, each airplane carried navigation charts and approach and departure procedures for almost the entire country. Every week, revisions added charts, dropped others, and revised or corrected many. In the Metroliner, it was the first officer's job on weekends to replace old charts with new ones in the airplane's half a dozen seven-ring binders.

I had the hotel van take me to the airport two hours early Monday evening. It took most of that extra time to make the revisions.

We got memos from time to time reminding us to pay our hotel bills for extras. Sometimes, hotels billed us for room charges that weren't ours. Hotels change days between posted check-out and check-in times. Because our occupancies bridged the two, we sometimes got bills the previous occupant had incurred. Sometimes a hotel couldn't find record of our charges, and I wondered if they came up on the next occupant's bill.

When my class was hired, first-year first officer pay was just under $20,000 a year. Metroliner captains earned a few thousand more, and second officers on the Boeing 727 started at around $28,000. Metroliner turnover was high in part because captains went to the back seat of the Boeing for more money. To keep Metroliner captains in the airplane longer, the company raised their pay and lowered back-seat Boeing pay to make them equal.

Airlines had jumpseat agreements with each other to give commuting pilots more options for getting to work. This was to the companies' advantage, as pilots who couldn't make it to work called in sick at the last minute. Some airlines insisted that riders occupy cockpit jumpseats. Others, with captain's permission and the lead flight attendant's concurrence, allowed jumpseaters to ride in passenger seats.

It was the captain's airplane, but it was the flight attendants' cabin. Captains often introduced me to the lead and asked if she or he had a seat for me in back. Sometimes, the captain gave me the lead attendant's name and told me to ask, with his blessing, if I could sit in back. I never sat in First Class unless it was offered.

Quebec speaks French, but English is the international language of aviation. I was able to understand radio calls through heavy accents, but Canadian terminology was not always the same as American. We had to pay close attention and be ready to question anything we weren't certain we understood.

At check-in at the Pavilion Hotel in Montreal, we were offered glasses of champagne. I was quick to refuse, as our layover was less than the company's 12-hour bottle-to-throttle rule. The captain also refused, but only because I did. He said most of the pilots accepted the wine because the FAA rule was eight hours, and ten hours was plenty for one small glass. I don't like champagne anyway, but I was sorry that, by example, I'd deprived my captain of his treat.

If we wanted to eat in Cincinnati in the middle of the night between flights, and if we had time, we walked half a mile to the passenger terminal where one restaurant stayed open all night. Sometimes, someone with a car took pilots to a Waffle House. There was no food available in the DHL building other than sugary snacks from vending machines.

When I flew to Detroit on Saturday morning, I was on my own for the weekend. The captain had family nearby and stayed with them. The company did not care where we stayed as long as they knew how to reach us. I didn't go anywhere or do anything. I had plenty to read and there were enough cable channels that I could always find a good movie or a program worth watching. I didn't watch much TV except in hotels. At home, there were plenty of things more interesting and productive to do.

We flew into Kansas City's downtown airport rather than the new one a few miles west. The hotel was full when we arrived, and only one room was ready. Our rooms were supposed to be available around the clock every day. The desk clerk tried to talk us into doubling up. My captain refused and told the clerk he presumed the hotel was going to buy us breakfast while we waited.

I tend to overeat when food is free. I stuffed myself with ham and eggs and potatoes and toast and orange juice and coffee. I'd been asleep only an hour when I woke up and ran to the bathroom to upchuck my entire free breakfast. I thought I'd eaten something that had gone bad, but then I realized it was more likely the full belly topped off with combined acids of coffee and orange juice. It was the first time in at least a decade I'd thrown up for any reason.

A few days later, I flew with one of the few pilots older than I was. Standardization ensures that everyone on a crew knows what everyone else is doing and will do. That captain was casual about standard procedures, so I tried to stay more alert than usual. He didn't give a takeoff briefing, didn't call for the After Takeoff checklist, and didn't run the Parking checklist when we landed. The autopilot flew and he slept. I stayed awake and paid attention.

In Charlotte, we ate breakfast in the hotel. The captain flirted with waitresses and female hotel staff and got away with things that would get most men slapped. Orange juice was expensive, so I didn't order it. The captain did and sweet-talked the waitress into not charging him for it.

I was flying with a friend on his birthday. We could legally have a couple of beers to celebrate when we got to Charlotte, but we didn't get to Charlotte. We waited in Greensboro for Charlotte weather to improve until the company released us to go to a hotel near mid-morning. The delay had cut into our beer time, but we'd cheat a little and go by the FAA's 8-hour rule. After dropping off bags in our rooms, we had only half an hour before we'd bump into the time limit.

The hotel bar wasn't open at that hour, but we explained that we wanted to celebrate a birthday. The desk clerk came in from time to time to serve us. Judgment and inhibitions fade when people are desperate for sleep. We drank beers and shots of bourbon, and we didn't stop after half an hour. We got only a few hours of sleep before it was time to fly, and we were both shaky and tired. We agreed that the day was not something we wanted to talk about to others, and for a long time, we didn't.

A few years later, the pilots of a passenger carrier were arrested for showing up drunk. A passenger had been in the same bar as the crew the night before and knew they could not be sober after the short interval between bottle and throttle. That was a turning point in most pilots' perceptions of drinking in relation to flying. I was sure those pilots who were arrested considered themselves merely hung over.

Uniforms for my class arrived. Trousers, coat, and cap were tan. The cap had a brown visor and band. Short-sleeved white shirts with brown pinstripes and a brown necktie completed the ensemble. I carried my uniform to the hotel in Memphis Saturday and wore for the first time Monday evening. I had trouble getting all the clothes I'd been wearing into my bag and considered that I might have to carry fewer books and magazines.

When DHL created DHL Airways to supplement its courier service, no one in the company knew much about running an airline, and work rules were generous. Some airlines give pilots the vacation they'd put in for months earlier, and if it happened to fall on days off, too bad. We worked week-on, week-off, and could slide vacation so that a week of vacation would block out a full week of work giving us three weeks off. Bidding to change between odd and even weeks could stretch a one-week vacation to four. Some pilots traded with others so they worked two weeks on, two weeks off each month, alternating the off weeks so they were home four weeks and at work four weeks. A pilot trading with a partner to work month on, month off, could be off twelve weeks straight for his four weeks of vacation.

When I started at DHL, we were entitled to four vacation weeks after only five years of service. We had six personal holidays we could take anytime we wanted, provided there were reserves to cover our trips. Floating holidays came in handy when commuters couldn't get to work. More than once, when the airplane I was going to ride was delayed or I was bumped from my jumpseat, I called Crew Scheduling to request a floater for my first day.

Early in November, I put in for a floating holiday for Thanksgiving. It was denied because pilots senior to me wanted to be home that day. A few days before the holiday, Crew Scheduling called me at home to tell me I had Thanksgiving off.

"Thank you, but I thought you didn't have enough reserves."

"We don't," the scheduler said. "But A—— J—— pissed me off, so he's going to Philadelphia and you're staying home."

The handful of men and women in Crew Scheduling had our lives in their hands, but some pilots didn't understand that simple reality. They either made no effort to be civil, or they whined and complained when they couldn't get what they wanted. Those of us who understood how the world works tried to stay on the schedulers' good side. If they needed a trip covered and one of us was scheduled to go home but could afford to be a day late, we'd volunteer to fly it. Little things like accepting without complaint last-minute changes we didn't like made schedulers' jobs easier, and they remembered.

I'd been warned about a captain I'll call Napoleon. He liked to show he was boss. Other pilots told me he'd tell them to do something just as they were beginning to do it, or he'd wait until they were involved in one task to tell them to do something else. The moment the new task was completed, he'd tell them to do what they were doing before he interrupted them. Napoleon didn't pull any obnoxious power plays on me, perhaps because we were the same age.

Snow and ice on the ramp in Toronto made turning into our parking spot difficult. The station agent marshaling us in didn't recognize our problem and turned us too tightly. When the nosewheel slid sideways, Napoleon stopped the airplane and shut it down. The agent opened the door and climbed in to ask why we'd parked where we did. Napoleon screamed at the young man, yelling that he had no business telling him how to park the airplane, and that he wasn't going to move it. The agent could tow it if he wanted it moved. Then Napoleon ordered him to get the hell off his airplane.

I was as shocked as the station agent and embarrassed to be associated with such a jerk. I followed the agent off the airplane because I didn't want to have to talk to Napoleon. The agent asked me what was up with the captain. I told him I didn't know, that I hardly knew the man.

I decided to avoid flying with Napoleon as much as I could. Trading away from him proved difficult. The first question was almost always, "Who's the captain?"

I didn't like winter flying, not because of weather hazards but because walking around airplanes with a flashlight in cold wind and blowing snow is not fun. Captains didn't have to do the dirty work, but I did not want to upgrade in the Metroliner. I wanted to be on a bigger airplane in any capacity, an airplane with a toilet to alleviate the discomfort that necessarily follows high coffee consumption.

I flew my last trip in the Metroliner late in January.

Boeing 727 Second Officer

We were supposed to study some sections of the airplane manual ahead of time and pass a test on that information the first day of class. Then came two weeks of lectures, slide presentations, movies, and multiple-choice tests. We'd learned 727 systems for our flight engineer exams before being hired, but we got it all again in ground school.

There were three in the class for each of the two pilot positions and twice that many for the back seat. Several of us stayed at the Drawbridge Hotel during ground school. Almost the entire class showed up there on Friday evenings to relax and drink beer.

Anytime pilots get together in a bar, talk turns to the job. A young man stopped me as I was walking past his table and said, "I couldn't help hearing you guys talking. Are you pilots?"

"Yeah, we are," I said. "We fly for Continental."

I wandered back to my seat wondering why I'd said that, wondering why I'd picked on one of the few carriers we could ride free.

As closing time approached and we began to leave, the man and his wife were still there. I walked to their table and said, "Excuse me, but I can't leave you with a lie. We don't fly for Continental. We fly for Federal Express."

DHL contracted Boeing 727 simulator time from USAir in Pittsburgh. We stayed in a La Quinta north of the airport.

We trained as crews, one captain, one first officer, and two second officers. The captain candidate flew the first two hours and the first officer was the non-flying pilot. One of the second officer trainees worked the first two hours and the other worked the second half when the first officer flew. Second officers took turns standing in the back of the simulator cockpit behind the instructors to watch.

Second officers managed fuel, pressurization, electrics, hydraulics, and other systems. Although major malfunctions in flight are rare, we had to learn how to deal with all of them. Instructors at panels behind the crew pushed buttons to create problems.

Second officers don't fly the airplane, but we were required to monitor what the pilots were doing and pay attention to takeoff and arrival briefings. The second officer kept the log and did some of the paperwork, but we didn't waste simulator time doing paper.

The second officer sits sideways behind the first officer facing a small desk. The systems panel extends the width of the desk and upward as far as the seated second officer can reach. The seat locks in place, but levers and pedals allow it to turn and move up and down, forward and aft, and left and right so the second officer can reach almost everything he ever has to reach without unfastening the seatbelt or releasing shoulder straps. To the right of the second officer's desk are a coat rack and the bulkhead separating the cockpit from the rest of the airplane. The half of the wall to the right of the desk and panel is covered with circuit breakers, buttons that can be pulled out a quarter of an inch to remove power from whatever they control. The cockpit door is in the center of the wall.

On the left side of the cockpit, behind the captain, are two cramped jumpseats, one behind the other. The one directly behind the captain is high enough that the occupant can see over his head. The rear jumpseat, the comfortable one, is adjustable vertically and directionally.

Each member of the crew had to learn flows, the orders in which panels were checked, switches flipped, and instruments set. Our checklists were not "do lists" but were read and responded to only to ensure that all items on them had been done. When everyone has finished building their nests—when everyone has settled into their seats, adjusted them to their liking, plugged in headsets, checked oxygen masks, and gotten out the charts they'd need—the captain asks for the logbook and the second officer hands it to him. The captain looks back a page or two to see if there were any pertinent remarks logged. He checks to see what mechanical problems previous crews had written up and what the disposition of each was. Most items are repaired or replaced immediately, but some are deferred because of lack of time or lack of parts. The airplane has a Minimum Equipment List, a manual specifying what can be missing or inoperative and what restrictions, if any, a defect might impose on performance.

The captain briefs the crew on what to expect in terms of weather and anything else that might affect the flight. The second officer tells the captain how much fuel is on board, having compared readings on the fuel gauges and to a total derived from what the airplane arrived with, how much was pumped in, and what the density of the added fuel was based on temperature. If the two numbers were within prescribed limits, we could assume we had the amount of fuel the flight plan and the gauges said we had.

Flight plan computers on the ground calculated expected fuel burn based on weight, altitude, and winds aloft. Bad weather required a planned alternate airport—an English teacher would insist on "alternative"—and enough fuel to get there if we couldn't land at our destination. We had to carry fuel for holding and expected delays plus forty-five minutes worth of "Now what?" fuel. During long flights, it was the non-flying pilot's job to compare actual fuel burn with planned burn at various points across the country.

When the captain is satisfied the log book is in order and paperwork is complete, he calls for the Before Start checklist. In the simulator, we began at the beginning only once or twice. Unless starting problems were on the schedule, engines would be running and all checklists assumed complete when we climbed into our seats.

I liked going second. Watching the first guy get more or less what I was going to get lent an advantage, which is why we alternated going first.

Standing behind the crew gives a perspective that sitting close to the panel does not. The instructor might elbow me gently and point at something the other second officer hadn't yet noticed, perhaps a warning light or a gauge out of limits. I'd wonder how it was possible that something so obvious could escape notice. Then, when it was my turn in the seat, the other guy got to watch me not notice obvious things.

Instructors insisted they didn't give us more than one problem at a time, although if we didn't handle that one problem correctly, it could lead to a cascade of others. Sometimes we crashed.

Sometimes we crashed in wind shear training. Sometimes it was when the crew didn't respond quickly enough to the ground proximity box's recorded warnings, "Terrain! Terrain! Pull up! Pull up!" as we flew into the side of a virtual mountain. We knew the simulator was bolted to a concrete floor, but once in the game, when a fire bell rings and red lights flash, adrenalin flows and hearts pound. We couldn't mentally separate ourselves from the mechanical box on hydraulic legs that was, to us, our airplane.

We flew the simulator more than thirty hours over eight training sessions plus checkrides. At the end of each day, crews often had dinner and a few beers together while we talked over the day's training—what we did right, what we did wrong, and what we could have done better.

I thought we were finished for the day when the fire bell began its shrill jangle. I saw no red light to indicate what was burning. We were parked and engines were shut down, so the only thing left was the Auxiliary Power Unit, a small jet engine inside the airplane that provides electric power and compressed air when those necessities are not available from ground equipment. With none of the engine fire handles lit up, I turned to the APU controls on the circuit breaker panel. There was no red light there, either, and the APU was running normally. That bell had to be a simulator glitch.

My instructor was a white-haired, red-faced man many students regarded as a tyrant. I started to ask what was going on, and he yelled in my face. "If you have a fire bell, you have to do something!"

With engines off, it had to be the APU. I pulled the fire handle, even though it wasn't lit red, then turned it to fill the APU compartment with fire suppressing chemicals. I was angry at what I thought was an unfair trick—not that the light in the APU fire handle was burned out, but that the instructor had given me the fire at the end of the session when we were packing up our books and headsets to leave the simulator. I was mad, but my instructor was madder. He screamed, "You lose your temper like that in the airplane, it'll get you killed!"

I understood, even in the heat of the moment, that he was right.

My checkride was easy after hours of emergencies and failures one right after another. Anytime nothing was going wrong, I looked around constantly, certain I must be missing something.

Modern simulators are so realistic that people can learn to fly without ever touching an airplane, but the simulator we used was not new. It had primitive visual representation through the front windows but none out the sides, so regulations required us to take a second checkride in an airplane. During the day, our airplanes were everywhere except in Cincinnati, so my entire class went to San Francisco to fly one for a few minutes.

It was vaguely unsettling, five of us flying a 727 in jeans and sport shirts. The absence of uniforms didn't look right, but the airplane couldn't tell the difference. The first day's short hops were warm up, and we had a day off before checkrides. The day after that, I was working the first of several trips of Initial Operating Experience with an experienced second officer watching until he was satisfied I could manage on my own.

I'd never been to New York City and didn't care if I never went there, but that's where I landed for the weekend layover. The car that picked us up at JFK Saturday morning was a sedan, okay for three passengers but crowded with four. We double-parked at a takeout store on the way to Manhattan and the second officer supervising me ran inside to buy a six-pack of beer which we all drank on the ride to our hotel.

We stayed in tiny rooms at the Milford Plaza on Eighth Avenue near Times Square. The captain went to bed so he'd be awake for Saturday night in the city. The rest of us changed into civilian clothes and met in the lobby. We walked across the street to Smith's Bar for breakfast. We took a booth and ate the Smith's equivalent of Egg McMuffins and washed them down with beer and coffee. Regulars drank, ate, and read newspapers at all hours.

After breakfast, we moved to the bar. A bartender with a strong Irish accent asked what we wanted and I ordered a beer and a shot. Sure, Jack Daniels was fine. We had several of what each of us was drinking and the world became wobbly. It was Saturday morning, and we didn't fly again until Monday evening, so we didn't care.

The Metroliner that went to Montreal came to JFK on weekends, and its captain found us at Smith's. The afternoon became fuzzy, and my umbrella disappeared. There is a gap between deciding to leave the bar and crawling around on the tiled floor of my hotel bathroom looking for a contact lens.

It seemed I'd been asleep only minutes when the phone rang. "Hey, Rush! You ready to pahty?"

I didn't want to party. I was still drunk and trying to sleep.

"Ah, too bad," my mentor said. "You shoulda puked!"

When he said that, I almost did, but I went back to sleep and woke hungry late at night. Not yet realizing that New York truly never sleeps, I wondered if anything was open.

Eighth Avenue was as crowded with traffic and people. More than one denizen of the streets tried to sell me something as I hurried back to the hotel with two slices of pizza in a bag. I expected to be mugged at any moment.

When I woke again, it was daytime and I needed coffee. I went into the first deli I came to.

"Reglah?"

"What?"

"Do you want *reg-you-lah*?"

Well, sure. Regular. He brought me a Styrofoam cup loaded with sugar and cream. I told him I wanted black.

"You didn't say that," he snarled. "You said reglah."

After sampling black coffee at several delis, cafés, and restaurants in Manhattan, I understood why "regular" coffee meant cream and sugar. It's the only way you could choke it down.

The rest of the crew slept late after their night on the town. When we got together Sunday evening for dinner, I became aware from the conversation that I was missing something. What taxi? What bar in Queens? A few days later in Cincinnati, the Metroliner captain who'd been with us handed me my umbrella. "You left it in the cab," he said.

It was raining in New York Monday evening when our driver took us to the airport, and it was snowing when we landed in Cincinnati. We stayed in the same airplane and flew to Salt Lake City and on to San Francisco where my week ended. My IOE supervisor signed me off, and I was on my own.

I rode the shuttle bus from the DHL building to the terminal and hopped a ride to Seattle and another to Port Angeles. I was home only one night before it was time to go back to work.

Flights out of Port Angeles were full, so I flew my Cessna 152 fifteen miles to Sequim Valley Airport and caught a ride from there to Seattle on a Cessna 402. Coastal Airways flew three round trips a day to Seattle, and empty seats were free to commuting pilots. Horizon had frequent flights from Seattle to Portland where my first unsupervised week began.

DHL maintained two pilot domiciles in the late 1980s, Cincinnati and San Francisco. Salt Lake City was a mini-hub where our 727 from Portland terminated after stopping in Seattle and where small, contract airplanes from cities in surrounding western states brought shipments to be transferred to a 727 from San Francisco for the rest of the ride to Cincinnati. The DHL building at Salt Lake City had a bunk room and a lounge for pilots. The Portland crew and contract pilots spent five or six hours there in the middle of the night between flights.

Crews that flew the route from Portland through Seattle to Salt Lake City and back were based in San Francisco. That looked like a good gig for anyone living in the Pacific Northwest, so I requested to be based there.

The trip was the same thing over and over, and I liked that. Each evening, we left the hotel in Portland and rode to the airport. Total flight time to Seattle and Salt Lake City was about two-and-a-half hours. In Salt Lake City, we could sleep for a few hours when normal people slept or stay up and read or watch TV.

I didn't like going to all the trouble to undress and dress again, so I slept in a comfortable chair. I found I liked sleeping twice a day for short stretches instead of trying to get enough sleep all at once during the day. Sometimes I slept more at night in Salt Lake City than during the long, daytime layover in Portland.

Manhattan in April was not an entirely unpleasant place to spend a weekend. I hadn't lived in a big city since I was four and couldn't imagine living where there was nothing underfoot but concrete and asphalt. As I spent more time exploring Manhattan, I found parks scattered among skyscrapers where people could escape confinement. Central Park must be what keeps New Yorkers sane.

The captain led us to Cabana Carioca, a Brazilian-Portuguese restaurant on 45th Street. Garish paintings of masked figures covered one wall. The most expensive steak on the menu was under twenty dollars.

I had trouble getting used to pedestrians who avoided eye contact, who didn't smile or nod a greeting when they passed. Where people are scarce, we value contact. In crowded cities, people are an impediment.

The first two Boeing 727s DHL Airways acquired were identical castoffs from United Airlines. Each airline has its own preferences in the way instruments and switches are arranged. Subsequent airplanes were covered in our manual under a Differences section. This was manageable when we had only a few 727s, but, in time, the original "standard" airplanes felt as non-standard as everything else. It was amusing, as we settled into our seats and built our nests, to hear a pilot say, "Okay, where the hell's the transponder in *this* airplane?" While variations provided moments of humor, in emergencies, differences are dangerous. Little by little, mechanics made changes to standardize cockpits.

All our 727s began life as passenger airplanes. To convert them to cargo, seats, galleys, overhead baggage lockers, interior walls, and aft restrooms were removed. Rollerball mats with side rails and lockdowns replaced carpet. A huge rectangular door, hinged at the top, was cut into the left side of the airplane a few feet behind the entry door and ahead of the wing.

Boxes and canvas bags went into compartments in the bottom half of the fuselage like luggage. Cargo on the main deck was loaded into aluminum or fiberglass containers flat on bottom and curved on top to just fit the cabin with little wasted space. Tugs pulled trains of flat trailers, each holding one cargo can, between airplanes and the sort building. Hydraulic K-loaders hoisted the cans and propelled them into the airplane where men and women pushed them aft and locked them down.

Most main cargo doors worked off the airplane's hydraulic systems, but one oddball had separate hydraulics. All doors had lights to warn if they were not latched. Airplanes were not expected to survive if the main cargo door opened in flight.

I didn't mind not having a window seat. Flying would have been more fun and it paid better, but I wanted to spend a couple of years in the back seat learning by observing. The biggest problem in not being the captain had nothing to do with money, status, or ego.

Pilots' feet were far from heated air outlets. I faced a large panel full of hot little lights and had trouble staying cool. Some captains liked it hot enough to bake bread. "Put another log on the fire, Mister Rush!"

Air aloft in older jet transports is dryer than the Sahara. Before DHL began stocking airplanes with cases of water, I carried a plastic bottle in my flight bag and looked forward to someday being a captain so I could control temperature.

The Skipper said to new captains under his tutelage, "Remember! It's the job of the first officer to make you late, and it's the job of the second officer to kill you! Your job is to prevent them from doing their jobs!"

As I began to get comfortable, I made errors. The first day of my work week was always a Monday, regardless of what the calendar said.

The hop from Portland to Seattle was short, and I felt rushed to get things done. I forgot to set cruise altitude, so the pressurization system tried to keep us at sea level. Once the pressure differential reached its limit, valves opened wide and the cabin "climbed" at an ear-popping rate. It was not a good way to impress a captain I'd never flown with.

Climbing out of Seattle on our way to Salt Lake City, I again forgot to set cruise altitude but caught it before relief valves dumped. I got away with that oversight, but I didn't get away with a serious fuel imbalance.

If a 727 airplane was fueled for a short flight, all three tanks had the same amount of fuel and each engine burned from its own tank from start to shutdown. For longer flights, wing tanks were topped off and enough more fuel was pumped into the larger center tank to reach the total required for the flight. After takeoff, the second officer opened valves and turned off pumps so all engines burned from the center tank until all three tanks were equal.

I'd looked up the power setting for cruise at our weight, altitude, and speed and handed the data card up to the pilots. Then I decided to balance fuel. The center tank had more fuel in it than either wing tank, but the difference was slight and within limits. I could have let it go, but I decided to even them up by having all engines burn out of the center tank for a very few minutes. It took a moment's thought to be sure of doing that right. Crossfeed valve open, then wing tank pumps off. If pumps are turned off first at high altitude, engines can flame out. Doing that wrong in a simulator *always* caused engine failure.

Just as I'd finished setting valves and pumps, the captain questioned the power settings I'd handed up to him. I opened the performance manual and looked up the numbers again. All three engines sucked up the small surplus in the center tank and then some. When I looked at the gauges, the amount of fuel in the center tank had dropped below the allowed differential with respect to the wing tanks.

I thought it through again, then turned on the pumps in the wing tanks and turned off the pumps in the center tank. I'd do nothing but stare at fuel gauges until balance was restored.

"Why is the fuel so far out of balance?" my alert captain asked.

I confessed I'd been balancing fuel and got distracted by paperwork. For the rest of that flight, the captain frequently twisted in his seat to look back at my panel to see if I'd found some other way to try to kill him.

Being based in San Francisco worked well. Weekends at work were Portland layovers and I spent them at home. Then, in June, flight schedules changed and the Salt Lake City mini-hub went away. San Francisco-based flight crews had only one trip, a three-leg, cross-country journey from San Francisco to Cincinnati and on to Dulles and Philadelphia for the day's layover. That night, the course was reversed.

The Portland flight originated in Cincinnati and went through Seattle to Portland. The time between the morning arrival and evening departure was too short for a crew to get legal rest, so two crews flew the trip in tandem, each with a Portland layover of more than thirty hours. The crew that arrived Tuesday morning would leave Wednesday evening, and the crew arriving Wednesday morning wouldn't leave until Thursday. The crew arriving Friday morning would depart Monday evening, and the crew arriving Saturday didn't go out again until Tuesday. Weekends in Portland would, for me, be long weekends at home.

American was buying AirCal, and DHL didn't have jumpseat privileges on American. Commuting to San Francisco was going to become difficult with fewer options for free rides. I put in a request to change my domicile back to Cincinnati.

The calendar's Monday was also my Monday, so I tried to pay attention as though it were my first trip ever. I did everything right on the first leg, but in Seattle, I found a new way to screw up.

After all engines are running, the second officer moves the toggle for each generator to put it on line. The first one automatically trips the APU or GPU generator off line.

We took on two jumpseaters in Seattle, a senior captain and a new second officer, two extra witnesses to my embarrassment.

I went through my flow to get ready for the Before Taxi checklist. When I turned on the first pack, I didn't see the expected increase in electrical load from the pack cooling fans. That was strange. The captain was looking over his shoulder, waiting for me to finish my flow, so I turned on the second pack. The airplane went dark except for a big red light on my panel signifying loss of essential power. My mind went blank. That had never happened in the simulator. The captain quietly said, "Turn on the generators."

I'd noticed on the short flight from Portland that generator frequencies were a little high, so, as we started engines one by one in Seattle, I tweaked the knobs on each generator to precisely four hundred cycles per second. Because my fingers had done something with generators, my brain checked that box on the clipboard in my mind and was satisfied. I'd observed no increase in engine generator load because the load was piling up on the single APU generator until it tripped off.

The captain kept a close eye on my panel after that, and, just to show he was on top of things, he asked me to close the pack cooling doors as we climbed through twenty-two thousand feet.

Those small doors in the belly of the fuselage are normally open at low altitude and slow speeds to allow extra cooling air to flow around the air conditioning packs. Our procedure was to close them as we climbed out of ten thousand feet to decrease drag and reduce fuel burn. I hadn't closed them promptly because the two toggles for the doors had to be held against a spring for thirty seconds to drive the doors closed, and thirty seconds seemed like thirty minutes when I was busy doing other things.

Exactly when the second officer closed those doors was not a detail captains normally paid attention to, but, after my error with the generators, I could expect close supervision.

I avoided reserve. Many pilots who lived near their domicile airport preferred being on call because they got to spend more time at home. Commuters hated reserve because they had to pay for living quarters, either hotel rooms or rent on houses or apartments called crash pads, rented with other pilots and filled with bunks.

One of the pilots based in San Francisco wrote schedules for the few of us based there. We told him our preferences and he did his best to accommodate everyone, but my first week in June was reserve. I planned to get a lot of reading done.

In Cincinnati, reserves wrote phone number where they could be reached on the schedule board in the crew lounge. It didn't occur to me to call Cincinnati to tell Crew Scheduling where I'd be. It didn't occur to me that I might be needed for anything other than the scheduled departure from San Francisco the next evening. I made a reservation at Comfort Suites and wrote the phone number on the schedule hanging on the wall in San Francisco, just as I'd seen pilots do in Cincinnati. When I checked in at the hotel, I called home to say where I was and went to bed.

The next morning, I went out for breakfast and took a long walk. When I got back to my room that afternoon, the message light was blinking. The company had needed to send me to Los Angeles so I could ferry our airplane from there to Portland, and Crew Scheduling couldn't find me. They called Barb at work, and she drove home to get the phone number of my hotel.

The San Francisco chief pilot called me that evening. He couldn't understand why I hadn't told Crew Scheduling how to reach me, as they couldn't see a note on a wall in San Francisco from their office in Cincinnati. I told him I'd never been on reserve before and had nothing to go by but what I'd observed others do. I thought where I'd left my number was the obvious place anyone trying to find me would look.

The chief pilot thought my aviation judgment might be faulty, so he pulled me off flight status and said the reserve would fly my trip. I pointed out that I was the reserve.

I was back in San Francisco the following week for a disciplinary hearing. The chief pilot could not believe that, with nearly a year in the company, I did not know I was supposed to let Crew Scheduling know how to reach me. I told him again that I'd never been on reserve and had never been told I needed to let Cincinnati know where I was. I copied what I'd observed others doing in Cincinnati. I argued that, if I'd not seen others writing their phone numbers on the schedule board, I'd have asked someone what procedure was, but I thought I knew what to do.

The chief pilot conceded that the company shared responsibility by not including reserve procedures in a manual or in initial training, so I didn't have to spend a month on punitive reserve. Punishment was a letter in my file.

Such letters didn't cost me money and didn't cause pain, so I didn't care.

The atmosphere was damp at Dulles in the hour just before dawn, damp and loaded with fragrance. My first breath of Maryland air took me back to a farm not far away where my family spent a weekend in the 1940s. I hadn't been to that part of the country in the decades since. I stood in the entryway as the hydraulic cargo door rose on its hinges, watching a slide show in my mind of walking down a country lane with my father, enjoying new experience at an age when everything in the world was new, smelling the sweet fragrance of dairy cows and hay, and watching white ducks splash in muddy puddles.

I slept in my cabin seat on a PSA flight from San Francisco all the way to landing in Seattle, and, because I was asleep, my ears and sinuses plugged on descent. I'd had sinus trouble all my life growing up in the dry air of Colorado and didn't know what normal breathing felt like until I moved to the Pacific Northwest. Dry air in the stratosphere caused trouble again.

The next time I went home from San Francisco, I rode in the cockpit with an AirCal crew using American Airlines checklists for the first time. American swallowed AirCal a few days later. Alaska and PSA were the only free rides left between Seattle and San Francisco, and competition for seats increased. I left home for work earlier than usual in the first week of July, and leaving two hours early almost wasn't enough. Jumpseats on non-stops to San Francisco were taken. I rode PSA through Reno and didn't get to San Francisco until just before my DHL ride to Cincinnati departed. Commuting was hard on nerves.

The Boeing 727 has a back door, the seldom-used passenger entry made famous by hijacker Dan "DB" Cooper when he used it as an exit with a parachute and a bag full of money between Seattle and Portland in 1971. Part of my preflight inspection was to be sure that door was latched, and I missed it. With late afternoon sun flooding the cockpit, I didn't notice the amber Doors light on my panel was on until after we'd started engines. It is not possible to get to the DB Cooper door from inside the airplane with cargo cans aboard.

The mechanic on the ground had not yet unplugged his headset. The captain told him about the door. The mechanic had to pop open an access panel to the aft airstair control, lower the stairs, run up and latch the door, and, outside again, hold the lever on the hydraulic valve to raise the stairs. All that made us two minutes late. The captain told me to log it as on time. We did not like to have to explain delays that were our fault.

The airplane we flew to Dulles and Philadelphia was the newest addition to our fleet, a discard from some European airline. It hadn't been with us long enough for mechanics to work all the residual bugs out of it, and many orange deferred-maintenance stickers decorated switches and gauges.

On our westbound trip, the captain farted frequently. He denied responsibility, but he'd munched peanuts on the entire eastbound trip the day before, and we smelled peanuts. The first officer and I took refuge in oxygen masks.

Even with constant airflow through the cockpit, close proximity made personal odors a problem at times. My nose rebelled at the ashtray stench of smokers' clothing. Almost as bad was cologne and aftershave lotion. Flatulence was a minor irritation in comparison.

Most pilots took turns taking naps on long flights. It was illegal to sleep, but it was safer than struggling to stay awake through the night and then nodding off during arrival and landing when workload was high. For a long time, I did not allow myself to sleep. I reasoned that two pilots could take turns resting their eyes. I sat behind them and could keep an eye on the one who was supposed to be awake. But there was only one of me, so I didn't sleep.

During takeoff and landing, my chair faced front so I could monitor flight instruments and what both pilots were doing as I read checklists. Sometimes I nodded off leaning forward into my shoulder straps when landing at dawn. After I fell asleep several times one morning between the San Mateo Bridge and the runway at San Francisco, I decided it would be better for me to doze a few minutes en route. After fuel was balanced, my job was little more than recording fuel and oil quantities every thirty minutes.

My father never used an alarm clock. He merely told himself what time he needed to wake up, and he always did. What I discovered in the airplane was, after logging those things I was required to log each half hour, I could sleep sitting up for twenty-nine minutes, wake up to make my log entries, check where we were, note that at least one pilot was awake, and lean my jaw on my fist and sleep another twenty-nine minutes. I woke instantly if one of the pilots asked me a question or said my name, and I woke if I heard our radio call sign on my earphone. And I was awake and alert for landing.

I was bored to the edge of insanity on long flights with captains who didn't allow the illegal practice of reading something other than airplane manuals. Sleep during those flights was a refuge.

Someone stole my typewriter out of the DHL pilot's lounge in San Francisco. The room was also our office, the place we received flight plans over a fax machine and did paperwork. We stored flight bags there rather than lug them home on weeks off. The lounge room was a thoroughfare between offices in the front of the building and the huge hangar behind the wall where freight was sorted and loaded into containers.

The building was locked and no one came in unescorted without company ID. I hate thieves in general, and especially those who steal from other employees. My anger lasted all the way to Philadelphia, and I made many minor errors.

I ate dinner with the first officer. He was a rarity among pilots in that I never heard him swear. When our food was served, he closed his eyes and bowed his head for a moment. I am not religious, but I tried to pay attention when dining with someone I didn't know so I could sit still and be quiet out of respect for those who are.

On the first of September, I was back in Philadelphia after being awake twenty-two hours. I'd gotten up early at home to write my weekly column for the Port Angeles newspaper before I left for work, and I didn't get a chance to sleep in the jumpseat on the way to San Francisco. The PSA crew talked for most of the trip about the impending takeover by USAir.

In Cincinnati, I learned I'd be domiciled there the first of October. A second officer who lived near Spokane and I would bid lines that normally started with the Friday trip to Seattle and Portland. One of us would bid to work weeks one and three, and the other weeks two and four. The plan was, after my scheduled last trip on Thursday, I'd fly his trip to Portland instead of jumpseating. He'd start his week Monday evening in Portland and fly my trip to Portland the following Friday. We'd work four nights on and ten off while drawing full pay and per diem. If the one of us planning to take over on Monday couldn't make it, the other would cover the trip.

Our arrangement would cost the company nothing. The same amount of flying would get done by the same number of people for the same amount of money. It gave the two of us more consecutive days off and lessened demand for jumpseats to and from Cincinnati. The only problem was, Crew Scheduling didn't write the schedules in such a way that we'd not violate flight time limitations by flying our own long last trip and the other guy's long first trip. The Thursday end-of-week trip had to be a short one. Months went by before Portland schedules became tradeable.

I'd flown nothing other than my Cessna 152 in more than a year. A long sentence in the back seat allows flying skills to rust. Many second officers took part-time flying jobs to stay proficient.

Coastal Airlines had two Cessna 402s and a small staff. The owner asked if I'd like to fly for him now and then. I studied his operations manual, took a short written test, and went up with him for the required few minutes of flight training. I flew four Coastal trips to Seattle on four consecutive days late in September. At twenty bucks a trip, I'd not get rich, but it felt good to fly a 402 again.

In Miami one Sunday, I rented a car to go see the Everglades. As I drove, I saw what appeared to be small clouds of smoke near the road. When I stopped and got out to take a picture, I discovered the clouds were mosquitoes. I stopped at the first store I came to see if they had repellent. They had stacks of it, and beer, too. I bought a stick of Cutter's and a six of Beck's and the trip was more pleasant thereafter.

I continued to Key Largo, just because I'd enjoyed the Bogart movie. After dinner, I sipped a gin and tonic and watched the sun set over silhouettes of moored boats on flat water.

A DHL pilot was on a jumpseat out of Portland going to work. When we landed in Seattle, two more jumpseaters were waiting to ride.

There was a flight attendant's fold-down jumpseat facing aft just inside the entry, but we weren't allowed to use it because the oxygen bottle and mask for that seat had been removed. The captain asked the first officer and me and the jumpseaters if anyone would object to the third man riding the flight attendant's seat and using the portable oxygen bottle if necessary. We didn't object. Maybe next time one of us would need a rule stretched so we could get to work on time.

I flew several trips with Napoleon when he was a 727 first officer. Our captain was close to retirement age, congenial and soft spoken. Napoleon hadn't been in the airplane long and the captain made suggestions, advising and instructing as we sailed through the night. It must have been hard for Napoleon to receive well-intentioned and necessary guidance with me sitting behind him taking it all in. I tried to be unobtrusive in deference to his ego, but I paid attention to absorb as much as I could of the captain's experience and knowledge.

Portland and Seattle were below our landing minimums one morning, so we landed on the dry side of the Cascades at Yakima to wait for fog to lift and to take on fuel. Outside temperature was below freezing, and we got cold waiting for the undersized fuel truck to pump us a thousand gallons. Air temperature at cruise had been a hundred degrees below zero, and the cold-soaked aluminum sucked heat out of our bones.
Seattle was still socked in. Dispatch wanted us to fly to Portland, then up to Seattle when weather improved and back to Portland for the day. The captain refused. We were too tired to extend our day with weather what it was. We flew to Portland and parked.

I had trouble getting a ride out of Seattle and arrived at work in Portland five minutes late. The captain was about to call Cincinnati. I apologized and hurried out to preflight the airplane.
We were using a new checklist for the first time. Somebody decided that redundancy would improve safety. I thought it would breed disrespect for the checklist. Anybody sloppy enough to miss setting trim the first time through would likely be sloppy enough to miss it the second time, but nobody asked me.
The first officer turned the transponder knob the wrong way, turned it off as we took the runway. Tower couldn't see our code on his radar. The first officer corrected his mistake, but

Tower still couldn't see it and asked us to try the other one. The captain turned the selector and waited for a response from Tower.

I didn't read manuals any more than absolutely necessary, so it was pure luck than I knew how long it took transponders to warm up.

"It'll be eighty seconds before he can see it," I said. "That's the warm-up time."

The captain was impressed that I knew that. Perhaps I had redeemed myself for having been late to work.

Emergency oxygen switches were guarded and pinned so they couldn't be turned on accidentally in all of our 727s except the switch at the second officer's station in one airplane. The unguarded switch was on the lowest part of the panel just above my desk. The oxygen gauge showed the bottle was full when I logged it on my worksheet before we started engines in Phoenix and again when we reached cruise altitude. It read zero on the ground in Denver. When I'd closed my performance manual after looking up cruise power settings, the cover of the binder flipped the switch up to the emergency position and let the contents of the oxygen bottle flow through the mask hanging in its clip above head. Ambient noise covered the hiss of escaping oxygen. We took a delay in Denver while mechanics refilled our oxygen supply. The next time I was on that airplane, the switch was properly guarded and pinned.

If we had a long taxi for takeoff and were not too heavy, it was company policy to start only two engines to save fuel. Then, when takeoff was imminent, we'd start the third one. Many captains would not taxi on two engines. One reason was the distraction of having to start an engine while on a taxiway and in traffic. The other was Murphy's Law.

So it was that, when we started the third engine in Portland one evening, the generator would not come up to speed. We had to get out of line and taxi back to our ramp at the other end of the airport. We wrote up the problem and the mechanic put an orange Deferred Maintenance sticker next to the generator switch. We reviewed the One Generator Inoperative procedure and left late for Seattle and Cincinnati.

On the way to Cincinnati a few weeks later, we got a call to divert to snowy Minneapolis to pick up freight there. The contract DC-8 there was down with a mechanical problem. We had a few problems of our own. The clock on my panel had been gaining three minutes an hour, but it fixed itself in flight. The #3 fuel crossfeed valve failed, apparently frozen. It fixed itself on the ground in Minneapolis. A leading edge flap appeared to have failed to extend, but the problem was a frozen indicator switch that fixed itself on the way to Cincinnati.

Loaders in Minneapolis weren't familiar with the 727 and wasted time trying to figure out how proceed. The contract mechanic DHL called out to handle our diversion was upset that we didn't have money to pay him on the spot.

When we got to Cincinnati, the crew lounge was abuzz with news of a PSA jet that had crashed in California. A fired employee kept his ID and got on the airplane with a revolver and shot the pilots. The airline community was small enough that, whenever there was a fatal accident, we tended to hold our breath until we knew who was flying.

The jumpseat in the MD-80 folds down from the bulkhead and blocks the cockpit doorway, and the closed door is the seat's backrest. As soon as the seatbelt sign went off on the way to Seattle from Phoenix one Saturday morning, the lead flight attendant opened the door and leaned in to ask the pilots what they wanted to drink. I tried to lean forward to get out of her way, but she leaned farther than I could, pressing her breasts into my back. I wondered if she did that for all jumpseaters.

I got back to Phoenix three hours early Monday evening. It was nice having full daylight to do my preflight inspection and to have more time than I needed. The mechanic had plenty of time to tighten loose screws I noticed in access panels on the wing.

The FM radio I carried to listen to classical music had gotten turned on in my bag and the battery was dead. I'd left my pocket calculator at home, and my good pen was gone forever, left at the gate in Seattle when I filled out a jumpseat pass. The week was not starting well.

It was our first stay at the Gateway Hilton in Newark. New layover hotels caused problems for us and we for them. We were tired and irritable when we checked in, and it didn't take much to set some of us off. One of our Metroliner captains had been fired for vaulting a check-in counter and threatening a clerk.

Reservation computers are geared to guests staying overnight, not overday, and the desk clerk in Newark had trouble checking us in. When I got to my room, the key card didn't work. A yellow light meant the deadbolt was engaged.

I went back down to the desk, luggage in tow, to get an unoccupied room. The desk clerk said the battery in the door lock must be low, and he sent me back up with a maintenance man who woke the room's unhappy occupant. I went back down to the lobby and got a different room. I went back up to my new room on a different floor. The key didn't work.

I picked up a house phone in the corridor and asked the operator for the front desk. I'd been awake twenty hours except for a short nap on the ride to Phoenix. I got tired of listening to the phone ring, so I hung up and punched zero again. I asked the woman who answered that my key didn't work. She told me to come down and get another one. I told her I was tired of riding elevators. She sent up the maintenance man. He opened the door with a pass key.

That evening, I went out in wind and rain for hamburgers. The kids who work at McDonald's in Newark were every bit as sullen as the ones in New York. I remembered to get a new room key when I got back to the hotel. That one didn't work either.

Newark crews began laying over in Manhattan. Our limo didn't show up at the hotel one evening. The captain on that trip was always one of the first with the latest electronics. He called Crew Scheduling on his newest gadget, a cell phone. Crew Scheduling told us to take a cab.

The driver did not speak English, but he knew where Newark was. The hard part was getting him to understand exactly where on the airport we wanted to go, which was not the passenger terminal. We finally got him pointed down the dark service road, but he was unhappy and perhaps even frightened. We got to the airplane late.

In Manhattan near the end of March, spring weather made walking pleasant. I still couldn't envision living in a big city, but, if I regarded layovers there as trips to a zoo, I enjoyed them. I was in Manhattan again on April Fools' Day. I went for a walk and a bird shit on my head.

I saw a micro-cassette tape recorder in a store window for thirty bucks. I went inside to look at it ended up buying a better one for more than twice that. I recorded conversation in the airplane all the way to Portland. When I played it back,

I was surprised at how much crew conversation is laced with foul language.

Crew Scheduling, tired of complaints about schedules, had invited pilots to offer suggestions. The latest schedule had been written by a pilot who lived in Cincinnati. He made no provisions for outstation trading on weekends. It was a good schedule only for the minority who lived near Cincinnati.

I thought I could write one that would enable trading without imposing on locals, but it was more difficult than I'd thought. Flight times on all the lines had to be reasonably close for fairness, but long and short trips had to be mixed in such a way that daily flight times weren't exceeded. And week-on, week-off had to be preserved.

The odyssey of getting to work in Portland one evening was like one of those frustrating dreams in which you desperately need to do something or go somewhere and are thwarted by cars that won't start, legs that won't move, or guns that won't shoot.

I left Port Angeles on San Juan's flight to Seattle early in the afternoon, as usual, but there was no room on Horizon to Portland at either three-thirty or four o'clock. Alaska had revised its jumpseat policy, and DHL wasn't on the new list.

I bought a ticket on Horizon, but the four-thirty had been canceled and the passengers rebooked for five and five-thirty. I could not get a confirmed seat until much too late. I went to an ATM to take out a hundred dollars so I could perhaps buy a seat from someone who could afford to go later, but the machine said I had only a few dollars in the account. I was beginning to feel desperation bordering on panic.

As I paced near the gate, hoping for a no-show, a Horizon agent I knew only by name walked past, his shift for the day finished. He asked how it was going and I told him. He stepped to the computer at the gate and tapped keys. Delta had a flight that would arrive in Portland at six-thirteen, and they'd accept my Horizon ticket.

I ran to the Delta gate to check in and then to a phone to call our contract cargo handler in Portland. I explained my situation and asked the man to ask the first officer to preflight the airplane for me and then pick me up in front of Delta at six-thirteen.

The first officer had been a second officer and could do a walk-around inspection and cockpit setup. I'd do a quick check of the interior when I got there and do paperwork during the long taxi. What was important was that we got out on time.

Delta blocked in one minute early. I was one of the first people off and only a step out of the airplane entry when someone yelled, "Hey!" It was the man I'd talked to on the phone, and his company pickup waited idling on the ramp at the bottom of access stairs from the Jetway. We sped down the taxiway and got to the airplane ten minutes before departure. We blocked out exactly on time, but I was a mental wreck.

I couldn't face another stressful airline commute to Portland, so the next time I went to work, I drove the 232 miles in my Nissan pickup. US 101 is two lanes almost the entire distance to Olympia, but Interstate 5 went the rest of the way to Portland. Most of the first hundred miles is dotted with small towns and campgrounds, and the highway is not straight. Even so, I could sometimes average a mile a minute over the entire distance. As I learned the road and my travel times became faster, I gradually delayed my departure from home, and the stress of being almost late returned.

I decided to sell my airplane. It was expensive to own, even if it never left the ground. It had earned its keep when I leased it for rental and training, but San Juan got out of the flight school business and my airplane generated no income. I flew it only about twenty hours a year, and fixed costs combined with operating expenses brought my hourly rate to more than double what I could rent a larger airplane for.

I become emotionally attached to vehicles, my little Cessna, especially. I wondered for many weeks if I could let it go. I reminded myself that the sorrow of letting a favorite motorcycle or truck go was entirely anticipatory. Once the object was gone, so was the attachment.

We were heavy leaving San Francisco one evening, so calculations for takeoff were critical. I made two errors.

At that time, we normally set flaps at five degrees for takeoff, although the airplane would leave the ground in less distance and at a slower speed at Flaps 15. Takeoff speeds for Flaps 15 came from a different page in the manual. The captain wanted Flaps 15.

We normally took off with air conditioning packs on, but we could get a little more thrust if we turned them off before takeoff and back on after we were in the air. The captain wanted packs off.

Because our weight was very near the maximum for the departure runway, the first officer checked my figures carefully. I'd used speeds for Flaps 5, and I'd neglected to add the power correction packs off gave us. Both errors were in our favor, but they could just as easily have been against us. As the first officer handed the data card back for corrections, I said, "Good thing I brought you along."

He laughed, but he said, "You shouldn't be making that kind of mistake this far along in your career."

I couldn't help but think that if I were a true aviator, if I had the Right Stuff, I would be better at my job. But there is just too much that interests me to be able to focus exclusively on any one thing, even flying.

The aurora borealis display as I rode jumpseat to Cincinnati in the middle of May was the most vibrant I'd ever seen. Shimmering streaks and curtains of light soared and swirled across the stars.

Our airborne view of the sky was an unexpected benefit of night flying at high altitude. Being above city lights and terrestrial obstructions made stars appear as sharp points of white on ebony. Meteor showers were more spectacular against such a sky, and the faint tails of comets were not lost in ambient light.

I'd never bothered to learn the names of more than a handful of stars and constellations. One pilot I flew with had a circular star map, a plastic wheel within a wheel the size of a dinner plate keyed to the middle northern latitudes. Turning the inner wheel to line up date and time aligned the map and its labeled stars and constellations with the sky. I bought one and carried it in my flight bag for the rest of my career.

Getting back to San Francisco after spending Memorial Day layover at home was expensive. The flight I wanted out of Seattle was full. I bought a ticket on a later American flight.

American and Alaska charged the same for the one-way ticket, but I spent my money at American because Alaska no longer allowed us to jumpseat. American didn't allow us to jumpseat either, but I felt more resentment toward the airline that had pulled the privilege than toward one that had never granted it.

The $13,000 I got for my airplane was the biggest chunk of money I'd ever had in my hand. I bought a salmon fishing boat from an old man who had grown too frail to manage it. I bought my daughter a used car, bought a winch for my truck, bought a cartridge reloader for my revolvers, and bought a tiny travel trailer. In late July, I found the sailboat I'd wanted since I was a teenager, a Columbia 22 for sale just south of Seattle. I bought that with what was left of my airplane money. What I should have bought was Microsoft stock.

After Labor Day, I was off six weeks. Two weeks of vacation eliminated a four-week bid period, and by bidding the correct lines, I would be off the week before and the week after. I almost always took vacation in fall. People with children in school could have the summer months. I preferred being off when highways and campgrounds weren't crowded. And I wanted to be off for hunting seasons.

Another reason for taking a long block of time off at that time of year was consistent weather on either side of vacation. I did not wear my uniform jacket because the lining irritated my skin. Shirtsleeves were acceptable uniform in summer, and in winter, the warm, rain-shedding trench coat covered the absence of uniform jacket. By taking vacation during the transition from warm weather to cold, I could go directly from no coat to overcoat.

I considered calling in sick the first week of December, but if I stayed home every time sinuses bothered me, I'd never fly. I got to Seattle for my jumpseat to Cincinnati with time to spare. The airplane from Portland landed with a problem in the inboard flaps.

Flap problems were usually in the gauges and easily fixed, but not that time. The mechanic found all screws missing from a splined shear collar on a flap shaft. Critical fasteners in airplanes are safety wired so they can't loosen, but someone either forgot to wire the missing screws or forgot to put them in. A couple of us held the flap in position so the mechanic could slide the collar back to where it belonged. Lacking the proper screws, he borrowed one from each of the other three couplings. In his signoff in the log, he attributed the problem to a broken transmitter wire. He called Maintenance Control in Cincinnati and told them the real problem and what they needed to fix it properly. Then we were on our way.

I'd taken Drixoral and had sprayed Afrin up my nose, so my sinus problem was temporarily suppressed. I thought it was legal to use Afrin while flying, but it wasn't. I didn't know about Drixoral.

A change in company policy made sinus trouble worse. As business increased, our airplanes were often required to carry the maximum weight they legally could. Dispatch would call on the radio as we sat in the cockpit and ask the captain what our maximum payload was. The answer depended on that particular airplane's operating weight, plus fuel on board, plus any spare parts being carried, plus jumpseaters. We were expected to calculate takeoff weight for air conditioning packs off. Too often, we'd forget to add the extra weight for packs off, so the company made packs-off takeoffs standard.

Before taking the runway, the second officer turned off both packs and set the pressure controller to one thousand feet above ground level. Once in the air with gear and flaps up and power reduced to climb thrust, the second officer turned on packs one at a time with several seconds between them. Ideally, the airplane would smoothly pressurize to the set altitude of a thousand feet and then begin climbing the cabin at the normal rate when the controller was set to cruise altitude.

Ear pressure easily keeps up with four hundred feet per minute, unless ears or sinuses are congested. But that first thousand feet of unpressurized climb followed by pressure surges as packs and outflow valves struggled to find equilibrium was not pleasant even for clear sinuses and healthy ears. For those of us chronically congested, it was painful.

The auxiliary power unit in the airplane we were taking to Seattle and Portland wasn't working, so we had no heat until engines were running. Temperature in Cincinnati was ten degrees. I turned on all lights in all instrument panels as high as they would go and turned on electric windshield heat. I had an earache. My feet almost never feel cold, but they did that night. Everything was behind schedule, so I sat in the airplane longer than usual waiting to be loaded. Pilots have less to do and didn't need to be at the airplane as early as the second officer. Because they knew there was no heat on that airplane and knew how late we would be, they sat inside drinking coffee while I froze.

I got two pair of dirty socks out of my bag and put them on over the ones I was wearing. I put on a jacket under my uniform overcoat. And I got out my orange and black and white Stihl Chainsaw stocking cap and pulled it down over my ears.

The first officer also had sinus trouble. Weight wasn't critical, so we took off with packs on, just the way the airplane was designed to do.

I had sinus surgery at the end of January. When the doctor pulled packing out of my nose the next day, my voice sounded to me as though I were in a vaulted cathedral. I closed my mouth and inhaled completely unrestricted for perhaps the first time in my life. I stayed home three weeks. When I rode jumpseat to Cincinnati for annual recurrent ground school, my renovated nose worked just fine.

My simulator checkride in Pittsburgh went well, but I almost failed it. We'd lost two engines, and I lost track of which one was still operating as I opened and closed fuel valves and turned pumps on and off to keep the airplane balanced. I heard my examiner whispering to the pilots' examiner as they stood behind me. When he muttered, "My hands are tied," I knew I was doing something wrong and saw my error in seconds. The fuel pumps to the only engine still operating were off and I'd set us up to become a glider. I turned the correct pumps on and prevented myself from doing what The Skipper considered my job to be—killing the captain.

When we got to Philadelphia one morning in March, all three of us walked to the Cold Beer Bar near the hotel, legal on the long layover. Talk turned to retirement, which didn't concern me because I seldom planned beyond next week. DHL did not have a pension plan, but we did have a 401K with generous matching contributions. I was not yet putting money into it beyond the small amount DHL matched dollar for dollar. I needed my income for living expenses.

When I went to work for DHL, friends asked if my being away from home so much was hard on our marriage. Barb and I both claimed it was good for us. By the time I'd been at work for several days, I was eager to get home and Barb was beginning to miss me. Then, after a several days, we began to look forward to my going back to work. Implications for my eventual retirement were far beyond the horizon.

Horizon Air surprised me with a change in its jumpseating policy. Universal airline procedure was for a jumpseater to introduce himself to the captain and request permission to ride. Horizon didn't want the flight crew interrupted, so the flight attendant took the jumpseat form and handed it to the captain later. I didn't like that. It was the captain's ship, an airship to be sure, but it was his. Going aboard for a free ride without his permission didn't feel right.

Unless heavily burdened with bags, I often used stairs in Cincinnati, and not only for exercise. I could walk up four floors with baggage and beat what had to be the slowest elevator in the world.

Many pilots worked out in hotel exercise rooms or nearby gyms during layovers, but nearly all of them used elevators rather than stairs and got rides to restaurants rather than walk half a mile. I used stairs, walked to dinner, and skipped the gyms.

I grumbled frequently about the lack of good food available on the turn in Cincinnati. Some meals in the machines weren't bad, if you liked spaghetti microwaved in the plastic container it came in. My weight began creeping up, not only because of the lack of good food but because, once in the habit of eating out of machines, my selections expanded to include cookies, chips, and other tasty junk. When the DHL enlarged the sort building, we got a cafeteria.

The earliest we could call to reserve jumpseats was seven in the morning Eastern time on the same date we wanted to reserve a seat a month later. We'd landed in Newark and were in the hotel van before seven, so as soon as we got to the hotel, I went to a phone in the lobby and called Crew Scheduling to book a jumpseat home thirty days later. I was surprised to hear that I'd gotten the last of the two seats, surprised because I was flying with the other two pilots who needed seats on that flight. I was on the phone and they were still checking in.

The Skipper had the first jumpseat. He said he'd called in at the same time I did, but with a phone at the check-in desk. I knew he was lying because I was talking to the scheduler while he was still in line to check in. The Skipper wasn't the only pilot who had his wife call in at precisely the right time when he knew he wouldn't be able to.

The airline worked on Greenwich Time, but I kept my watch on Pacific. It was easier to make mental conversions from just one time zone to Greenwich than to change my watch every time we landed. My brain hadn't yet fully adjusted to Daylight Savings, and on the turn in Cincinnati, I set my alarm incorrectly. I woke up twenty minutes after I was supposed to be at the airplane. There was no time to brew coffee, and I hadn't had my ration of caffeine the previous day.

I hurried the preflight inspection and made mistakes. I missed the calculation of our Seattle ETA by an hour, put the wrong year in the date on the aircraft log page, missed an item while reading the Taxi checklist, and forgot to set the CSD oil cooler switch to Off for takeoff. I figured that was what laying off coffee for a full day did to my brain. It would be another decade before I realized that caffeine is, for me, non-prescription Ritalin.

Cabana Carioca, my favorite Manhattan restaurant, would not issue separate checks. Getting enough money from a group of pilots to pay for dinner was almost impossible. Too many rounded down, forgot sales tax, and figured others would cover the tip. I'd heard we had at least two pilots who would sneak back to the table as the group was leaving and pocket part of the tip. It amazes me that so many airline pilots, well paid and on per diem, are some of the cheapest sons of bitches on earth.

True or not, there are stories of pilots taking burned out light bulbs to work to exchange with good ones from hotel lamps. We had a pilot who once refused to pay for a restaurant meal he'd eaten without complaint because the vegetable was not the same one as in the picture on the menu.

I wasn't that cheap, but I saved soap and shampoo. Rather than use hotel soap once and leave it to be thrown away, I took it with me and used it until it was a sliver. Then I stuck it to a new hotel bar and used that. Sometimes my bar of soap had four or five colors in it. On days I didn't need a new bar of soap, I took them with me. It was the same with shampoo. With not much hair, a little bottle would last me all week. I took the others home, reasoning that if I, like most people, used a little and left the rest behind, it would probably be thrown away. After I retired, I didn't have to buy hand soap for a couple of years, and, with even less hair now, I still have more than a gallon of shampoo in plastic jugs.

I'd ordered almost everything on the Cabana Carioca menu over the years and had settled on two favorites. One was a huge sirloin steak, and the other was six large shrimp grilled in garlic sauce. In time, waiters didn't bother bringing a menu. As soon as I sat down, a cup of coffee appeared, unless it was old, in which case they'd brew a fresh pot and bring it to my table. They'd ask with Portuguese accent, "What you like today, the sirloin or the shrimp?"

When I was there before the dinner crowd came in, I didn't feel uncomfortable lingering over coffee while reading a book. When the restaurant was busy and I was by myself, I was often shown to a cramped table for two around a corner and behind a glass dessert case. That became my favorite table. It was the last table used, and there was a lamp on the wall beside it perfect for reading. When dining alone, I requested that table even when the restaurant was empty.

A few years after my routine at Cabana Carioca had become well established, I didn't get to New York for several months. When I walked into the restaurant in the middle of the afternoon, the manager was sitting at a table near the door doing paperwork. He looked up, smiled, and stood to greet me. "It's nice to see you again," he said. He stepped aside and swept an arm toward the interior of the near-empty restaurant. "Your table is waiting."

An engine in a United DC-10 exploded in 1989 and ruptured all hydraulic systems. The crew managed to get the airplane down on the airport at Sioux City, Iowa, but it broke apart on landing and many passengers died.

Nearly a year later, I went home for the weekend from Chicago and returned Monday on a United DC-10. When I stuck my head in the cockpit to introduce myself, I was stunned and perhaps awestruck when the captain introduced himself and his crew. Al Haynes was a national hero not to be eclipsed until Chesley Sullenberger landed dead stick in the Hudson River years later.

I'd wondered about one thing ever since the DC-10 incident. Left alone, the airplane wanted to turn right. Only by running the right engine at higher power than the left could the pilots keep the airplane flying straight. What I wanted to know was, did the crew consider dumping fuel out of the right wing to lighten it and perhaps prevent that wing from dropping and turning the airplane?

Even if I'd ridden in a jumpseat rather than the cabin, I would not have asked Captain Haynes that question. Knowing whether fuel balancing was considered and rejected or not considered at all might help me cope with a similar situation someday, but asking it could have been construed as second guessing, and I would not, as a guest aboard his airplane, have risked insulting a man who had managed to avert total disaster against impossible odds. When the situation was later replicated in simulators, no crew survived. I was glad the Boeing 727, with its old technology, could fly under control if all hydraulics failed.

Unless I had a good reason for refusing, I accepted extra assignments. The additional money was nice, and helping out schedulers made them more likely to do me favors.

The company would have bought a ticket from Port Angeles to Seattle, and I should have let it, but I rode free to Seattle and picked up my Alaska Airlines ticket to San Francisco. I realized too late that I should not have ridden another carrier's jumpseat when my company was sending me somewhere. Jumpseats were benefits for flight crews, not for businesses. By taking the jumpseat, I'd deprived Horizon of revenue and jeopardized our jumpseat privilege. I'd not do that again.

Finally, late in August, Portland weekend schedules meshed so I could trade out there and work Monday evening through Friday morning and be off ten days. No more would I waste time jumpseating to and from Cincinnati. As we acquired new airplanes and established new routes, I passed up opportunities to upgrade to first officer. The difference in pay between the back seat and the right seat was not huge. My trading partner and I had too sweet a deal to give it up for more money but with less time off and less control of our lives.

I went to work the evening of 11 September and landed in Newark the next morning, my birthday. I told the pilots I'd buy them a beer at Smith's to celebrate. They insisted that, it being my birthday, they would buy. With a 14-hour layover, we could spend a couple of hours in the bar. We were tired after crossing the country on the first trip of the week, and it seems I am not the only one who loses the ability to make sensible decisions when exhausted.

The bartender was the same man who had served me on my first weekend in New York more than two years earlier. He asked what we wanted and before I could order a beer, he stared at me and said, "Beer and a shot. Jack Daniels."

My jaw must have dropped. How could he have possibly remembered one customer from one prolonged binge in a city that size after so much time? Well, hell, I couldn't say no to that. Or to another when the first one was gone. After two hours, we decided to go by the FAA's 8-hour rule rather than the company's twelve. Then we lost track of time.

I hadn't yet realized what would dawn on me after two Northwest pilots were arrested months later for doing exactly what we were doing. Hung over often means still drunk. I was glad I didn't have to fly the airplane.

The departure profile from Newark requires a slight left turn as soon as it is safe to maneuver, and then a right turn a couple of miles from the airport, that distance measured by one of two DME transmitters, unless it wasn't broadcasting, in which case we took the distance reading off the other. While we're doing all that, the tower hands us off to departure control. The non-flying pilot calls Departure as soon as he can get a word in on the busy frequency, and Departure assigns a new heading, a higher altitude, and perhaps a speed restriction. As we taxied out that night, the captain threw up in a sick sack.

All things considered, our departure went pretty well. The first officer flew, and we were late contacting Departure because the captain clicked in the wrong radio frequency and it took several seconds of no response to his call before we realized the error. When we got to cruising altitude and could relax a little, we agreed that perhaps we'd overdone my birthday celebration.

Our new system chief pilot had held that position for a time before I was hired. When he was appointed chief pilot again, the reign of Pharaoh II, in The Skipper's parlance, began. One of the first things Pharaoh did was borrow several pages from the section in Delta's manual on personal appearance. He issued edicts with all the fervor of a new kid on the block announcing his rules for a game the other kids had been playing for years: Nothing in shirt pockets except a maximum of two pens. No member of a crew will wear a topcoat out of the airplane unless all crewmembers do. Mustaches must not droop below corners of the mouth.

I was ironing a uniform shirt in my room in Philadelphia when Pharaoh called to confirm that I wanted to be in the next upgrade class beginning the end of January. We didn't need more 727 crews, but the flight department wanted to get ahead of the game, to be ready to crew more airplanes when they began to arrive later in the year. After training, I would continue in my present seat at present pay until needed. I'd get the pressure of training over with and still keep my sweet schedule for a few weeks or months. There were already enough 727 first officers junior to me that I'd be able to avoid having to sit on reserve for days at a time in Cincinnati when I moved up to the right seat.

During the turn in Cincinnati, we attended an informational meeting on random drug testing, part of President Reagan's program to get government off the backs of the people.

I had no objection to taking a drug test prior to employment. I had no objection to being tested if there was reason to suspect drug use. But the idea of random testing infuriated me then as it does now. The Constitutional guarantee of freedom from unreasonable search was sacrificed to a problem so infinitesimal as to be nearly non-existent. If I'd had a little less need for my career and the lifestyle it provided, or if I'd had a little more self-respect, or if I'd had any belief at all that it would make a difference, I'd have refused to accept random drug tests.

The doctor conducting the meeting advised us to avoid eating poppy seeds, as the morphine in them could trigger a positive on the test. If the routine test came up positive, a more expensive test would be done to see if the positive result indicated a significant amount of opiate or a poppy seed bagel. I resented that the nation's airlines hadn't refused en masse to have anything to do with random testing. I resolved to eat poppy seeds at every opportunity in hopes of driving up costs for my employer.

Barb drove Art Stark and me to Seattle on the last Friday in January 1990. Ground school would begin Monday morning. Art had been chief pilot at San Juan Airlines, and we San Juan pilots who had preceded him to DHL joked that he'd made the job change because he couldn't stand seeing us come and go with so much time off. Art was in second officer class after serving as Metroliner captain. We shared a room at the Drawbridge.

On Friday evening at the end of the second week, we relaxed and celebrated with too many beers and paid for it the next morning. I ate four aspirin and drank lots of water. Art and I met a new-hire at the airport, and I walked them through the second officer's preflight inspection.

The third week, training crews worked together in cockpit mockups at the training center to learn flows and checklists. The last day of the third week, we all met at the hotel swimming pool to learn how to clamber aboard the inflatable life raft carried in the airplane on overwater flights. After ground school, we all rode USAir to Pittsburgh and checked in at La Quinta.

The Skipper was pilot instructor for our training crew, and in his heart, he was a drill sergeant. My first session flying USAir's 727 simulator was grim. My difficulty in flying the damn thing came from complete absence of experience flying a jet. The inertia of an airplane more than ten times heavier than anything I'd ever flown, the lack of drag, and the slow response times of jet engines to power adjustments compared to pistons and propellers contributed to my ineptitude. Efforts to control speed and altitude took so much concentration, I wasn't able to keep up with procedures. I was so far behind the airplane I wouldn't have been hurt if it crashed. That night, I dreamed of flying the simulator. In my dream, I flew it well.

I tended to fly by feel more than by numbers. It took me a long time to make the mental transition from strapping on wings and going flying to operating a full-motion video game, and I never completely succeeded.

I flew better the second day, but I could not land. Every time wheels touched down and I pulled power to idle, the airplane skipped back into the air. "Fly the nosewheel down!" my instructor commanded.

I'd always held the nosewheel off as long as possible, and then eased off back pressure to gently set it down. In the 727 simulator, it took several high bounces, several exasperated commands to fly the nosewheel down, before I snapped, "I *am* flying it down. I'm not *dropping* it!"

That was the problem. My immediate response to the main gear touching down should have been to relax back pressure just a little, then, slowly *push* on the yoke to fly the nosewheel down, the opposite of what I'd been doing since my first flying lesson.

Knowing that did not erase years of habit. For my first few months flying the Boeing 727, I had to talk to myself through every landing: "Don't pull back, don't pull back, don't pull back..."

My crew had afternoon sim sessions the first two days and then mornings. In spite of the early hour, I flew much better, well enough to think that perhaps I hadn't chosen the wrong line of work after all. The next afternoon, the captain, both second officers, and I all had a bad day. It didn't help that I'd flown first instead of watching the captain. It also didn't help that I was coming down with a cold.

Several of us had colds, and the wet, snowy weather didn't help us get well. The next day's sim session went better for all of us, and the next day was a day off. Several of us stayed up most of the night drinking bourbon and listening to The Skipper tell stories of his life as a young Marine Corps infantry officer and pilot.

The session after our day off was a disaster. I tried too hard to do everything exactly the way DHL wanted it done and got too involved with those trees to see the forest. I set the outbound course instead of the inbound for a holding pattern, and then made left turns when I should have turned right. I fell for a trick I knew was coming, a situation involving what appeared to be one kind of landing gear problem but was really a different problem. The next morning wasn't good, either. My biggest difficulty continued to be inability to control the airplane precisely. The Skipper scheduled me for an extra session that afternoon.

Another first officer upgrade passed his checkride easily and said it was a piece of cake. Training was always more strenuous than the checkride, but it was hard to keep that in mind.

Four of us drank copious amounts of bourbon the evening before my afternoon checkride. What I may have lacked in alertness as a result, I more than made up for in calmness. My first landing was perfect, and I passed without significant error.

That evening, several of us drank beer and listened to The Skipper tell more stories. Captain Scamahorn seldom drank, but when he loosened up a little, he was a magnificent entertainer. He could have told stories on a bare stage and people would have paid to listen. I thought I should sit down with him and a tape recorder someday and write his biography.

I thought that several times over the years, but I felt no urgency. There'd be plenty of time later.

The company put us up at a Holiday Inn near JFK for airplane training. Razor wire atop a chain link fence reinforced warnings from hotel staff not to walk in the neighborhood. Our check captain and a second officer from the training department took three of us to Stewart Field, northwest of New York City and west of the Hudson River. The former Air Force base had instrument approaches, long runways, and little traffic, ideal for training flights and checkrides. Most of first officer airplane training was takeoffs and landings. The first officer who flew first did well. The second man flew well enough. I went last and did poorly. The captain passed me anyway and said I'd pick it up on the line.

In two weeks at home after my checkride, I went fishing and sailing, tended crab pots, cut firewood, and lost three of the ten pounds I'd gained in training. Not knowing my schedule, I packed to be away from home for a full week, but my first trip of Initial Operating Experience was to Portland for the weekend. My IOE captain gave me the first leg to Seattle. I flew by hand until several minutes into cruise before setting the autopilot. Then I poured coffee and watched morning sun flood the land from over my right shoulder, happy to have a window seat again.
Touchdown on my landing in Seattle was light and smooth. The captain thumped it on in Portland. I said, "You didn't need to land hard just to make me feel good, but I appreciate it anyway."
The captain let me do all the flying the rest of the week, probably because he realized I needed all the practice I could get, and I already knew how to work radios.

DHL bought me a ticket to Pittsburgh for my annual simulator check as second officer. I'd continue to serve in the back seat until I was needed in my new position in April.
The airplane in Portland was scheduled for maintenance and wouldn't be available for the return to Cincinnati Monday evening. Crew Scheduling booked the pilots on the chartered airplane's jumpseats and bought me a ticket to Cincinnati. The first officer was just out of training and hadn't been home in

eight weeks, so we called Crew Scheduling and swapped rides. He got the ticket so he could go home for the rest of the weekend, and I drove to Seattle for a ride on the charter Monday evening.

The Skipper rode the Express One 727 from Portland. When I climbed the stairs and got on the airplane in Seattle, the crew was involved in discussion, so I kept quiet. The captain was new at his job and very conscious of his position. I stowed my suitcase, sat down behind him, and strapped in. Ten minutes later, the young man feigned surprise that I was on his airplane. The Skipper rolled his eyes. He'd explained to the captain when he got on in Portland that I'd be getting on in Seattle.

I told the pipsqueak that he'd been busy in conversation with his crew and I hadn't wanted to interrupt. Once we were leveled off at cruise altitude, I waited until all three crewmen had opened soft drinks before getting out my Thermos and asking if anyone would like coffee. No one did, of course, but I got points for the offer.

We had a jumpseater from Cincinnati to Boston, a woman from DHL's sales department. She asked The Skipper if he would carry her bags to the airplane. I tensed, fearing his response. He looked her in the eye and said, "We have three women pilots who have been trying for years to prove they're equal to us. You could undo all that in one night."

She carried her own bags.

Seat belts and shoulder straps in our old airplanes had been handled by countless hands over the years. They left smudges on white shirts and tan trousers. Some pilots laid towels across their laps and buckled seatbelts over them. I talked a captain into writing up shoulder straps for being dirty, and the maintenance department's solution was to replace the entire harness at God knows what cost. I didn't write up any more shoulder harnesses.

Our restraint system had five straps meeting in one round aluminum buckle—the two halves of the belt, the shoulder straps, and a crotch strap that clicked into the bottom of the buckle. All were required to be fastened for takeoff and landing, but only the belt had to be worn all the time. When we left an airplane, we fastened all straps to the buckle to keep them off the grimy deck. The Skipper went further and mandated a specific way of folding loose ends of belts—left over right, the same way the Marine Corps laced shoes.

One new second officer, a young man we called Nissan, didn't fasten his crotch strap when seated but let it flop on the floor to be dragged to and fro as he moved his seat. I chided him in the crew lounge about his not using the strap. Nissan claimed he never used the crotch strap. I told him I was sure it was required, but that, regardless, when he let it drag on the deck, it got the next guy's uniform dirty.

The Skipper happened by and I asked him if the crotch strap was required when the shoulder straps were. He said it was. Nissan insisted it was not. The Skipper did not like being contradicted by a junior, especially by a junior from another country. He marched the spluttering Nissan into the flight manager's office. The flight manager looked up the regulation and showed it to Nissan, and that would have been that, if the young man had not kept arguing. The Skipper got in his face and told him he'd not last long at DHL with his attitude.

He didn't.

Boeing 727 First Officer

First officer was a good position. The guy in back did most of the work for less money, and the pilot on the left had all the responsibility and the pay to go with it. All I had to do was fly alternate legs, talk on the radio when the captain was flying, and take care of paperwork.

It was the first officer's job to pick up the weather and flight plans from Dispatch and look them over to be sure they were complete and accurate. Some captains liked their first officers to highlight those parts of the weather package that applied directly to the flight. The first officer gave the paperwork to the captain who looked it over and signed both copies of the flight release. One copy of the release stayed in the building. The first officer took the rest of the paper to the airplane.

Once aboard and settled into his nest, the first officer reviewed the load sheet for accuracy and ran the numbers through a small computer to be sure the load was within limits and to calculate the trim setting. The second officer verified proper takeoff trim from a chart.

We all had different brands and styles of headsets. Radio panels in nearly all of our airplanes had separate volume controls for each radio at each seat, but not the one we flew to Orlando and Miami on one of my first trips as first officer. My headset had external earphones, but the captain's had a molded piece that fit inside his ear. With the radio receiver volume set as high as he could stand it, I couldn't hear well enough unless I pressed an earphone tight to my head the moment a controller started talking. Even then, I sometimes missed things.

Writing up that radio problem did no good for a long time. Nothing was broken, so there was nothing to fix. We began to stress safety in our written complaints, and the antique radio panel in that airplane was eventually replaced with the independently adjustable kind.

My favorite part of flying was looking out the window, especially in summer when days were long and we were often in the air before sundown and after dawn. I especially liked looking down on the American landscape—mountains, rivers, and deserts a huge relief map.

Looking down at Nebraska and Wyoming, I imagined what it would have been like in 1850, crossing the same ground in a covered wagon, plodding in one day the distance we flew in one minute. Looking down at Grand Canyon or Monument Valley just after sunrise never failed to inspire awe. Irregular sleeping hours, meals at odd times, and days away from home were small prices to pay for earning a living in airplanes.

On a day off in Cincinnati before flying to New York Saturday morning, instead of going to a hotel, I jumpseated to Dallas to visit aunts and uncles and cousins for the day. I slept an hour on the way down and on the way back, enough rest for the short trip to JFK. Except that when we got to New York, we had to fly back to Cincinnati empty and take a second load to New York. We didn't get to the hotel until early afternoon. I slept sixteen hours.

It was my leg to Cincinnati Monday evening. ATC kept us high because of conflicting traffic, so I had to improvise. I slowed with speed brake and called for landing gear down. The captain said we were going too fast. We weren't. I said again, "Landing gear down!" He whipped out his flashlight so he could read the speed limitations placard by the landing gear handle and put the gear down.

That captain had a large and fragile ego. He'd made an error, so he rode me hard all the way to the runway, criticizing everything that wasn't exactly right, which, given the circumstances, was a lot. He was so busy picking nits that he missed his hundred-foot call, and I flared late and landed ungently.

The captain slept for an hour or more on his leg to San Francisco, which was nice for me because I didn't have to endure his demonstrating how great he was. He liked to be seen as superior, a sure sign of an inferiority complex, and he enjoyed critiquing first officers. I had much to learn and appreciated all the help I could get, but he wasn't a good pilot or a good captain. If I pointed out any error on his part, which I was required to do in many regimes of flight, he would then be extra picky when I was flying to re-establish his superiority. Many first officers did not like flying with him.

Our new CEO and his management staff had experience running airlines. The new team thought we had too much time off. They wanted to reduce vacation and take away our personal holidays. A few pilots began talking about forming an in-house union. I thought labor unions had been a good thing when working conditions were terrible a century earlier, but in modern times, I didn't think they were necessary.

Management got word of union talk and backed down, but not for long. They insisted that week-on, week-off had to go, that we'd have to work three blocks a month rather than two. They did not like paying us for sitting around on weekends. We protested that the schedule was a big reason many of us worked at DHL and the reason we didn't grumble much about lower pay than UPS or FedEx.

A couple of pilots wrote schedules that produced the productivity the company said it needed, but management wouldn't consider them. Week-on, week-off, had to go. Mutterings of unionizing began again.

My commuting luck ran out after four years of not going to work a day early in case something went wrong. I drove to Seattle to catch my ride to Cincinnati, but the airplane broke down in Portland. Crew schedulers were still amenable to instant vacation in such circumstances for those of us on good terms with them. I called, got the day off, booked a seat for the next night, and drove home.

Luck ran out again the following week. Not until the airplane arrived from Portland did we learn that an oxygen mask at one of the jumpseats was broken. Another pilot was going in a day early, but I had a trip. The other guy had a hot date in Cincinnati, though, and exercised his seniority. In his position, I'd have given up my seat to the guy who had to get to work, but I didn't argue. Crew Scheduling said they'd cover my trip, so I booked a seat for the next night and drove home.

My weekend trip to Newark was in a new—to us—727-200. I sat in a jumpseat and observed the minor differences between that longer airplane and the one I was qualified in. After checking in at the hotel in Manhattan, I walked to the bus station for a ride back to Newark. I got on Continental Express and flew to Maine for a weekend of lazing around with friends at their log house in the woods. Weekends in New York were nice, but weekends in Maine were nicer.

I was off two weeks in October for deer hunting. When I got back to work, tension was high between management and union organizers, between the VP in charge of the airline and the quiet captain who had been urging us to form our own union. We had no intention of gouging our employer. We just wanted to protect our quality of life.

My attitude all my life had been, if I didn't like the way I was treated at work, I'd get a better job. But I was no longer young enough to start over. I was stuck with DHL for the rest of my flying career, just as I'd promised in my hiring interview.

I got off the elevator on my way to the crew lounge, and the first person I saw was the union agitator. "Where do I sign up?" I said. He smiled and said, "Step into my office." I followed him into the restroom and signed a card calling for an election for union representation.

Again the company backed down. It demanded only that reserve lines would not consider weekends to be duty days when nothing was flying anyway. Reserves would be on call two weeks plus two days.

We almost never saw the executive team because we were seldom in Cincinnati during the day. After we had enough support for an election, big shots were out almost every night, making nice and arguing against unionization. The VP said they had seen the light, that we didn't need a union, that we could work together without one. I said to him, "What are we supposed to do, have another union drive every time you guys want to take something away from us?"

A senior pilot with management aspirations made a presentation complete with posters and charts showing we were better off without a union. He implied that we were flying freight only because we couldn't get hired by passenger carriers. That argument angered one pilot who had chosen DHL over American Airlines and pushed more than one other indifferent pilot off the fence.

I couldn't get the hang of landing the longer 727-200. The main gear and wings were farther back from the front of the airplane. Whether that made a real difference or only a perceived one didn't matter. The -100 I was used to almost landed itself, but, when applying the same technique to the -200, wheels hit hard.

When my eyes were at the accustomed height above the runway, the main wheels, farther back, were closer to concrete, close enough that a little bit of back pressure to slow descent came too late, and the wheels, behind the center of rotation, hit the ground descending faster than they would have had I not added back pressure.

That explanation may not be mathematically or aerodynamically correct. Flying is more science and less art than in decades past, but perception is still a factor. I learned to get consistently smooth landings out of the -200 by creating an illusion for myself.

In the last hundred feet or so before touching down, I pretended nothing existed behind the cockpit door and mentally moved the nose gear forward a few feet until it was directly under me. All I had to do was land my imagined hovercraft, set the dual nosewheel gently on the runway, and the rest of the airplane would take care of itself.

What that delusion did was eliminate the bit of back pressure that worked well to slow descent in the shorter airplane. I continued to fly my little hovercraft down. Ground effect cushioned the wings and slowed their descent while I kept the nose going down. Instead of pivoting downward around the center of lift, the main gear's descent rate lessened in the last few inches of flight and touched down gently.

My system worked fine when I remembered to start the hovercraft movie in my mind. When I flew the airplane as an airplane, landings were not smooth.

Union debate intensified through November. Management promised seven-on, seven-off forever. A few pro-union pilots wavered. Although the original push was for an in-house union, support for the Air Line Pilots Association grew.

Management plied us with food. After one particularly good midnight meal, I wrote a thank-you note to the vice-president responsible. I saw no reason for incivility just because of the union struggle.

We endured a barrage of letters and memos from management as election day approached. We needed 50% of the votes plus one to unionize. We got that and one vote more. A majority of the yes votes were for the Air Line Pilots Association. Almost all of us joined ALPA immediately.

Napoleon had made it through upgrade training somehow and was my captain on a flight from San Francisco to Cincinnati. Weather was marginal in fog and drizzle when we arrived. Napoleon elected to fly the approach on autopilot, but he turned it on late, and it didn't have time to stabilize before we intercepted the glideslope and started down. The airplane began porpoising, chasing the glideslope signal up and down. Napoleon clicked the autopilot off and went around for another try. He did the same thing and the autopilot did the same thing. Napoleon turned it off and flew manually to the landing. Then he wrote up the autopilot as not working properly.

Any time I had occasion to doubt my own competence, all I had to do was think of Napoleon to feel better about myself.

I was scheduled for a day of reserve Friday, but I volunteered for the short trip to Newark with its long layover. After landing, we spent nearly an hour waiting for snowplows to clear a path to our ramp. We didn't get to our hotel until almost noon.

We didn't learn until we got to the airport that evening that Cincinnati was socked in solid with fog. Saturday morning business deliveries weren't critical, especially on a holiday weekend, so DHL cancelled the day. When our limo returned to take us back to the hotel, I had the driver drop me at the passenger terminal. When I got home at noon, the water heater wasn't heating and the washing machine wasn't washing. I spent the weekend fixing those instead of spending the end of grouse season in the woods with my dog.

I was at the Port Angeles airport long before dawn Monday to ride the early flight to Seattle. I called Dispatch to confirm that the Newark airplane was still scheduled to depart that evening. I got on United to Denver and then on United's only flight to Newark, a 767 that went out full. The only empty seat on the airplane was the second cockpit jumpseat. I continued to be amazed I didn't develop ulcers.

I took the bus to Manhattan, walked to the hotel to change out of my uniform, and went back to 45th street to eat dinner. Crowds were already beginning to drift into Times Square for New Year's Eve. I was glad we were getting out of there before 1990 ended.

Arriving at different hotels every night in a fog of fatigue scrambled room numbers and floor plans in our brains. Pilots have stories of getting up half awake and walking into the closet thinking it was the bathroom, which that door was the day before. I sometimes had trouble finding the bathroom, but I never peed in my shoes.

My job gave me time to read about seventy books a year plus the thirty magazines that came to our house each month, but there were bits of time that were too short to get involved in a book. I noticed pilots spending break time with little plastic boxes in their hands, pushing buttons and focusing intently on tiny, monochrome screens. Tetris had become a raging fad.

I bought a Gameboy with Tetris for ninety dollars in Manhattan. The batteries would last fifteen hours, certainly more than I'd need over the weekend. I used them up and went out to buy more and ran them down, too. I realized I was going to have to ration myself if the novelty didn't wear off.

Fear of running out of batteries was like an addict's fear of running out of drugs. Even at home, when I had plenty of things to do, I played Tetris. I'd get home mid-morning when I had the house to myself, frazzled from fatigue, and I'd play just a couple of games. Two became uncounted dozens, and the world around me might not intrude until late afternoon.

When I quit smoking twenty years earlier, I didn't taper off or allow myself a cigaret now and then. I just quit. Tetris was the same. I couldn't play it just a little bit. I gave the damn Gameboy to my daughter and son-in-law and never played Tetris again.

My number came up for a random drug test. I was shaking with rage when I walked into the room selected for pre-piss paperwork. I did not know even then if I would refuse the unconstitutional search. I turned on my mini-recorder and set it on the desk in front of the technician who would collect my urine. I wanted a record in case... I didn't know in case of what. A woman from our human resources department stood behind the technician seated at his desk, her function apparently to witness. I quoted Benjamin Franklin's, "Those who would sacrifice essential liberty for temporary safety deserve neither liberty nor safety." But I caved in and pissed in their fucking cup.

I got a talking-to by the 727 chief pilot for my language. He wanted me to apologize to the HR representative. I said I'd listen to my recording and, if I'd said anything to apologize for, I would do that. During my weekend in New York City, I wrote letter to the HR woman apologizing, not for my attitude, but for having taken my anger out on her.

The chief pilot said he didn't like random testing, either, but if he didn't go along, he'd be out of a job. I told him Adolph Eichmann had the same problem.

That was only my first random drug test, but once a threshold between principle and expediency is crossed, doing it again is easy. First-time prostitutes probably know the feeling.

Fog covered most airports in the Northeast Saturday morning. JFK was below minimums, so we diverted to Boston to refuel and wait for fog to lift. We went inside the DHL building to pick up new paperwork and sit. Someone brought us a box of donuts. I dozed in a chair. Though it was Saturday on the calendar, it was my Monday and past my bedtime.

Visibility improved, but so many airplanes were holding, we couldn't get clearance to depart Boston until much of the backlog aloft had landed. JFK went below our minimums again, but Newark was up. Dispatch filed us to Newark. We'd change the destination to New York en route if weather again improved.

After more than two hours on the ground, ATC allowed us to leave Boston. I went out to the airplane to review approach procedures before we took off. The flight would be short and busy and I'd be flying.

Our departure clearance included a wheels-up time. We couldn't take off before then, and, if we were late, our clearance would be canceled. We took the nearest runway with the shortest taxi to beat the clock and took off in a 30-knot crosswind.

Air was rough across New England. Controllers talked fast, sometimes stringing instructions to different airplanes together without giving pilots time to acknowledge. New York weather became good enough for us to land. We set up our navigation radios for the ILS to Runway 22L at JFK. In our collective fatigue, we forgot to tell ATC that we wanted to go to New York, not Newark. Both airports have runways 22L, and both airports were landing airplanes on those runways that morning.

As the busy New York controllers vectored us for approach, our ILS receivers didn't come alive. We were in unbroken cloud without a glimpse of the ground. The captain asked Approach to verify the ILS frequency. ATC's response was not what we had dialed in. All three of us realized at the same time that it was the frequency for Newark's 22L, not JFK's. The captain explained our situation, and the exasperated controller pulled us out of the Newark line and vectored us to New York.

Because visibility was right at our minimums and crosswind was strong and gusty, I expected the captain would want to fly the approach and landing, but he let me do it. I flew one of my better approaches with autopilot off, needles crossed in the center of the ILS receiver all the way down.

The flying pilot does not look out the window. He flies on instruments while the non-flying pilot watches identical instruments on his side of the panel and calls out deviations. The second officer is supposed to crosscheck pilots' panels.

The flying pilot is required to respond orally to normal calls and called deviations and to make necessary adjustments to course, altitude, or speed. If the flying pilot does not respond, the non-flying pilot takes control of the airplane. If the non-flying pilot does not call, "Approach lights in sight," by the time the airplane reaches two hundred feet above the ground, the flying pilot initiates a missed approach, a go-around.

At two hundred feet, a Three Stooges skit began with the three of us fatigued almost to delirium. The captain called, "Minimums, approach lights in sight." I looked up and saw the lights, but I was concentrating on flying and forgot to respond. The captain said, "I have the airplane," and took control. I said, "I have the runway," and he said, "You have the airplane."

One hundred feet above the ground in near zero visibility in swirling fog and gusting wind was not a good time to be handing the airplane off back and forth, but there was no time for discussion. "I have the airplane," I said. My landing wasn't bad, all things considered.

We stopped for a six-pack on the way to the Park Central hotel and drank it as we discussed the flight we'd just survived. After checking in and changing clothes, we continued the discussion at Mulligan's. The captain, being wiser than his crew, soon retired to his room.

Monday afternoon, I was in my room high in the hotel reading when the smell of dirty smoke drifted in, I assumed through the open window. I'd paid no attention to the sirens, as emergency equipment was always running somewhere in New York. The sirens grew louder and stopped.

No fire alarm had sounded on my floor. Smoke was visible in the corridor and elevators weren't working. I started down the stairwell, but smoke became thicker. I hurried to the stairwell at the other end of the building and went down three or four steps at a time until I caught up with other people in less of a hurry. Firefighters filled the lobby. Soon the fire in the kitchen was out and normalcy resumed.

I'd always considered people who refused rooms on floors higher than fire ladders can reach to be overly cautious. The smoke-filled stairwell changed my perception from overly cautious to prudent.

Pharaoh called me at home to order me to be in his office the following Wednesday. He thought my drug test tantrum had to be dealt with more severely than an oral dressing down. A reserve would fly that day's trip.

I had a concealed pistol license and carried a small .380 in my fanny pack when not at work. When jumpseating out of Port Angeles, I left the pistol locked up at home. When I drove to Seattle or Portland to catch a ride or continue my work week, I locked the trigger-locked gun in my truck.

Hundreds of times a year, airport security finds a gun in a carryon bag or on a passenger. Almost always, the guilty party claims to have forgotten it was in there. Many people find that impossible to believe, but to people who carry a weapon all the time, it's as much a part of them as a wrist watch or a ball point pen. It's not something that's on top of one's mind every minute.

I was preoccupied wondering what punishment the chief pilot might inflict on me as I drove to Seattle and did not realize I'd not taken my pistol out of my bag until in the air and on the way to Cincinnati. After I started breathing again, I realized it was no big deal. I wouldn't have to go through security at any of the airports on my schedule that week.

Because we didn't go through security to get to our airplanes at most airports, some pilots carried things with them they shouldn't have. One friend, a charter pilot in a western state, carried a .45 pistol in his flight bag. He reasoned that, if a charter was bent on suicide by plane crash or wanted to steal his airplane, he might be able to save himself. I thought that was a solution looking for a problem until a man in Colorado chartered a Cessna 402, overwhelmed the pilot, and dove the airplane into a back yard in Boulder.

Why Pharaoh thought it necessary to pull me off my trip and replace me with a reserve so he could tell me he was putting a letter in my file was beyond my poor powers of understanding. He could have read me the letter over the phone.

The day after my come-to-Jesus meeting with the chief pilot, I flew to Windsor Locks, Connecticut. Signs at the state line warn of a mandatory one-year jail term for illegal possession of a firearm in Massachusetts. I renewed my resolve to never make such a mistake again and put the pistol out of my mind. It stayed out of my mind until we got back to the airport that evening.

The office where we received paperwork and filled our Thermoses was in the Windsor Locks passenger terminal. Our limo dropped us at the curb on the ticketing level, and we carried our bags inside and down a flight of stairs to the office at ground level. That stairway was the one charter flights used, but we didn't know that. Never had the security station at the top of the stairs been staffed in all the times I'd been to that airport. People on their way to the Caribbean were going through the electronic arch that evening. The chartered jet usually departed in the afternoon, but it had been delayed. The three of us walked past the line at the metal detector to go downstairs.

We told the security man who stopped us we always used those stairs and we'd never gone through security. He said that, if security wasn't there, we didn't have to go through it, but, if it was, we did.

We went to the back of the line to wait our turn, glancing at our watches and grumbling about institutionalized stupidity. My suitcase was moving toward the X-ray machine and I was swinging my small bag up onto the belt, the bag that contained my fanny pack, when I remembered and froze. A stern young woman manning the scanner stared at me. The captain turned to see what she was looking at. I whispered, "I can't go through security."

He rolled his eyes and sighed, "Oh no..."

I told the security woman, "I've got to go to the bathroom."

We weren't in Massachusetts, but whatever rules Connecticut had about concealed weapons couldn't have been good. My plan was to put the pistol in a coin-op locker and trade for the same trip the next night so I could retrieve it, but the terminal had no lockers.

I didn't have much time. I ducked into a men's room to think and to see if there was any place I might hide a gun for a day or two. The counter holding the small restroom's two sinks was open underneath, pipes exposed except for foam rubber insulation loosely taped around them to prevent condensation from dripping on the floor. I took the pistol out of my bag and unloaded it. I tucked the empty gun into the insulation around the drain of one sink and the magazine and cartridges into the other. Unless the sinks had a plumbing problem, I could probably come back months later and find my gun still there.

I hurried back to the stairway. The passengers had disappeared. Only my captain and two security people remained.

"I'm sorry," I said as I put my bag on the belt to be scanned. "I had a sudden urge to go to the bathroom." That was not a lie.

I hurried downstairs to get started on paperwork and brew coffee and explained what had happened.

"You should have said something," the captain said. "You could have gone outside and down to ground level and we could have let you in that door,"

"You don't understand," I said. "I didn't remember I had a problem until a millisecond before I put my bag on the belt."

After I'd looked over paperwork and filled my Thermos and my pulse had returned to normal, I looked up the stairway. The security people were gone. I retrieved my pistol and ammunition, glad to be on my way out of there and not on my way to jail.

En route to Atlanta the next morning, a crack appeared in the captain's front window. After landing, we realized it was only the outer layer that had cracked. We could fly with a cracked outer pane as the window's strength is in the inner layer. We wrote it up and the mechanic deferred repair. Instead of going to the hotel, we'd return to Cincinnati for window replacement. Right after takeoff, the outer pane shattered. We returned to Atlanta and unanimously refused to fly the airplane until the window was replaced. We went to the hotel to wait for mechanics to round up a new window and install it. What would take the most time, assuming they could find a window quickly, was waiting several hours for sealant around the new window to cure.

I hoped the airplane would be ready to go soon. If the company decided to airline us back to Cincinnati, I'd have to throw away cartridges, take my pistol apart, and stow parts separately in a bag I could check. Not all airlines allowed guns in checked luggage. I figured gun parts weren't a gun.

Our airplane was ready by departure time.

I took six ham sandwiches with me when I went to work the following week. I'd not have to go hungry between restaurants and I'd save money. I forgot my toilet kit and spent saved lunch money replacing essentials.

The nose lifted too easily taking off from Seattle, and the captain had to roll in nose-down trim as soon as wheels were off the ground. That happened now and then when, hurrying to avoid a late departure and the inevitable blame game, loaders misread numbers and loaded cans in a different sequence from the one on the weight-and-balance paperwork. But that wasn't the last load error of the day.

As we rolled down the runway after landing in Newark with a different airplane and a different load, we heard a rumble and a heavy bump behind us. Strange sounds in airplanes are never good, but at least we were on the ground.

The airplane wasn't full, and one of the cargo containers toward the rear had not been locked down. The can hadn't moved during taxi, takeoff, climb, cruise, or even during descent, but it rolled forward through an empty space and slammed into the can ahead as reverse thrust and brakes slowed the airplane.

I wanted to take time to watch the unloading to see which can was loose and how far it had rolled so I could write an incident report. The captain didn't want to bother with it, and he was the captain.

Cargo has to be secured so it doesn't fly around and damage the airplane in turbulence and so it doesn't shift in flight and change the center of gravity, which is what happened in 1997 to a Fine Air DC-8 taking off from Miami carrying pallets of denim to Santo Domingo to be sewn into blue jeans. Unlocked pallets rolled aft in the partially empty airplane when it lifted off, and the airplane stalled and crashed.

On the way to Dallas the next day, radios were silent for perhaps half an hour. Late at night, there wasn't much going on in the sky, and sometimes several minutes passed in silence. But not half an hour. We checked connections, switches, and volume controls and discovered the captain's hand mike was lying on its transmit button. A transmitting radio blocks the frequency completely for anyone nearby trying to use it, and the receiver of the transmitting radio is silent.

Most of us used headsets exclusively and seldom checked to see if hand mikes were stowed properly. The captain released the button and I called ATC to apologize for jamming the frequency. The exasperated controller scolded us and handed us off to the next sector. We unplugged the hand mikes.

The airplane I was to ride home had erratic indications on one engine inbound to Cincinnati. Mechanics checked connections and replaced parts. Nothing changed. Instruments that fed information to the computer that ran the bad gauge were all working normally, and it would have been legal and safe to fly, but the captain elected to have it fixed before we left for Seattle.
I didn't know that. I was strapped into a jumpseat, sound asleep. The crew went inside the building to be out of the way. Mechanics came and went, ran the engine, and couldn't find the source of the problem. I slept through it all. After four hours, they gave up. The crew came out to get their gear and woke me. I thought we were in Seattle.

FAA regulations prohibited us from flying more than thirty hours in seven days, but using the company's bizarre logic, with concurrence of our POI—Principal Operations Inspector in FAA parlance; Privately Owned Inspector in ours—we could legally fly thirty-eight hours in six-and-one-third days. Most airlines used a rolling clock and looked back one full week to see if a crew was legal to fly. DHL used a calendar and dropped time by the day. In advance.
Those of us who were picky about such things were tempted to protest, until we realized that our week-on, week-off schedule could not exist with a rolling clock. Our schedule was important for quality of life. Logic and arithmetic were not. Every now and then, some new-hire pilot brought up the company's flawed application of the rule, and the rest of us would set him straight.
The matter of crew fatigue has only in the past few years been allowed out of the closet. It wasn't until a Kalitta DC-8 crashed attempting to land at Guantanamo Bay in 1993 that pilot fatigue was cited as the primary cause of an accident, but that didn't mean pilots before that time didn't get tired. Flight and Duty Time regulations tend to reflect airline needs more than human physiology. Time in the air was not, in itself, fatiguing.

I'd have cheerfully flown fifty hours a week, if flights were long, non-stop, and on a consistent schedule.

I used a cell phone for the first time in Los Angeles when the ATC computer lost our flight plan. Normal procedure was to call a communications facility on the radio and have them call Cincinnati on the phone and patch us through. Our mechanic pushed a button on his cell phone and handed it to me. Pretty slick, I thought. Within a few years, most of us had cell phones, and the company began to rely on our phones for communicating with us. That was convenient for them and for us, but some pilots resented the company doing business over cell phones we were paying for. In the early days, when every call cost money, we could submit phone bills with expense reports to be reimbursed for company calls.

When the simulator training schedule didn't have enough people for all seats, we could volunteer to fill out the crew and fly the sim with no jeopardy. We were expected to be competent, but we weren't being tested and couldn't fail while flying support, in theory, but major screw-ups could get a volunteer relieved from flight duty until he received remedial training. Sim support was overtime and good practice for when it counted.

I spent six hours one day flying support. The next day's session was my scheduled training as well as Captain Napoleon's warm-up and proficiency check. I packed up and checked out of the hotel so I could go straight from simulator to airport and catch a flight home.

The pilot being checked must perform some elements himself, but he can have the other guy do everything else. Napoleon was shakier than usual, perhaps because he'd been hit by a car a few days earlier, an incident that earned him the nickname Speed Bump. After being instructed to fly to a fix and hold there, Napoleon gave the airplane to me. My stuff was done and I was thinking about alternatives if I missed my flight home instead of paying attention. I entered the holding pattern exactly backwards.

The simulator failed before Napoleon's checkride was finished, so he had to stay over to complete it. A training department pilot volunteered to fly right seat for him so I could go home on schedule.

Napoleon busted his ride. He told me later I was lucky I wasn't there. From then until he retired, his name for me was Lucky. Better Lucky than Speed Bump.

A commuting United Airlines pilot rode our jumpseat from Chicago to Cincinnati on his way home from work. We couldn't help but try to be at our professional best with offline jumpseaters, knowing they'd mentally critique our procedures and performance.

Some captains, when the rider was female, transformed themselves into proud roosters, and that made life unpleasant for junior crewmembers playing supporting roles for His Lordship. I was pleased now and then to see a woman all but roll her eyes at a captain's over-acting. The weakest captains put on the biggest shows.

After checking into the Minneapolis hotel one Saturday morning, I went back out to the airport and rode a 747 to Seattle, riding in the cockpit and listening to the crew trade jokes featuring Peewee Herman, Jeffrey Dahmer, and blondes. I managed to sleep a couple of hours anyway.

I got up early Monday for the long commute back to Minneapolis and caught the first Horizon flight to Seattle. I couldn't get on flights I wanted and had to settle for Detroit. The closer I was to Minneapolis if I had to buy a ticket, the cheaper it would be.

A 747 was the last non-stop out of Detroit that would get me to work on time. A DC-9 was boarding for Minneapolis with a stop at Midway, and I took it on impulse, hoping I'd not be bumped in Chicago. A flight attendant told me that the 747 was overbooked, and I'd not have gotten on even with a ticket. I got to the hotel with only an hour to spare.

Since high school, I'd wanted to someday build a house. Barb and I had bought a lot of nearly two acres on a hillside overlooking Sequim Bay a couple of years earlier, and we decided to build a Lindal Cedar Home kit, a chalet roofed, prow fronted, solid cedar house over a walkout basement and garage tucked into the hill side at the high end of the lot. It would go together fast, like Lincoln Logs, with each thick red cedar plank tagged to show exactly where it fit. I figured I could build it in three months of days off, vacation time, and weekends at home on Seattle layovers. We got a construction loan for six months.

We didn't start building until June. I spent almost every day of my life that I wasn't at work until May 1993 building that house. The eleven-month period between moving dirt and moving in is a hole in my memory. Vacation time, weekend layovers, days off, and occasionally sick days, when such problems as mild tendinitis or sniffles demanded it, all went into the house.

My naïve and optimistic idea that I could build a house in three months was, in retrospect, delusional. Friends and visiting family members helped, and a contractor did much of the work. The bank had expected the construction loan to become a mortgage after six months and became impatient. I was under personal pressure to finish the damn house, too. I was high enough on the seniority list for upgrade to captain.

There is an unwritten rule among airline pilots that one does not attempt upgrade while in the midst of divorce or building a house. Delays in construction meant delays in my other dream and the large jump in pay that would come with it. We moved into our new house but didn't have time to unpack before I was off to Cincinnati for captain upgrade class.

I'd put myself at a disadvantage in flying with the same captain almost exclusively during the time I was building the house. My seniority guaranteed me Seattle weekends, as did The Skipper's. By the time I started upgrade training, I'd flown more hours with The Skipper than with all other captains combined. I'd grown to like the man in spite of his Teutonic ways.

DHL had its procedures and The Skipper had his. One morning after landing in Seattle, I said, "Skipper, I'm going to be in upgrade soon, and when the FAA examiner asks me why I do something in such and such a way, I'm not going to be able to say, 'That's the way The Skipper wants it done.' I need to do everything DHL's way from now on."

He was silent for a moment, and then he nodded.

A training company near the Cincinnati airport had acquired a suitable 727 simulator, so we'd stopped going to Pittsburgh. Many pilots in upgrade rented an apartment together or stayed in the same hotel. Most of ground school covered subjects I'd been over many times in five years on the airplane.

I'd logged fourteen hundred hours as second officer and nearly that many in the right seat. I was comfortable in the 727 but flew more by feel than by numbers. The simulator moves in such a way as to impart a sense of flight, but feel is imperfect. If you put in the correct numbers, you get the desired response, but you have to know the numbers.

My first officer in upgrade training came straight from the Metroliner and had no experience in the 727. Jay pumped me for numbers before we began flying the box. He wanted to know precisely how many degrees of pitch to hold for various conditions of flight and what power settings worked for different configurations. He was astounded that I didn't know. After our first day in simulator, the instructor said to him, "Don't let this go to your head, but that was the best first first-officer ride I've ever seen."

I asked Jay how he did that. "I just watched everything you did," he said. "And then I did it different."

It is normal for progress through simulator training to be uneven, but I didn't just have ups and downs. I had steep climbs and freefalls. My poor days were often followed by unusually good days, as if fear of failure stimulated my brain to extra effort. A good day allowed me to relax again.

The course allowed a small number of extra sessions for those who need more time. I used up my allotment flying makeup lessons with members of other crews who were also having trouble.

We flew two models of the Boeing 727, and there were variations between airplanes within models. The simulator cockpit was different from all of our airplanes, and the cockpit mockup was different from all the airplanes and from the simulator. I attempted my oral examination with an FAA examiner in that oddball mockup.

The first question my examiner asked stumped me. When I couldn't immediately find familiar switches, my brain froze in panic as I drew a complete blank. I answered another question on another system correctly for the airplanes we flew, but the layout in the mockup was not the same, and, for the mockup, my answer was wrong.

"I can't believe you have that much time in this airplane and know so little about it," he said. He left the room to find an instructor.

The examiner was astounded to learn the mockup, simulator, and airplanes were all different. "I won't write you a pink slip," he said. "I'll be conducting your checkride, and then I'll find out if you know the airplane."

I envisioned him perching like a vulture on my shoulder to see if he'd made a mistake in signing me off, but my examiner in the simulator was not the man who had passed me on my disastrous oral exam.

On checkrides, the support crew can make the ride easy or difficult. Regardless of support, competent candidates pass. I failed. I had two days off to think about things before a two-hour warm-up and another checkride the day after. When I woke on doomsday, my mind was calm and I knew without doubt I would do well.

When I got to the simulator building, I had a new crew and a new Fed. In the break room going over paperwork before we went into the simulator, the genial examiner, knowing it was do or die for me, tried to put me at ease. I told him I was fine, that I knew I'd do well, and I did. I may have been the only one not surprised. The hard part was finally over. All I had to do was fly a couple of approaches in the airplane, just as I'd been doing for years.

We stayed in our layover hotel in Springfield, Massachusetts, and used the airplane parked at Windsor Locks during the day. Stewart Field, just across the Hudson River in New York, had little traffic and all the instrument approaches we'd need. With a training department crew, I flew the same approaches I'd fly the next day with the FAA on board. We first flew the ILS to Runway 09, flew a missed approach, and circled back to the west to fly the NDB to the same runway. Any crosswind component needed for the ILS would be the same I'd apply to the NDB heading. Those two approaches, one precision and one non-precision, were key components to the checkride. After nearly two months away from home and away from my new house, I was almost finished.

The next day, when we landed at Stewart to pick up the FAA examiner, we discovered a minor problem with the airplane that could have been deferred over the telephone in five minutes, but the company wanted it fixed then and there. The only mechanics available were not familiar with the 727, and, after wasting much of the day, they gave up and Cincinnati deferred the repair.

Mine was the last checkride of our class. We were all eager to go home, and my support crew had flight reservations for early that evening. While we stood around waiting for the airplane to become flyable, the training captain acting as my first officer said he wanted to modify the plan to save time. We'd fly the ILS as planned, but, instead of circling back for the NDB I'd practiced, we fly a straight-out missed approach from the ILS and fly the VOR approach from the east to Runway 27. VOR approaches are simple. I looked at the unfamiliar approach plate while we waited.

The VOR radio beacon provides a course to a point from which you land or execute a missed approach. Time from the final approach fix defines the missed approach point. Even if DME is not part of the approach, sometimes distance information is printed on the chart. I failed to notice that the final approach fix was not the VOR more than ten miles from the airport but an intersection much closer to the runway.

I flew the ILS to a touch-and-go wearing the plastic instrument training visor and headed straight out in clear weather to line up for the VOR approach. ATC vectored us to intercept the final approach course inside the VOR. I said we needed the turn on outside that beacon, thinking that was the place I'd start the clock. The training captain in the right seat relayed that to the controller exactly as he should have done, although there are support pilots who, in his position, would have found a way to steer me straight without the examiner's noticing. Turning off the course to circle for another entry ate time, and we were trying to save time.

I should have realized when I looked at the approach plate on the ground that two minutes was not enough time to cover the ten miles from VOR to airport. As miscalculated time ran out, I finally saw my mistake.

Had I announced my error and immediately broken off and gone back for another try, I'd probably have passed the ride, but time was tight and people had flights to catch, so I said, "I started time at the wrong fix, but we can use DME and continue."

DME is more accurate than time anyway, so what I did was not unsafe. It wasn't correct, either, and captains are supposed to know how to read an approach plate. We landed and the Fed whispered with my crew in the entryway as I unplugged my headset and put away my charts. The FAA man could not pass me on that last approach, and I was so tired of it all that I didn't give a damn. I just wanted to go home.

I was a full-time babysitter while Barb was at work, taking care of my first grandson while his parents took a short vacation. As I walked through the countryside with Tim on my shoulders, I realized it was the first time since we'd begun building the house more than a year earlier that I'd not been under constant stress. In that moment, I realized why I'd had so much trouble in the simulator with such extreme variations in performance, why I let my guard down before the airplane checkride. I'd been too goddamned tired. I resolved that I would not attempt upgrade again until everything that needed to be done to the house was complete so I'd have no distractions or outside pressure during training.

Failing an upgrade meant returning to the previous crew position, but only if that position was open. I was sure I'd not lose my job, but that confidence was due more to my optimistic nature than to objective analysis.

I was home only a week. After a session with the chief pilot discussing my failure, I went into the simulator for an easy, two-hour requalification ride as first officer. I went back home for two more weeks before I was back on the schedule as one of the more senior first officers. By company rule, I could not attempt upgrade again for a year. If there was a bright side to failure, it was that I would have been too junior as captain to avoid flying to Mexico City.

As months went by, pilots lower on the list moved into the left seat. I didn't mind flying with junior captains, some of whom were years younger than I and had less time in the airplane. On my birthday in September, I realized I had only nine years before mandatory retirement from a pilot's seat to earn enough money to pay off the house and fatten my 401k enough to avoid retiring to the back seat.

Time off work was unpressured. I built a storage building and an equipment shed and installed an irrigation system. The one house project left to do was replacing temporary carpet with hardwood flooring.

I was eager to get home for elk season, but my hunt almost ended before I left Cincinnati.

Part of pre-takeoff procedure was to check movement of flight controls just before the Taxi checklist. When the captain said, "Control check," it was a signal for the first officer to pull his feet back from the rudder pedals. The captain didn't say anything and drove a pedal into my right instep. I yelped in pain and surprise. He said, "Watch your feet."

I flew the trip with my shoe off, and after a couple of days, pain and swelling subsided. I was in the woods most of a week, enjoying solitary respite from the world and from the job. Coming home once again without an elk didn't even register on my disappointment scale.

DHL Airways began acquiring half a dozen DC-8s, ancient four-engine airplanes that carried much more cargo than 727s and could fly to Europe non-stop. Many pilots eager to fly the larger airplane were those the rest of us didn't like to fly with. Someone referred to the DC-8 as "The Sweeper" because it swept all the assholes out of the 727, and the name stuck.

I had no desire to learn a new airplane and no desire to fly the heavy, ungainly thing. It would have been like trading a peppy car for a lumbering bus.

United Airlines was the last big customer for the pinstriped uniform shirts we wore, but they'd changed uniforms a few years earlier and it was becoming difficult for us to find shirts. Our tan uniforms showed dirt, so we settled on dark blue replacements with white shirts. Many wanted to delete hats, but that idea was nearly twenty years away from general acceptance among airlines.

Right after takeoff from Pittsburgh, we turned right ninety degrees. In the turn, I got distracted and the airplane began to descend slightly. The Ground Proximity warning began yelling at us: "Pull up! Pull up! Terrain! Terrain!" I resumed climbing, but not decisively enough to make the box happy. "Don't sink! Pull up!" it said.

I'd never heard that warning before, and the novelty was another distraction. My response was slower than it would have been if the captain or second officer had said "Altitude!" as they should have the instant the climb became a descent. We were all tired enough we should have begged off the trip, but claiming fatigue would have meant buying hotel rooms in Cincinnati for the weekend, and we'd almost rather crash than suffer that cruel and expensive fate.

We were the first flight to land in Cincinnati Monday night, and we didn't have time to get out of the airplane. As it was being unloaded, Dispatch sent someone out with flight plans and weather for a run to Minneapolis with a mechanic on board. The airplane there had a bad smoke detector and couldn't fly until it was fixed. We got back from Minneapolis just in time for our scheduled departure to New York.

Wind was fierce and directly across the active runway at JFK. Traffic backed up, and everyone was holding. A TWA pilot asked for a smoother altitude. The controller said other altitudes were unavailable. TWA said, "Well, make one available. We're not gonna hold in this shit." The controller asked him to call when he got on the ground and sent him and other complainers way to hell and gone somewhere to hold at the altitudes they wanted. We were glad to be flying freight. Boxes don't complain and don't get airsick.

We didn't have enough fuel to hold long, so we diverted to Newark. We'd flown almost eight hours and had been in the airplane nearly twelve hours straight. It had been fifteen hours since we'd eaten. Dispatch wanted us to wait out the weather and continue to New York. The captain refused and we got to the hotel late for a minimum-rest stay. I spent the first hour checking in and eating and the last two eating and getting ready to leave. Eight hours rest allowed only five for sleeping.

On the return to Cincinnati—my last leg before going home for Christmas—we told our second officer to delay his call to the company as long as he could. He was supposed to call in to give our ETA as soon as we were in radio range, about thirty minutes out, but we'd heard a crew ahead of us call and be told to stay in the airplane because they were being sent to some city where an airplane was broken. The same thing happened to the next airplane and to the third. We landed ahead of those last two, but we were only a few minutes out when our second officer called in and we didn't have to go anywhere.

I slept soundly all the way to Seattle. Right after we landed, ice fog closed the airport. Luck was with me again when I got stopped by a very young state patrol officer on my way home. He clocked me at sixty-seven in the ubiquitous fifty-five zone. I was polite and so was he. I got off with a warning.

Philadelphia was enjoying a January ice storm to begin 1994. Runways were clear, but taxiways were slick. A coat of ice closed highways and bridges. The van took deserted back roads and side streets to the hotel. I unplugged the phone and set an alarm for late afternoon.

The phone rang when I plugged it in. Crew Scheduling told us to go to the airport more than three hours early to try to get out before the worsening storm trapped us. It didn't occur to us that the early report meant we'd not have enough duty time remaining to fly to Seattle for the weekend.

There was time to eat or take a shower but not both. I gobbled a turkey dinner next door at Shoney's and hurried back to the hotel to pack.

The others were waiting for me when I got to the lobby. I had to pay for a couple of phone calls and lines were four deep at the desk. We didn't get to the airport until half an hour after we were supposed to. We waited two more hours to get de-iced. That was good because we could lie about our report time and have enough duty time remaining to fly to Seattle.

Because we left Philadelphia early, we had time to kill in Baltimore. We called the FBO on the radio and a van came out to pick us up. We waited inside the warm building drinking coffee.

We'd left the APU running to keep electric power on the airplane. When the van returned us to the airplane after our break, the second officer began his preflight walk-around. The captain turned on a pack for heat and we settled into our seats. A burning odor wafted out of the vents. Our second officer ran up the stairs, reached into the cockpit, and yanked the APU fire handle. "We're on fire," he said. "Get out."

Pulling the fire handle shut off fuel and generator and closed air ducts. It takes a twist of the fire handle to discharge the extinguisher, and I did that on my way out of the suddenly dark and silent airplane.

The fire was on the outside of the APU exhaust duct. The mechanic had noticed steam or smoke before flames erupted. We thought something had dripped onto the duct, and when we turned on the pack, the load on the APU caused exhaust temperature to rise enough to ignite whatever it was. I called Cincinnati from the mechanic's office to explain what had happened.

Maintenance Control gave me a list of things to check that could have been affected by the fire. The mechanic was already checking things from his own list. As soon as all paperwork was done, we left an hour and a half late. That left no time for a nap in Cincinnati, so we took turns sleeping on the way to Seattle.

It was eighteen below zero in Cincinnati one night. Snow and ice closed highways. Tugs and K-loaders ran out of fuel because trucks couldn't get to the airport. Only a few small contract airplanes and three or four of our 727s departed before DHL said to hell with it and shut down for the day. Several of us went to a nearby Hilton with a stop at a liquor store on the way. I sipped Wild Turkey and went to bed. Cold weather doesn't usually bother me, but Miami felt especially good the next day.

Fog began to thicken in Seattle as dawn lightened the sky on Saturday morning. We wanted to fly fast to get there while we could still land, but the airplane had not had engine modifications to reduce noise. If we landed before the overnight noise curfew ended, DHL would incur a fine.

I suggested we call the company and let them make the decision. We got a phone patch over the radio and the okay to land. The folks with the Big Picture must have figured a fine was cheaper than landing somewhere else.

The phone at home rang early one Tuesday morning before coffee had primed my brain. "This is your fairy godmother."

I was slow to understand that I was getting another week off. I'd just finished one free week off because my seat was needed for a check airman flying with captain fresh out of upgrade training. They needed my seat for another week. Before I went back to work, I bought smoked salmon for my fairy godmother in Crew Scheduling.

After landing in New York one morning near the end of March, we were going to Atlanta as soon as normal freight was taken off and a charter cargo loaded. Our airplane didn't have a working APU. The first ground power unit the JFK crew plugged into us wouldn't stay on line, so we sat with an engine running until they rounded up one that worked. After freight was unloaded, we started two engines and taxied across the airport to Japan Airlines Cargo to pick up our charter. Cincinnati had assured us there'd be a GPU and an air cart waiting for us. There was neither.

We called Dispatch on the radio. They wanted us to taxi back to DHL and swap airplanes. We all voted No, and the captain shut down engines. He figured it would take less time for JAL to round up sparks and air than it would for us to change to an airplane that hadn't been fueled yet. We finally got out of there in full daylight after more than two hours on the ground. Atlanta didn't have external power ready for us, either, but we didn't care.

Hotel clerks couldn't find the sign-in sheet for us, likely another oversight from our support departments in Cincinnati. A clerk found rooms. They were occupied. We went back to the lobby to try again.

I put in a request for a floating holiday on the day that same wretched charter was on my schedule for two weeks later. I was surprised when the day off was granted. Maybe it was the smoked salmon.

I stayed up late on the first Sunday in May so I could sleep late Monday before going to work. A bad dream woke me early, a dream that I'd busted my checkride on a second attempt at captain upgrade. I couldn't remember the error I made in the dream, but it was something that couldn't happen in the real world. Even so, I couldn't go back to sleep.

The return to Cincinnati Monday night was my last leg before recurrent training. I checked into the Signature hotel with several others who'd be in class that week. Because so many arrived on jumpseats after midnight on Tuesday morning, the first day of class wouldn't start until after lunch. Instead of going to bed immediately, I watched a movie and read for a while, knowing I'd pay for the indulgence by falling asleep in class.

I'd been on the airplane seven years, so I knew the systems as well as I ever would. Regulations were something else. Our instructor was enthusiastic about his subject. He talked fast and buried us in details none of us cared about or would remember. Time dragged. Someone moved the clock ahead an hour on the first break after lunch. Our instructor talked even faster the rest of the afternoon trying to catch up.

I flew the simulator much better than usual. I got a wind shear on takeoff at maximum gross weight and survived. We sank so close to the ground, the radar altimeter indicated zero. The instructor was amazed we stayed in the air, but I'd never crashed in wind shear training. I wasn't the most precise pilot, but my survival instinct was strong.

The next day, even though I'd stayed up late watching a movie on TV, I flew the simulator better than I ever had on a checkride. The confidence builder started me looking ahead to another shot at the left seat.

We flew to Orlando and Miami in one of the six -200 models we'd acquired from Air France. When the second officer did his preflight in Cincinnati, standby power didn't work. The battery was good, so failing the check likely meant the standby inverter wasn't working. Maintenance said Air France wired its airplanes for the battery to power the first officer's side, not the captain's. We'd never heard of such a thing. Maintenance checked four of the other five Air France airplanes that were on the ramp and all were like the one we were in. The mechanic pointed out that my side was powered on the check.

Well, of course it was. The only instruments de-powered on the standby check were the captain's. Mine were powered normally, not from the standby inverter, but that fact didn't enter our minds. In the heat of battle at four o'clock in the morning, with mechanics spinning theories and departure time fast approaching, we didn't realize that we had no standby power at all.

We could find nothing in the books that prohibited flying with what we thought we had, but the captain refused to take the airplane without higher approval. The flight manager called the chief pilot at home and woke him up. He said we could go with standby feeding my side if we were comfortable with that and if the weather was good, so we did.

On the way to Miami, the second officer and a new-hire jumpseater analyzed the problem. They concluded the inverter was bad and we had no source of standby power. If all three generators failed, we'd have nothing to fly by except the view out the window.

The chance that all three generators might fail was slim, but one reason airline travel in the USA is among the safest in the world is that flying with even a slim chance of disaster is not allowed. High standards are expensive, but crashes cost more.

We wrote up the standby inverter after we left Orlando for Miami. Nobody could prove we had figured out what was wrong before we landed the first time, and our hotel was in Miami, not in Orlando.

When in uniform, I carried my wallet in my small bag so it wouldn't wear a print into the back of my trousers. I had time to stop at a Safeway in Seattle for snacks, and when I got back into my truck, I put my wallet on the seat. It fell on the floor and I didn't notice.

Not having money was easily remedied. I borrowed enough to get me through the day in New York. On Saturday, I'd be back in Seattle. My license and medical certificate were in my wallet, and I couldn't legally fly without them, but the chance of being ramp checked by the FAA was remote.

I'd already checked in for my trip to Newark when the captain learned he'd be conducting a line check. He'd check the entire crew for licenses and medicals, so I took him aside and confessed. He said I couldn't take the trip. I rode jumpseat back to Seattle to get my wallet, even though there was no open jumpseat back to Cincinnati that evening.

After sleeping three hours on the ride to Seattle, I retrieved my wallet and got to the United gate five minutes before a departure. I told the agent I was embarrassed to ask so late, but would it be possible for me to get on? Forty-five minutes after landing in Chicago, I was on a 737 bound for Cincinnati.

I went to the bunk room and slept six hours before rejoining my crew to fly right back to Seattle for the weekend. I never went to work without my license again.

Friends invited us on a weekend trip to the San Juan Islands on their sailboat. Barb had things to do and didn't go. With only a light breeze, the boat required little attention. They told me about their teenaged daughter and ADD.

The girl had read a couple of books on attention deficit disorder because a friend of hers had been diagnosed with it. She told her parents it sounded like the book was talking about her. Mom and Dad read it and hustled her off to a specialist. What they'd thought was an extreme case of generational war aggravated by Dad's stern nature had another explanation.

They had a book on ADD aboard. I browsed through it as the boat rode gentle swells. It sounded like the book was about me, but I wasn't a kid. I read the chapter on how to recognize ADD in adults. Adults didn't get over ADD. They learned ways to cope with it.

At the public library, I found a book on attention deficit disorder in adults. By the time I'd finished reading it, I realized I could be the poster boy for adult ADD. I wondered if I should be flying airplanes at all.

I called ALPA's aeromedical department and learned Ritalin is prohibited for pilots. The doctor said that if I'd made it that far in life without medication, I was doing fine. Maybe after I retired I could experiment with the drug.

I mentioned to my friend with the sailboat that I wondered if I should be flying. He said, "You'll screw up little things and the paperwork, but when something goes wrong, some emergency you haven't been trained for, you'll be more likely to survive than the guy who just knows the books and follows them."

I thought about that and remembered the times I forgot to sign log pages, the times my mouth got ahead of my brain, the times in small airplanes when unorthodox responses to serious problems had saved my life. Maybe I wasn't in the wrong line of work after all.

Flying with managers and training department pilots who did not regularly fly the line was always interesting, in a minefield sort of way. I flew to Baltimore and Philadelphia with our training department manager, a man new to DHL. Our second officer hadn't been with the company long, either.

We had temporary data pages for construction-shortened Runway 28 at Baltimore and the three of us discussed the takeoff. The numbers said we could use reduced thrust, but reducing to the limit would leave us no margin. We could reduce less than the full amount, a compromise that would make the engines happy and give us a ten-thousand-pound buffer, so we agreed to do that. Because the departure end of the runway was lower than the middle, we wouldn't be able to see red lights marking the temporary end until we were well into our takeoff roll.

After I pushed up the power to approximately the correct setting, I lifted my hand while the captain trimmed the levers to the numbers the second officer had taken from her performance manual. He was still doing that when we topped the rise and saw runway end lights looking much too close. The captain shoved power up to go-around thrust without waiting for me to command it. To reject a takeoff was a captain's decision, not mine, and I was glad he didn't try to stop. We'd have run off the end of useable runway and into the construction zone and God knows what kind of surface and construction equipment. I rotated normally when we reached the proper speed and lifted off in the last few hundred feet of concrete. As we climbed through ten thousand feet, I asked the second officer if we'd used the wrong page, the full-length data instead of the page for the shortened runway. She said she'd used the correct one.

Normally, both pilots check the numbers the second officer writes on the takeoff data card against the numbers in the manual, but they almost always are correct, so our checks were often more casual than careful. The captain had checked the numbers, but I had not. After our discussion of what pages and settings to use, how could there be any confusion?

The captain asked me what I thought had happened. My first guess was we'd used the wrong data page. The only other explanation was that we were heavier than the load sheet said we were. Before he could respond, the second officer said she'd used the wrong chart. She felt like hell for screwing up. I told her *she* didn't screw up, *we* did. The captain agreed and added, "What happens in the cockpit, stays in the cockpit."

I didn't like that. I thought we'd better serve ourselves and other crews if we described what had happened and talked about how we could have prevented the error. But I wasn't the captain.

The crew who'd brought the airplane in at Cincinnati had written up the first officer's sliding window for air leaks. Maintenance replaced the window, but we soon discovered the new one leaked, too. I thought of the British pilot who'd been sucked halfway out of his airplane when a window blew out. I tightened my seatbelt and kept my shoulder harness on the entire trip.

The next time I went to work, the pilot on the other jumpseat was one who had beaten me to reserving a jumpseat on a day we were both in the air. He'd called in on his cell phone in flight. I decided to get one.

There would be two 727 upgrade classes, early January and late February of 1995, but there was only one bidding window for both classes. Which class an applicant got depended on seniority, but, in Pharaoh's twisted logic, the first class would be filled by the most senior, regardless of preference.

I would not be ready for a January class coming hard after holidays and hunting seasons. I wanted time to study the books and buy a few hours of simulator training before class began. I wrote a grievance contending my seniority rights would be violated if I was denied choice of class. If I couldn't be sure of being in the February class, I'd have to pass on both.

I assumed the captain would want me to land on the long runway in Dallas, as he'd once made a disparaging comment about first officers and short runways, but he wanted us to land on the short one, closer to parking. I reminded him of what he'd said and said that was why I'd chosen the long one. He said that if he'd been concerned about my landing on either runway, it would have been his leg. I was surprised at the compliment, as he was a sharp captain with high standards.

A few days later, flying to Minneapolis with a different captain, I was absorbed in a detective novel and made a mental arithmetic error when calculating where to start down. The captain kept quiet to see what would happen.

When I realized my mistake, I had only twelve miles to lose seventeen thousand feet and make a crossing restriction. A normal descent required forty miles. I pulled the speedbrake and pointed the nose down. Air was smooth, so I flew only a hair below redline. Approach asked if we were going to make it. I told the captain to say Yes. If I'd thought to put the landing gear down for more drag, we'd have made it easily.

While we waited for the hotel van to pick us up, I told the captain I was surprised he'd let me go so far before starting down.

"I wouldn't have with just anybody," he said. After the captain's comment in Dallas earlier, I wondered if yet another compliment from another captain I respected might be the beginning of an auspicious trend.

We touched down in New York at exactly seven o'clock. As soon as we cleared the runway, I turned on my new cell phone and called Crew Scheduling and booked a jumpseat for thirty days later.

We were between Detroit and Minneapolis one Tuesday morning not long after that when I got out my cell phone to call for a jumpseat. When I got my phone bill a few weeks later, it took me a couple of minutes to figure out why I'd been charged for a call from Saginaw, Michigan.

The first time I went to work in December, I forgot my belt. I was wearing my optional navy blue sweater, so the absence of belt didn't show. A greater concern was that my pants stayed up just fine without a belt. I don't like tight clothes and ordered my uniform an inch larger in the waist than the tailor measured. I thought about that as I fed coins into the vending machine in Cincinnati. I wasn't hungry, but I pushed the button that turned the carousel in the Wheel of Death and bought a hamburger and a pie.

First we were going to go non-stop to Miami because Orlando was socked in with fog, but the plan changed. We'd go to Atlanta and Miami. We sat for an hour on the Cincinnati ramp waiting for fog to lift in Atlanta. By the time we got there, weather had improved in Orlando, so we'd go there and then to Miami.

All those changes required mental reset, tiring in itself. We were on descent into Orlando when we got a call on the company radio with another change. After offloading everything in Orlando, we were to return to Cincinnati. We refused. It was late and we were tired, and to return would take us over our contractual duty maximum of fourteen hours. Only the south end of Runway 35 in Orlando was visible in a cloak of fog so dense it took twenty minutes to taxi to parking.

The plan for that evening was to stop in Saint Louis on the way to Cincinnati. We got to the airport early and were ready to go, except we hadn't been loaded. Seven minutes after departure time, the mechanic got on his headset and asked when we'd be ready. The captain said we were ready, except we hadn't been loaded. The mechanic said we were going empty. Pilots were always the last to know. We dug out a blank weight and balance form, filled it out, and dropped the station copy out the window.

Because the company seemed to take delight in using our contract to make our lives miserable, a growing number of pilots were returning the favor by flying by the book. Normal operations were not illegal or unsafe, but by not requesting shortcuts en route and refusing them when offered and by not flying fast to make up for late departures, we hoped to show management that both sides could play dirty.

I'd never flown the published arrival into Baltimore. At the hours we flew, traffic was sparse, and we almost always got vectors direct to the airport or to a radio fix near it. The captain flew the full approach and made the short trip to Baltimore and Philadelphia almost as long as the flight to Saint Louis and Houston.

The next night, we had a captain from the training department to Denver and Phoenix. With by-the-book flying slowing the entire operation, management pilots had begun flying every night. The second officer and I had no way of knowing if our captain was flying because he needed the time for currency or if he was a company snake. Neither of us urged him to do anything contrary to normal procedures, but we tried to leave everything open so he could do the right thing if he wanted to.

After visiting family in Colorado after Christmas, I slept on the jumpseat all the way to Cincinnati. In Philadelphia, I ran the tub full of hot water through the shower to put some moisture in the air, took my last two Sudafeds, and went to bed.

I woke up after only four hours and walked to a store to buy cough drops and a spray bottle of Afrin. For almost my entire flying career, I was under the mistaken impression Afrin was on the list of medications pilots could use while flying. I piled hot peppers on my spaghetti dinner at Romano's, snorted Afrin, and was yawning when it was time to leave the hotel.

By the time we landed in Seattle, I was sicker than I realized. Because of the extra day of New Year's weekend layover, I thought I'd be well enough to fly by Tuesday evening.

On Sunday morning, I still thought I'd be able to go to work Tuesday. By Monday evening, I knew I'd have to call in sick from a layover, something I'd never done. Crew Scheduling was not staffed on weekends, so I called the message line and hoped someone bothered to check it now and then.

A bronchial infection lingered for more than a week, and forced inactivity was hard to take. I began 1995 by watching six bowl games and developed back spasms. I normally didn't watch six football games in a year. At four o'clock Tuesday morning, I struggled out of bed and called Crew Scheduling in case they hadn't gotten my message.

I was home two weeks. The last few nights at home, I had anxiety dreams involving running late, getting lost, and not being able to get back to the hotel. At my semi-annual physical exam and a cholesterol check, I weighed twenty-five pounds more than when I'd been building the house two years earlier.

Barb had the day off and fixed dinner early so I could eat before driving to Seattle. I stopped on the way for a hamburger I didn't need because I'd be hungry later if I didn't. No wonder I was heavier than I'd ever been.

I skipped breakfast in Houston Tuesday and slept eight hours. I was scheduled to fly the same trip the next day, but when we got back to Cincinnati, I saw that the captain on that trip would be our unpopular 727 chief pilot. I knew I wouldn't be able to read while flying with him, so I looked for a trade. A Texan was scheduled for Seattle. I asked if he'd like Houston. He enthusiastically agreed before asking who the captain was. The crestfallen look on his face when I told him cracked up everyone within hearing. I was surprised when he accepted the trade anyway.

When I got to work a week later, a new upgrade class for six captains in "late spring" had been posted for bids. My grievance over the weird way Pharaoh interpreted seniority had not yet been adjudicated.

DHL sold off the fleet of Metroliners to a contractor who flew them in DHL colors and with DHL cargo, so new DHL pilots went directly into the back seats of the DC-8 and 727. A class of new hires would begin late in April for a week of indoctrination into DHL's ways before training with the upgrade class began the first of May.

A friend, upgrading from second officer to right seat, would be my simulator partner. He and I would be flying side by side for the first time since he was in high school and I was his flight instructor.

STI in Seattle had a simulator training course designed to familiarize pilots making the transition from propellers to jets. The course was ten hours of no-motion 727 simulator time for nine hundred dollars. My second upgrade attempt would be my last, pass or fail, so the cost was a bargain.

Normally, an STI instructor sat in the right seat. A second officer was not required. We explained we'd like to fly together in the seats we'd train in. Our instructor agreed to our plan and we got on the schedule.

Barb and I drove to Seattle to an RV show in the Kingdome. I was already thinking of ways to spend my captain's income. A slide-in camper was going to cost as much as my Nissan pickup had, and we'd need a bigger truck.

We pushed back in Seattle Monday evening, started engines, and the lower rudder wouldn't work. The second officer reset the breaker, but the rudder still wouldn't move. We taxied back into the blocks and shut down.

It took three hours to get the airplane fixed. We landed in Cincinnati too late for our outbound trip and were rescheduled to Miami. Not just to Miami, though—Baltimore first. And there was more bad news. The next day, instead of our scheduled Saint Louis and Houston, we'd inaugurate a new route through Houston to Guadalajara.

My entire leg from Baltimore to Miami was in broad daylight, and I was the only one of us reasonably awake. Daytime flying was miserable—speed up, slow down, turn left, turn right, climb, descend. Daytime flying was almost like real work.

The captain was so tired, it took some explaining to get him to understand that we were landing to the east, not to the west, and that we wanted Runway 12, and if we couldn't have that, 9R but not 9L. Duty time for the day came to three minutes under our contractual maximum fourteen hours. When we got back to Cincinnati that night, I told Crew Scheduling I was too tired to take a long trip, especially one to a new destination in a foreign country when the entire crew needed to be especially alert. I could either trade Guadalajara for a short trip or for reserve, or I could take a fatigue day. I said I'd do whichever would cause the least trouble.

A reserve replaced me on Guadalajara. He'd been scheduled for Mexico City the following night but couldn't do two long trips back to back. I realized that might put me in line for his Mexico City trip and ruin my record of never having gone there, but I was too tired to care. I went to a hotel and slept.

The next day, I flew to Detroit and Minneapolis, changed clothes, and went to breakfast. When I got back to my room, the plastic key would not fit the slot. That made no sense, as I'd already used it once. I went back down to the desk. The clerk pointed out that it wasn't their key. I'd walked off with the hotel key in Cincinnati, and the Minneapolis key was in another pocket. I could almost see the clerk thinking, "They let this guy fly airplanes?"

I rode a Southwest flight home from Sacramento for the weekend. The two-year-old boy in the center seat did not want to keep his belt fastened, and Mom was having a tough time with him. I lent a little uniformed authority to the situation, and the kid shut up and sat still.

The first Monday morning in April, my training partner drove us to STI, just south of SeaTac airport. I flew the simulator pretty well, sticking with the instructor's instruction to pay attention to the ADI—the artificial horizon—90% of the time and never take my eyes off it when it was moving, basic stuff I'd no doubt been told many times before. Our instructor taught us a way of visualizing holding patterns that made choosing and flying the correct entry so easy, it would be hard to screw it up even when tired and distracted.

After our third session, the instructor said that, unless I just wanted to spend more money, he couldn't see that he had any more to teach me. That was the confidence booster I needed. My partner finished his ten hours without me.

The captain wasn't happy with the way I put the airplane on the ground. He was afraid I'd touch down on the nosewheel instead of the mains because I rolled the airplane on instead of holding it off and landing with the nose high. I pointed out that when the airplane is sitting on the ground, the nose is nearly a full degree down, so any positive pitch in the air ensured the main gear would touch down first. But, always willing to learn something new, I held the nose higher landing in Cincinnati that night. We finally landed a few thousand feet down the rain-slick runway and used more of what was left to get stopped than I was comfortable with.

The captain flew the next leg. When he landed at Baltimore, he floated forever, too, but I didn't say anything. When I landed next in Philadelphia, I did it my way and easily made the early turnoff that took us straight to our parking spot.

Before I drove to Cincinnati for upgrade class, I told Barb I did not want to hear about any problems while I was away unless the house burned down or there was a death in the family—our immediate family. I rented a studio apartment near the airport with no TV. I wanted no tempting distractions from the only thing in my life that mattered for those few weeks. Instead of coasting through ground school, I tried to pay attention. For relaxation, I rode my bicycle in the Kentucky hills and along the Ohio River.

I remember little of the nearly forty hours in the simulator because it was uneventful. My sim partner had trouble with NDB approaches, and our instructor began to worry. Until he mastered following that ADF needle and turning the correct direction to stay on course, he couldn't advance.

We had a break of several days in the simulator schedule while captain candidates studied for oral exams. Other crewmembers got to go home. Before my training partner left, I made him an ADF simulator out of a beer carton. I drew a compass rose and pinned a strip of cardboard to the center of it. One end of the strip was the head of the needle and, to the other end, I pinned a symbolic cardboard airplane. I showed him how he could pretend he was off course going to the NDB and turn in the direction the arrow was off, and how it was easy to visualize dragging the tail of the needle over to the course when past the station. I told him to play with it at home until understanding and visualization was as ingrained as holding pattern entries had become at STI.

The day before that break was over, our instructor showed me a training aid he'd made. His cardboard ADF simulator was almost identical to the one I'd made. When my partner got back, I told him what our instructor had made for him and suggested he not mention he already had one. Better to let the instructor take credit for his improvement.

I didn't bother to put names of my checkride support crew in my log, and I don't remember who they were. I remember nothing about my checkride because nothing went wrong. All hurdles were behind me except the one I'd tripped over two years earlier.

Three days after my simulator checkride, another new captain and I were in the hotel in Springfield, Massachusetts. We flew the airplane from Windsor Locks to Stewart Field in New York with our instructor, just as I'd done two years before. We took turns flying maneuvers and instrument approaches. The Fed was a man I'd never met. On our checkrides the next day, we flew the same approaches we'd practiced. We passed our rides, but I almost flunked debrief.

I should have listened to the man and said nothing beyond, Yes sir, No sir, and You're absolutely right sir, as he critiqued my performance and offered suggestions. I was accustomed to debriefing as discussion, but my contributions sounded to the Fed like excuses. He became irritated. I got the message and shut up. All that mattered was, I had a type rating in the Boeing 727.

When the other new captain and I walked back out to the airplane with our support crew, I pulled out my little camera and handed it to someone to snap photos, including the one on the cover of this book. I don't remember who took the pictures.

Boeing 727 Captain

It was still possible to be denied the left seat. New captains flew with captains designated as check airmen for several hours of Initial Operating Experience and then received a line check from the FAA.

My first line trip on IOE came after twelve days at home. We flew from Cincinnati through Atlanta to Saint Louis for the weekend in the only 727 in our fleet that did not have a toilet. It had a Port-a-Potty in the entryway between cockpit door and cargo bay, much to the disgust of everyone. Female crew members, when they knew they'd be flying that airplane, avoided drinking anything before or during flight, especially coffee.

After simmering in midsummer sun, the foul soup in the little toilet stank unbearably. My IOE captain wrote it up in the log and called Maintenance Control to have it emptied and refilled with blue water. Maintenance was peeved that we'd take a delay over the toilet, but they didn't have to fly with the damn thing. Mechanics finished cleaning and replacing the toilet before late loading was finished, so loaders took blame.

Steering the airplane on the ground was the only completely new part of switching seats. Our 727s had a nosewheel steering tiller only on the captain's side in the sidewall next to his left knee. It is an arc of a steering wheel, about a third of a circle the size of a dessert plate. Rudder pedals controlled nosewheel steering with limited range and authority and worked fine for maintaining direction on the runway. The tiller had positive hydraulic control of the nosewheel, and handling it smoothly took practice.

I slept only five hours in Sacramento, then turned on CNN long enough to get an update on Hurricane Erin. The storm would hit Florida the next morning at about the same time we were scheduled to arrive. But we didn't go to Miami. The company wanted a fresh crew on that trip in case of delays, so we flew to New York instead.

The next day, we flew the Orlando-Miami trip we'd been pulled off of the day before. I spent my couple of hours in Cincinnati reviewing things in our operations manual that my IOE captain thought the Fed might ask me. An examiner from the FAA office in Louisville rode with us to Orlando and didn't ask anything I'd reviewed. We had a good airplane, one that flew straight and had no non-standard instruments or switch locations. The flight to Orlando was one I was thoroughly familiar with, but I'd stumbled over simple things before.

When we reached cruise altitude, the Fed asked, "Which engine instruments were in the yellow arc on takeoff?"

I'd been looking out the window and down the runway and had no idea, but it was a hot night, and I knew exhaust temperatures would have been high, so I guessed EGTs. Then the Fed asked which ones, and I didn't know. One and three were close to redline, he said, but his asking wasn't an oral exam. He said, "Wake me up when we land."

In spite of gusty crosswind, or perhaps because of it, I flew a good approach and landing, and, after a foot-tap warning on the rudder pedals to slow my taxi speed, I turned smoothly into our parking spot and set the brake. Finally, a month short of my fifty-third birthday, I'd reached the pinnacle of my late-entered career twenty-one years after deciding to learn to fly.

The check airman could have signed me off, but he wanted to fly out the last of our scheduled trips together as he was drawing check airman pay and overtime.

Our landing in Denver was my first arrival at the new airport miles northeast of the city. The cargo ramp, apparently an afterthought in the airport's design, had a long, steep, downgrade in and an equally steep uphill climb to get out. There was only one way in and out for all airplanes using the ramp, and one short section was like a one-lane bridge on a two-lane highway.

I flew my first unsupervised trip as captain to Los Angeles. We parked in front of the old terminal building where the final scene in *Casablanca* was filmed, where midgets scurried around the model of a C-47 getting it ready to fly Ingrid Bergman away from Humphrey Bogart forever. Our maintenance office and parts stores were in that old terminal. The building housing DHL's sort facility and gateway offices wasn't there when the movie was made.

I thought the most difficult and delicate part of my new job would be finding the proper line between running the show and allowing other crew members to use their own judgment. On my first flight in the left seat as the non-flying pilot, I'd told the first officer before we took off that, when it was his leg, it was his airplane, just as though he was the captain.

I soon expanded my briefing and said to first officers flying with me for the first time, "When it's your leg, it's your airplane. You've had the same training I've had, and if you don't get in the habit of thinking and making decisions, you'll have a hard time in upgrade. So, unless you make me late or try to kill me or do something so stupid I can't stand it, decisions are yours."

I included the second officer in that briefing. "When it's the FO's leg and you have a question about how high or how fast we want to go, ask him, not me."

Then I added, "The only thing you guys don't get to do on your own is change temperature in here. I don't like it hot, and I swore that, when I made captain, I'd never be roasted out of a cockpit again. If you want more heat, ask me. Maybe I'll say yes, but don't count on it."

I always wore thick white socks under my thin, black uniform socks. When crewmembers complained of cold feet, I asked how many pairs of socks they had on. The answer was always One.

On a flight several years later, I had jumpseaters and a green first officer who had apparently been flying exclusively with control freaks. After telling her to stop asking me every little thing, to simply fly the airplane the way the company had taught her to, one of the jumpseaters, also a woman, chimed in and said most captains didn't expect the first officer to act as captain when flying. She said people appreciated the way I treated them.

I'd jumpseated a few times with captains who dictated every move their first officers made, so I knew those guys were out there, but I didn't realize how many. I'd not run into that sort of micro-management as a junior crewmember—except with The Skipper—perhaps because I was older than most of the captains I flew with and was not female.

Training never ends. I was assigned our scheduled day charter from New York to Santo Domingo for overwater training. I wasn't planning on flying over oceans, so I hadn't bothered to read the sheaf of papers explaining how our Omega navigation system worked. I studied the instructions before deadheading to New York.

A factory in the Dominican Republic was idle, waiting for whatever was on our airplane, and the company whose cargo we carried wanted us to leave early.

The scheduled captain supervised from the jump seat. Weather along the route that day was the worst the regular crew had seen all year. We spent more time off course than on, finding paths between cumulonimbus clouds that didn't show on radar unless we pointed the antenna down. Either the radar was screwed up, or all the water in those fast-building clouds was in the bottoms.

In spite of the request that we leave New York early, there was no urgency in unloading us. The supervising captain slept in his jumpseat. I listened to Spanish music on the ADF receiver. No one was in a hurry to load us for the return, either. When we realized we weren't going anywhere soon, the rest of the crew walked across the ramp to the terminal building. I stayed in the airplane to make sure nothing walked away.

The first officer flew the return leg while I played navigator and made required position reports to Oceanic controllers. By the time we got back to New York, I'd pretty well learned the routine, but I'd not have wanted to try it without an experienced crew.

I had the next day free before deadheading from New York back to Cincinnati and flying to Newark for the weekend. Crew Scheduling called to say I'd been switched from Newark to Mexico City for the weekend because there'd been a lot of sick calls and I was the only one available and legal to fly that far without time problems. I protested that I wasn't prepared for a weekend out of country and had adjusted my sleep times for my scheduled short trip. I got out my copy of the contract and reviewed the section that allowed the company to switch pilots around when necessary in inverse seniority order.

I called Crew Scheduling back, apologized for being gruff earlier, and asked if I understood correctly that I was the most junior captain available who could legally take the Mexico City trip. The scheduler said I was.

I'd hoped to finish my flying career without ever going to Mexico City. I didn't like flying where English wasn't the first language of other pilots and controllers, didn't want to deal with that high-altitude airport, and I didn't want to have to breathe the infamously foul air. And there was a new component in my desire to get out of that trip. Pilots knew I'd managed to avoid it and were eager to see my record fall.

After studying charts and approach plates and several pages in the manual concerning paperwork and other requirements for the international trip, I walked to Rockville Centre for dinner at a Mexican restaurant, certain that, unless my ride to Cincinnati broke down during the stop in Detroit, I was doomed. I realized I was being a butt about the assignment, knew I should relax and enjoy it, but, dammit, I didn't want to go to Mexico City.

In Cincinnati, I checked the sign-in sheet. A reserve captain junior to me had been assigned the Los Angeles trip, and if he had enough time for that, he had enough time for Mexico City. The scheduler had assumed he was senior because he'd been a captain for three years. I expected her to tell me I was out of luck, but she checked the seniority list and said, "You're right. I'll change it."

I was amazed. Mexico trips were usually unchangeable late in the game because crew names had already been sent to Customs.

Crew Scheduling had called the reserve captain that morning to tell him he was going to Los Angeles. That was fine with him because he lived there. When he arrived in Cincinnati and learned he was going to Mexico City, he was not pleased. He told me he thought he'd been screwed. I couldn't disagree. He wanted me to go with him to talk to the scheduler and get our trips swapped back. I argued that I had not asked that our trips be changed, that I'd merely pointed out that I was senior.

I was stalling to be sure crew names had been sent to Customs. Then I remembered that the man had gotten me on a flight out of Denver when jumpseats were taken because he knew the captain. I owed him a favor. I relented a little and said that who should go where should depend on who had been assigned first.

We went upstairs to talk to the scheduler. There had been a jumble of reassignments that morning. Jim had been assigned to Los Angeles only because the scheduler had made a mistake in thinking him senior to me. She said the error was hers, that she'd corrected it, and it was too late to change the paperwork back anyway.

He still felt shafted, as I would have in his place. I was thirty-four numbers down the captain's list and could not always get lines I wanted, but I was senior enough to avoid Mexico City.

Our weekday hotel in Guadalajara was the Holiday Inn on the airport next to the parking lot where a priest was shot down a year or so earlier. I went to sleep hungry and slept five hours. We met for dinner in the hotel restaurant.

Some tourists and pilots avoid eating salad in Mexico out of fear that water lettuce was rinsed in would make then sick. I ate salad and stayed healthy. Worrying about such things was more stressful than an occasional alien microbe, I reasoned, forgetting how miserable I'd been when bugs in water attacked my guts on a vacation in Dominica ten years earlier. Maybe that illness had given me immunity to such waterborne invaders.

Outbound flights began with the digit 4 and inbounds with 1. Second and third digits were the same both directions. Flight number to Boston was 449. The Newark trip was 445, and the two airplanes were in the same controllers' sectors at the same time. On the radio, 449 and 445 sound alike, and the two crews continually responded to each other's call signs. One of the better-humored en route controllers sometimes dropped the numbers and called us, "The DHL out of Boston" and "The DHL out of Newark."

With DHL 445 right behind us, we all listened carefully as we climbed out of Cincinnati on our way to Boston. We were kept at twelve thousand feet longer than usual. When I heard an airplane behind us cleared to climb, I asked Departure for higher. The controller snapped that he'd cleared us higher three times and to pay attention. None of us had heard a clearance for our flight number, but I refrained from lipping off. Then, when he neglected to give us an expected turn to join the published departure course, I kept my mouth shut. By the time ATC got us sorted out, we'd cut many miles and minutes off our usual dogleg.

When we got back to Cincinnati, I asked the crew of the Newark flight if they had heard us cleared out of twelve thousand the night before. They hadn't.

We were hijacked in Sacramento one November evening, not our airplane but our limo. All three of us were standing outside the hotel waiting for our ride to the airport. The car wasn't there. A clerk came out of the hotel and said the limo company was on the phone and wanted to talk to one of us. I followed him inside and took the call. It wasn't our limo service, and, no, there weren't any other pilots waiting.

If our ride didn't come soon, we'd be late getting off the ground. I was wondering who would get the blame for the delay when the clerk came out again and said our limo service had called to say our ride would be here soon.

Our driver told us the story as she drove fast to the airport. She had been on the job only a few days, and she was not the one who'd driven us to the hotel that morning. She'd pulled up to the hotel ten minutes early and was surprised to see two pilots already waiting.

The driver asked the pilots if they were DHL. They said they were and climbed in. On the way to the airport, she asked why they were only two instead of the three she'd expected. The captain mumbled an answer she didn't quite hear. Our driver didn't know she'd been had until she pulled up to the security gate at the DHL ramp.

"Where's our airplane?" the captain asked her.

"Right there," she said.

"That's not ours. Ours is on the other side of the airport. At FedEx."

The driver yelled at them for lying. They said it must have been a misunderstanding. The story would be better if she'd returned them to the hotel, but all she could think of was losing her job. She took them to FedEx and radioed her dispatcher.

I was slow to put all the pieces together. The FedEx ride was late, and when ours pulled up, the resourceful captain took it. It was a neat trick, something I might have done myself in the same situation, if only I thought faster.

I said, "I hope those other guys tipped generously."

"They didn't tip at all," she said.

To combat dry air in hotels, I ran the shower full hot until the bathtub filled. Exhaust fans in most hotel bathrooms were in series with the light switch, and the fans defeated my purpose.

When exhaust fans weren't hardwired but merely plugged in like a lamp, all I had to do was unscrew the grille and pull the plug. Sometimes, I'd return to those rooms weeks or months later to discover no one had complained and the fans were still unplugged.

Bathroom fans in our Boston hotel couldn't be disconnected. For a weekend stay, I unscrewed the grille from the ceiling and refastened it with a folded towel inside to block air flow, but I always removed that sort of modification before leaving. I stood on the toilet seat one Monday evening to screw the grille back to the ceiling after removing the towel. I was off balance and leaning a little on the shower curtain rod when it fell. My feet and the toilet seat flew out from under me and I went down backwards into the tub, thinking as I fell that people get killed that way.

I tucked my chin into my chest and landed on my butt and back. Neither my head nor the tub suffered, and bruises remained tender for only a week. I stood on a chair, refastened the fan grille, reinstalled the curtain rod, snapped the toilet seat back into place, and made it to the lobby on time.

It's traditional for pilots to spend money as soon as they make captain. I ordered a new truck, a four-wheel-drive diesel. Because of options I wanted, I'd have to wait six months for it.

Barb and I had been walking on temporary carpet for nearly three years while bundles of maple sat in the loft. In February 1996, I spent a week nailing down flooring. By Tuesday morning, I'd finished all but the last couple of rows next to walls where there was no room to use the rented nailing jig.

We broke out of clouds as we intercepted the localizer for Runway 17R at Denver and saw one airplane climbing toward us and another on the same runway waiting to take off. My first officer thought we'd lined up for the wrong runway. We rechecked the localizer frequency and called the tower. The controller said to continue and expect landing clearance on short final, that there'd be one more Lear departure off 35L with a quick right turn. I slowed down to avoid conflict with the head-on traffic. We were landing at a brand new airport with a gazillion runways, and they were using one piece of concrete for takeoffs and landings in opposite directions. We lost several minutes sitting on the entryway to the cargo ramp waiting for a dozen little airplanes to come out through the one-lane choke point.

I ate dinner with my second officer. He and other new hires were wondering if they were at the right airline for a career. I didn't know what to tell him. I was optimistic, but I always am. I didn't know how I'd have felt if I'd been thirty years younger.

The day after I got home, I worked on shaping and nailing in the last few pieces of flooring until I ran my hand through the table saw.

Three small pieces of maple had to be undercut to overlap carpet in a bedroom doorway. My mind wandered ahead to the next step, and the whirling blade snatched a piece of hardwood out of my left hand and my fingers followed it across the saw. The circular blade extended up through the table only a quarter of an inch, and my fingers, being thicker than that, stayed on.

There was no pain at first. I found it interesting that my hand had been snatched through the teeth so fast that the parallel cuts on two fingers looked like shark gills. Ring finger and little finger had only minor cuts. As the doctor looked my hand over, my mind was working a couple of days ahead, pushing back renting a floor sander to the first of the week, trying to figure out if I could finish the job before I had to go back to work.

I got no stitches, as it would have been like sewing up hamburger. The doctor said I could forget about going back to work or doing anything else with that hand for a few weeks, and my fingers would be tender for a couple of years. Time would tell how much nerves had suffered. With that bit of news, it finally sank in that I'd done more than cut myself. Finishing the floor would have to wait. The only good thing was, I had material for the next week's newspaper column.

I could have milked disability insurance for several weeks, but I wanted to go back to work when sick leave ran out so I wouldn't have to fill out insurance paperwork. Once fingers began to heal, the only thing keeping me from returning to work was inability to grip the steering tiller. I knew I was going to get tired of reading and one-handed typing, so I reinstalled Minesweeper in my computer.

By the time I went back to work in March, I'd been off six weeks. On the jumpseat to Cincinnati, I watched the captain to see if he had to do anything with his left hand that I hadn't thought of. I could grasp with my thumb and two smallest fingers, but my tender index and middle fingers were bandaged in aluminum splints.

Because I'd be flying back to Seattle, I left everything but a book and Thermos in my truck when I rode to Cincinnati. I woke up as we descended over Indiana and looked at the landing data card perched on the console. With hundred-foot ceiling and quarter-mile visibility, the crew discussed their alternate. If we had to go to Detroit and wait for better weather, I'd miss my trip to Seattle and be reassigned to a later-leaving trip. I resolved to never again leave my toothbrush where I thought I was going to be. Weather improved, we landed, and I forgot about my new resolution. I spent all my time on the ground catching up on memos and manual revisions.

I discovered I couldn't reach into my flight bag next to my seat to pull out manuals. I had to raise the left armrest and reach across with my right hand. I didn't fly until my fingers healed, but my first officers did not object.

Fingers improved. I cut firewood and began typing with both hands again. The trip to Miami at the end of March was the first time I'd taken my turn flying the airplane since January.

I got brave enough to finish undercutting the last three pieces of hardwood flooring and nail them in. While at home that week, I oiled and rode both of my bicycles, trying to decide which one to take to Boston and keep in the hotel there. I rode my bike many miles that spring and summer, to Lexington and Concord, to Walden Pond, and along the Charles River. My weight began to edge down.

I insisted on listening in when the first officer called for our clearance. A mistake in hearing or copying could cause us to screw up a heading or an altitude, and the captain was responsible. If I was going to catch hell for an error, I wanted it to be my error.

We were loaded early for a change and were trying to get out of Seattle early. I told the first officer I'd get the clearance while he was calculating weight and balance. I wrote down the clearance on a note pad. Soon after takeoff, I remembered I needed to write the clearance on the flight plan for records, so I copied it from my note. A little later, the first officer questioned our heading. He said that wasn't what the clearance said.

I looked at what I'd written on his clipboard and then at my note pad. I'd misread my scrawl. My first officer smiled and said, "And you're the one who wants both of us to get the clearance."

The flight from Boston was one of the first airplanes to land in Cincinnati each night, so if someone needed to go somewhere because an airplane was broken, the Boston crew was often tagged for the rescue. We were on the ground only long enough to unload and refuel. Our dispatcher said he'd bring flight plans and weather out to us. I told him we needed food, too, and he asked why. I said it had been six hours since we'd eaten and it would be four more before we got back from Kansas City. He brought sandwiches from the cafeteria with our paperwork.

It was too late for us to go anywhere when we got back to Cincinnati, but it was our last day, so Crew Scheduling released us. I rode United to Chicago and Seattle. After I drove home, I'd had less than three hours sleep in the previous forty and was too tired and wired to take a nap. I fell asleep walking down the stairs.

I'd poured bourbon over ice, walked upstairs for something, and on the way back down, I thought I was at the bottom before I got there and stepped out into space. I crashed in a heap on the landing with not even a bruise to show for it. My barely tasted drink was all over the wall, but the glass didn't break, and bourbon is the same color as cedar.

Most pilots I flew with and rode with lined up on the centerline stripe for takeoff. That put one of the nosewheel tires in line with all the recessed centerline lights next to the painted line, and the bump-bump-bump during takeoff roll drove me nuts. I got pretty good at keeping the line of lights between the nosewheel tires. I told my first officers they didn't get extra points for hitting all the lights. Some of them took the hint.

One evening, my first officer mentioned his difficulty in landing the -200 smoothly. I explained my mental movie to him, told him to pretend the cockpit is a hovercraft or a lunar lander with only one landing gear. I promised him that if he just set the nosewheel down gently, the rest of the airplane would take care of itself. He did and it did.

A first officer in the training department flew the trip to Phoenix and Los Angeles. In the van to the hotel, he got started talking politics and became irrational. He was incapable of listening to the second officer and me trying to calm him. There were no other passengers, so we stopped trying. He kept ranting, even as we checked in at the hotel, even as we walked down a corridor to our rooms. I couldn't persuade him to think of guests still sleeping and lower his voice.

I considered calling Cincinnati and having him removed from flight duty for psychological evaluation, but I decided that would be an extreme response to what was, so far, an isolated incident. Fatigue brought out the worst in all of us.

That evening at dinner, I informed my crew we would not talk politics then or on the return flight. The first officer apologized for his behavior that morning. Even his apology was intense. I couldn't remember knowing anyone as high strung as he seemed to be, but there was no trouble from him on the return trip. A few years later, he killed himself.

Our assigned landing runway had a slight tailwind at the surface, but wind was strong at the initial approach altitude. The first officer was flying. All three of us were assessing wind and discussing expected shear. We were so focused on wind, I forgot to call Cincinnati tower and we landed without a clearance. We didn't realize the omission until we'd cleared the runway and the first officer keyed his mike to ask if we should change to Ground. "DHL 149, you're still with Approach."

I asked a couple of other captains how they avoided forgetting to call the tower. I adopted their technique and turned on the taxi light on the nosewheel strut only after we'd received landing clearance instead of flipping that switch the moment the gear went down. If that switch was off, it meant we hadn't received our landing clearance yet.

A few months later, Approach Control cleared us for a visual approach but didn't tell us to contact Tower. We were preoccupied with the autopilot's failure to intercept the localizer and didn't notice the omission. When he finished reading the Before Landing checklist, the second officer added, "Cleared to land." I then turned on the taxi light, thinking I'd forgotten to do it when we received landing clearance.

When we'd cleared the runway and the first officer switched frequencies, Ground said, "DHL 1742, cleared to land. Taxi to the ramp."

I asked the second officer what had given him the impression we'd been cleared to land. He said he always turned the galley power switches on (in our airplanes, those switches did nothing) when we got landing clearance as a reminder in the same way I used the taxi light. He'd glanced at his switches when he reached the end of the checklist and they were in his cleared-to-land position, so he added confirmation to the checklist as many second officers did.

While we were discussing that, I taxied past our turnoff to the parking ramp and had to come in from the other end. No harm done, although we confused the marshalers. It illustrated why non-essential talk was prohibited when the airplane was below ten thousand feet, including while moving on the ground.

After years of pilots' complaints, Crew Scheduling changed the start time for booking jumpseats from early morning to early evening. Everyone was on the ground then and had a fair chance at reserving seats. The new time hadn't worn a groove in my brain yet, and I was too late calling for a seat home. I put myself on standby. A lot could happen in thirty days.

We got out of Boston more than an hour late. DHL's scales broke, and all our cans had to be weighed at the other end of the airport. In Cincinnati, the union held an informational meeting comparing Airborne and FedEx contracts to ours. I needed sleep more than information, so I didn't go.

Miami was landing to the east, so our approach was from over the Everglades. We all tried to find the hole in the swamp that ValuJet crash had made three weeks earlier, but controllers kept us in tight and we didn't fly over the scene.

Anytime I had to ask myself before starting down whether I'd need to pee before we parked, the answer was Yes. I violated the rule one foggy morning going to New York. I didn't really need to go, and we'd be on the ground soon.

Fog rolled in and we had to hold with everyone else while controllers changed to a runway with better visibility. By the time everyone was sorted out, fog shifted and the airport had to switch runways again.

The airplane was one of three we had with antique flight directors that did not have controls on the first officer's side. The autopilot heading mode was also only on my side. With dense traffic and frequent heading changes, I didn't want to leave my seat, as the first officer would have had to fly the airplane by hand and handle communications and make decisions. I regretted not having peed before we began descent. It's difficult to land an airplane with your legs crossed, even if crossed only mentally.

We were scheduled to go through Detroit on the return from New York. Any more weather delays might eat enough time that I couldn't fly my scheduled trip to Phoenix and Los Angeles.

When we got to JFK that evening, our airplane wasn't there. It was inbound from Haiti with a load of mangoes, and fog was so dense, it took the crew forty minutes to taxi in. Even so, we blocked out six minutes early, but we were about number fifty for takeoff. We listened to almost an entire basketball game on the ADF as we poked along on taxiways wasting fuel. That put us just far enough behind schedule that we didn't have to go to Detroit.

Wind was negligible in Cincinnati. Runway 27 would have been quickest for us, but it required flying low over residential areas. Landing from the west was mostly over forest, so Runway 9 was preferred for noise abatement.

The first officer, whom I'll call Bryce, heard Tower clear a light airplane to land on 27 and asked if I wanted it.

"Yes, but only if it's offered. Don't ask for it."

"Why not?"

"Because"—you idiot—"nine is the noise abatement runway for turbojets and if we don't accept nine, I'll have to explain why."

But the controller offered 27. The change in plan required a steep descent, so I pulled the speedbrake, slowed, and called for landing gear down. Bryce said, "Airspeed two-seventy." That was the upper limit for gear extension. I ordered him to put the gear down and he did. I asked what the problem was. Noise level was high with gear down at high speed and I didn't understand his reply.

After the brake was set and checklists completed, I asked again what he'd said that I hadn't heard completely. He replied that he'd called Airspeed because we were still fast and going through ten thousand feet.

After he left the cockpit, I asked the second officer. He said Bryce had called Airspeed before putting the gear down when we were well above ten thousand, and his amended explanation was covering his error in thinking we were going too fast for gear extension.

I don't know why some people can't simply admit a minor mistake.

I'd spent most of the weekend riding my bicycle around Boston and its suburbs, and, on Monday, I ended the afternoon's ride in Back Bay. After dinner, time was tight as I started my long ride to the hotel. It was almost dark when I ran over a nail. I couldn't remember the last time I'd had a flat tire. I repaired the obvious hole in the tube and tried to pump it up. I took the tube out again and found two more holes opposite the one where the nail went in.

Time was short, and I could not make myself wait for cement to set up before sticking a large patch over the other two holes. The patch came loose immediately.

I pushed the bike to a coffee shop to call a taxi and call the hotel to have them tell my crew I was running late.

Minutes ticked by and anxiety rose. The feeling was the same as in occasional dreams in which obstacles prevented me from getting to work on time. I had never been the cause of a delayed departure, at least not officially. The cab finally arrived and I had to remove the rear wheel to fit the bike into the trunk.

I knew the area around Chelsea better than the cab driver did, and I realized he wanted to get on the highway, a route that would have taken too much time. I insisted he follow my directions through residential streets, and he did. I tipped him generously.

My arms and hands were black. Tire-changing grime smeared my face. I showered, dressed, and packed in less than twenty minutes and put my crippled bike in the bus with our bags.

The driver had to drop off passengers at the terminal on the way, and it was almost departure time when we arrived at our building. Paperwork wasn't there because the fax machine had jammed and nobody noticed. We got out nine minutes late. The fax machine took the blame.

The truck I'd ordered in December arrived in July. Driving the big Dodge was not unlike transitioning from a small airplane to a large one. I had to think about where the unseen bumpers were in relation to other vehicles and fixed objects. After years in a little truck, using cruise control was the only way I could keep speed down for the first few months.

After sleeping a few hours on my next weekday Seattle layover, I went out to drive my new truck around. I spotted a slide-in camper on a trailer lot near Tacoma. It was exactly the make and model I wanted, a trade-in only a year old.

On descent into Miami, we all heard descent clearance to four thousand feet and I read back four thousand. The first officer pulled the speedbrake and we descended fast. As we went through six thousand, the controller said our assigned altitude was ten. He told us to maintain six and traffic was a 757 at three o'clock just above us.

I told him we'd heard four thousand, read back four, and were climbing back to six with traffic in sight.

We had trouble regaining the few hundred feet to get us back to six thousand. I glanced at the console and saw that the speedbrake was still deployed. It was an error many of us made sometimes, the same error an American 757 crew had made while trying to clear a ridge near Cali, Columbia. It amazed me that Boeing hadn't installed some kind of interlock between throttles and speedbrake to prevent what amounts to pushing the accelerator and the brake pedal at the same time while going uphill.

The approach controller didn't sound angry, and I favored letting the incident slide, but my crew wanted us to call the tower on the phone and to file NASA reports. NASA reports were an avenue for pilots to report their mistakes and thereby gain immunity from penalty, if reports were filed before the complaint was. After we parked, I phoned the control tower.

The supervisor had listened to the tape. He said we were assigned ten, but that I'd read back four and the controller didn't catch my error. That made it his error. The supervisor said it appeared we had traffic in sight "before we lost the three-mile separation" and that the 757 had us in sight, so there was no separation violation.

That airplane was one of a few new to our fleet that had the kind of radio panel that did not allow separate volume control at each crew station. The second officer could barely hear the radio, and it's his job to be a third ear backing up the pilots. If he could have heard better, he might have caught my read-back error, if it was an error.

When I wrote my incident report for the company, I stressed danger caused by that radio panel. Safety was a hook that got things done.

My first trip after a short vacation was to Boston, and I planned to go home from there for the weekend. Dispatch told us we'd be coming right back to Cincinnati to get the airplane out of New England before Hurricane Bertha got there. I was glad I'd slept three hours on the ride to work.

The New York and Newark airplanes returned, too. The one in Windsor Locks stayed there because the airplane got so full of rain during its stop in Philadelphia that some instruments stopped working.

We wanted to return to Boston early enough Sunday to get there before restaurants closed, but leaving Cincinnati in the afternoon would have made our trip east a daytime flight, and our contract required sixteen hours of rest between day and night flying. We taxied out in late evening as a squall line moved in from the southwest. We were number seven for takeoff. All airplanes ahead of us were going the same direction, and ATC wanted twenty miles of separation. We watched the mass of clouds roll in as we waited.

When the Lear ahead of us took the runway and we made the right turn to hold short, our airplane and radar were pointed at a wall of solid red on the screen. The Lear's captain declined to take off and taxied clear. We took the runway just as the tower began broadcasting wind-shear alerts.

Ordinarily, I would have refused to take off under those conditions, but the first officer was flying the leg, and he had far more experience flying large jets than I had. He said we could do it if we got an immediate right turn. We were empty and had plenty of reserve power.

I didn't think to ask the second officer what he thought, but he heard our discussion and didn't say anything. Departure was uneventful, aside from large airspeed fluctuations on the takeoff roll.

When we reached cruising altitude, I apologized to the second officer for not asking his opinion before takeoff. He said not to worry, that he'd have said something if he had any objections.

I flew to Raleigh, North Carolina, late one Saturday morning in September right after the eye of Hurricane Fran had passed over the airport. Our hotel was flooded and closed. The first few hotels we called said their computers were down and they didn't know if they had vacant rooms. I called the weekend crew scheduler at her home and explained our plight. She authorized a rental car and whatever accommodations we could get.

The second officer lived in Raleigh and drove home, though power was out at his house. The first officer hopped a ride to Cincinnati, and I rode a shuttle bus to Alamo to pick up a car. If I'd been thinking, I'd have gotten a mini-van to carry my bike.

I called every hotel in the yellow pages. Half didn't answer. The other half had no rooms because locals had moved in from powerless homes. The last listing was William Thomas House. The bed and breakfast had a cancellation, but I'd have to check out before noon Monday.

I stuffed my bike in the trunk and tied the lid down with a scrap of string I found on the ground. Carefully copied directions did me no good because so many streets were closed. I used the free map from Alamo.

I drove to Durham the next day, my first time there since 1949. Oak Grove School, where I'd attended first grade, had been replaced with a new building a few years earlier. One house we'd lived in was gone, displaced by a highway. The other was still there, and renters let me wander around and revive memories.

My first trip when I went back to work after a hunting season vacation in November was to Houston and Guadalajara. I boiled tap water with my new immersion coil to make oatmeal and went to bed for the day. When I got up, I boiled water for coffee before going down to dinner. While I was putting on clothes, I put the coil in a coffee mug of water with my contact lens case to boil it clean, just in case Mexican tap water had bugs in it.

I mentioned to my crew during dinner that I'd destroyed my first immersion coil years earlier when water boiled away and the coil burned out. After dinner, when I got back to my room, my new coil had boiled the water away, melted my lens case, and burned itself out. I gave up on immersion coils.

Our Hotel Committee persuaded the company to change hotels when complaints warranted. Noisy locations, uncomfortable rooms, and lack of nearby restaurants and other amenities were all valid considerations. Every time we moved to a new hotel, it took some time to break the staff in to our schedules and routines.

I went home for the weekend after checking in at our new hotel in Chicago and drove to Seattle Sunday evening to return. The United agent wasn't at the gate yet, so I set my license and ID on the counter and sat down to wait. When the agent appeared, people got up to get in line. I was right behind a young blonde pilot in uniform. We exchanged a few words and the agent, who hadn't yet gotten set up to process passengers, held up my ID and called me to the head of the line to fill out a jumpseat form. I hadn't seen any pilots around, other than the one in line, so I assumed we would both get on.

When the other pilot saw the agent hand me my pass, she picked up her bag and hurried away, probably to try for an American flight leaving at about the same time. I was puzzled for a moment until I looked out at the airplane. It was a 757 with one jumpseat. If I'd realized that, I'd have asked her how tight she was on time, as I was flexible for once.

I didn't catch the captain's name when I stepped into the cockpit to request permission to ride, but I knew the first officer from his delightfully opinionated posts on the ALPA National online forum.

My seat in coach was between a skinhead with rings and studs in ears and face and a nerdy young man with one cheek swollen to the size of a softball. I stayed awake and read a book. The pilots left the airplane before I had a chance to thank them for the ride.

On the ALPA forum, I wrote a note to the first officer asking him to convey my thanks to his captain. He replied with a private email saying the captain was a scab, so he wouldn't be talking to him at all.

United had hired strikebreakers a decade earlier, and many union pilots still shunned scabs as completely as working side by side allowed.

A pilot at Pearson Air in the late 1970s had been an active union man at his previous airline. He flew for Pearson for a short time after being furloughed. I ran into him in the terminal in Seattle not long after the United strike and was amazed to see him in United Airlines uniform. I asked why he had crossed the line. He said, "I needed a job and United was hiring."

I asked if it was as bad between union men and new-hires—I couldn't bring myself to say "scab" to his face—as stories I'd heard indicated.

He looked away and said it was, that he had to frequently check his back in mirrors for gobs of spit, things like that.

My dinner companion was perhaps too smart to fly airplanes. Too much thinking prevented quick action. The man I'll call Sidney became wrapped up in detail and couldn't see the big picture. He almost failed training for second officer in the 727 after DHL sold the Metroliners. I liked him but I'd never flown with him before he upgraded to right seat. I tried to avoid letting negative things I'd heard influence my evaluation of him. That first trip, I saw nothing wrong with his flying, though I chastised both him and the second officer for letting me get twenty knots over the low-altitude speed limit going into Atlanta. The second officer had been busy with his work and hadn't noticed. Sidney said captains jumped on him for calling such things, and he'd become reluctant to do so.

I told him that if it's something our book says to call, he should call it, unless the flying pilot was already correcting or if the deviation was so small it didn't matter. But if speed was too fast and increasing, that demanded a corrective call.

Sidney said one captain would not let him fly, but he wouldn't tell me the man's name. I wanted to know so I could gently pump that captain for information about his relationship with Sidney to see if perhaps the problem was skin color. On the first trip the next week, I began to understand the problem: Sidney had brains but no sense.

We were sitting in the airplane in Cincinnati getting ready to fly. I asked Sidney if he'd deselected stations three and five on the Omega. He hadn't gotten to that yet. He was busy and I wasn't, and it was one of the few things I knew how to do with what was, to us, a new navigation system. I said I'd do it for him, but he watched and took issue with one step I made in the procedure. I was certain I'd done it the way we'd been taught.

I looked it up and showed the manual to Sidney. He whipped out a copy of an Eastern Airlines procedure that contradicted the way DHL did it.

I suggested he throw away the Eastern shit and use our books. After all, Eastern was gone and we were not, so our information must be right. Sidney merely noted the difference amid the many notes he'd made on that worn piece of paper.

All seemed normal on a visual approach at Phoenix when, at five hundred feet above the ground, Sidney said, "Airspeed."

That startled me, and I almost added thrust before sizing up the situation. Speed was good, and a quick check of Sidney's airspeed indicator showed no discrepancy between them. I said, "I show three knots above approach. What's wrong?"

Sidney mumbled, "Okay, you don't want me to call it."

"No, Sidney. I want to know what *made* you call it."

But we were landing, and it was not a time for discussion. When we were parked and the second officer had left the cockpit to open the cargo door, I asked again why he made the airspeed call.

Again he said he wouldn't call it if I didn't want him to.

"No, goddammit, Sidney, I want to know what you saw that I didn't see that prompted you to make that call!"

It turned out that the book said that, on visual approaches, the airplane should be stabilized and on approach speed at five hundred feet above the ground. I was still a hair above the allowed five knots over approach speed at five hundred feet, but speed was still decreasing toward the target. It was a real nothing as such things go.

By the book, Sidney was right. No, not right—he was correct. I told him to use some judgment. "If speed has been decreasing throughout the approach and is that close to the proper speed at five hundred feet, don't scare the flying pilot by calling 'Airspeed' even if it's technically correct. Call gross errors, or minor errors that are trending in the wrong direction, but use some sense."

As we descended into clouds on approach to New York a couple of days later, I began banking into a turn and leaned over to look at the true air temperature gauge on Sidney's side of the panel to see if we needed engine anti-ice. I should have asked Sidney what it said, and because I'd taken my eyes off my instrument panel, I banked too much and Sidney called it. It was the first legitimate call I could remember him making, and when we got on the ground, I told him that was the sort of thing he should call.

The departure procedure off of JFK's Runway 31L began with an immediate left turn while climbing to five thousand feet. Sidney took off, turned left, and leveled off in the turn while accelerating to twenty knots above climb speed. Because of the G-load in the turn, the vertical speed indicator showed we were climbing, and I wondered if Sidney had focused on that instrument and hadn't realized he'd leveled off. I planned to ask him about it in private when we got to Cincinnati, but I didn't get a chance to, and that was a good thing.

We flew to Orlando a couple of hours later in a different airplane with a different ADI. The little lines in the instrument indicating how many degrees the nose is pitched up were in a different configuration from the airplane we'd just flown. Right after takeoff, as I began to lower the nose to nine degrees for climb, we hit some turbulence in a heavy rain shower. The airspeed needle was bouncing around so I ignored it and held nine degrees nose-up pitch. Sidney called, "Descending," and we were. I pitched up a few degrees more and resumed climbing.

While bouncing around in the transition from takeoff to climb, I'd lowered the nose to what would have been nine degrees in the previous airplane but was only four degrees nose up in the one we were flying. The result of my error was almost identical to what Sidney had done coming out of New York.

* * *

I drove to Seattle the last Sunday evening in 1996 to find a ride to Newark after spending the weekend layover at home. The first flight going my way was a United to Chicago.

The flight from Chicago to Newark was crowded. A few seats were open in back, but I rode in the cockpit. People aren't at their best in the early morning, especially on a Monday, and passengers were arguing with each other and with flight attendants over carryon luggage space.

The captain was about my age but short and fat. He would have made a classic Santa with eyes half hidden above chubby red cheeks. His first officer was several years younger. The captain pushed up the power and our takeoff roll began. The first officer followed the levers with his left hand to trim power precisely after the captain had set it.

"Don't touch my hand!" the captain yelled. "Goddammit, Ed, I told you that yesterday!"

As we sped down the runway, the captain continued, "I'm sorry, Ed, but that is extremely disconcerting when you touch my hand on takeoff," and more in that vein as we climbed. It was hard to refrain from laughing. Poor Ed must have felt like hell, getting yelled at in front of a jumpseater. I did not speak unless spoken to throughout the flight to Newark.

When we blocked in, the captain grabbed his hat and jacket and zipped back to the exit door to personally see each passenger ashore. It was a gesture from the old days, and one he clearly delighted in.

We had leveled off at ten thousand feet temporarily after taking off from Houston for Guadalajara one Saturday morning. My first officer was flying. We'd had just begun to climb again after traffic passed over us when #1 engine flamed out. The sudden loss of one-third of our thrust felt like driving a car into a snowdrift. We completed memory items for the engine failure before I declared an emergency and told Departure we'd lost an engine and would return to Houston. I hoped the engine problem was something quick and easy to fix. We were already late, and my wife was sitting in the terminal in Guadalajara waiting for me.

Company procedure required the non-flying pilot to continue communicating with ATC while working through emergency checklists and procedures with the second officer. I thought that was stupid. It divided attention between yakking with controllers and working to systematically and accurately complete vital procedures. The company didn't want the flying pilot distracted by the radio, but nearly all of us had thousands of hours in single-pilot airplanes walking and chewing gum at the same time. I worked with the second officer on the rest of the checklist procedures while my first officer flew and responded to radio calls.

There was no visible damage to the engine pod and no obvious cause for the failure. The mechanic guessed high-pressure fuel pump. We went to the hotel. I called Delta and learned there was no way to page passengers in Guadalajara. I called the DHL cell phone and talked to the man who met our airplane in Guadalajara each morning. Diego said he'd try to find Barb.

DHL dispatched a spare airplane from Cincinnati to pick up our cargo and continue our trip to Guadalajara. We were almost out of duty time and couldn't continue. I asked the scheduler to ask the captain to try to find Barb to give her the Houston hotel's number. Then, when I could think of nothing else to do, I called Diego again. He handed the phone to Barb.

I told her I'd lost an engine for the first time in my career and was stuck in Houston for the weekend. She said she'd see what she could do about either going back home or coming to Houston. Meanwhile, I was watching TV in my room and trying to stay awake, wishing I could go out for lunch and a beer or four. When the phone rang, it was someone at DHL in Houston. Guadalajara had called to say Barb was on a Continental flight arriving in twenty minutes. I waited for her to call me.

After an hour, I called the airline to see if the flight had arrived on time. During the two minutes I was on the phone, Barb called and left a terse message. "I'm in Houston at the airport. Come and get me."

I'd told her it would be warm in Guadalajara and that women there did not wear pants. Barb had sat shivering in a light dress in the terminal and watched Mexican women in jeans and slacks come and go. Houston was also cool and breezy. We went across the street to a mall to buy her jeans and a warm shirt.

I treated my crew to dinner and told them I was pleased with the smooth way we had interacted. I was particularly impressed that the first officer not only did his job but monitored what the second officer and I were doing and corrected us when a badly worded procedure began to lead us in a wrong direction.

Salvaging what we could of the weekend, Barb and I rented a car Sunday and drove to Galveston. Glen Campbell's version of

Jimmy Webb's song began playing in my head and stayed with me for the rest of the day. I drove to the airport that evening to turn in the car and put Barb on her flight home.

The next time I flew to Guadalajara, I gave Diego a gift box of smoked salmon when Customs wasn't looking in appreciation for his having taken care of Barb when she was stranded there.

It was the first officer's job to take care of paperwork and turn it all in when we got back to Cincinnati—flight release, flight plan, load sheets, fuel receipts, and the file copies of log pages. A first officer I'll call Darrel took paperwork seriously. My assessment was, he was very, very thorough. Art Stark's assessment was, he was an idiot.

If I got to the paperwork before the first officer did, I'd look at the weather, make sure the flight number and airplane number were correct and the same on all forms. I'd sign both copies of the release and put it all back in the proper pigeonhole for the first officer to pick up. If the first officer got to it first, he'd check to be sure it was all there, read whatever parts of it interested him, and take it to the captain in the crew lounge or cafeteria for signature before putting the station copy of the flight release back in the pigeonhole and taking the rest of it to the airplane.

Some first officers highlighted important items such as weather at destination and alternates. Darrel highlighted almost everything. I told him he should use transparent spray paint to save time. He approached me one night with paperwork in hand and said something about runway closures in Tampa. He'd put in his usual time and effort into highlighting almost every line. I'd already signed it and told him so. He said, "I'd like you to look at it anyway."

I refused. The closure he thought so important was a short runway for little airplanes. Maybe Art Stark was right.

A note on the New York arrival chart said to expect a speed reduction to 250 knots crossing Lendy intersection. We were late and I was flying fast. The controller hadn't mentioned the speed reduction. Darrel asked him if he intended to give us the restriction, and the controller immediately did.

I pulled power back to idle in disgust and said, "Never ask a question you might not like the answer to. That's not just an aviation rule. It's a life rule."

I began to develop a bias against former Air Force transport pilots.

* * *

It was my first officer's leg from Newark to Cincinnati. He was a former Air Force transport pilot I'll call Corrigan. When we took off, we were cleared direct to East Texas VOR and then on course. After crossing East Texas, we'd need to turn left a few degrees to track J-80. Just before reaching the fix, I turned both CDIs to the outbound course of 249 degrees and told Corrigan I'd done that. I spent a few seconds putting charts away, and when I looked at the panel again, we'd made the left turn and then some. Needles showed we were left of course, and the airplane was still turning.

Ever the diplomat, I said, "I show us left of course and going left."

Corrigan immediately made a correction and mumbled something about not having turned much at all.

Then, when briefing the ILS approach to Cincinnati, he said we'd set the bug at one hundred feet on the radar altimeter. I said, "We can't set it below the published two hundred." That's about as basic as instrument flying gets.

Then he said we couldn't shoot the approach because the ceiling was only one hundred feet. I reminded him that the ceiling could be zero, that all we needed has half a mile of visibility.

I put a mental flag next to his name.

I didn't have time for a nap in Cincinnati between Baltimore and Guadalajara, so I was tired on the way south for the weekend. I flew with two people I couldn't relax completely with. The second officer—I'll call her Annie—confirmed that as we started the first engine when she announced that the #1 A-system hydraulic low pressure light had failed—that is, it went out. Well, yes indeedy it went out, and a good thing, too. It was the normal indication that the engine was turning the pump.

The first officer flew to Houston. I'll call him Jock. When we arrived, visibility was at our minimums under a hundred-foot ceiling.

Jock established the airplane on the inbound course and was holding a correction angle to the right for crosswind. Because the airplane was pointed a few degrees to the right, I expected to see approach lights just to the left of the nose, if I saw lights at all.

I kept my eyes on instruments with only quick looks outside until I made the required "One hundred feet above minimums" call. Then my eyes went outside to look for lights, glancing back in to monitor altitude during that last hundred feet before we'd have to go around.

When approach lights appeared, they were not to the left of the nose but were way off to the right. Visibility underneath the low ceiling was good, though, and we could see how we were oriented. Jock banked right and then left to move over and align with the runway. Near the ground is not the place to be making large corrections, and we should have flown a missed approach. It was only because we could see clearly that that I didn't take the airplane and go around. If a check airman or a Fed had been aboard, we'd have been in trouble.

Jock said the flight director gave him false information at the last, right when my concentration was shifting from inside to out. He said he was getting ready to fly the missed approach when he saw the lights. I had no basis to say he was, uh, mistaken. I didn't bother to ask Annie where she was looking in the last hundred feet, but I'd have bet she was looking for lights instead of backing up the flying pilot with eyes on instruments. Many second officers looked out the window when they expected to see lights. It was difficult not to.

I couldn't stop analyzing the approach to Houston over the otherwise relaxing weekend in Guadalajara. Even if the flight director had burped, we were supposed to back it up with raw data. I thought my first officer had screwed up, though I couldn't prove it.

I almost got killed walking to a restaurant Monday evening. Most streets I had to cross were one way, so that was the track my mind was on. I watched traffic coming from the right as I approached an intersection. I couldn't see anything to the left because a thick hedge along the sidewalk went to the curb. A gap in traffic coming from the right appeared and I stepped into the street. Only then could I see fast traffic coming from the left on the only two-way street between hotel and restaurant. I stepped back onto the curb as cars shot by. Had the gap in traffic been shorter, I'd have started to run across rather than walk and I'd be dead. I always carried my airline ID with me when outside of hotels to avoid a John Doe toe tag.

* * *

Jock was flying when we left Guadalajara Monday night, so when we got a differential fault—a short circuit—that kicked #1 generator off line, I worked through the problem with Annie. She immediately wanted to reset the generator, the last thing in the world to do with a differential fault. Shorts in big wires cause big fires. I got her slowed down and we went step by step through the procedure in the book and wrote it up in the log. The generator distraction had made me forget I wanted us to fly the same approach into Houston that Jock had on the way south to see what the flight director did.

System Operations Control comprised three men who worked nine-hour shifts and controlled the entire DHL flight operation. They had God's authority and no accountability, as we understood it, except to the company VP in charge of the airline. SOC appeared to go out of its way to make life miserable for pilots, even when doing so cost the company money.

A Denver-bound airplane broke at its stop in Kansas City one Saturday morning. Cincinnati launched a spare airplane with a reserve crew. All three crewmembers on the Denver airplane lived there and planned to spend the weekend at home. All the reserve crew lived near Cincinnati and would have liked to spend their weekend at home. The simple solution would have been for crews to swap airplanes, the Denver crew continuing west and the Cincinnati crew returning home with the broken airplane, one that could be ferried empty but not flown with cargo aboard.

SOC overruled Crew Scheduling. The scheduler explained to SOC that the Denver crew was going home and would do everything possible to complete the flight. The reserve crew had similar incentive to get the cripple back to Cincinnati. He said the Denver crew, if not allowed to continue, would claim fatigue and stay in Kansas City at company expense rather than return to Cincinnati and pay for lodging for the weekend. SOC refused to allow the change. The original Denver crew unanimously fatigued and went to a hotel, angry and bitter at the obstinacy on the part of one powerful jackass. We did not just imagine that SOC hated pilots. They'd been overheard more than once making snide remarks about us.

Some pilots believed Crew Scheduling liked to make us unhappy, but schedulers hated SOC, too. We had no idea why SOC had power to override managers of other departments such as Crew Scheduling and Load Planning

A new procedure required dispatchers to sign releases. My first officer saw a signature, assumed it was mine, and took all the paper out to the airplane early so he could finish his work and sleep for a few minutes.

I couldn't find him. I had him paged throughout the building. Ramp Tower called the airplane, but there was no answer. I rode the crew bus to the airplane in something less than a good mood, got the paperwork, and told the second officer to have the airplane a lot cooler when I got back.

I rode the bus back to the building and went inside to look over weather and flight plans in good light, sign the releases, and drop off the station copy. We got out late and it would have been our fault, except for a loading delay that took the blame.

The lower rudder's yaw damper didn't work when I tested it. We stopped on the taxiway, called Maintenance Control, deferred the yaw damper, and got amendments to our flight plan over the radio for a lower altitude and speed to comply with restrictions imposed by the defect, and I forgot to call for the Before Takeoff checklist.

As we approached the runway, I noticed the first officer reach up and turn on the transponder. When I was in the right seat, I didn't turn on the transponder until the checklist was called for. If it wasn't on, we hadn't done the checklist. So when the man reached up and turned it on, my mind, out of rhythm because of dealing with the yaw damper, turned its checklist page. I explained all this to my crew as we flew. I was pleased to notice the next time I flew with him, that first officer had adopted my old procedure of waiting for the checklist before turning on the transponder.

The desert was beautiful in light and shadow from low evening sun as we flew east from Sacramento to Salt Lake City. We found a basketball game with the ADF, found it again on another station when the first one faded.

We took off to the north out of Salt Lake City just after the sun had gone down leaving the thinnest possible crescent of moon hanging near the horizon above the Great Salt Lake. In Cincinnati, my first officer got one of the nicest landings I judged he'd ever get. Flights like than reminded me of why I loved my job.

I rode our jumpseat to San Francisco and changed to a clean shirt in the DHL building before taking the bus to the terminal to find a ride to Seattle. When I got home, I realized I'd left my Leatherman tool in San Francisco when I took it off my belt and set it down while changing my shirt. It was a gift, and my name was engraved on it, but I never saw it again. Maybe the guy who stole my typewriter years earlier still worked there.

The day after I got home, I headed east to Cincinnati with truck and camper. The plan was to leave the rig parked in the DHL lot while I worked a week and attended recurrent training. Barb would fly out and we'd drive home after picking up our six-year-old grandson at his dad's home in Illinois.

Ground school began Tuesday at noon. I drove to the school parking lot to camp there. At the end of that first day, our director of operations came into class and asked us if we'd fly some short trips out and back that evening. Too many scheduled pilots had timed out in fog delays the night before. We could either cancel ground school and reschedule it, or we could shift Wednesday's class to the afternoon and stay late. We didn't want to reschedule. Atlanta was a short trip, so I'd be back early.

I made a couple of sandwiches to take along, just in case. Just before we left, a manager brought us sandwiches and apologized for not having brought soft drinks! We marveled at what appeared to be an element of humanity creeping into management. The catering came in handy. We sat on the ground in Atlanta more than four hours.

UPS pilots went on strike. We would not carry UPS cargo, but many UPS customers changed temporarily to other carriers, so our loads were heavier than usual. Our sort system ran late every night. We were nearly ninety minutes late out of Cincinnati, and we never got to Seattle.

Engine starts were normal, but during taxi, the second officer noticed that #3 engine was idling too low. Pushing the thrust lever up a little corrected idle speed, but when it was pulled back to the stop, turbine speeds dropped.

We should have evaluated the minor glitch further, but I was on the radio talking to Dispatch about a discrepancy between our printed flight plan and the one in the ATC computer, and then we were at the runway. I told myself to remember to write up the low idle when we got to Seattle.

Sidney flew. I carefully checked engine instruments during takeoff roll and saw nothing out of line, although it's hard to detect minor differences because of vibrations and bumps imparted by imperfect pavement.

Tower handed us off to Departure immediately. Before I checked in and before we'd reached a thousand feet, the fire bell rang. The small fire light on the annunciator panel lit red, but we saw no other light indicating what was on fire. Nearly all of our 727s had large, red, engine-fire handles high in the center of the instrument panel, impossible to miss when one lit up. We were in one of three airplanes that had fire handles overhead, too far back for pilots to see without turning their heads. Even the second officer, leaning forward to monitor engine instruments on takeoff, could not see them until he sat back. We all hesitated a moment wondering why we had a bell and master warning but no indication of where the fire was.

One of us pushed the button to silence the jangling bell. The second officer called out that #3 engine fire light was on and that it was still running.

Fire or not, if the engine was producing thrust, so we should have left it alone. The procedure we practiced over and over in the simulator was to level off at a safe altitude, clean up gear and flaps, accelerate to engine-out climb speed, set maximum continuous thrust, identify the problem, call for the appropriate emergency checklist, perform critical first items from memory, and then declare an emergency. We didn't do it that way, in part because we'd all been mentally derailed trying to figure out what the fuck was wrong.

In the simulator, if an engine does not catch fire or fail on takeoff, it's a pleasant surprise. But, in the simulator, engines always fail at V1, the point beyond which the airplane must continue the takeoff because there is not enough runway left to stop. Because nearly all simulated fires and failures occur at that point, a failure or fire after the airplane is in the air and climbing presents a scenario different from the one grooved into our brains.

Our airplane was flying just fine. All three engines were running. Sidney, as flying pilot, should have directed us through the emergency procedure, and I should have seen to it that he did.

I may have jumped in and hurried Sidney into the procedure and bumped him out of proper sequence. Had we done things in proper order at the proper time, we'd have had three good engines separating us from the earth until we were at a safe altitude. But either the second officer or I pulled the fire handle first, shutting off fuel to the engine, and there we were, still near the ground with a full load of fuel and only two engines. I told the second officer to dump fuel, though that was the flying pilot's call. Gear was up, but flaps were still at fifteen degrees.

We were lucky to be in an advanced 727 with big engines. It climbed nicely on two, in spite of flaps not being up. The second officer and I ran the Engine Fire checklist, and then I noticed we were through three thousand feet and still climbing, still at Flaps 15. I told Sidney we needed to level off and get cleaned up, then climb. I declared an emergency and asked for seven thousand feet to dump fuel down to landing weight. That altitude would ensure the oily jet fuel would evaporate before it reached the ground.

We were vectored for an ILS to Runway 27. Sidney offered to give me the airplane, but it was his leg. He was flying just fine, as far as handling the airplane went. He was no more deficient than I was in procedural errors we, as a crew, had just made. It was my job to run the show and see to it that everything was done correctly and in proper order, and I had failed miserably. It would have been a terrible blow to Sidney's battered confidence if I'd taken the airplane from him so soon after the union had won his job back after he failed a simulator checkride in recurrent training.

We landed to an audience of crash trucks and taxied in. Mechanics popped the cowl and saw no sign of fire. A bleed air leak had caused the low idle speed. When we increased power for takeoff, hot engine bleed air escaping into the cowl heated the fire detection loop. We'd shut down a perfectly good engine long before we needed to. I was disgusted with myself.

The first officer flew to Seattle and I played with the video camera I'd bought in Boston, recording lightning as we dodged thunderstorms and, when the sun rose behind us, taping scenery and mountains from Wyoming to Washington. Rather than wait for the van in Seattle, I drove us to the hotel. When I got to my room, I realized I didn't have my video camera with me. I'd set it and my Thermos down while I fumbled for my truck key. I drove fast back to the employees' parking lot.

Camera and Thermos were sitting in my parking space where I'd left them.

Desk clerks were busy when I checked out, so I just tossed my room key on the counter. I wanted to tell them about the shower head that sprayed water all over the bathroom unless it was wrapped in a towel, but someone else would eventually.

My room in Manhattan's Park Central Hotel had been refurbished not long before. I got out my video camera to record mushrooms growing in damp carpet under the air conditioner.

I ate dinner with Sidney at Cabana Carioca Sunday evening. Out of the airplane, he was enjoyable company, a bright and thoughtful man. He was just in the wrong line of work. After our botched engine fire procedure the week before, I had to consider that maybe I was, too.

Our van was stopped at a red light in Guadalajara on the way to the airport. A beautiful little girl about eight years old in a clean pink dress took advantage of traffic stopped there to sell chewing gum. She held out her wares to us and yelled "Money" over and over in English. I shook my head No. She didn't move to the next car but continued to yell "Money" at us. Her pushiness didn't detract from her smile and general appeal, so I rolled down the window and gave her a ten-peso note for a package of gum. The size of the bill stopped her incessant chant, if only for a moment, before the light changed. I wondered what life held for her, wondered if her teeth and smile would be as lovely in another ten or twenty years.

As soon as we were aboard our airplane, lightning began flashing all around. We sat in heavy rain until three hours past departure time, updating our flight plan from time to time so it wouldn't drop out of the system. FedEx taxied out, thought better of it, and returned to the ramp. A couple of Mexican airliners took off in hard rain, gusty wind, and near-continuous lightning. I wondered if they had plastic Jesuses on their glare shields.

When FedEx finally took off, we called to ask what their radar showed. It looked good in the direction we'd be flying. We started engines and took off.

In Houston, I phoned Crew Scheduling to say we expected to be in half an hour past our check-in time, and would like not to be replaced on our Boston trip. The scheduler said she was glad I called, as they were just at the point of making that decision.

We were loaded and fueled and ready to go, but the Customs agent took his sweet time clearing us. That cost us twenty minutes. We dodged small storm cells all the way to Cincinnati flying as fast as we could. We deviated as little as possible for weather, although a few more degrees of turns would have given more comfortable margins.

The Boston airplane was only two spots over. It was departure time, but all cargo doors were still open. We jumped on the crew bus and asked the driver to drop us at the Boston airplane. We ran up the stairs and discovered a crew in the seats.

We went inside and learned all eastbound flights were delayed half an hour, so there was time to swap crews without adding to the delay. I asked Crew Scheduling if the reserve captain wanted my Boston trip or would rather stay in Cincinnati. He wanted to fly, so after grumbling in front of schedulers about how our reward for doing everything we could to make up time was no trip, no per diem, and hotel rooms at our expense, I gave up. As I waited outside for the hotel van, I realized that, as much as I disliked whiners, I was capable of being one myself.

I was off from mid-September until the first week in November. When I woke up in a hotel my first day back at work, I looked at the clock, noted the sky was still dark, and went back to sleep. When I woke again a little later, I was surprised that no light was coming through the curtains. Then I realized it was evening, not morning, and that I was in a hotel, not in my own bed.

When we arrived at Cincinnati that night, wind was light from the east. The airport was landing Runway 9, but the ILS was out of service for that runway. Weather was not a factor and we'd get a visual approach. I told my first officer we'd refuse that runway and accept any with a working ILS.

A year earlier, I'd have landed on the same runway everyone else was, but another captain, a good friend, considered it stupid to accept a runway without an ILS if one with it was available and suitable, especially at night and especially when we were tired. I'd always considered him an overly prudent pilot, but the older I got, the more inclined I was to drop the adverb.

One night in our cafeteria, I noticed a couple of pilots peeling the buns off egg-and-cheese sandwiches. They were on a low-carb diet that a lot of the pilots were using to lose weight. I asked if there were any side effects.

"There are," one said. "My cholesterol is down, the ratio has improved, and triglycerides are way down."

My cholesterol had always been high, except for several months a few years earlier when I'd driven it down with liver-destroying levels of niacin. I decided to cut back on pasta, potatoes, and bread to see what happened.

The company began installing GPS receivers in our airplanes, and that meant ground school to learn how to use them. It did not instill confidence to learn that our GPS units were being installed by student mechanics at the company that did scheduled heavy maintenance on our airplanes in Florida. In two airplanes, they had installed the keypad above the screen and we couldn't see what we were doing while entering data.

After GPS training class, several of us went to a steak house for dinner. The other guys ate ribs, fries, and bread. I ordered a T-bone with vegetables and salad with oil and vinegar. I didn't eat the croutons. I ordered the same meal again for dessert. My goal was to lose twenty pounds. When I got home, I bought the Atkins' diet book.

The week before Thanksgiving wasn't the wisest time to start a diet. Atkins' program didn't allow alcohol, so I cut out my evening drink. I indulged in a glass of wine with Thanksgiving dinner at home. Dinner, for me, was turkey, celery, carrots, and olives.

There was only one airplane in Seattle the last weekend in November instead of the two that had been flying the trip for weeks. Four of us were confirmed for jumpseats Monday evening, and I'd been booked on the airplane that wasn't there. I considered calling in sick, but I was scheduled for my first trip to Puerto Rico on Tuesday and didn't want to miss it. I left home early and left suitcase and flight bag at DHL with a note asking the crew to put both bags on the airplane. I got a ride to San Francisco for a jumpseat to Cincinnati from there.

With a scheduled stop in Miami, the Puerto Rico trip arrived too late for the same crew to return that evening. So, as with Portland a few years earlier, two crews leapfrogged with a 30-hour layover and a three-night, four-day weekend. A taxi service provided transportation. The Colony was a small hotel at the end of a short street paralleling the public beach in Isla

Verde. All we had to do was walk out the door, and we were a few steps from a white sand beach shaded by coconut palms.

We met in the lobby for dinner and walked to a nearby restaurant. I had two rib steaks and gave my rice and beans to the second officer. After dinner, we went to the casino in a hotel not far from ours. My first officer tried to explain Caribbean Poker to me.

I was too tired to stay out late with the others, so I went back to my room and called home. I explained the weekend setup and suggested we keep San Juan in mind for holiday layovers. The crew that had arrived on Thanksgiving stayed six days, a nice break in a seven-day work week.

In Miami on our return the next day, we got word we'd stop in Orlando on the way to Cincinnati. While the first officer was inside getting new paperwork, I put the Orlando flight plan into the GPS from memory and confirmed it when he returned with the paper copy. On the ground in Orlando, I quickly punched in the route to Cincinnati and the GPS came up with more than four thousand miles. I decided to be very careful about relying on memory for putting identifiers in the machine. I'd punched in CEC thinking it was Cecil VOR, and the machine wanted to take us over Crescent City, California.

Our airplane to Phoenix and Los Angeles was one I'd considered refusing to fly because of the communications difficulties and resulting safety hazard of non-standard radio panels that did not allow individual volume control. I'd been told that airplane was scheduled to have the panels replaced, but I didn't know in what year. I went out to the airplane a full hour early so I could write up the radios without causing delay. That prompted a long discussion with Maintenance Control and the flight manager. There was nothing wrong with the radios. They operated as designed. We chewed that bone for a few minutes, and I told them there was a memo from me on the subject upstairs in a manager's mailbox if they wanted to save time and conversation. The mechanic asked if I was just trying to make a statement. I said I was and would continue to do so until the radio panels were changed.

We took the airplane, but we used the overhead speakers instead of our disparate headsets. The problem with using speakers was, when the second officer keyed his mike to make his reports to the company, speaker volume was muted and we sometimes missed calls from ATC.

The GPS wouldn't couple to the autopilot. We didn't write that up on the first leg for fear the mechanic in Phoenix would defer the autopilot or GPS or both, leaving us with neither for the rest of the trip. We were supposed to write things up as they occurred, but we decided we could legitimately wait until we were on our way to Cincinnati, having taken time during the first three legs to troubleshoot and be sure the problem wasn't operator error.

I wasn't able to spend much time hunting deer and elk during my week at home. Getting ready for Christmas always took more time than I thought it should, even though we'd spend it away from home that year. I filled an extra suitcase with gifts to take to Colorado. I didn't realize I didn't have my wallet until I got to Cincinnati. After the first time I'd done that, I began carrying my licenses and medical certificate in a plastic folder held inside my shirt-pocket logbook with a rubber band. I borrowed money from other pilots to get me through the week.

Weight came off fast on the Atkins diet. I had to cut three inches off my belt. Uniform pants bunched up at my waist, but I was on schedule for two new pair later that winter.

Snow was turning to light freezing rain and the de-ice truck that normally served us in Seattle broke. Because I was riding to Cincinnati to turn around and fly back to Seattle, I'd left everything in my truck except Thermos, coffee, a cup, and a book. I'd arrive in Cincinnati in time for my trip if our delay didn't last much longer. I called Crew Scheduling to say I'd be pushing my check-in time when we arrived and asked the scheduler to hold the trip for me as long as possible. She asked how late I was comfortable with. Arriving twenty minutes before departure would suit me fine.

I called Crew Scheduling from the air when we got low enough that my phone wouldn't be trying to talk through cell towers all over the Ohio Valley. I said we were there, though we were still a few minutes from touchdown. When we got on the ground, we learned the entire system was running half an hour late. I thanked the scheduler for holding my trip for me, made a Thermos of coffee, turned in an article for the union newsletter, and went out to my airplane.

In Seattle, I made an absolutely flawless touchdown in gusty wind, and the nosewheel tires settled to the runway astride the centerline lights. The line about blind pigs and acorns crossed my mind.

A jumpseater waited for us in the maintenance shack at Newark, a young Dutchman who'd flown from Brussels to New York on our DC-8 for a week of vacation and shopping. Newark to Cincinnati was the first leg of his return to Brussels. His name was penciled in on the release. Our mechanic said he'd called Cincinnati to confirm he was booked for the seat. He was, but for the previous day. I told Rubin we often made the same mistake until we got used to DHL's day beginning on Greenwich Time.

He showed me his passport and pilot's license. I asked to see his company ID. He had none. He said that he flew for a company with only two small airplanes, and his company didn't issue ID.

I asked Rubin how he'd gotten aboard our airplane in Brussels with no company ID. He said the captain asked only for his license and passport. He didn't remember the captain's name.

I called Dispatch, explained the problem, and was transferred to Crew Scheduling. I explained again and asked who had authorized Rubin's travel with no ID badge. The scheduler said the flight manager had.

In the past, captains who had denied seats to people who were approved to ride had been chastised, and the unwritten rule became, if the name was on the flight release, the rider had been approved by someone who had authority to approve. I told Rubin he was welcome to ride, but that I wasn't sure it was legal. My thinking was, we'd brought him across the ocean, and we had a responsibility to get him home. When we boarded our airplane, I checked the manual. Nothing in the book gave anyone authority to list a rider who did not have company ID.

The first person I ran into in Cincinnati was the flight manager. I told him I couldn't find in the book where it said it was okay for our man to ride. He didn't know anything about it. He hadn't been asked to approve anyone that night. I said the approval was probably four weeks old. The manager said he definitely would not have approved anyone without proper ID. He said Rubin could not ride.

I said that whoever let him on the airplane in Europe had screwed up, but that we were responsible, at least morally, for getting the guy home.

The problem turned into a Big Deal. Someone called the 727 chief pilot at home. He came out to the airport to be the Big Chief on the Scene. He, the flight manager, and a union jumpseat committee member, all got on the phone with the DC-8 chief pilot. The 727 chief pilot seemed to want to Exercise Authority. The DC-8 chief pilot seemed to want us to resolve the issue without official intervention or knowledge.

A check of the schedule identified the captain who'd flown Rubin to the United States. He said he hadn't thought to ask for company ID because that was the one thing jumpseaters always had, and he was more concerned with checking his license and passport.

I hung around the decision makers and stressed at every opportunity that, as the man had not tried to deceive us and was the innocent victim of our failure to deny boarding in Brussels, we were responsible for getting him home. If we wouldn't take him, we should buy him a ticket.

I didn't say so, but I'd have put an airline ticket on my credit card and worried later about collecting money from either the company, the union, or contributions from the pilot group. What I said to Rubin in front of the flight manager and the union representative was, if DHL would not either take him home or send him home at company expense, he should call US Immigration and a good lawyer and I'd help him explain the situation.

After all that hullabaloo, the solution was simple. We would ask the captain flying to Brussels that morning if he'd allow Rubin to ride home on his airplane without ID. The captain was an easygoing good guy, but that was no guarantee he'd stick his neck out. He was in the bunk room and wouldn't be awake for another couple of hours. I needed a nap, but I wasn't going to risk not being in on the last chapter of the story.

Rubin seemed embarrassed. He was only a part-time pilot for his company, but he'd heard from a friend he could ride cargo carriers. His friend gave him DHL's phone number, and he called to book seats for his American vacation. The crew scheduler told him he had to have a passport and pilot's license with him, but nobody said anything about company ID. To the scheduler and to the captain, the ID requirement was so obvious neither of them thought to mention it.

I told Rubin we'd get him home somehow, and that, if nothing else, he'd have a good story to tell when he got there. He was asleep in a recliner when the Brussels-bound captain woke up and heard the story. He readily agreed to let the man ride. Rubin was still asleep when domestic flights departed, so I didn't get to say goodbye.

Crew Scheduling made a new rule that we couldn't ask to pull last-day reserve at home until after all flights—and all rides home—had left. They were too busy to be bothered by such requests. Since our presence disturbed them, instead of signing in for our trips as soon as we arrived, we began waiting until the last minute, precisely one hour before departure. Crew Scheduling would have little notice on how many reserves they'd have to call out.

We got out ninety minutes late Saturday morning. The weekend before, it was two hours. Lots of crews claimed fatigue. Managers thought it was a job action. The union suggested they compare fatigue calls to system delays.

In Boston Saturday, I bought a paper and went to the hotel restaurant for breakfast buffet. Scrambled eggs that late in the morning were as dry as foam rubber and just as tasty. I ate a pile of bacon and sausage instead. I ate the same thing Sunday and Monday.

I got home Tuesday morning and went in the next day for my FAA physical and a cholesterol check. I'd lost twenty pounds since my exam six months earlier. A couple of days later, my doctor called. Total cholesterol was well over three hundred.

I explained that I'd been on the Atkins diet and was almost to my target weight. I told him about the mountains of bacon I'd eaten the previous weekend and said I said I'd come in for another check after I was back to a normal food intake, except no sugar and little starch.

We were being held below our planned cruise altitude coming out of Newark. Winds aloft were strong against us, so I told my first officer to tell the controller we'd like to stay at the altitude we were at. It should have been a short, simple request, but Corrigan rattled on in an obsequious manner until it sounded like we wouldn't mind staying low if that made things easier for ATC. The controller said he'd get us higher in a few miles.

I told Corrigan he hadn't conveyed that we *wanted* to stay low, that he'd given the controller the impression that we *could* stay low to accommodate ATC.

Corrigan said he was trying to be nice.

I said, "Don't be nice. Be direct. Nice is confusing."

I had time for a short nap in Cincinnati and drank tea instead of coffee westbound so I could sleep well in Los Angeles. I slept a few minutes more in my seat in Phoenix while mechanics attended to a maintenance problem.

Climbing through twelve thousand feet, the cabin altitude horn began beeping, indication that air pressure inside was equivalent to above ten thousand feet. I turned my head to check the second officer's panel just as he realized he hadn't turned on the second pack after we started engines. One pack couldn't keep up with air leaks in the old airplane.

The second officer said he couldn't figure out why he couldn't turn the air mix valve off the default full-cold setting, but he figured, since his captain liked it cool anyway, what the hell. I said, "It's a good thing I don't like it hot, or if we'd caught fire, you'd have let it burn."

I hadn't slept enough during the day, so I made coffee instead of tea for the eastbound trip. I didn't want to sleep with Corrigan flying. He flew the first leg and didn't call for the Approach checklist as we descended toward Phoenix.

The non-flying pilot calls, "Flight Level one-eight-zero" reaching that altitude and both pilots reset altimeters, either to the standard 29.92 inches when climbing or to the local setting when descending. If descending, the flying pilot then calls for the Approach checklist. I waited until I was sure he'd forgotten before I said, "Are we gonna do the approach list or what?"

That wasn't a big deal, but that week was the first time I'd flown with Corrigan since he'd made the weird wrong turn coming out of Newark the year before. Memory of that kept me more than normally watchful. After our break in Cincinnati, we continued to Boston. Corrigan flew.

Unlike many captains, I let first officers set interior lighting to their preferences when they were flying, all except my own instrument lights. I wanted engine instruments bright during takeoff, regardless of who was flying, so abnormalities would be clearly and instantly readable.

When it was my leg, I kept all panel lights bright until after leveling off at cruise. Only then, when nothing was changing, would I dim the panel floods and instrument backlights for visual comfort. But I kept the altitude alerter light bright all the time. In level flight, that light was off anyway.

The amber altitude alerter light on the front panel comes on when the airplane climbs or descends through a thousand feet from target altitude and goes out when the airplane is three hundred feet from that altitude. It doesn't come on again unless the airplane deviates three hundred feet from the altitude set in the alerter. The non-flying pilot calls, "One thousand to go," and the flying pilot repeats that to acknowledge he's heard it.

My attention span is shorter than the couple of minutes it takes to climb or descend that last thousand feet, so I needed the alerter light bright to get my attention when it went out a few seconds before we reached the selected altitude. If I wasn't flying, all I had to do as we approached assigned altitude was monitor the first officer's leveling off. I could concentrate on that for two minutes, if that's all I had to do.

As usual, soon after takeoff, Corrigan dimmed the lights lower than I liked, but it was his leg. We were first cleared direct Dayton. Our outbound course from Dayton was a twelve-degree heading change. Just before crossing the VOR, I turned my heading knob to the outbound course and told Corrigan the number. He mumbled something I took for an acknowledgement and reached to his dimly lit panel and turned a knob.

We crossed the VOR a moment later and he began the slight turn. I was on the radio acknowledging a handoff and changing to the new frequency. When I checked instruments again, I saw we were right of course and diverging from it. Because I couldn't see Corrigan's darkened instruments clearly, I asked him if he had forty-seven degrees set. He did not. I'd seen him turn the heading knob to make a minor adjustment, not to change his course setting to the outbound.

Next, he shot through our assigned altitude. Being more than three hundred feet high or low is a violation, and we were already two hundred feet high with no hint of leveling off. I crosschecked altimeters and they were the same.

"Where are you going?" I asked.

"Trying to level off," he said, and just then he realized the situation. Because he had the altitude alerter dim, neither of us had noticed the light go off.

I never again let him or anyone else dim that light.

I didn't sleep well on my jumpseat to work one night early in March. The captain kept the cockpit hot enough to glaze pottery. As a jumpseater, I was a guest and didn't complain. I looked forward to the long weekend in Puerto Rico's soothing, moist air.

We were tired in late morning as we approached San Juan. Traffic ahead was getting the usual clearance to cross Beano Intersection at eleven thousand. We didn't realize immediately that we were past the point we normally got the same descent clearance. At least my crew had an excuse. They'd never been there.

The first officer asked me if I wanted him to ask for lower at the same time ATC asked if we'd gotten clearance to cross Beano at eleven. We had not.

I pulled power to idle and pulled the speedbrake handle to the stop and, when speed dropped to the extension limit, I called for landing gear down. When three green lights came on, I shoved the nose down to let speed build to more than three hundred knots and we screamed downhill.

The Boeing 727 was fun to fly because it was versatile and forgiving. Pilots who went to the DC-8 quickly learned they had to plan descents precisely.

The first officer and I walked to Metropol for dinner and ordered smoked chicken, a house specialty. We wondered if we were eating the losers from the cockfight arena next door.

I basked in sunshine Monday until clouds filled the sky. I burn easily and was pleased that I'd paid attention to time and was only a little red on my shoulders and the top of my head. I was sorry to be leaving. I didn't know when I'd ever have San Juan weekends again. I thought everyone would want long layovers there.

I flew to Puerto Rico again the last Tuesday in March. When I turned down the bed in my room, the sheet was full of short hairs. The only explanation my groggy mind could come up with was, maybe it had been washed with barbershop linen. I was too tired to consider the fact that there was no barbershop in the hotel. I called the desk and soon a maid came to change sheets.

Some maids in some hotels don't always change sheets. After one of our pilots was stuck in the leg by a hypodermic syringe in a hotel bed in New York, I'd made a point of pulling bed covers all the way back to check.

When we got to the airport the next evening, paperwork wasn't there. Dispatch said they'd sent it, but they'd fax it again. After a few minutes, the machine began pushing out paper, but it stopped before it spit out our last pages. The display said, "Out of ink, memory full, fax disabled."

Nobody around at night knew where ink was or how to put it into the machine if they found it. The man on duty gave me a SITA number, whatever that was, and I called Dispatch and gave them that number. Another freight handler, not a DHL man, turned on the SITA printer, and we finally got all our paperwork five minutes before scheduled departure.

While taxiing to the runway, we got no warning horn on the takeoff configuration check. That horn sounds when power is increased for takeoff if flaps or trim are not in the correct range. We could not take off with the warning not working.

We pulled and reset the circuit breaker and cycled the flaps. I got out my phone and called Cincinnati to ask if we were overlooking something. The maintenance supervisor told us to taxi back in.

We explained our problem to the contract mechanics. There were variations in the 727 in how the warning horn was activated, and we had to explain that ours didn't work the way they thought it did. Then one of them pulled out an old Eastern Airlines manual and said the system didn't have to be tested. I pointed out that we were not Eastern Airlines.

They finally found what they surmised was a defective module and said they'd try to locate one. It would take at least three hours to get another part and another hour or two to install it. By then, we'd be well into hunger, and there was no place to take a nap.

For once, we were not kept on duty until we were contractually and legally dead. Crew Scheduling called our hotel. We checked back into the rooms we'd just left, and I was glad of my habit of leaving rooms neat and orderly when I checked out. The classical FM station I'd left on greeted me softly as I walked in. The last towel I'd used was on the rack instead of in the neat heap of used ones on the floor.

After changing clothes, we all walked to Lupi's for late dinner. That late at night, bouncers frisked young men for weapons with electronic wands as they entering the restaurant and bar. I didn't know whether to feel honored or insulted that they didn't check me.

The first trip after my week off was a weekday trip to Puerto Rico. Both jumpseaters out of Cincinnati for Miami showed up late and we had to re-calculate weight and balance. We had two DHL jumpseaters' names on the release from Miami to San Juan, neither of them flight crew. We were ready to go fifteen minutes early, and one jumpseater hadn't shown up. We were ready to close the door when one of the ground people ran up the stairs to say the jumpseater had just arrived. Would we take her?

I didn't give the young woman a hard time about showing up late, but I didn't try to hide mild chagrin. Maybe a little frosty air would convey the message. Halfway through the flight, I offered both jumpseaters coffee to show I wasn't a bad guy.

We were not far behind our DC-8 after leaving Miami for Cincinnati and were on the same radio frequency most of the time. When heard it divert to Atlanta because its radar had failed, we knew we were doomed. A few minutes later, Cincinnati called us to tell us to go to Atlanta and load up with all the DC-8's freight we could carry.

While we were in Atlanta, severe thunderstorms closed Cincinnati. Most of our airplanes diverted to Nashville. We hung out in the freight office for a couple of hours. I bought a gristle sandwich from a vending machine and slept in a chair. We didn't have to take on DC-8 freight. Mechanics borrowed a radar from Delta.

When Cincinnati opened again, we took off. Before we got there, more storms moved into the area. Some airplanes were finding gaps between cells and getting in. We set our radar to its extreme range of three hundred miles. It looked like we could get around the northeast end of the line and come in behind it. Indianapolis Center didn't think so, but I wanted to have a look. We asked how far we'd have to go to get past the end of the line of storms. The controller said weather extended to Buffalo. It didn't, but we were reluctant to disregard the controller and believe our radar and our eyes.

Soon our radar showed a forty-mile gap between cells. Only a little lightning was visible in the directions radar showed clouds, and it appeared the storm line was dissipating rapidly. I thought we should turn toward the apparent gap for a better look. The second officer didn't want to.

My policy was not to override vetoes from anyone on my crew. My second officer was, I thought, being too cautious. I'd proposed nothing more than turning the airplane and the radar toward the weather for a better look at what appeared to be a wide gap between rapidly dwindling red blotches.

We could see lights on the ground dozens of miles ahead with no radar echoes from that direction and no lightning. I explained my analysis of the rapidly improving situation and asked the second officer if it looked better to her out the front windows and on the radar screen, now that we were pointed in that direction and she could see from her seat. She didn't answer, and we either had to turn away or go ahead, so we went ahead. All we encountered was light turbulence with a few moderate bumps. The only lightning was an occasional flash in clouds far below us that lit up the thin cirrostratus we were flying in.

Before we left the airplane, we talked about the decision I'd made. My second officer wasn't happy. She said she thought we'd been lucky. I felt bad that she'd been dragged along reluctantly, but she said she hadn't been unhappy enough with the situation to exercise her veto. I'd rather have had us all comfortable with what we did, but my decision was neither unwise nor unsafe.

I thought the Indy Center controller was out of line with his dire warnings and exaggerated descriptions of the extent of the weather. We didn't have to go to Buffalo to get around. We didn't even leave Ohio. But things were changing fast, and I couldn't know what it looked like from where he sat.

I did not want to fly the long trip to Phoenix and Los Angeles with a Fed on board conducting a route check because I knew I'd need to sleep some on the way. I traded my Los Angeles for Sacramento, even with the Fed thrown in.

I flew the first leg, as I always did with someone I'd not flown with recently or at all. My first officer was a serious, methodical, thorough, by-the-book pilot. Our assigned departure off Runway 16L in Salt Lake City began with a right turn of more than ninety degrees. The first officer climbed straight ahead to precisely four hundred feet before beginning to turn, and the controller had to amend our heading to get us pointed in the right direction.

The four-hundred-feet-before-turning rule comes from instrument departure procedure calculations. Absent specific instructions, if you climb at two hundred feet per mile to four hundred feet above the airport before turning, you won't hit anything.

My diligent first officer didn't lower the nose to increase speed and call for flap retraction going through a thousand feet. I thought he'd forgotten and mentioned it. He said he had a personal rule against retracting flaps in a turn.

I liked flying with him in spite of our different styles. He caught little things I tended to miss.

Our Holiday Inn in Sacramento was jammed with school kids for History Day and with police officers and firefighters for a convention. Elevators were busy and service was slow. When I checked out in the evening, my second officer was already in the car. I assumed the first officer was late because of the elevator crunch and waited a couple of minutes before going back inside to call him on the house phone. I asked the operator to ring his room number. She needed a name. Somebody answered, but she'd rung the wrong room.

A different operator answered when I called again. I told her the name and room number. She said that room wasn't occupied. I asked her to ring it anyway. She refused.

I slammed the phone down and walked the few steps to the busy front desk. They young woman behind the counter looked stern and prim, about the way you'd expect Dennis the Menace's friend Margaret to look when she grew up if she turned out not to be happy.

"Will you please call room nine hundred for me? That goddam bitch on the house phone won't do it."

She said, "Excuse me?" with the look and tone of a grade school teacher of generations past. I apologized and revised my request.

She said she'd checked us all out. I said I didn't care, that my crewman was not downstairs, and that I needed to be sure he'd left his room. She put the call through, handed me the phone, and strode off. There was no answer, so he was either on his way down or dead. I went back outside.

Two or three minutes later, he came out of the hotel. I asked when he'd checked out. "About fifteen seconds ago," he said.

It occurred to me on the drive to the airport that Margaret the Clerk had not said we'd all checked out but that she'd checked us all out. I wished I'd held my temper better so I'd have been in a position to write a letter to the hotel manager.

A wall of thunderstorms covered Pennsylvania and extended southeast into Maryland. Air traffic in New England was stopped. Some flights had been waiting to get out of Boston several hours past departure times.

Weather improved and we took off from Boston after only an hour's delay. My first officer—I'll call her Sandra—was new to the right seat, but I didn't realize how inexperienced she was. Sandra seemed reluctant to trim the airplane, even after I explained how to watch what the autopilot was doing for guidance on what trim the airplane needed to be happy. That airplane was a twisted one that required retrimming with every change of power, speed, or configuration. When hand-flying the arrival, she struggled to keep the airplane from rolling into a turn. I finally reached down and cranked in some rudder trim. She immediately noticed the improvement. I said, "Sorry, but I just couldn't stand it any longer."

We had a noticeable drift from a left crosswind, and Sandra tried to use a small-airplane technique to correct for it, flying in a slip with the upwind wing down, rather than accepting the crab angle with wings level and then using rudder to align the airplane with the centerline at the last moment.

I sat in the company cafeteria with my second officer on the trip just completed and said I was pleased that I'd remembered all three of my after-landing flow items five flights in a row. Richard said I was doing better than someone he'd recently flown with who couldn't even remember the one item a first officer had to do after landing—turning off the pitot heat switch on the overhead panel. Richard had reached up and turned it off on both legs. I asked who that was, mildly curious but not expecting an answer. Many pilots would not name names when telling of others' shortcomings. He said it was Sandra.

I told him he wasn't doing her a favor by doing her job for her. I suggested he read the checklist and, if the switch wasn't off when she responded that it was, he should repeat the item until she caught her mistake.

He said a friend of his in her upgrade class said that, if she'd been a man, she'd have busted out of training.

Airlines were rife with stories of sub-standard female or minority pilots advancing because companies didn't want to be sued for discrimination. I told Richard that, when I heard negative critiques like that one, I always made allowances if the subject was female or had skin not as light as his and mine.

* * *

A captain failed a drug test and was fired.

It was astronomically unlikely that all three members of one crew would have their names drawn at the same time for a random test, so we surmised someone had turned in a tip. I couldn't believe any pilot would be so stupid as to smoke a joint when it could mean the end of a hard-earned and lucrative career, so I suspected a setup. Maybe someone had slipped him a doctored snack and then called the FAA.

A few years earlier, one of our pilots had lost his job after testing positive for marijuana. He spun a tale of having eaten marijuana brownies without knowing what was in them at a party, and the party's host backed him up. He kept his license, but DHL didn't take him back. I, being naïve, believed his story. I didn't know he'd bragged that he took a supplement that removed traces of the drug from his system. I hope he got his money back.

Boston was below minimums when we took off from Cincinnati, so we were released to Windsor Locks with all the fuel we could carry so we could hold and wait for Boston to come up.

I was flying, so Sidney was on the radio. Luckily for me and for the controller, Sidney was on a bathroom break when ATC asked our intentions. I explained in one sentence that, although we were flight-planned to Windsor Locks, we intended to go to Boston if weather improved. It would have taken Sidney a couple of paragraphs to perhaps get the point across.

The controller re-cleared us to Boston. I shouldn't have accepted that because Boston wasn't yet legal for us. If our radios died, we'd be expected to comply with that clearance. We held at Gardner VOR and stayed high to burn less fuel. Soon, visibility came up to our minimums.

We flew a Monitored Approach, one in which the captain is flying the airplane but he isn't, and the first officer isn't flying the airplane but he is. The first officer flies with the autopilot, but he makes altitude calls as though the captain were flying. The captain looks out the window all the way down and takes the airplane only if he sees lights or the runway. The second officer monitors instruments to back up the first officer. If the captain doesn't say he is taking the airplane by the time it reaches decision height, the first officer begins a missed approach.

It was confusing when we began training for Monitored Approaches several months earlier, and we didn't do them often. The idea was a good one, to eliminate the visual transition from inside to outside at a critical moment just above the ground.

That particular airplane required continual changes to aileron and rudder trim as speed and configuration changed. I'd learned to trim it so that, although the ball indicated it was not trimmed, the airplane flew straight and the autopilot didn't fight the heading bug. Sidney trimmed the rudder to center the ball with wings level because that's the way the book said to do it.

I saw lights and took control of the airplane. We were near the ground in dense fog with no visual reference except approach lights. I clicked off the autopilot and, because the airplane was out of trim, it dropped a wing and tried to turn. I returned the wings to level just as we touched down.

We got out of recurrent training class early one day, and a couple of us drove to Sporty's Pilot Shop across the river in Ohio. The new headset I bought then was probably the last one I'd ever need with four years, one month, and twenty-four days to go before I turned into a pumpkin.

Time remaining to mandatory pilot retirement age was meaningless to me, but I was always aware of it. I wouldn't be able to afford to retire, even if I wanted to, and I didn't want to. I'd retrain as a second officer and downgrade to that entry-level position and ride sideways until I got tired of it or until DHL replaced old airplanes with new ones requiring a crew of only two. Income wasn't the only thing that would keep me working. My wife and I weren't entirely joking that my schedule probably made our marriage workable. The prospect of having to put up with each other full time sometimes floated to the surface of conscious thought.

I finally crashed the simulator. On an engine-out go-around the first day, I let the nose get too low right after the gear came up and we hit the runway. The simulator tumbled and slammed around as much as being bolted to the concrete floor would allow. Our instructor said it was the best crash he'd seen. We climbed out and took a short break while Flight Safety technicians rebooted the computer, or whatever it was they did to get the machine working again.

In the afternoon session, we were supposed to practice avoiding unexpected encounters with the ground. I survived wind shear, as usual, even when we got a sudden tailwind too late to get stopped. I shoved power to the stops and kept the wheels on the ground all the way to the end of the runway. We were still well below normal rotation speed, but the airplane flew. Our instructor seemed disappointed that we survived. In debrief, an instructor suggested I try to avoid over-controlling. I told him that's what instructors had been telling me from my first flying lesson.

After lunch, we were back in the box for my checkride. It was the easiest one I'd ever had. The instructor didn't bother to check my flight bag to be sure I had all the required equipment, and that was a good thing.

The flight computer, a circular slide rule, was still in the original shrink wrap. It was a company-approved model when I bought it, but DHL's new rule required a bigger one. I saw no reason to waste money on something I'd never use. The Skipper advised leaving the things in the original packaging to preserve resale value.

I got to Seattle on time for my jumpseat Tuesday evening after a week at home, but the takeoff warning system wouldn't test and the airplane was grounded. I had to call in sick and book a jumpseat for the following evening.

I was uncomfortable using sick leave improperly, but the days of instant vacation were long past. I told the scheduler I'd be in the next night and booked a jumpseat. Then I called Barb to let her know I was coming home so she wouldn't be alarmed when our dog barked in the night.

We were at maximum landing weight when we got to San Juan, and I made the hardest landing I'd ever make in a Boeing 727.

My crew and I were glassy-eyed zombies. The autopilot didn't intercept the localizer because I forgot to turn the selector knob to Approach after I made that change in the flight director. I clicked off the autopilot and flew by hand.

Anytime instruments showed me exactly on speed and on flight path for more than a few seconds, I assumed they were broken. Tired as I was, the approach was probably the most stable I'd ever flown. Speed was precisely on the bug all the way down.

When we landed on Runway 10, wind, disrupted by airport buildings, sometimes dropped to almost nothing just above the ground. I had no extra speed for Ma and the kids, and we were at maximum landing weight. Airspeed dropped a few knots below the bug in that last few feet above the runway, and I didn't react quickly enough to add a brief burst of power to cushion our arrival.

Neither crew nor jumpseaters said anything about the landing, a bad sign, I thought. Moderately lousy landings usually drew sarcastic comments. I walked around the airplane to check tires for flat spots or other damage and told the mechanic why.

Our return to Cincinnati from Los Angeles a few days later was a nightmare of errors. When I got to the airplane, the second officer was trying to figure out which of the several deferred maintenance items we'd arrived with had been cleared. The old DMI page had been filled and removed. The top line of the new one in the aluminum logbook case said, "All previous DMIs cleared."

I looked back a few pages in the flight log, but the several most recent pages were all maintenance entries documenting routine servicing and minor repairs. Pages that stayed with the airplane were fourth copies and hard to read. I didn't go back far enough to see a flight page with crew names.

The aluminum case that held the pad of log sheets had the airplane number painted on it, but it had become chipped and scratched over time and was illegible. The DMI sheet said all discrepancies were cleared, and no orange stickers remained on panels. That was good enough for me. It was time to fly.

When we blocked in at Phoenix, our mechanic came aboard and asked to see our logbook. The DC-8 captain in Los Angeles was more alert than I and noticed the mechanics had put our log on his airplane.

Thunderstorms caused departure delays out of Phoenix. That gave us time to wait for required recent pages from our log to come over the fax machine from Los Angeles. The long weather delay saved me from being blamed for the delay out of Phoenix. We flew fast and got to Cincinnati with a minute to spare before I'd have been replaced on my weekend Boston trip. Then the entire system was delayed because the DC-8 from Los Angeles had not arrived.

I thought it would be right behind us. Its captain, though, had wanted confirmation from higher up that he'd be legal flying with faxed copies of only the previous ten days of the log. That took time and phone calls. They were delayed further because, when Phoenix sent the required pages, the Los Angeles fax machine was out of paper.

I wondered what effect, if any, the long, tiring trip west followed by the short layover in Los Angeles may have had on our collective thinking, such as it was, while we puzzled over that logbook, trying to identify trees in the wrong forest. I had to explain to the flight manager how I'd screwed up. I expected a summons from the 727 chief pilot to come in on a day off without pay to explain my error to him. That was at least a few days in the future, too distant for me to worry about just then, and, as it turned out, too distant to worry about at all.

The long night continued. I was the only one going to the hotel in Boston. After my second call to the hotel, the clerk admitted she'd forgotten to radio the bus driver. I waited an hour for my ride.

A second officer I often flew with picked me up in his truck Monday morning, his canoe strapped on top and a lunch for us both in a backpack. We spent the day on a lake near his home in New Hampshire, and Tom grilled burgers when his wife got home from work. The day was a delightful break in weekend routine.

We were over New York that night when my second officer overheard a conversation on company radio between New York and Cincinnati. The right landing gear on one of our airplanes had collapsed on landing and the airplane caught fire. We speculated it was a DC-8, as no 727 was scheduled to arrive in New York at that hour.

I tuned the ADF to New York's all-news radio station and didn't have to wait long for the story. It was a DHL 727. The fire was small and crash trucks quickly extinguished it with foam. The crew got out unhurt, except for a minor injury to one while sliding down the escape rope. I hoped the airplane wasn't N722DH, the one I'd landed hard in San Juan a week earlier.

When we arrived in Cincinnati, the building was abuzz. All sorts of managers we never saw in the middle of the night were there. We learned the airplane had been leaving New York, not arriving, with five on board, including two jumpseaters coming to work.

Number two engine had failed right after takeoff. The crew declared an emergency, ran through procedures and checklists, dumped fuel, and returned to land. A 747 was on their runway, cleared for takeoff and not moving. The 727 had to go around on two engines and set up for another approach.

The landing was smooth, but the right main gear collapsed. The captain kept the airplane on the runway as long as he could before the dragging wing swerved it off into the dirt. Crash trucks were there immediately and put out a small fire. The airplane was N722DH.

I'd landed the airplane hard by my standards, but not hard enough to require a log entry and an inspection of the landing gear. I thought I should tell the director of operations about my landing, but other pilots advised me to keep my mouth shut and see what came of the investigation. If the cause was ruled previous damage from an unreported hard landing, I could re-evaluate my position. They reminded me that I didn't know what may have happened to the airplane during the week between my landing and the airplane's ultimate one. Still, it bothered me that what happened may have been, in some way, my fault. When I talked it over with the second officer who was with me on the San Juan landing, he said he'd been through much harder landings at DHL, usually with former military pilots.

When I saw the captain several days later, I told him the whole story. He said inspectors found so much corrosion in the airplane, it could have happened to anyone at any time.

In early September, I went in for my FAA medical exam. I passed the eye tests without correction for distance, though I'd begun wearing glasses more than thirty years earlier. After becoming increasingly myopic, as bookworms often do, I'd reversed the trend and was back to normal in less than two years of rebending the proverbial twig. All I'd done to reverse nearsightedness was wear drugstore reading glasses nearly all the time, the corrections always a bit stronger than I needed for what I was doing.

October weather triggers in me an urge to prepare for winter. I busied myself cutting firewood, bringing in the last of the vegetable garden, and getting ready for hunting season.

I screwed up my bid and got Mexico City weekends in November, but I had enough sick time to cover both. Because of a spate of schedule glitches, I'd softened my resolve to avoid using sick leave for other purposes. I'd begun to refer to sick days as schedule reconciliation days. Meanwhile, the woods awaited. Deer season was open and soon it would be time for elk.

I'd been off seven weeks when I drove to Seattle late in October. Big news at work was, a system bid was out for a new airplane. Rumors that DHL would add Airbus A-300s to the fleet appeared to be true. The model we'd acquire was of the last generation of airliners to require a crew of three.

Rumors are the lifeblood of airlines. We were always either about to buy UPS or to be bought by it. We were going to buy Airborne Express. We were going to get more 727s, or more DC-8s. Some pilots started outrageous stories, just to see if they'd fly. I tended to discount all rumors. They changed every few days and most were wrong anyway.

The last Friday in October was a reserve day, but I was far enough down the list to sneak out on the airplane to Seattle. My truck and camper were in the SeaTac parking lot loaded with hunting gear. I didn't go home but drove to the eastern Cascades for elk season. I almost forgot to call in sick for my Mexico City weekend.

My first trip of 1999 was a six-day New Year's layover in Puerto Rico. When I saw the long New Year's layover on my schedule weeks earlier, I suggested that Barb come to San Juan.

When I was at home, I didn't feel like going anywhere, so inviting her to join me on long layovers in interesting places seemed like a good way to give her vacations from homebound routine. I was surprised when she wasn't enthusiastic and disappointed when she eventually declined. Maybe memory of our Guadalajara debacle was too strong.

Snow in Cincinnati made everyone's departures late, so Crew Scheduling had ordered box lunches for us in Miami. They hadn't arrived when we were ready to go, so I told the mechanics to eat them. We were tired and wanted to get to the hotel.

At Lupi's that evening, the waiter with short bleached hair and a stud in his tongue remembered me. I ordered my usual burrito dinner and two Coronas and read a Zane Grey western while I ate. I ordered the same thing again and considered eating a third, but sanity prevailed, and I was falling asleep by the time I'd finished eating.

I unplugged phones and slept fourteen hours. Year's end noise did not penetrate my earplugs.

I spent part of Sunday afternoon lounging on the beach. The first officer on the other weekend crew went with me to Lupi's, and soon his captain joined us. I ate two burrito dinners. The other two weren't yet hungry and planned to eat later at Outback Steakhouse in Embassy Suites, then gamble a little in that hotel's casino. I was tired and didn't want more beer, but it was only a little out of the way, so I tagged along. We sat at the bar and I ordered a vodka on the rocks, something I could sip and make last a long time. I watched amazed as the young woman tending bar tossed a few ice cubes into a glass and filled it to the brim with vodka.

My two companions talked as they ate and drank their beers. I couldn't hear well over noise and clatter of the bar and restaurant and didn't pay attention to the conversation. I was still behind on sleep and eager to get back to our hotel.

Three seats across from us at the horseshoe-shaped bar opened up and were immediately taken by three women, two twenty-somethings chatting merrily with each other and another woman, several years older, who sat quietly studying the menu before ordering.

I sipped my vodka, waiting for my companions to finish eating and move to the casino. My mind wandered as I looked around at people coming and going, eating and drinking, laughing and talking. Now and then my eyes lingered on the quiet woman sitting directly across from me. She looked around as she ate her dinner and sipped her drink, not as though expecting someone, just taking in everything around her, much the way I was. When she finished eating and appeared to be getting ready to leave, I asked the bartender to give her another of whatever she'd been drinking, but, if she asked, to tell her it was from all three of us. I didn't want her to think I was trying to pick her up. She glanced at us from time to time as she drank her margarita, and I didn't notice when she left.

In the casino, I saw her playing a slot machine and tried to strike up a conversation. She insisted, in English, that she spoke no English, and, when I called her on that, she laughed. We walked over to a small bar in the lobby and talked, she with rusty, public school English and I with non-existent Spanish. We talked about our families and showed each other photos of children and, in my case, grandchildren. I couldn't understand her name and asked her to write it on a napkin. Nereida. When I mispronounced it, she corrected me: Neh *r-r-ray* dah.

Time and alcohol caught up with me and I told her I had to go to my hotel. She saw I wasn't sober and offered a ride. The thought that she could have been setting me up for robbery or worse crossed my mind. Perhaps an accomplice was hiding behind the seat of her car. I thanked her for the offer and declined, but, when I stood up, I realized I was probably in greater danger walking down a dark street alone. I looked around the casino, hoping my companions were ready to leave. I didn't see them, so I accepted the ride. I fell asleep on the short drive to the hotel but woke up when the car stopped. I asked if she'd like to walk on the beach.

I realized that I'd put myself in an unfamiliar and perhaps dangerous situation—I a married man and she a recent divorcée, enjoying a walk in the moonlight on a tropical island. But, no harm done, and I'd never see her again.

The only part of the parking ticket on the windshield I could read was the amount of the fine. I had assured her it was okay to park there and insisted on paying the fifty dollars, but I didn't have that much cash. She said it didn't matter. I insisted on paying it and asked her to come to the hotel the next evening for the money. And I invited her to dinner.

Monday evening in San Juan a couple of weeks later, I was in the lobby on time and the second officer arrived a minute later. Our driver pulled up out front. I called my first officer on the house phone and woke him up.

The driver had to pick up a Continental crew at another hotel and we were making him late. When we got to the airport and reached for the customary tips, I told the first officer to dig deep because he and I owed the driver big time. He owed because he'd made the driver late. I owed because my crew was my responsibility. I told our driver to tell the Continental crew that FedEx made him late.

It was a typical Monday, worse because it actually was a Monday. My second officer that month wasn't much older than 60, but he seemed ancient in his lack of speed and general forgetfulness. The loader in Miami had taken his copies of the paperwork and left the airplane. In peripheral vision, I saw the stairs being rolled away from the door. We were ready to push back, I thought, but I hadn't turned far enough in my seat to look past the second officer to double-check that all the lights on his doors annunciator were out.

I rattled off the before-start litany to the mechanic on the ground: "A-pumps off, ground interconnect closed, beacon's on, brakes released, cleared to push."

Nothing happened and the guy on the ground didn't say anything. I leaned forward to look down and saw the mechanic talking to another man and pointing up at the side of the airplane. I twisted to my left and looked back through the side windows and saw the entry door standing open.

Flustered and embarrassed, I almost started to taxi without calling for the Before Taxi checklist, but my second officer caught that. I was pleased that he had, but I'd have been happier if he'd remembered to close the damn door.

I wasn't surprised that I didn't get Seattle weekends when the schedule came out for March, as there were many captains senior to me living in the Pacific Northwest. I was surprised to get my third choice, short San Juan weekends.

Short meant normal. Instead of both weekend crews staying three nights and four days, the crew that arrived Saturday morning would leave Monday evening, a normal weekend layover. The crew that arrived Friday morning would not leave until Tuesday evening after five days and four nights in paradise. The caveat was, if the charter department lined up any weekend work in that part of the world, the crew with the extra-long layover had to fly it. Any charters would be scheduled before the crew left Cincinnati, so they wouldn't have to hang around the hotel in case something came up.

For the next year, I got long San Juan weekends more often than not and never had to fly a charter during layover. Lying on a tropical beach, drinking beer, eating good food, and wandering around Old San Juan visiting museums, art galleries, and shops was a great way to earn a living. I was able to get those weekends because many pilots senior to me didn't like sitting around five days with nothing to do.

Another reason few bid San Juan weekends was the trips that went along with them. Beginning a week with the long grind to Los Angeles was a tough way to transition from time off to night flying. West coast pilots, particularly, liked to start the work week with a short trip. Yet another reason for avoiding San Juan weekends was a change in the way we were paid. Under our new contract, we earned more for flying than for sitting, and many pilots bid for pay.

That was fine with me. They could take years off their lives with the stress of night work. They'd make more money than I would while I held down their spots on the beach and slept nights like a normal person. If I couldn't be home on weekends, I'd settle for a tropical island.

At home one morning, I woke after a vivid dream of taking off from San Juan. The airplane would not leave the ground. I slammed power to the stops and yelled at the second officer to dump fuel. We lifted off but could barely climb. I was thinking in my dream that, if we got down alive, I'd demand a re-weigh of our cargo.

I was busy getting a collection of my newspaper columns ready for publication. I painted a cover for the book and spent several days fighting with computer, scanner, and printer. Every re-reading of what I thought was a clean manuscript turned up more typos. Going to work the last Friday in January was welcome respite from frantic days off.

I was beginning to think perhaps 60 was a good age to stop flying. Half a dozen of our pilots had retired to the back seat. The three I flew with most often were asleep at the switch half the time, too often literally.

One could have passed for 45 with unlined face and no trace of gray in his hair. After starting engines in Cincinnati, I looked back at his panel, waiting for him to put generators on line and go through his flow so we could do the checklist and get going. He was jotting down notes and tending to paperwork. I asked if he was planning to put the generators on line before we took off or after. He had it in his head that we would be pushing back, in which case his post-start chores would commence after the towbar was disconnected.

It was a minor brain fart, but I'd keep an eye on his panel until I'd flown with him enough to know if such lapses were common. Then I forgot to call for the Taxi checklist until the first officer reminded me.

Another old second officer was slow like an unwarm reptile. The third was both slow and not mentally in the game. I wondered if those three were a large enough sample on which to judge the age group, or if perhaps riding sideways after being pilot-in-command was such a letdown that they couldn't muster enough interest to do the job well.

Our route to Austin was a gantlet of cumulonimbus to nearly twice our altitude with continuous lightning on all sides. We kept twenty miles between the airplane and red blobs on the radar, but a couple of bumps bounced books and coffee mugs around the cockpit and disengaged the autopilot. I put it back on but neglected to re-engage altitude hold. My first officer caught it as soon as altitude began to drift. That and my failure to call for the Taxi checklist made two beers I owed him.

Our regular driver in Guadalajara hadn't waited for our late arrival, it being the weekend and his contract with DHL not requiring him to wait. Only on weekends did we stay at a hotel off the airport, the Fiesta Americana. One of the loaders said he'd take us after they finished with the airplane. As we drove out of the airport, a man with a briefcase tried to flag us down. Eduardo told us to never pick up riders, especially pretty young girls. "They'll slit your throat and rob you," he said.

We saw young women trying to hitch rides along the highway. If they were carrying knives, we couldn't figure out where they could be hiding them.

My scheduled trip for Thursday was the short hop to Atlanta, and I was scheduled for a line check. Instead of the check airman riding my scheduled trip, I was assigned to fly his to Houston. There was no fog in the forecast, but soon after we took off from Cincinnati, Houston socked in. We continued in hopes visibility would improve. When it didn't, Dispatch re-released us to Austin. The entire crew was fresh except me, so my start time in Sacramento the evening before determined when we had to park the airplane.

We sat with an engine running for an hour after landing. Our APU was deferred and it took that hour for the Austin ground crew to find a ground power unit for us. While we waited, we tried to calculate my drop-dead time. The second officer found a seldom-invoked and unfamiliar rule that he thought applied. With lawyer language stripped away, it appeared that, because I'd flown more than nine hours in twenty-four without a required eleven hours of rest afterward, at no later than twenty-four hours after the short rest began—layover in Sacramento—I had to go off the clock for twelve hours.

Because of the way the rule was worded, it was difficult to understand, even for wide awake people. Crew Scheduling didn't understand it when I called them on my phone, and I was too tired to construct clear sentences. I handed the second officer the phone and asked him to explain. He spoke slowly, calmly, and clearly, much as a parent might in trying to convince a toddler it was time to go to bed.

Because Austin wasn't then a destination, we had no regular hotel. Crew Scheduling made reservations for us, but the taxi took us to the wrong Red Lion. That hotel's van took us to the correct one. We all ate breakfast and I washed my uniform shirt and called Crew Scheduling to work out my rest period start and stop times. Then I called each crewmember and told them what time we should leave the hotel that evening and went to bed.

I woke after only two hours because the room heated in the sun. I turned on the air conditioner and went back to sleep and did not awaken again until five minutes after we were supposed to meet in the lobby.

Heart pounding, I called Crew Scheduling to tell them I'd overslept and to confirm departure time was ten o'clock. Then I called the hotel desk and asked if the DHL crew was in the lobby. Who? Three pilots. Blue suits.

I told the check airman I'd be right down. I brushed my teeth, put on my clean but wrinkled shirt, and packed fast.

Paperwork was waiting for us at the cargo handler's office. We waited ten minutes for a van and driver to take us to the airplane. We had only half an hour before departure time, and that would have been enough, except that the airplane was dark and no one was around. There was no ground power unit in sight.

The stairs were gone, too, but the airplane was empty, so we lowered the aft stairs and went in through the DB Cooper door. The battery switch was on and the battery was dead. The unloading crew had turned it on for interior lighting and hadn't turned it off.

I called Cincinnati and explained our situation. We needed a power unit and perhaps a new battery. Maintenance advised trying to charge the battery as soon as we got a power unit. It would take thirty to forty-five minutes to fully charge, they said. Meanwhile, they'd try to locate a new battery, already charged. We needed electric power to operate valves and gauges before fuel could be pumped aboard.

After the GPU arrived and we had power on the airplane, we began to get ready to fly. The auxiliary vertical gyro wasn't working. The mechanic deferred it. When we tested wing anti-ice, lights wouldn't show the left wing's valve was open. When I released the test switch, the lights wouldn't show it was closed again. While we were pondering that, the light came on indicating the valve had closed.

I held the test switch again for a longer time, gave up and let it go. The Closed light came on again, though in less time than before. We figured the valve was hung up on pigeon shit or something and kept trying. Finally, we got a valid test.

While all that was going on, the airplane from Guadalajara landed to clear customs and take on cargo en route to Cincinnati. There was only one tug, and we both needed it to push back. We got out first and headed for Houston to pick up cargo.

Our dispatcher had asked us to call him before we got there. The through flight from Mexico City was able to take on all the Houston freight, so we were re-released to Cincinnati, the first good thing that had happened in nearly twenty-four hours. Before we got to Cincinnati, the #1 VOR receiver began to fail, not locking onto navigation signals until we were near the stations. Then, on final approach, the #1 ADF failed.

During debriefing—the flight was a line check, after all—the check airman asked about the departure out of Cincinnati. I told him I couldn't remember departing Cincinnati. What he was getting at was, we'd taken off with fuel distribution improperly set, and neither the second officer nor I had noticed.

I'd looked back at the Doors panel and the yellow Tail Skid light on the Doors panel caught my eye. It was the only airplane in the fleet that showed a light when the tail skid was down when it should be down. I hadn't noticed pump-off lights on the fuel panel a couple of feet away from the light that had grabbed my attention. I asked the second officer if he'd had his fuel pump lights dimmed, and he conceded he had. He said he wouldn't do that again.

The check airman was generally pleased with our performance under abnormal circumstances, especially our teamwork. I couldn't remember a worse day in my career.

I'd been assured that a fully drained aircraft battery would be fully charged after less than an hour, and, sure enough, it had appeared to be fully charged. We relied on a full charge in that battery to give us twenty-five minutes of useful life to power vital instruments long enough to get the airplane on the ground if all generators failed. A pilot I'd known for years was more cynical than I. His experience had taught him that management and mechanics will tell pilots all sorts of lies to get an airplane off the ground. After hearing about my diversion to Austin, he researched NiCad batteries. What he learned indicated it would take the dead battery *a full day* to recharge, that what we'd thought was a full charge was surface charge only, good for maybe five minutes.

We almost took off for Phoenix and Los Angeles on time. We'd started engines, but when the first officer reached up to turn on pitot heat, he noticed one of the six indicator lights was out. It would take only a moment to change the bulb. I reached up to twist off the amber lens and the entire light socket came out of the overhead. We shut engines down and mechanics wheeled stairs back up to the door. Three came aboard to fix the light, one to work and two to watch.

In Los Angeles, I got a call from the flight manager asking for our version of why we'd had to take a delay. He needed to have the flight department's argument ready for the daily blame assessment meeting.

My first officer got a prime room on the front corner of the hotel overlooking the beach in San Juan. My room stank of smoke and had one window and no view. I went downstairs to request a change and got a corner room with good ventilation. When I said something to the first officer about his getting a good room while I, the captain, got a dump, he confessed that he tipped the desk clerk ten dollars every time he stayed there.

We'd been deiced in Cincinnati to remove light frost. The book said the wing had to be checked visually within five minutes before takeoff. The second officer, a former Air Force transport pilot, reminded us as we taxied.

Without precipitation, the chance new ice had formed in the few minutes between being hosed off with hot fluid and takeoff was zero. Both for my legal protection and for crew comfort, I never told my crew to do something contrary to the book. I made some remark that the second officer could interpret as permission not to bother. He said he preferred to check.

We stopped before we took the runway. The second officer turned off the packs to depressurize the airplane so he could open the door. He left the cockpit, unstrapped the big flashlight stowed on the airplane just for checking for ice, donned a safety harness clipped to a ring on the sidewall, and opened the door to lean out and shine the light on the wing. There was no ice, of course, but he'd followed the rules.

The newspaper I wrote for published a collection of my weekly columns, and I began taking books to work to sell. I'd sold several dozen before a senior captain took me aside to tell me he thought I was being too pushy, that junior crewmembers might feel they were being coerced into buying books.

I had not considered that possibility. I toned down my sales pitch.

I had a vivid dream of flying a 727 with my brother in the right seat and no second officer. In my dream, we were landing in Cincinnati with a strong tailwind and had to abandon the approach. As we climbed straight out, Jon got sick. I was busy taking care of him and trying to find out what was wrong. The airplane continued to climb east and we didn't talk to anybody. By the time my brother was restored to normal health, we were several states east of Cincinnati and out of radio range. We turned the airplane around to head back, but headwind was so strong, we were stationary over the ground. I landed the airplane like a helicopter on a dusty, sandy field and shut down. My brother was okay, but it was two or three days before we were discovered. I was upset that I'd missed my weekend trip to San Juan.

Puerto Ricans drove in what seemed like chaotic anarchy, but their way seemed to work well and with less anger and horn blowing than in New York City. I soon realized Puerto Ricans drove the way I would if I didn't have to worry about traffic cops. Puerto Rican drivers were assertive rather than aggressive. To enter bumper-to-bumper traffic from a side street, a car crept forward until someone stopped to make room. Such a maneuver in the states would prompt shouting and rude gestures. Puerto Ricans accepted it as normal.

I rented a Toyota the next time I was in San Juan for a weekend, finally brave enough to drive there. I pulled into traffic on the expressway and accelerated to fifty-five. Everyone zipped past at sixty to eighty miles per hour. I speeded up to go with the flow and soon felt right at home.

We were closed up and ready to leave Miami before someone realized two cans that San Juan loaders had tagged Cincinnati were supposed to be taken off in Miami. Different people had different solutions to the problem. One said to open the airplane and unload the Miami cans. The other said to fly it all to Cincinnati as the tags instructed. I called Cincinnati on my phone. They didn't know anything about it.

The Miami crew didn't like the idea of unloading and reloading in heavy rain, so we'd leave as we were. Rain had soaked the mechanic's headset, so we pushed back and started engines on hand signals. The mechanic and tug driver didn't know which runway we'd been assigned and we had no way of telling them. They turned us the wrong way, but there was room to make a tight one-eighty on the ramp. As we began the turn, we heard and felt a hard bang. The tiller froze and we couldn't steer.

The ground crew had run inside to get out of the rain. No one noticed when I flashed landing lights. I phoned Cincinnati and they called Miami.

We sat in the airplane for an hour. One of the mechanics came up the stairs with a message for us to call Cincinnati. Crew Scheduling had gotten us rooms and the hotel van was on the way.

Crew Scheduling called after I'd returned to my room from an early afternoon breakfast. Our airplane wouldn't be ready until after midnight. I called my crew and told them the new plan. I reminded them that it was no more certain than any other DHL plan, and if it changed, I'd let them know. Later, I went back to El Tropico to eat again. If we arrived in Cincinnati too late for our scheduled trip to Houston, I'd probably ride home on Delta or United, so I skipped the garlic.

Our airplane was across the airport at the heavy maintenance facility. We had to go to DHL to get our flight bags, but the building was locked and deserted. We found a guard who had a key to the office complex, but none of us knew the combination to the room where our bags were. We'd never seen that door closed before.

I was getting out my phone to call Cincinnati when the guard slid the window open on the cargo side of the wall, climbed through, and handed our flight bags out.

The van driver then drove us around to the other side of the airport where our airplane was. We were towed out nineteen minutes late. We'd have been a few minutes quicker if my first officer had been anyone but Darrel. It took time to convince him we didn't need a signature on the weight and balance form to verify all cargo locks were up. That the airplane was empty was irrelevant to his way of thinking.

I was in San Juan when I learned The Skipper was dead. Captain Scamahorn flew gyroplanes for recreation. He and his passenger were descending to land. An ultralight took off and climbed into him. I called my crew and told them the news. We repaired to the rooftop bar for a wake and the other crew joined us. We told Skipper stories and toasted his memory. It turned into a long night.

A tropical storm threatened to become a hurricane. It didn't pass over Puerto Rico, but it came close enough to make it a wet weekend. When we left San Juan Tuesday evening, Grand Turk radar was out of service, damaged by lightning. Because controllers couldn't see us over the middle of the flight, we'd have to actually navigate and fly the route we'd been assigned instead of being given a radar vector direct. Our flight-planned route took us south of our normal path and through Dominican Republic and Haitian airspace to avoid Tropical Storm David.

My first officer had come from the DC-8 and was familiar with international flying rules I hadn't bothered to learn in ground school. He knew we had to make radio contact with Santo Domingo and again with Haiti ten minutes before entering their air space. Had I been flying with someone of marginal competence—someone such as myself—I'd have looked closely enough at the chart to notice all those rules printed along the route of flight.

It was the first officer's leg, but he suggested that I fly and he talk. I confessed I was thinking the same thing, but that I hadn't wanted to appear to be weaseling out of the hard part.

When we were getting ready to leave San Juan one evening, the load manager complained that my second officer had yelled at his men about shoving cans too hard and throwing sill guards around. He said we should talk to him, not to his men, many of who didn't speak English well. I agreed and went further. My crew should talk to me and I should then talk to him. I said I'd speak to the second officer.

He conceded he'd been sarcastic and forceful. I explained the concept of chain-of-command and suggested that, if he had problems with ground crews in the future, he inform his captain.

We had to detour south of our course between San Juan and Miami to avoid a mass of thunderstorms. GPS warned we were near Havana airspace, and soon we were in it. I checked the chart to see how far we were from Cuba. We were within a hundred miles and in the Outer Zone but not yet near the Inner Zone. I had no idea what those zones signified. Miami Center was too busy rerouting airplanes around weather for us to ask how close to the island we could go before Fidel invited us to land. Tension in the cockpit ran high, more from fear of a fighter escort to a Cuban airport than from fierce storms on our right. Nothing happened, and soon we were able to turn north toward Miami.

Just before we started down for Cincinnati, I saw a tiny frog clinging to the wall next to the toilet, a coqui, a ubiquitous amphibian from Puerto Rico. The frog was no doubt colder than it had ever been and probably dehydrated.

We put the frog in a coffee cup with a wet paper towel and snapped on a lid. I gave the stowaway to the crew going to San Juan that morning. They let it go in the hotel lawn. I chuckled, imagining the story of alien abduction the coqui might tell his friends if frogs could talk.

I was busy getting the truck and camper ready to drive to South Dakota to hunt pheasants with friends. I cut firewood and stacked it in the boiler room, enough that Barb wouldn't run out during the two weeks or more I'd be gone. After returning from South Dakota, I was home again only a couple of days before heading into the Cascade Mountains to hunt elk.

I slept late into my first morning home after nine days of slogging up and down mountains in snowy woods with a rifle and pack. I began to consider that, at age 57, I might be past my prime.

Barb said she hated those three fall months when all I thought about was hunting and guns. I thought, if she hates three months, she's going to love my retirement. After breakfast,

I went down to my workshop in the basement to put a new barrel on my muzzle-loading rifle.

When we got to the airport to leave San Juan after a long Thanksgiving weekend, my second officer gave me a pound of Puerto Rican coffee. He was the only crewmember who had drunk my coffee over the years who contributed in any way. I was touched by his thoughtfulness, as it had never occurred to me to expect anyone to chip in.

We almost didn't get out of San Juan. The EXIT light over the entry door was powered by the airplane's battery. In my thirteen years on the airplane, I'd never known the light had to be checked during the second officer's standby battery check. Although voltage looked good at the gauge on the panel, the light faded rapidly. Mechanics had to install a new battery before we could fly.

I flew, dozed, and read Hemingway on the trip to Seattle. We clipped twenty minutes off the flight plan without trying and were on the ground early, so I drove home for the day and slept nearly six hours, about as long as I'd have slept in the hotel. I'd hoped a jumpseater could fly the return for me, but there were none.

We arrived in Cincinnati more than an hour late because we had to stop in Salt Lake City. Snow backed up arriving traffic there, and as soon as we turned off the runway and got clearance to parking, a UPS jet stopped on the taxiway with a mechanical problem. The captain refused to move until he was sure it was safe. A moment later, the #3 engine of a Delta L-1011 caught fire and ground control stopped all movement for half an hour while they sorted things out.

Loaders and fuelers worked fast getting us ready to go. We pushed back for de-icing and sat for nearly an hour waiting for our contract de-ice people to finish hosing down an Airborne Express DC-8 and refill their trucks.

We usually took off on Runway 34R, a short distance from our ramp. That night, we had to use Runway 35 on the other side of the airport. The long taxi ate up more time, and we were so late when we finally got to Cincinnati, the early flight to Seattle—my ride home—had taken off.

I signed the log, grabbed my bags, and ran down the stairs and across the ramp, hoping there was an open seat on the late flight, then almost ready to close doors and leave. One of the riders booked on that second airplane had taken my seat when I didn't show up for the early one, so I got his.

I called the jury-duty phone line. The clerk told me I didn't have to call again for a week. I loved jury duty, days off with full pay. My views on crime and punishment were well known in the community because of my newspaper column, and the chance I'd be allowed on a jury was almost zero.

As I drove down our long driveway on 23 December after three weeks off, I realized I'd forgotten my necktie, and I lost a few minutes going back to the house for it. Even so, I got to SeaTac in plenty of time to renew my parking pass for the next year. When I got to DHL, I learned the airplane had landed at Boeing that morning because of fog at SeaTac. After several minutes of indecision, someone somewhere decided to truck freight to Boeing Field rather than ferry the airplane to SeaTac. A mechanic drove the other jumpseater and me to Boeing.

We got out nearly two hours late and would arrive, at best, only half an hour before departure to San Juan. I called Crew Scheduling and said I did not want to lose my trip. I said I'd call when we blocked out to give them our ETA.

The captain was glad we were late. If we blocked in even one minute after four o'clock in the morning, he'd get an extra day's pay. I explained how much I didn't want to miss my trip. The captain said he'd try to hurry. It was snowing in Cincinnati and the system was running late enough that I got there in plenty of time.

Our hotel in San Juan was sold out and overbooked for Christmas. Because of a misunderstanding as to how many crews would be there, my crew and I were supposed to check out Christmas Day and go to the Ramada in Condado for one night. I asked at the desk who the first crew was. Two of them had checked out and gone home, but their rooms had been resold.

I thought our contract with the hotel was for six rooms every day of the year. We did not want to have to pack up after one day, move to Ramada, and move back after one day there, but we were too tired to deal with the problem until Christmas morning.

We went down at noon to check out. The hotel manager, a young woman who spoke unaccented English, listened respectfully as the elderly second officer and I argued that the two rooms of the pilots who'd checked out should be available to us. She countered that Crew Scheduling hadn't notified her there'd be two crews over Christmas until it was too late to reserve rooms. We'd been accommodated in another hotel, so the manager's problem was solved. When we got back to the Colony just before noon the next day, the lobby was crowded with people checking out, but our rooms were ready, nice ones on the front side of the hotel overlooking beach and ocean.

After spending Sunday on the beach, Nereida and I walked to Outback Steak House for dinner to mark a full year since we'd met there. I had not expected our relationship to last that long, but Nereida, even more than I, lived in the moment. I stayed with my lifelong pattern of not dealing with problems until I had to. We both knew DHL could change plans with little notice and that I had only a few years left in my career. I'd explained all that in the beginning to be sure she understood we had no future.

I'd always held myself to a high moral standard, and it was difficult to accept that I was no better than anyone else in that regard. The one thing I could do to preserve a shred of self-respect was to keep a high wall between home finances and personal money.

Pilots in the training department didn't like our new pay structure in the proposed contract. Because training pilots seldom flew, they'd miss out on higher pay. We line pilots had no sympathy. Training pilots worked days mostly and were home nearly every night.

At a union meeting, a training pilot argued that, by not boosting pay for trainers in the deal, we were dividing the pilot group and being unfair. A line pilot responded that trainers had always had better pay and better working conditions, and he wasn't interested in hearing pleas for equal treatment.

We airline pilots were like little kids whining because our cookies didn't have as many chocolate chips as some other kid's did.

Company called us in the air and told us to fly the airplane to Los Angeles as soon as it was unloaded in Sacramento Saturday morning. They needed it there for an urgent charter. Then Sacramento weather went down and we couldn't land. Company said nearby Mather Field was good and told us to go there. We checked. Mather was worse than Sacramento.

ATC gave us holding instructions. I had to draw Corrigan a picture of the holding pattern or he'd have turned the wrong direction and held in the wrong place. Fuel ran low. Company told us to go to Los Angeles.

I asked ATC for direct Los Angeles, not an unreasonable request had it still been the middle of the night. The controller laughed and said we couldn't do that, but he'd give us a clearance if we wanted one.

The first part was direct Linden. Corrigan, who liked to do everyone else's job while neglecting his own, punched LDN into the GPS, saw Linden VOR come up, and didn't notice the distance was nearly three thousand miles in the wrong direction.

I punched in the correct identifier for California's Linden and we were on our way. Corrigan had us going to Virginia. A recent crash of an Air Force airplane in Wyoming was fresh in my mind, and I said without thinking, "Now I see why you Air Force guys keep running into mountains."

We were assigned Runway 24R on the north side of the airport. That required us to cross the other three runways to get to our ramp. Ground rattled off our taxi route including a hold point and instruction to monitor Tower. Tower told us to taxi up to the hold bar. Corrigan told Tower we were at the hold bar, which we weren't. Tower told us to turn right and hold at the next hold bar which was about a hundred feet away. I did that, and Corrigan told me to keep going. I asked him to confirm which hold bar. It was the one I'd stopped at, the one he'd insisted we should cross to enter an active runway.

"You do a lot of guessing, don't you," I said.

The Los Angeles airplane had broken in Phoenix and ours was needed to fly the London Philharmonic's instruments to Fort Lauderdale for a concert the next day. The charter crew was there waiting for us, but our airplane had developed a fuel leak and wasn't going anywhere.

Corrigan hopped a ride home for the weekend. The second officer and I went to our hotel in El Segundo. I called Cincinnati to see if they had a plan for us. They didn't.

Over dinner and beers, we talked about our first officer and flying into mountains. I was most upset about Corrigan's punching in Linden from memory without checking to see if distance and direction made sense. My second officer was more concerned with his trying to convince me that we were cleared to cross the busy runway we were told to hold short of.

I slept well with delightful but unremembered dreams about roads in the woods, hiking, hunting, beaches, and flying small airplanes. When I woke up Sunday morning, I started the coffee maker and called Cincinnati to see if anyone had a plan. The dispatcher handed me off to Crew Scheduling. We'd fly the scheduled inbound through Phoenix on Tuesday evening.

I stayed up late but woke early Tuesday and went to the lobby for free breakfast. The inbound crew was there, so I joined them and got caught up on gossip. One of our pilots had been arrested for soliciting minor girls in a park in Cincinnati. We were shocked. It was *January*—too damn cold to hang out, as it were, in parks.

As we approached Cincinnati, we were cleared to descend and Corrigan pulled the speed brake. I pointed out that we had forty miles to lose eleven thousand feet, a dozen miles more than we needed. He stowed the brake and mumbled something about wanting to get started down.

When I was setting up the radios for our approach, I noticed both ADF receivers were turned off. It was the first officer's job to check all radios. I said, "Nice radio check."

"Hunh?"

"ADFs are off," I said.

"Oh, that's okay."

"No, it isn't," I said.

Corrigan landed slightly sideways in the crosswind.

My pay stub showed six extra days, not the three I expected. I'd forgotten about three carryover days for the San Juan trip that extended into the new bid period. After deductions, that netted me nearly 2500 over my standard pay, almost enough to bring my checking account up to zero.

My wife was a saver and I was a spender. To avoid conflict, all regular income went into a joint account and we each drew an identical allowance for personal spending. That prevented arguments over whether I really needed a new shotgun or fishing rod. Any money either of us earned beyond basic salary was ours. I needed overtime because I spent more than my allowance.

When controllers told us of other airplanes in our area, my first officer reached up and turned on two landing lights. Most pilots turned on a light when passing other airplanes, and the other crew usually turned one on in reply. I seldom turned on lights unless there was potential conflict, and then I'd use just one.

I asked why he turned on two when one would serve. No reason, he said. He just did it that way.

Later, when I was flying, he turned on both lights in response to a traffic call. I turned one off and said, "When it's my leg, we'll use one light."

I wondered why such a small thing seemed a big deal to me. Then I remembered my Cessna 152.

My airplane had two lights in the nose, a landing light and another pointed down a few degrees for taxiing. It's good practice to turn on big lights near airports, day or night, to help other pilots see the airplane, but big bulbs cost money and have a short life. In my Cessna, replacements came out of my pocket. I instructed students to use only one light and save the other for when the first one burned out. I explained all that to my first officer by way of apology for being a prick about the lights.

I saw a copy of the company's trip plan for the rest of the year. The Airbus would fly to San Juan beginning in May, and only Airbuses and DC-8s would go to Miami. The only way I could get to Puerto Rico would be to bid weekends in whatever east coast cities had frequent non-stops to San Juan.

I considered changing airplanes, but there was no guarantee the Airbus would stay on the San Juan trip, and a fall class and subsequent annual recurrent training would interfere with hunting seasons. I realized with mild shock that I'd have only one more recurrent training as a pilot after a fall or winter Airbus class. I was pushing mandatory retirement age, but I still felt like a kid.

With Nereida's marginal English and my non-existent Spanish, I had a difficult time explaining DHL's changes to airplane assignments and how they would affect my ability to get to Puerto Rico. Earlier, I might have welcomed a forced break in our relationship, but a point of no return had passed unnoticed some time before.

I was glad I hadn't bid the Airbus. San Juan would become a DC-8 trip starting in May.

When I got to San Juan late one Friday morning, I went to the store and bought a case of beer. The second officer chipped in a few dollars in penance for having given us grossly incorrect takeoff numbers out of Cincinnati, an error that could have killed us had it not been so obvious that even I had noticed.

We had a jumpseater from one of the inter-island airlines going from San Juan to Tampa to spend Easter with her mother. She was surprised to learn we were going to Orlando, not Tampa. I told her we were surprised, too. We got her a ride from Orlando to Tampa on a DHL truck.

The Weather Channel had shown a line of severe thunderstorms sweeping toward Cincinnati. Our radar was painting the ground on the left side of the screen and some unknown elevation in the sky on the right. We could see lightning ahead over Georgia and Tennessee, but we couldn't see echoes on radar. We heard the controller talking about someone going through a hole in the line, so we asked where that airplane was. He was talking about us.

Weather moved east fast and had passed Cincinnati by the time we got there. We had to hold half an hour, though, joining the flock of airplanes that had been waiting for the storms to go by.

We didn't have enough fuel to hold for more than a few minutes with distant Saint Louis as our alternate. We called Dispatch and had our alternate changed to nearby Louisville. Our dispatcher said we could hold until fuel reached eleven thousand pounds. We told him thirteen thousand was as low as we'd go. People in airplanes tended to be more conservative with fuel estimates than people on the ground.

After we landed, I told our dispatcher that I didn't mistrust his fuel figures, but that I didn't want to arrive at Louisville with minimum fuel at the same time a dozen other airplanes were doing the same thing.

We got to Cincinnati in time for a pilots' meeting to learn how to track our hours and trips with a new computer program Crew Scheduling had begun using. The new system explained why I didn't get a Guadalajara trip I'd put in for. With training days that month, the extra trip would have put me over the 85-hour monthly cap, a greed control measure put in to prevent senior overtime whores from hogging it all.

When Deutsch Post bought DHL, the airline had to be spun off as a separate company to comply with federal law regarding foreign ownership and control of a United States airline. Ramifications of that change were not immediately apparent.

After pushback in Boston one evening, the marshaler stood in darkness without lighted wands. I flashed the taxi light to signal we were ready to roll and thought I saw him signal us forward. I released the brake and both my crew said, "Stop!" The mechanic's van was still next to us in front of the right wing and landing gear, out of my field of view. I wrote a trip report when we got to Cincinnati and got a response from Boston a day later. The marshaler apologized for not using wands and denied having signaled to taxi.
A few days later, I was in Boston again and talked with our mechanic about the incident. I showed him the report I'd written and the response to it. The mechanic said the marshaler did make the taxi signal. He was a new guy, and it was his first time directing an airplane.
When we taxied out that night, the marshaler had bright red lighted wands and a man close behind him shouting instructions in his ear.

I flew to San Juan for the last time on a Wednesday morning. Nereida did not cry before I left, but I knew she would after. Our life together—if 'together' was a word even remotely suited to our situation—would become much more difficult. CBS newsman Charles Kuralt maintained a triangular life for many years before he died, but he died young, and I wondered if the stress of his situation helped kill him.

Several weeks later, after a week at home planting a vegetable garden, writing, working on a sailboat model, and shooting at the rifle range, I slept all the way to Cincinnati on the last Friday evening in May. By the end of Memorial Day weekend in Sacramento, I was coming down with a cold. I fought it with cough drops and Sudafed, but my ears plugged descending into Cincinnati and again into Boston. I slept well for only four hours. I'd have stayed in bed, but my second officer had never been to Boston and I'd promised to show him around. I didn't need a lot of sleep. I'd dropped my Sacramento trip the next day and booked jumpseats on the DC-8 to and from San Juan.

My ears stopped up a little on descent into Cincinnati. Between my head cold and lack of sleep, I was glad I didn't have to fly to the west coast. I'd dropped my Sacramento trip and was on my way to San Juan for the first time in weeks, riding a DC-8 jumpseat. I rode with the crew to the hotel and walked two blocks to the apartment Nereida and I rented high in a building overlooking the beach. That evening, she drove me to the airport.

The airplane needed a replacement for a bad outflow valve, one of two that maintained proper pressurization by regulating how fast air escaped the airplane. San Juan maintenance had notified SOC that the airplane would be down until nearly midnight, but SOC didn't pass the word to Dispatch and Crew Scheduling. The captain for the return flight had called Dispatch earlier to check the status of the airplane. So had I. We'd been told the flight would leave on time with a stop in Atlanta where we'd pick up two must-ride jumpseaters. I'd be bumped there.

The scheduler said he would put me on AVL—a form of reserve—because I'd be bumped and asked if I'd prefer stay in San Juan or to get off in Atlanta. He must have been joking. After learning we weren't going anywhere for a while, we all rode back to the hotel to await developments. I gave the captain my local phone number.

Nereida and I ate dinner again, leftovers from our earlier meal. The captain called. Lobby time was midnight, and we were going non-stop. The good news was, I wouldn't be bumped in Atlanta. The bad news was, we'd land too late for my trip to Minneapolis.

When I walked over to the hotel in uniform, the van was there waiting. The captain stepped out of the elevator in shorts and T-shirt. The airplane was still broken and the flight was canceled. I walked back to the apartment again.

Between the dropped Sacramento trip and the missed Minneapolis, I had several hours to make up to prevent the shortage from cutting into normal income, money I promised myself I'd not use to support my island life. I put in for a long trip on my next days off. Because my grandsons would be visiting then, I wouldn't fly that trip but would call in sick for it, something a few pilots did regularly but something I considered an extreme abuse of sick leave. The situation I'd put myself in pushed me to make uncomfortable compromises with ethics.

Nereida was in New Jersey visiting relatives. On Labor Day weekend, I met her at the bus depot in Manhattan. On Monday, we walked downtown all the way to the financial district. The view from the observation deck of the World Trade Center was worth the price of the tickets, although rainstorms with a cold front drove us inside. It felt strange, looking down on swirling clouds from something other than an airplane. Nereida thought an airliner passing nearby was too low. I explained that it was on approach to JFK.

My month ended with trips Thursday and Friday after a week off, and then I'd be on vacation for a month. Rather than go in for two days and interrupt preparation for hunting elk in Colorado, pheasants in South Dakota, and elk in Washington on the way home, I called in sick. I'd become as casual as some others in abusing sick leave to modify my schedule, but I didn't feel good about it.

We began picking up ice on descent into Cincinnati. Turning on engine anti-ice was routine, but my crew prompted me to use wing anti-ice as they had the day before going into Boise. After we landed, I told them that I'd used wing anti-ice as much on that trip as I had in all my time as captain. The second officer was right to have suggested it, as there was still ice on the wings when we parked. I told him I'd flown with The Skipper too long. Captain Scamahorn had viewed using anti-ice almost as a personal weakness, a character defect.

The flight director in the airplane we flew to Austin that morning had a manual approach mode unique to that airplane. We hadn't been trained on it and I never used it, at least not intentionally.

It was the first trip to Austin for all three of us since we'd changed airports. We had traffic we were to follow in sight. The controller cleared us for a visual approach to follow that airplane. Without looking at the knob, I turned the flight director selector to what should have been Approach mode.

The flight director display indicated the need for an immediate turn toward the runway. Lights were green, meaning we'd locked on to both localizer and glideslope. We'd lost sight of the airplane we were to follow in city lights as it descended. The autopilot didn't begin a turn, so I did.

Tower saw the turn on radar and asked if we were lining up for the wrong runway. We said we were not, but I widened the turn when the localizer needle did not begin to move toward center. We were also descending, as we had a green light on the glideslope and a centered needle. The problem was, it wasn't the glideslope for our runway, and we were lower than we should have been for where we were. We were in no danger, though, as weather was clear and the sky was growing light with the dawn. We got it sorted out and landed on the correct runway.

I told the crew we'd write up the flight director. When the mechanic came on board and I began to explain the problem, I realized I'd clicked the flight director to the manual approach detent, not auto. Even there on the ground, far from any runway, the damn thing showed green lights with Manual Approach selected.

I hated non-standard anything. I couldn't help but wonder how many crashes written off as pilot error were caused by just that sort of difference.

I'd worked a three-way trade that put me in Miami for the weekend. We were empty from Atlanta, and the airplane didn't have maintenance scheduled. We flew it to Miami so it could be washed. At the hotel, I packed a small bag and rode the van back to the airport to catch a ride to San Juan. I returned early Monday to be sure of getting back to Miami on time and rode in the cockpit of a full flight.

We were scheduled for an early departure from Miami that evening. I called Dispatch to ask why we had to leave early and sit two hours in Atlanta. They wanted us at the airplane early enough to discover any problems that might have been caused by scheduled maintenance. I pointed out that there had been no maintenance, that the airplane had merely been washed. I told the dispatcher we may be a little late getting out of Miami, and then I said, "I didn't say that." The dispatcher laughed and said, "I didn't hear it."

Even though we got to the airplane an hour later than scheduled, paperwork wasn't there. Even after that delay, we got to Atlanta an hour before scheduled departure and left for Cincinnati ten minutes early.

The flight manager asked why we were late out of Miami. I told him exactly why and explained my reasoning. He said people upstairs were upset.

After landing in New York, we wrote up a trivial pressurization problem that became a big problem on the daytime charter to Santo Domingo. When we got to the airport that evening, our airplane was down. A reserve crew was flying out from

Cincinnati to haul our freight, and we were to fly empty and unpressurized at ten thousand feet to Orlando for repairs.

I got on the phone to Crew Scheduling and suggested that they let us fly it to Cincinnati and have a reserve crew take it from there to Orlando, as I was not going to babysit a broken airplane in Orlando or anywhere else over Christmas.

Maybe they heard between the lines that I'd call in sick to preserve my Christmas weekend, or maybe they came up with the same plan on their own. We flew to Cincinnati.

Our new contract required the company to have a scheduling system that allowed pilots computer access and participation by the end of the year 2000. The system was full of errors and incorrect information. The union solicited and collected documentation from all of us so it could argue that the company had not met the requirement and should, therefore, pay a 78-hour guarantee as penalty. That high guarantee was bad for me because I needed time over the guarantee to boost my personal share of each paycheck.

We won our grievance claiming the computer scheduling program did not work well. The first trip I picked up from open time in 2001 wouldn't put me over the higher guarantee, so I'd be flying it for nothing. I had to pick up enough trips each month to put me as close as possible to the 85-hour maximum our contract allowed.

On departure from Cincinnati to Atlanta, the airplane gave us a false Takeoff Configuration Warning horn. I checked my shirt-pocket logbook. It was the same airplane that had done that to me a month earlier. We taxied clear of the runway, called the company to report our rejected takeoff, cycled the flaps a couple of times to free the switch, and took off.

We wrote up the problem and the mechanic in Atlanta cycled through flaps, speedbrake, and trim a few times until he was satisfied all was well. He signed off the write-up, "Ground Checks OK." As soon as engines were running, I put flaps down and shoved the #3 thrust lever up and we got the horn again. We had to cycle the flaps several times before we could take off for Miami.

We parked at the heavy-maintenance hangar and went to the hotel. My crew went home for the weekend. I packed a small bag and caught a ride to San Juan. Rumor was, American was going to buy TWA. That would reduce my options for getting to Puerto Rico.

I had a message from Crew Scheduling when I got back to the hotel Monday. Our airplane was down indefinitely. I didn't know whether to take a nap or drink more coffee. I took a shower and got ready to leave the hotel in case the airplane was fixed. Finally, at two in the morning, I lay down for a nap and the phone rang. I called my crew and we met in the lobby a few minutes later. The Airbus crew was there, too. Their airplane was also at the maintenance hangar, and it was ready to fly. I didn't know what their problem was. I didn't even know what ours was.

A jumpseater was waiting for the Airbus crew, a pilot for one of our contract feeders. She had white-blond hair about an inch long and a Dutch or German accent. She'd been waiting seven hours.

I told her we'd be out first and she'd be welcome to ride with us. She took us up on that when the Airbus second officer came off the airplane complaining that his seat wasn't on its tracks and had turned over when he sat down.

We couldn't find our paperwork. Dispatch said they'd faxed it, but to what machine in that huge building, nobody knew. I read the dispatcher a number off a machine in an unlocked office. As we walked through the hangar, a man came running up with paperwork in hand. I told him we'd called for a new copy. He told us the paperwork always went to his office. I didn't bother to ask where that might be.

We got to Cincinnati too late for my jumpseat home. I caught a TWA Express to Saint Louis and TWA to Seattle. I thought it might be my last ride on the nation's oldest airline.

I put in for a west coast trip at the end of my week. One more long trip would put me up to the cap for the second month in a row. I needed the money to pay down my credit card.

In Baltimore, I was assigned a Smoking room that stank. I went back to the lobby to insist on a No Smoking room. When I opened the door to the new room, it hadn't been made up yet. The clerk offered me breakfast while I waited. I didn't want food. I wanted sleep. The clerk said it would be an hour or so. I pointed to a couch in the lobby and asked that he wake me when my room was ready.

Camping out in hotel lobbies worked magic for me more than once during my career. It made rooms appear when none existed. Before I pulled off my shoes, a manager asked me to come with him to check two available Smoking rooms to see if one might be acceptable. One was.

I ate a greasy pizza in Cincinnati, forgetting that the El Paso flight was catered because the trip was long and the layover was short. Then I set my alarm and went to sleep in the crew lounge. When I woke up, the slot for the trip's paperwork was empty. I thought the first officer was somewhere nearby reading it. I couldn't find him, and someone told me he had gone out to the airplane.

I'd wasted my coffee-making time looking for my first officer. I rode the bus out to the airplane and began chewing him out for taking the paper I needed to sign.

He'd wanted to go out to the airplane early but didn't want to wake me. The weather had been marked up with highlighter, and he naturally assumed I'd looked at it but had forgotten to sign the release. He left a copy of the release for me to sign and had our copy and everything else with him.

Someone had grabbed our pile of paper, gone over it with a highlighter, and put it back after realizing his error. The dispatcher had picked up his copy of the release without noticing it lacked my signature. The whole incident was the result of lots of little things piling up in one direction, just like most airplane crashes. I apologized to my first officer for tearing into him.

We got out on time in spite of it all, but we were two minutes late out of Dallas. The ground crew asked us to fudge the time so they wouldn't get dinged for a delay. I refused on grounds that contractual changes meant we were paid based on log times. If a trip went beyond its guarantee, padding time was the same as stealing from the cash register.

Instead of taking airplanes to Miami for maintenance on weekends, we began going to a facility in north central Florida. The only instrument approach to Lake City was an NDB approach, the least precise of non-precision approaches made less safe by being below ATC radar coverage. The nearest city with scheduled air service was Jacksonville, sixty miles away.

That there was nothing to do in Lake City but read and watch John Wayne movies on TV made not being able to escape to Puerto Rico even worse.

When I signed paperwork for Saint Louis and Boise Tuesday morning, I realized duty time would exceed our contractual limit, though not federal regulations. I asked Crew Scheduling how that had been approved. They didn't know. I could refuse the trip because of the contract violation, but no one could tell me with certainty that I'd be paid for it. There wasn't an open jumpseat to Seattle, and I was better rested than usual, so I flew.

We landed at Boise in fog. The airplane had a useless flight director and a marginal autopilot. Instruments gave us conflicting information, so we broke off the approach to try again. The second officer noticed I'd set an incorrect course in my HSI when setting up for the second attempt. I told him I owed him a beer for that. I had two bottles of Michelob in my bag, leftovers from the weekend. As soon as we were out of the airplane, I pulled one out of my bag and handed it to him.

In New York a week later, the first officer discovered during his checks that the #1 communications radio didn't work. The mechanic was baffled. Everything had worked when he did his cockpit checks just before we arrived. There was no backlight in the radio, an indication no power was getting to it. The mechanic pulled the radio out of the console and shoved it back into place and it worked again.

The radios were face up in the center console. Our sexy second officer said maybe it was her fault. She'd been taught to save time by sitting astride the console instead of sitting in pilot seats one at a time to set up pilots' panels. Perhaps, she suggested, her weight on the radio disturbed the connection. "That explains it," I said. "Those old radios can't stand that much excitement."

While taxiing out in Cincinnati, heading indicators were ten degrees different with the first officer's being correct, according to the compass and alignment of the taxiway. I reset mine to agree with his and we took off, but it quickly drifted until it was twelve degrees off. If we'd written it up immediately, we might have been stuck in Saint Louis, so we agreed to evaluate the problem further on the second leg.

We wrote it up and called it in to Maintenance Control en route to Boise. They said they'd notify an avionics tech in Boise, but if it wasn't working right by flight time, the airplane couldn't go. That made us glad we'd waited to write it up. If we were stuck in Boise long enough, we might get out of having to go to Syracuse the next day.

When we got to the airport that evening, mechanics were waiting for a part. We were to hang around Boise Air Service for half an hour, then call Cincinnati for an update. The new part didn't fix the problem.

I made coffee and sat down to read a book. A mechanic came in at ten o'clock and said they'd quit for the night. I called Cincinnati again and gave them the news. Crew Scheduling asked if we'd be willing to fly in the daytime if the airplane got fixed early. I asked what the rules on that were, but I couldn't get an answer beyond, "You can do whatever you want." The scheduler refused to read the applicable section of the contract to me, and my copy was in my flight bag in the airplane. I said we'd call back from the hotel.

After discussing it with my crew, I said we'd do it, but we didn't want to be called early to go sit at the airport for twelve hours. We didn't want to be called until there was reasonable assurance the airplane was about to be ready, and, as I'd be illegal to fly my Boston trip the next day, I wanted the company to buy my hotel room in Cincinnati. The scheduler thought that was fair. We went to the hotel bar and drank ale with an America West pilot.

I slept until nearly noon and plugged in my phone, happy to see the message light remain dark. I called Crew Scheduling so I could plan my day. Our report time was late enough in the evening for it to be a night flight, so we'd be legal for our trips Friday morning.

I was walking out of my room to check out that evening when the phone rang. Our flight was canceled. Crew Scheduling asked again if we'd fly in the daytime if the airplane was ready. I told the scheduler that would make it illegal to fly our weekend trips, but that we'd discuss it and let him know. The scheduler said he'd never seen a day trip materialize from our situation.

We changed out of uniforms and met in the lobby. We agreed we'd accept the day trip on condition we could all be AVL at home for the weekend. I called Crew Scheduling to tell them that. I asked that we not be called before noon as we wanted to sleep late to be in shape for an evening departure. Then we went to the bar.

We ordered and ate a pizza, but the kitchen was closed when a Southwest crew arrived. We thought they were out of luck, but two huge platters of nachos materialized. They'd called ahead from Saint Louis.

After several mugs of ale all around, a flight attendant bragged she could manipulate her toes independently, like fingers. Soon we all had shoes and socks off to compare feet.

The maintenance company in Lake City, Florida, provided free transportation to and from civilization. I checked into the hotel, threw some clothes into a small backpack, washed my face, and got a ride to Jacksonville. I walked right onto an American Eagle flight to Miami. The 757 to San Juan was oversold, but they had one open seat in First Class.

I woke early Monday morning when my alarm went off. The morning was cool and wet from rain in the night. We sat on our apartment balcony in the breeze drinking coffee while we watched the rising sun flood the world with light. I did not want to leave San Juan.

The flight to Miami was full, so I rode in the cockpit, my first ride up front in an Airbus. As we made the climbing turn over the blue Atlantic with the entire sunlit city of San Juan in view, the captain sang out, "Yippee!" A moment later, he said, "Monday morning. Somewhere down there, some poor son of a bitch is going to work." His first officer and I knew exactly what he meant.

In Cincinnati one night, the chairman of our union's Professional Standards committee took me aside to ask about a complaint. The second officer had reported my screwed up visual approach into Austin, an anti-icing issue, and said I'd banked too steeply going into Boise. I said my crew and I had thoroughly debriefed the Austin debacle and that I couldn't remember what the other two things were about beyond my being aware that that second officer was quicker than I was to want anti-ice turned on. The complaints were no big deal, but the committee provided a venue for handling differences and complaints among pilots while keeping management out of it.

I'd forgotten what it was like to fly with Sidney. Forecast called for low clouds, drizzle, and marginal visibility in Austin. I asked him which leg he wanted to fly. He chose the first one.

Distant lightning was visible before we descended into cloud. All red echoes were too far away to interfere with us except one cell so small it didn't show on our radar. The controller mentioned it, and I turned the range down on the radar and saw a red dot. ATC said to deviate to the left.

Five miles is nothing in a fast airplane, but Sidney started messing with the radar as we barreled along straight at the cell. "Sidney," I said. "Just turn the airplane."

We were coming in from the northeast and landing to the north. Sidney did everything right, including asking me if we'd been forgotten as we crossed the localizer course at right angles. I'd never landed on that runway and thought perhaps the vector that took us through the approach course was either normal procedure or for spacing on another airplane. About that time, the approach controller apologized and gave us a right turn to intercept. A new voice came on and gave us more of a turn and asked if it was okay with us to intercept the localizer just outside the marker. I looked at Sidney and he didn't say anything, so I said that would be fine.

He was flying on autopilot with the flight director. Our vector to intercept was a 45-degree angle, much too sharp a turn for the autopilot. Sidney left it on as the airplane went through the localizer, turned and overshot it again, and again turned back toward it.

I told Sidney the autopilot would never catch up that close to the runway. He clicked it off and quickly got us stabilized with needles centered.

He was exactly on speed, but the airplane was half a dot low on the glideslope. I said, "Glideslope," and Sidney replied, "Correcting." Nothing changed. I said, "Correct more." He pitched up a little but didn't add thrust, so speed decayed five knots.

I'd always discounted the general opinion that Sidney was dangerous. He was one of those people that somehow invites being picked on, and I knew that some animosity was racial. But he was dangerous.

I almost never took the airplane away from a first officer, but we were in cloud and too close to the ground for further discussion. I said, "I have the airplane, go around," and shoved the power up.

Pilots are supposed to be mentally prepared to go around if the runway lights aren't in sight at decision height. In training, go-arounds always come at the last second, not hundreds of feet in the air. I hadn't thought it through and disgraced myself by calling for gear and flaps out of order and abusing the engines because I didn't call for go-around thrust after I shoved the levers up, and the new second officer didn't take it upon himself to pull the them back to the proper setting.

We were high enough that my botched procedure hadn't put us in danger. We had a jumpseater, a dispatcher on his annual familiarization flight, so we couldn't discuss our growing collection of errors just then. I kept the airplane and flew the next approach and landed. Sidney's feelings were hurt and he made required calls so softly I couldn't hear him.

Once on the ground, I told the jumpseater to go ahead and bail out, that he'd only be in our way as we cleared the cockpit. Then I asked Sidney if he'd noticed the speed decay when he tried to regain the glideslope. He hadn't. He thought he was right on the bug. I told him he was, until he pitched up to acquire the glideslope. In explaining why I'd taken the airplane from him, I said I could accept being off glideslope or being off speed, but not both. Sidney looked away and said, "It's your prerogative," as if that answered anything. We debriefed my completely screwed up go-around, the error-filled procedure itself and my lack of mental readiness. I tried to remember if and when I'd ever flown a go-around correctly other than in a flight simulator.

A scheduled maintenance weekend in Lake City was canceled and we returned from Atlanta to Cincinnati. I walked to the terminal and got on a Delta 727 to Miami on my way to spending the weekend in Puerto Rico. I rode in the cockpit jumpseat. The airplane was loaded and ready to leave on time, but just before the door closed, an elderly man went into the bathroom just behind the cockpit. He was in there nearly fifteen minutes, and the airplane couldn't move until he was in his seat. A couple of times, we heard a flight attendant asking him through the door if he was okay.

The gate agent had run the Jetway back from the side of the airplane as soon as the door closed. She stood in the opening, staring at the crew through our rain-streaked windows and looking more perplexed with each passing minute. The second officer made a sign for me to hold up to the window: "There's a pax in the lav taking a dump." The agent squinted to read the sign and laughed.

I turned on the TV in Boston one day to see if there was anything new in the effort to raise the mandatory retirement age for airline pilots from 60 to perhaps 63 or 65. With many airlines merging or going out of business and pension plans evaporating, pilots who had opposed raising the limit were pushing for additional years to save enough money to retire.

I slept soundly on the jumpseat from Seattle to Cincinnati. I slept another hour on a recliner in the crew lounge before taking off for Kansas City and Denver because I'd have to be awake and alert flying with Sidney and Annie. When I got to the airplane, one of the loaders said they'd be finished in a couple of minutes. I said we'd be ready. A pilot going home rode the rear jumpseat and a ground operations trainer rode the other.

My crew and I were discussing the flight when a ramp worker banged his hand on the side of the airplane below the windows, their usual way of getting our attention to ask with hand signals if they could unplug ground power. We were in the middle of discussion and I didn't immediately look out the window to signal the okay. The ramper banged again like an impatient cop knocking on a miscreant's door.

I unbuckled and ran down the stairs to show the man how to interpret the lights at the airplane's GPU plug that indicated whether or not the airplane was on ship's power or still drawing electricity from the ground unit. My heated manner intimidated the poor guy and others nearby. Turnover was high on the ramp, and there were always new people who weren't up to speed.

When I strapped in again, I told the jumpseating trainer that ramp personnel should be trained to read the lights and not bang on the airplane. They didn't realize how loud and irritating it was. I didn't notice we needed to be pushed back.

Normally, we didn't start engines until after we'd been pushed back and turned. The airplane was heavy enough without the tug having to overcome idle thrust. My outburst had not only distracted me, it apparently cowed ground personnel and my crew into silence. The man on the headset informed us doors were closed. I said we'd be right with him. We ran the Before Start checklist and I said, "Start one." Nobody outside and neither of my crew reminded me that we had to push back. We started all three engines.

After we'd pushed and the man on the headset informed me that steering was connected, I apologized to him and asked him to convey my apology to the rest of the ground crew. I gently chided my crew for not having said anything when I called for the first engine start, but the problem was caused by my overreacting to the guy pounding on the airplane.

Crew Scheduling asked for a 727 captain to volunteer to sit hot standby for a few hours. It would have meant an extra two days' pay, well worth missing my jumpseat and having to find my way home, but I couldn't risk being assigned a trip. I'd promised to talk about writing to a grade school class the morning after I got home, and I'd be late and sleepy if I had to work a full day.

I called the newspaper later that week and spoke to the publisher about ending my column after fourteen years. A day or two later, Barb asked me why I was so quiet. I wasn't aware that I was quiet, though I was taking life easy for a change, not scurrying around to get things done. With warm weather, I didn't have to deal with firewood, and I wasn't fretting over the next week's newspaper column. I had only one more to write, and it was already composed in my head. I spent the weekend reading during the day and messing around in the pond with the canoe. Instead of dealing with income tax, I filed an extension. I sent my final column to the newspaper's computer, sad to be done with it but happy to be free from the deadline.

I was waiting near the door of the TWA flight from Boston to San Juan one Saturday morning. While passengers filed past and boarded, a flight attendant walked down the Jetway behind me and asked if I was jumpseating. She began scratching my back lightly through my uniform shirt as we waited for the last few passengers to board. It felt marvelous. I couldn't think of anything to say, so I kept my mouth shut.

Three drivers stopped to offer me rides as I walked in hot sunshine from airport to apartment. Cold beer greeted me when I opened the refrigerator.

My situation at the apex of a triangle of my own making was becoming more stressful even as it became more comfortable. I sensed doom of one sort or another, unavoidable without perhaps the luck of a Charles Kuralt.

We deviated around a huge thunderstorm over Texarkana, and the ride was rough. We were in cloud, and lightning appeared to envelop our airplane, even though the storm was a hundred miles away. My first officer thought perhaps the radar wasn't showing everything, but when we popped out of the cirrostratus, we could see the storm in the distance, right where our radar said it was.

When we went to dinner in Austin that evening, our waitress had no visible tattoos or piercings, and she laughed when we complimented her on that. After dinner, we wandered up and down 6th Street, a lively place on a pleasant Saturday night. We stopped at a music bar and had a few more beers. We asked our waitress why she had a stud in her tongue. She smiled and didn't answer.

I was only mildly hung over Easter Sunday. A cousin picked me up at the hotel and I spent the afternoon with him and his family.

My time at home was short after Barb and I flew to Colorado for my dad's 90th birthday. After a frantic couple of days catching up on things at home and buying a small tractor, I ran errands before driving to Seattle. As I made a U-turn out of a parking space at the end of a block downtown, I was watching a couple of kids on bicycles and turned in front a bus that had come out of a parking lot behind me. I ran down my window and yelled, "Sorry!" The driver yelled back, "I hope you don't fly like that."

Most of the week was recurrent training. I screwed up handling the second engine failure in the simulator by forgetting to intercept the glideslope higher than normal to allow time for the second officer to crank down each landing gear by hand. With only one engine, when the gear started down, the airplane started down. We survived, though, only because I flew the airplane at precisely the best speed, well below proper approach speed and one I arrived at on the spot by feel. We touched down on the first few feet of runway.

We got out of Atlanta two hours late. The standby attitude indicator read four degrees high. It wasn't a big deal to me, as they all seemed to be off a little. My first officer was adamant that we couldn't go without it working properly. I didn't override vetoes unless they were extremely unreasonable, and that was only mildly unreasonable and perhaps not unreasonable at all. The delay ate up nap time I'd looked forward to in Cincinnati.

We had several write-ups, including radar malfunctions, on the airplane we flew to Sacramento. Also, the nosewheel wanted to turn right rather than track straight. The airplane had just come out of D-check. Scheduled major maintenance at contract facilities often seemed to leave airplanes worse off than before they went in. Our engineering crews were supposed to catch those problems.

That airplane had been scheduled to be returned to the leasing agent, but new management had put such things on hold. We'd be acquiring no more airplanes and hiring no more pilots for a year. Construction of our new sort building in Cincinnati stopped, too. Many pilots were in a tizzy, but I was too old to care.

The trip that had terminated in Austin was revised to continue to Monterrey, but nobody told Austin. The fuel truck wasn't standing by the first day, and the inaugural crew arrived late in Monterrey and had to wait two hours for the hotel van. I flew the trip its second day. The fuel truck in Austin didn't have enough for us after filling a UPS airplane, so we had to wait for the truck to refuel and got out an hour late.

The arrival at Monterrey was a DME arc to a VOR approach. We'd fly a circle segment a fixed distance from the VOR in cloud as we descended. The penalty for screwing up was mountains.

Two pickup trucks carried us from airplane to terminal. We went in through the door our drivers indicated, but no one was there. We wandered around and found a woman who spoke no English, but we were able to convey to her what we needed, and soon the Immigration officer scurried in as fast has her too-tight skirt allowed.

Next, we had to find Customs. A bilingual security officer pointed us in the right direction. After the agent's cursory inspection, we went outside to wait for our ride to the hotel, though it had probably come and gone. We couldn't see any place for ground transportation to park and wait, and the driver probably had more important things to do than wait for late flight crews.

Knowing of the fiasco the day before, we were eager to get something going. I tried to call the hotel with my cell phone using international access numbers listed on my calling card, but I couldn't understand the Spanish recordings explaining what I was doing wrong. I went inside to use a pay phone. I punched zero but nothing happened.

My first officer went inside to try. He got someone to tell him the code for Operator and called Crew Scheduling collect to ask them to call the hotel. By the time he got back outside, the second officer had flagged down a small DHL truck. The courier spoke little English, but we got him to understand our predicament by showing him the name and address of the hotel on our trip sheet. He offered to take us, riding on a pile of boxes in his van. We declined.

He came around again a few minutes later followed by an unmarked pickup truck with a bilingual driver who offered to take us. We didn't know who he was, and we weren't going to ride in back. Then a white van pulled up and the driver talked with our two rescuers. We got into his van and went to the hotel. On the highway, we passed the hotel bus headed for the airport.

We had no idea who our driver was or who he worked for. I asked him if ten dollars was enough. He tried to decline, but accepted my ten and the usual tips from my crew. We didn't know if the hotel paid the driver or what, as his discussion with the doorman was in Spanish. A bellman took our bags to our rooms while we ate a superb buffet breakfast, free to airline crews.

From my room phone, I called Crew Scheduling collect. The scheduler started to tell me we could report late, but I told her we were willing to start our rest time when we got in the van so we could report as scheduled. I didn't want to change the time and risk further confusion and delay. After sleeping only three hours, I was wide awake.

It took exactly thirty minutes to get to the airport and another ten to clear out with Immigration. Our ride to the airplane showed up twenty minutes late. The driver expected two of us to ride in the back of his small pickup with the bags. He didn't understand much English, but he understood No. He made three trips across the ramp to the airplane.

There was no weather in paperwork a man handed to us. He asked if we needed it. We did. He left to go find it. We were all ready to go except we didn't have a fuel receipt. Fuel receipt? Yeah, we needed that, too. We got out only five minutes late.

My first officer flew. I'll call him Woody. The departure included flying a DME arc while gaining enough altitude to clear surrounding mountains. Woody was not turning tight enough to maintain the 12-mile arc, and the radius was increasing. I mentioned that. He made a slight heading change in the right direction. The DME read fourteen miles. I told him to turn left a whole bunch. Again he turned less than what was needed. I told him to turn more. He did, and we were almost back to the 12-mile arc when we reached safe altitude and turned on our outbound course.

After we landed in Cincinnati and the second officer had left the cockpit, I asked Woody if he had a sense of what was going on with that arc. He was adamant that he was no more than one mile outside the published arc on *his* DME. He said he'd noticed the discrepancy between DMEs earlier but had forgotten to mention it.

I was trying hard to be conversational, not accusatory, but the man bristled. I hated the thoughts going through my mind. He and another first officer had similar deficiencies and they were both from the same country. I didn't know if similarities in their lack of situational awareness was cultural or coincidence. It was convenient to conclude it was coincidence, so I did.

I was so tired when we landed in Cincinnati in a torrent of rain that I knew I wouldn't get enough sleep to keep going. I told Crew Scheduling I was fatigued and went to an appointment with the 727 chief pilot to be chastised for failing to sign a couple of pieces of paper. My deficiencies had turned up in an FAA audit.

Another problem was, we'd left no station copy at Newark after a recent departure. I remembered what had happened. The second officer had forgotten to hand out station copies of the release and flight plan before closing the door. The stairs had been pulled away by the time she noticed her oversight, and it was too windy for me to drop paper out the window. I said, "It only matters if we crash, and if we crash it doesn't matter." I'd intended to send the paper back to Newark with the next crew, but I forgot.

Boston was cool and rainy Saturday morning. The American flight to San Juan was lightly loaded and I had a row in First Class to myself. Leaving my island home on Monday was more difficult than usual because I didn't know when I'd be back. I had no Boston weekends the rest of June and probably would not in July.

The American flight I wanted Monday morning was on time. The flight crew saw me in line at the check-in counter and introduced themselves. I sat in the boarding area until the last paying passengers were on the Jetway. An FAA inspector was riding, so I assumed I'd have to ride in the cramped, second jumpseat. The Fed was a jovial man who agreed with the crew that I'd be more comfortable in First Class.

Two DHL pilots rode with us from Boston to Cincinnati. We had to alter our assigned route descending into Cincinnati to avoid thunderstorms, but I didn't ask for a large enough heading change to avoid a small cumulus building into the night sky, visible in moonlight but with no lightning and no radar return. Rather than bug the controller with another request, I thought we'd just pop through the small column of cotton.

We were hammered hard in some of the roughest turbulence I'd ever been in. The experience gave me increased respect both for cumuliform clouds and for Boeing airplanes. I apologized to crew and jumpseaters. To top it off, I made a lousy landing.

I was tired when we left Boston for Cincinnati one Monday evening, having been up since early morning to catch a ride back from San Juan. I considered taking a fatigue day, especially when I discovered the airplane for my Minneapolis trip still had radio panels I hated. But there were no open jumpseats westbound, so I traded the trip for the shorter one to Newark.

As I ate dinner, I wondered how many more times I'd be able to dine at Cabana Carioca. There were no more 727s going to JFK, and rumor said the Airbus would soon be flying Newark.

Our radar wasn't working right, and, with thunderstorms in the area, we couldn't leave Newark without it. Two jumpseaters would miss their trips if we didn't go. Cincinnati said a rescue airplane was on the way. That would get the jumpseaters to work on time, but I wouldn't get back in time for my jumpseat home and my appointment to renew my FAA medical. The jumpseating captain volunteered to babysit my airplane and let me have his jumpseat on the rescue. He lived in New York, and if the airplane didn't go, he could just drive home. By replacing me, he could be late and miss his trip without penalty.

Crew Scheduling called me at home a week later to tell me I'd been bumped from my jumpseat to work two days later by a SOLO, a Second Officer Line Observation. That was something new, training department pilots riding jumpseats to observe second officers and gather data on what areas of the job weren't being done correctly. SOLOs were supposed to be scheduled around commuting pilots. I asked if there was a seat the night before, but they were taken. I booked a seat out of San Francisco instead.

I was driving to Seattle the next morning to catch a ride to San Francisco when my phone rang. A training department pilot wanted to buy my Sacramento trip. I cheerfully agreed and turned around and drove home.

Managers and trainers had to fly now and then to maintain currency. They offered to "buy" trips when they needed flight time and landings. They flew the trips but the scheduled pilot got paid anyway.

I left home half an hour earlier than usual the next day in my unending effort to be on time, but I didn't get out of the driveway before hearing on the radio of a head-on collision. I hit the backup eight miles down the highway, and the wreck was still five miles ahead. I called in sick and turned around and drove home.

Napoleon rode jumpseat to Florida with us. While we waited for loaders to finish, we talked about airport security and the indignity of having to be searched like the average terrorist or passenger. Napoleon said it was all the fault of "the nigger that worked for PSA" who took a gun aboard and killed the crew in flight.

I told Napoleon I'd appreciate it if he wouldn't use the word nigger in that manner on my airplane. Everyone shut up instantly. Then Napoleon said he was sorry, that he didn't know it offended me. I said, "It doesn't offend me. It pisses me off."

He didn't thank me for the ride.

The jumpseating second officer worked the return from Miami so the man scheduled could go home. He'd just finished his post-60 downgrade training, and I noticed he was still wearing four-stripe captain's epaulets. I didn't ask then if that was by choice or by error, but I was pretty sure it wasn't proper for him to be wearing insignia for a rank he no longer held.

After a few weeks, he was still wearing four stripes, so I asked him why. With some bitterness, he said he'd been a captain most of his long career, and he wasn't going to quit wearing stripes he'd earned.

I mused, not for the first time, about people whose jobs were who they were, not what they did.

With two jumpseaters, I had to sit forward of my usual position, and my imperfect landing was in contrast with the rest of the flight. I'd noticed over the preceding few months that, after years of imprecise control of speed, altitude, and approaches, something had changed. I'd begun routinely flying with a degree of precision that I'd never been capable of before. I tried not to think about that. Sometimes too much thinking screws things up.

On looking ahead at my schedule for autumn of 2001, I realized I could take nine days of sick leave to extend my last vacation as captain and be off after the first week in September until early December.

I'd not been to New York for several weeks, and my waiter at Cabana Carioca asked if I'd been on vacation. I told him I hadn't yet and mentioned how long I'd be off when I did go. He couldn't believe I'd be off nearly three months. His reaction made me realize again how lucky I was to have such a job, and I resolved, not for the first time, to be more sensitive to the working conditions most people endure.

I flew to Boston and hopped a ride to San Juan Saturday morning. I treasured that Labor Day weekend because I knew that, with my long vacation, I'd not be back in Puerto Rico before December, and perhaps not even then.

I spent Sunday and Monday working on a landscaping project in the yard, glad I'd started my vacation a few days early by abusing sick leave so I'd not have to leave for work on my birthday, the 12th. Barb woke me Tuesday morning to tell me what was happening in New York and at the Pentagon. I watched TV for only a few minutes before going downstairs for breakfast. I spent the day working in the yard.

In November of 1963, while most of America was frozen in front of television sets in the aftermath of President Kennedy's assassination, I watched very little. Maybe because so much of what we see on TV is not real, it was difficult to accept the reality of exceptions. I thought of that as I wondered what it was that made me not want to watch the events of that September morning in 2001, why, when confronted with tragedy of huge proportions, I withdraw into familiar and mundane activities.

It was a good time not to be at work, not that anything was flying those first few days. As probably every airline pilot in the world did, I wondered what sort of preparedness could have thwarted those hijackings. The greatest vulnerability that day was the recommended response to hijackers: Do what they say, go along with their program, and everyone will be home in time for dinner.

In earlier times, captains of airplanes carrying US Mail were required to carry guns. If pilots had been armed on 11 September, perhaps the hijackers would have learned that you don't take a knife to a gun fight.

I was back at home a couple of weeks later after hiking into the Olympic Mountains with camping gear for an early deer season. I wasn't sleeping well, too agitated about the FAA's and some airlines' mostly inane responses to what was already being referred to by its date. What worried me most was that both United and American had stopped allowing jumpseat riders. New restrictions would make it more difficult to get to Puerto Rico.

I was glad I wouldn't have to deal with work and air travel for several more weeks. Maybe the people charging madly off in all directions would have time to settle down before then. When an acquaintance called to invite me to go salmon fishing with him and his brother, I declined. Then, as we talked more, I changed my mind. Maybe a day on the water would dispel the dark cloud that had enveloped me. We motored out in dense fog that hugged the strait all day. When we returned to the dock, I realized I'd gone several hours without thinking once about terrorists and airplanes. I went home with salmon, a sunny frame of mind, and a compulsion to buy another fishing boat.

Fishing and crabbing kept me from dwelling too much on the state of my world and of the larger one. Hunting seasons kept mind busy and body tired until time to go back to work at the end of November. After years of coming home with no elk, I had a freezer full of meat, and I was back down to my fat-free weight of 166 pounds.

I was out of currency and had to go to Cincinnati a couple of days early to fly three landings in the simulator with a full crew. When I shaved my vacation beard, I left my mustache longer than usual in hopes a flight manager would tell me to trim it so I could say, "Gee, if we were allowed to carry scissors, I could do that."

I drove to Seattle earlier than usual, not knowing what to expect. I had yet to encounter the utter stupidity of security procedures regarding flight crews going to work. We were searched as thoroughly as passengers on our way to our most destructive weapon, the airplane.

A DHL employee searched crew bags and mine, presumably for guns and grenades. It was good that he gave the procedure only the respect it deserved, as I'd forgotten to leave my new Leatherman tool with its small knife and tiny scissors at home. A DHL van transported our bags to the airplane. Some kid with an electronic wand frisked us before we boarded, perhaps looking for box cutters we might hold to each others' throats while ordering ourselves to fly the load of freight into the side of a Walmart.

In Cincinnati, I went outside to wait for the hotel van. A tent had been set up just inside the gate complete with bag search, walk-through metal detector, and a wand to frisk anyone who set off the detector.

When I woke in early afternoon, it took a few seconds to figure out where I was. After three landings in the simulator on Thursday, I walked to a post office near the hotel to mail my Leatherman tool home. I went out to the airport a few minutes early to ride our airplane to San Juan Friday morning. I told the man in the circus tent I'd been off three months and hadn't been through the routine. I emptied my pockets, walked through the detector, and asked, "What's next?"

"Bag X-ray."

"Where?"

"That guy will show you." He called over to the guard shack a few feet away, "This guy doesn't know where to go."

The guard pointed at the front door of the DHL building and said to go inside, take the elevator to the third floor, and go down the hall and to the left. I did exactly what he said to do, exactly what I always did, all the way to the crew lounge. I asked the flight manager what was up with that. He just shook his head. I should have taken my bags to Door 6 where the X-ray machine had been set up.

Even the proper procedure was a farce. I could have had a gun in my bag and transferred it to my person between personal check and bag inspection several yards away and inside the building.

My first flight since early September was an overdue line check. The 727 chief pilot would fly right seat to Austin Saturday morning and the scheduled first officer would ride jumpseat. Our chief pilot at that time was widely disliked because he had less experience flying the 727 than most of us and his skills were considered substandard. The man wasn't my favorite person in the world, but I got along with him as I do with almost everyone. He didn't even tell me to trim my mustache.

The flight was routine. I started down a few miles too soon and landed a little long, but the man complimented me on the way I ran the show. He noted that I even checked my smoke goggles before flight. I couldn't remember the last time I'd bothered to do that.

That trouble-free flight was followed by one at the other extreme. I looked forward to free breakfast buffet and a long day for sleeping after the short flight to Toronto. Fog formed and we held as long as fuel allowed before diverting to Rochester, New York. We took on fuel and sat there. I'd been asleep in the seat half an hour when my phone rang. Toronto was up. We took off.

By the time we got there, Toronto was down again and we held again, not at a VOR but at an intersection defined by distance from a VOR. Our DMEs failed, so we had to ask the busy controller to tell us when to begin our turn each time we came around the racetrack pattern. Then a fuel pump failed.

We got a phone patch to our dispatcher and told him we could hold for only another thirty minutes, and that wherever we landed was where we'd spend the day. I asked if they'd like us to return to Cincinnati so they could put a fresh crew on the trip.

Dispatch said Toronto was up. ATC said it was down. We reached bingo fuel and were about to ask for clearance to Rochester when Center cancelled our hold and put us in line for landing.

The day after Christmas, I had to get to Sacramento to begin my holiday-shortened week. I'd traded out with the other captain who had Sacramento weekends so he could go home from there Saturday morning for Christmas. Rather than risk getting bumped in the chaos of holiday travel, I'd bought a round-trip ticket from Seattle on Alaska. Three hundred dollars seemed a cheap price for peace of mind. I took nothing I wouldn't need. Everything I did need, including required items and manuals from my flight bag, fit into a small backpack. I could do without a computer for three days. I had room in the backpack for sandwiches, but I was afraid the airport insecurity folks would paw through them to make sure elk meat wasn't explosive.

I didn't go to the hotel when we landed in Sacramento Saturday morning. I waited, boarding pass in hand, for my flight to Seattle. When the gate agent asked for a volunteer to give up a seat on the overbooked flight, I wasn't quick enough. I'd have cheerfully waited a couple of hours in exchange for a new round-trip ticket.

I stowed my small pack under the seat in front of mine and put my shoulder bag and overcoat in the overhead. After I'd finished all that and settled into my window seat, the young woman in the center seat asked if I'd mind trading with her friend farther back so they could sit together. I grumbled and said it would have been nice if she'd asked before I'd settled in and stowed my bags.

Her friend and I passed in the aisle as I made my way aft. An elderly couple had just resettled into their seats when I got there to take the window seat. I stowed my bags and coat again and the three of us had just gotten comfortable when a flight attendant called over the PA system for a volunteer without checked baggage to give up a seat. I punched the overhead call button before she got three words out.

The old folks unstrapped and got up again while I gathered my gear and headed for the exit. The teen-aged girl waiting for my seat had thought she'd checked in for the flight with the skycap who checked her bag. She stood in the airplane entryway with tears streaming down her face as I stepped past her and the grateful gate agent on my way to the waiting area. The airline gave me an open round-trip ticket to anywhere it flew and a First Class seat on the next flight to Seattle.

Crew Scheduling called me at home early in 2002 to ask if I could go to San Francisco to fly from there to Los Angeles and on to Cincinnati. I could have, but because of the amount of time required to clear screening with ink still damp on a one-way ticket, I couldn't get to San Francisco on time. I hated to turn down what would have been a lot of extra money.

We landed in Boston Saturday ahead of forecast snow. After checking in at the hotel, I rode back to the airport for a jumpseat to San Juan and got in line to go through security. Before I got to the screening machines, an agent caught up with me and said I had to get a pass at the ticket counter. She escorted me to the head of that line and got me a seat assignment and a boarding card. Jumpseaters were no longer allowed to ride in the cockpit. I got the last seat on the airplane.

I called American reservations and listed myself on a Monday morning flight back to Boston. There were plenty of empty seats. Nereida dropped me at the airport two hours early, but the flight filled. I went to the gate for the next flight and got the last seat on it. Stress was intense, and perhaps the trigger for frequent dreams of not being able to get to work on time.

The morning was not yet light when we arrived in Rochester. Power was out at the hotel. The clerk issued us chemical light sticks. I read Patrick O'Brian by light stick and slept four hours. I had no idea where I was when I awoke.

On descent into Cincinnati, we heard a funny rumble. A-pumps were sucking air. That was my first hydraulic failure. We declared an emergency and elected to land on Runway 36L, as that gave us the shortest distance to be towed to our ramp.

Because of the way we trained, the control tower didn't understand our problem. In the simulator, we announced precisely what the problem was to our imaginary controllers. Real controllers hear "We have a total A-system hydraulic failure," as "We have a total hydraulic failure." I told my first officer to clarify, to say we had a partial hydraulic failure, that we'd have brakes but no steering on the ground.

I tried very hard to stop us with the centerline lights between the nose tires, steering with rudder and brakes, but we drifted a couple of feet off the line as we stopped, ruining perfection and bragging rights.

Bright sun on the last Tuesday of February seemed to confuse Washington drivers after weeks of gray. Traffic on my way to Seattle was dense and slow. I got to DHL a few minutes late, and the crew was already on the airplane. A mechanic drove me across the ramp in his truck. Because I hadn't gone out with the crew, I didn't have to stand there while somebody ran a wand over me looking for box cutters.

After takeoff from Orlando, the three-position landing gear handle would not come up past Off. There was an override trigger on the handle that would allow it to move past Off to Up, but we'd been told not to use it without following the procedure in the book. I couldn't recall at that moment what the possible consequence was, but I remembered it was bad.

The first officer was flying. I turned and asked the second officer to dig out the procedure for that gear handle problem and told Departure that we'd like to level off at three thousand feet, as we might have to return. The controller gave us a turn to the west to get us out of traffic. I put the handle down again and tried to bring it back up. Again it stopped midway.

While I was turned around in my seat to listen to the second officer read the steps of the procedure, the first officer raised the gear handle and the wheels came up. I asked how he'd done that. He said he pulled the override trigger. After a stunned pause, I said, "It didn't sound like anything broke, so we were lucky."

If we'd followed the procedure in the book to the end, we'd have learned whether the airplane thought it was on the ground or in the air. If the ground-logic box knew we were in the air, the problem was a bad solenoid and it was okay to override and raise the gear. If ground logic thought we were on the ground, a likely reason was a broken mechanical link between landing gear and logic box. Raising the gear with that link broken could drive a metal bar up through the wing, and the wing is a fuel tank.

It was our good luck that we had the more common bad solenoid and not a broken link. I did not distract us in flight by grilling my first officer as to why he'd done such a stupid thing. Even if I'd been flying and had told him to override the lockout, he'd have been right to refuse until we'd gone to the manual.

After we landed in Cincinnati, my crew went straight to the bunk room to rest up for their trip to Sacramento, so I didn't have an opportunity to talk to the first officer. It wasn't until I relaxed on the jumpseat to Seattle that full realization sank in of what a serious breach of cockpit discipline the man was guilty of. It demanded that I talk with him to be sure he understood that his action could have killed us.

The next time I saw him, I took him aside to talk. He'd realized he'd done a wrong thing the moment he did it, knew it was improper procedure, and understood it could have destroyed the airplane. He was genuinely contrite and had no explanation of why he'd done what he did.

He was a bright young man and an excellent pilot. The incident had been completely out of character for him, and we both knew it. I was confident he'd never do something like that again, so I took the incident no further.

At Toronto, Runway 24R is on the left side of the airport, and 24L had not yet been built. The controller said he'd try to get Runway 23 for us, which was on the right side of the airport and very near our parking ramp. So when we were cleared for a visual approach to 24R, my first officer lined up on the right runway, which was the wrong runway. My mind was in silent agreement with his reasoning until Tower asked if we were not, in fact, lining up on Runway 23. I replied that we'd just caught the error.

We sidestepped left to the right right runway and landed with no harm done except to our pride.

Tuesday was the first day of my last recurrent training as an airline captain. The class was unusually dull for those of us who had to endure the same hazmat training we'd had the first time a few days earlier. We were getting it again to synchronize all of each pilot's annual training to the same month.

Transporting hazardous materials was subject to books full of regulations and limitations on what could be carried, how much, and how it should be packed and labeled. There were restrictions on what combinations could be carried in what proximity to each other. Some things could be carried on dedicated cargo airplanes but not on airplanes with passengers. All of that was taken care of by shippers and by our people who accepted shipments and checked paperwork, but pilots were supposed to know all that stuff to be able to ensure that hazmat they carried was legal and that paperwork was complete and correct. It was exactly the kind of tedium my mind is incapable of absorbing.

Because it was recurrent hazmat training, those who hadn't yet had initial training got to go home early that day. Airbus people wanted class to run late because they'd all get an extra day's pay. They'd had to start their day early, driving to Louisville to demonstrate they could open the airplane door they opened and closed every time they flew.

The instructor who came in to conduct hazmat training in late afternoon didn't know the Airbus crews stood to make money if the class ran long. They asked lots of questions and managed to drag the class into overtime.

Pilots say most airlines give captains free rides on their last simulator checks. I surmised that DHL wasn't among them. My first session early Thursday morning after four hours of sleep was less than stellar. After a short nap during a lunch break made longer by a simulator breakdown, we all did much better, except that I crashed during windshear for the first time.

I talked with a couple of other 59-year-old pilots about the company's request that some of us consider downgrading before our birthdays. We were short of second officers but overstaffed with captains, so they'd rather have us old guys fill vacancies rather than hire more people.

Napoleon didn't want to be a second officer. I thought he was afraid he'd not make it through training, a reasonable fear in his case. He wanted a $250,000 buyout, a precedent no one thought the company would accept.

The director of operations wanted two volunteers for the back seat of the Airbus. Ken, a DC-8 captain, said he'd take the offer, but only if they'd pay him eighty-one hours a month during training, the amount he'd been averaging with overtime. The company offered 727 captains the higher pay of DC-8 and Airbus captains until our birthdays, but all I cared about was, the Airbus had replaced the DC-8 on the San Juan trip.

Ken called me to discuss how we should talk terms with the company. On Monday, I called director of operations to say that we were generally amenable to the proposition if it didn't hurt us financially or disrupt scheduled vacations. We'd wanted a guarantee that, if we failed training, we'd revert to our captain positions. Getting the higher pay of an Airbus captain until my birthday sounded excessive to me, and I'd have accepted maintaining my 727 captain's rate. I didn't think I averaged enough overtime to make it worth calculating, but the company figured it in.

There was a downside to downgrading early. For those who waited until their birthdays, there would be no pay interruption if there was no class available at that time. On a captain's birthday, pay would drop to the second officer rate at his seniority, and he'd be paid even if he sat at home for weeks or months waiting for a class.

Airbus training was set for six weeks in May and June. I planned to drive the truck and camper to Cincinnati rather than pay for a hotel.

We were on the ground more than two hours after landing in Charlotte one evening and had no idea why we'd been sent from Cincinnati so early. The mechanic drove the first officer and me to a nearby convenience store for sandwiches.

The first officer rode in the back of the mechanic's van. A metal partition separated the back end from the front seats, but there was a gap between partition and roof. When we got back to the airport gate near the cargo area, we had to show ID cards and driver's licenses. The first officer handed his forward through the gap. The guard did not look in the back of the van to see if the first officer matched his ID photo. There could have been half a dozen terrorists back there with rockets and machine guns. The mechanic said guards never looked in the back. That casual approach to security only reinforced pilots' perceptions that security measures passengers saw were mostly for show.

I didn't sleep well the night before my final proficiency check in the simulator, but I passed in spite of myself and went to the terminal to catch a ride home. It took fifteen minutes to get through Delta security.

I'd carried a short, double-ended screwdriver bit on my key ring for more than twenty years and security people had never objected. It wasn't sharp and was too short to use as a weapon. The security man that evening said I couldn't take it through. The only tools a passenger could carry were the tiny screwdrivers that come with eyeglasses repair kits—miniature stilettos. I could go back out and mail my screwdriver home, but that would make me miss my flight. I shook with anger as I took the screwdriver bit off my key ring. Standing in my socks, I said without thinking of consequences, "It's a good thing Richard Reid had that bomb in his shoe instead of up his butt."

The security man laughed.

Crew Scheduling called me at home one Wednesday morning to ask if I could go to Sacramento that afternoon to fly the inbound to Cincinnati that evening. I was ticketed on Southwest's three o'clock flight from Seattle to Sacramento. That gave me plenty of time to drive, be delayed by work on the Hood Canal Bridge, and go through the extensive security that last-minute, one-way tickets triggered. TSA didn't seem to realize any new wave of terrorists would buy round-trip tickets, in advance.

The ticket agent warned me I'd be singled out for additional screening. I hid my ticket and went through security easily as uniformed flight crew on duty. At the boarding gate, the agent noticed the code on my ticket and told me I'd be pulled from the line for additional screening when we boarded. I held my receipt and boarding pass with the pass covering the code on the receipt. The agent waved me through to the airplane.

I knew it would be my last landing in Salt Lake City. I flew the airplane by hand through the climb and didn't turn on the autopilot until we had leveled off. I got an extremely nice landing and marveled at how well I could fly when I concentrated.

I detected an undertone of hostility from a couple of pilots because I'd accepted the company's early downgrade offer. The situation wasn't addressed in our contract, and the union was grieving the procedure by which Ken and I had been selected.

Old captains returning to the back seat angered junior second officers. Instead of moving up, they lost bidding position every time a senior old guy moved back. One second officer half my age had been pushed down four numbers by old captains. We didn't lengthen their distance from an upgrade class, but losing bidding position affected quality of life.

A young second officer and I exchanged long emails. He wasn't angry at us, but he didn't like what the system did to him. He recognized that losing our seats by government fiat years before we qualified for Medicare and Social Security required many over-60 pilots to stay on the job.

* * *

My final flight was mechanically uneventful but emotionally laden as I realized with each phase of flight that it was my last. Passenger airlines make a big deal of a retiring captain's last arrival with fire trucks spraying arches of water over the taxiing airplane as it approaches the gate. DHL didn't do that, but there was nobody to see it in the middle of the night anyway.

I told people that I was at peace with the end of my flying career, but I wasn't sure that was true. I felt a little like I had when I realized, at 35, that I was too old to become a policeman or a fireman.

Airbus Second Officer

I put the camper on the truck, loaded bicycle and kayak into the cargo trailer, and left for Cincinnati early in May for downgrade training. Five days later, after stopping in Boulder to visit family, I pulled into River Ridge RV Park overlooking the Ohio River near Rabbit Hash, Kentucky, where I'd stayed five years earlier. After unhitching the trailer and driving out from under the camper, I hooked up electricity, water, and sewer in my temporary home. I grilled elk steak, heated green beans, and boiled potatoes. Thunderstorms interrupted sleep, but I didn't dare put in earplugs because I needed to hear my alarm in the morning.

I packed my old black steel lunch box with elk sandwiches and drove the eighteen miles to school on narrow Kentucky roads through wooded hills. The first day of Airbus school including watching *The Caine Mutiny* as an illustration of the need for cooperation among crews.

The next morning, ten of us got into a van for the ninety-mile drive to the UPS simulator in Louisville to demonstrate we could open an Airbus door. It was our first airplane with inflatable evacuation slides. The four of us new to the airplane also had to go down the slide.

Morning session the next day was short because the instructor had personal business to take care of. With three hours off for lunch, I studied for the afternoon session on the electrical system. After the 727, it looked simple.

School was dull, not because the information was boring but because our instructor had never served on the Airbus or any other large airplane. Much of the instruction was PowerPoint presentations, all of which were on our training CD. Another instructor told Ken to study hard on his own, as we'd be self-taught.

Bank statements had not arrived before I left home, and there was a check on my personal account that I didn't want to have to explain. I called Crew Scheduling and was amazed that seats to Seattle Saturday morning were open.

My dog was ecstatic when I drove up the driveway in a rental car. I spent the day reading mail, taking care of bank statements, and reading newspapers. I called American to list as jumpseater on a flight from Seattle to Chicago Sunday morning.

Our small class didn't take anywhere near the time allotted to cover scheduled material, so, even with wasted time and long breaks, we did not fall behind. I spent evenings going over what we'd covered in class, especially the parts I'd slept through after lunch.

One afternoon, we four second officer trainees drove from the training building the short distance to the airport and climbed all over an Airbus that was on the ramp for the day. The large entryway had a warming oven and an electric pot for heating water. Four seats against the bulkhead faced aft, one just inside the door and three on the other side of the cockpit entry. There was a restroom on the left just behind the cockpit and a coat closet with room to store baggage on the right. After 727s and DC-8s, the Airbus cockpit felt large and roomy. The second officer's seat almost fully reclined. I considered that an indication of how little the third crewmember had to do in the mostly automatic airplane.

After dinner, I was tempted to take my kayak out of the trailer and paddle around on the Ohio River, but I went over review questions instead. I was weakest on the electrical system.

I drove to the airport to ride our Airbus to San Juan. The trip had been changed to a non-stop, so there was time enough in San Juan for legal rest during the day. I went out to the airplane with the second officer to follow him around and observe how preflight inspections and cockpit setups were done in the real world. I stayed on my feet most of the flight both to stay awake and so I could observe better. I was the only one in the airplane who had flown to Puerto Rico, so I briefed the pilots they'd probably get the Lagoon Visual to Runway 8. The ATIS broadcast told us to expect the shorter Runway 10.

The captain told his first officer to ask for Runway 8. I said that sometimes they closed a runway for iguana removal. Tower said Runway 8 wasn't available. It was closed for iguana removal.

Class ran late one day because we had two hours of hazmat training tacked on to the schedule. That was the third time in two months I'd had that annual training, first when it became required, again in recurrent training, and again in Airbus training. Nothing I had ever studied interested me less.

A real pilot replaced our ground school instructor for the class on the Autoflight system. As I absorbed his explanations, I got excited about how neat the system was and took notes. From time to time, I reminded myself that was pilot stuff I'd never use.

One morning, we watched an entire movie in class. The only remote relevance was, Anne Heche made the mistake of inflating a life raft inside an airplane.

After lunch, we went out to the parking lot to practice putting out fuel fires. Then we drove to a nearby motel to use the swimming pool for life raft training. Never mind that Airbus life rafts are the inflatable exit slides. We trained with the standard round raft—jumping into the pool, flipping it upright, and climbing in.

Ground school was finally finished. I drove to the airport to get a ride home for the weekend to mow the lawn.

My innate laziness had allowed me to believe that, since I'd been a second officer on the Boeing and had fifteen years' experience on that airplane, the Airbus, with its simpler panel and automatic functions and only two engines would be simple. I'd forgotten what every second officer figured out for himself, if someone hadn't told him, that the job had nothing to do with flying skill. I'd become complacent because, in the last generation of airplanes requiring a second officer, there was not much to do.

The second officer's job was like a video game in which things had to be done in a certain order. Posters and diagrams showed the correct order in which to check the panel and flip switches, and the flow was different from that in the 727.

I taped posters of cockpit panels and controls to the inside walls of the camper in approximately the same relative positions as the panels in the airplane and did what I should have been doing weeks earlier—rehearsing flows and checklist responses. I had a lot of catching up to do in a training program that, aside from ground school, moved fast. We were supposed to be up to speed before we got to the simulator.

A normal training crew was one captain, one first officer, and two second officers. The captain flew two hours with one second officer at the panel and the other observing. The first officer flew the second half of the session with the other second officer at the panel. Our crew had two captain upgrades who swapped seats and roles. Each had to spend half an hour at the second officer's panel.

We second officer trainees got to fly one takeoff and landing each from the left seat while the captain candidates took turns at our panel. The airplane felt squirrelly when flown by hand, but I liked the pushbutton operation of the thing. Ken didn't like automated systems. He'd rather have been back in the DC-8, or perhaps even a DC-3.

Homework was filling out takeoff and landing data cards for various weights and weather conditions. The cards, about the size of a paperback book, were fill-in-the-blanks with spaces for weather conditions, flap settings, trim, speeds for different flap positions, and power settings. I filled out three cards we were supposed to take to the simulator to use the next day. In cleaning up clutter, I threw away all three cards and had to do them again in the morning.

In the simulator, I screwed up a few things by unconsciously reverting to Boeing procedures, a frequent occurrence in the heat of battle. In the 727, pushing up on the APU master switch starts the APU. In the Airbus, all it does is arm the start button, and I forgot to push the button. Then, with an apparent anti-skid problem, I did what we did first in the Boeing—push the lights to see if they tested okay. In the Airbus, the procedure was different, and testing the lights before going to the written procedure was a no-no. I spent the weekend studying and practicing cockpit procedures with the posters on camper walls.

To save expensive simulator time, we usually skipped preliminaries such as cockpit setup and engine starts. That made it difficult to make the mental leap to where we were in the scheme of things.

I asked my instructor if he wanted me to check circuit breakers, part of setting up the cockpit. In the simulator, circuit breakers frequently popped at the instructor's touch of a button, just to see if we were paying attention. He said not to bother, and I thought that meant for the entire session. When he noticed later that I wasn't checking them from time to time, he popped one to fail a fuel valve.

After starting the APU in the air—something we could not do in the 727—I forgot to turn battery switches back to Normal, and not for the first time. Naturally, my instructor overheated the batteries and we got a smoke warning. What I did to solve my problem of forgetting to reset switches I'd moved temporarily was to keep a pad of yellow Post-it notes on the table top and slap one on the panel next to any switch I had to come back to.

One captain and my partner passed Sim 5, but the other pilot and I would repeat it the next day. Sim 6 was pushed back a day for all of us.

My biggest problem in the simulator was trying to do things too fast. When the airplane is on fire or the wings are falling off, it's difficult to stay calm. Watching my methodical training partner reinforced the notion that haste makes waste. I wasn't paying for sim time, so there was no incentive to hurry. I went into the simulator for my repeat session feeling confident and competent. My plan to stick Post-it notes to the panel worked perfectly. I forced myself to speak slowly, read slowly, and to really see what I was looking at.

In the airplane, excessive rate of climb is obvious because ears pop. With the simulator's lack of pressurization, we had to check the gauge frequently on days when such problems were scheduled. I misread the gauge, different from the one in the 727, and thought our climb rate was normal.

After correctly following procedure for a manifold fault, I looked at the air conditioning pack not running and said to myself, "I can fix that," and proceeded to violate a rule I'd made for myself when I was a radio station engineer: Never mess with good enough.

Restoring the second pack was not necessary, and I used my head instead of following written procedure line by line. A few minutes later, when I had time to get back to that problem to make sure all was well, I asked aloud, "Why did I do that?" just as my instructor leaned over my shoulder to ask, "Why did you do that?" I couldn't answer either one of us. I'd do Session 5 a third time.

I spent that afternoon going over every possible problem that I might have to deal with in that familiar Sim 5 scenario. I spent most of my time on things that I hadn't seen in the first two attempts. Training department pilots would fly, so my session would not be complicated by problems up front. A third attempt was do or die.

Training called to say I'd been rescheduled with a different instructor. Whether that was because my regular instructor had the weekend off or because he'd had enough of me, I neither knew nor cared. An instructor I didn't have history with would be to my advantage. My new instructor was an Irishman with a great sense of humor and an inexhaustible supply of jokes. Stephen had been a school teacher before he became a pilot. My second repeat of Sim 5 went well.

Wednesday morning, I performed a cockpit setup with posters on the camper walls without the book in my hand. After breakfast, I settled in to study for my oral exam. I studied another couple of hours in early afternoon and closed the books. If I wasn't ready, I didn't know what I'd use for an excuse.

I thoroughly previewed the next day's simulator agenda and ran through the entire session in my head. I felt confident for the first time since the end of ground school.

I thought it was my best day in the entire simulator course. When we were finished and waiting in the debriefing room for our instructor, Ken and I agreed that I'd only muffed a couple of minor items. Both of us were stunned when our new instructor came in and said I'd have to take Sim 8 again! Ken and I wondered if Stephen was dyslexic and had gotten us confused.

I'd exposed ignorance of the two landing gear warning systems. They'd not been explained well in ground school, and I apparently hadn't absorbed the paragraph in the manual that explained how the two systems were inter-related. Boeing systems were still in my mind, and I'd applied that knowledge to a problem in the Airbus. Strike one.

While solving a fuel system problem, I didn't consult the book line by line when I flipped switches and turned knobs to restore normal operation. I'd read the procedure and the book was still open to it on the table, but because I used logic and memory instead of referring to printed instructions for each step, I didn't close one valve the book said I should have. Even though that omission had no negative consequences, it was strike two.

Then, when we got hit by lightning and lost all generators, I couldn't find the knob I was supposed to turn.

In the Boeing, the electric system switches and gauges are at eye level. In the Airbus, they are near the bottom of the panel, just above the table. My poster in the camper was higher than the panel in the airplane because that was a convenient place to hang it. That put the electrics on the poster at eye level, just as they'd been in the 727. Strike three.

My instructor and I would be on our own for my repeat session with no other students in the simulator. He made some remark about having to slow me down. I joked that maybe I should drink only a quart of coffee in the morning instead of half a gallon. He said I should drink decaf. It occurred to me he may have been right. I always drank all the second pot of coffee before I left the camper only because I knew it would be cold in the carafe before I got back.

I caught myself speeding up a couple of times during my makeup session, then started doing everything with what seemed to me exaggerated slowness. The session was good and I enjoyed myself. After all those years, after all those training programs, after all those upgrades, on the last one of my career, I finally learned to slow down.

After sleeping eight hours, I woke to a cool, foggy morning. I brewed only half the usual amount of coffee and ate a big breakfast. Then I reviewed checklists and flows and listened to Car Talk on NPR.

I got through the day, though that was about all I could say for it, and my instructor recommended me for a checkride. He admitted he'd driven me harder than necessary. He didn't want me to be complacent.

Less caffeine seemed to have made a difference, but Stephen said I should drink none before my checkride. Then he got on my case for not going faster on checklists.

My company oral exam was short and simple and I knew everything until my examiner asked me to show him how to test the pressurization on preflight. My mind went stone blank as I tried to remember in what order buttons were pushed and what I was supposed to see when I pushed them. It was a far simpler procedure than I was trying to make it, and I'd not forget again.

Aside from not noticing a fuel problem that gave no lights or flags, I did well on my checkride until dealing with a hydraulic problem. I was ready to stop in the complicated procedure when the problem seemed resolved before I got to the last line that would send me to another checklist. I knew something was missing and was trying to figure out what it was when my examiner said, "Get out that procedure again and let's go over it again. I opened the book and saw what I'd missed and finished the procedure correctly.

* * *

After a week at home, I rode our jumpseat to Cincinnati conscious of the three-stripe epaulets on my shoulders. I signed in for a series of daytime transcontinental flights and met the second officer assigned to supervise me the first few trips. We went over paperwork and headed out to the airplane. Wayne's procedure was to have me do nothing the first day but observe him doing the job. He found more things wrong with the airplane before we got off the ground that day than would occur in an average simulator session.

We had an easy two-hour daytime flight to Dallas-Fort Worth, and, after less than an hour on the ground, we were on our way to San Francisco with a lovely view of Monument Valley in late afternoon sun.

Wayne noticed I was drowsy as he showed me what paperwork I needed to do en route. I told him I was running a caffeine deficit, so he showed me how to operate the hot pot in what had been the forward galley when the airplane carried passengers. The only thing in the galley drawers was instant decaf, so I got coffee out of my suitcase and brewed Ethiopian espresso.

We stayed at the Nikko hotel in downtown San Francisco. As usual, Crew Scheduling hadn't thought to reserve a fourth room.

While out walking the next morning, I stopped at Tully's and bought a stainless steel one-quart French press. I preferred coffee that had gone through a paper filter, but the press would be easier to use in flight.

Wayne took me out to the airplane earlier than normal that evening so I'd have two hours to do what I would learn to do in one. We flew to Los Angeles and then to New York. Crossing three time zones eastbound made the night short. We wouldn't fly again until the next afternoon. After the grind of weeknight flights in the 727 with daytime sleeping on short layovers, Airbus duty felt positively civilized.

Wayne took time to show me things that either hadn't been covered in training or that hadn't sunk in. We blocked out exactly on time for the six-hour non-stop daytime flight from New York to San Francisco. My scheduled week with Wayne would be over when we got back to New York, but I'd have had only four preflights in the week of long flights and long layovers. I was still muddling through fuel verification computations, one of several paperwork things that could have been taught during wasted hours in ground school. Wayne wanted me to have another supervised flight or two after our week off.

I slept on the DC-8 to Seattle. I dreamed I was on my first unsupervised trip in the Airbus and had no idea what to do.

During days off, training and procedures had time to organize themselves in my brain, and I did much better on preflight and paperwork when I returned to Cincinnati. Much of the paperwork we'd done in training wasn't necessary in the real world, and when I realized that, getting ready to fly was easier.

I was still worried that Wayne might insist on more time with me. That would make me miss my trip to San Juan. When he asked if I was feeling comfortable, I said I was. He said he'd cut me loose. Before I went to the hotel for the day in Cincinnati, I went out to the airplane with Wayne once more to observe how he did the job when he didn't have to explain what he was doing.

My first flight on my own in the back seat of the Airbus went smoother than any of my IOE trips, but, after landing in San Juan, I completely forgot to do the post-flight inspection that mechanics duplicated anyway. I was just happy to be there.

We got out of Cincinnati a couple of minutes early on my first trip to Los Angeles, even though I'd called Maintenance because brake wear indicators appeared to be out of limits. They weren't. A mechanic explained that there were two different types of indicators. I added that to the list of things they hadn't told us in ground school.

I didn't remember to begin filling out the log until we were taxiing to parking in Los Angeles. It was a point of pride for second officers to be able to hand the completed log to the captain for signature the moment the brake was set.

We had a long distance to taxi, time enough for me to print crew and jumpseater names, fuel added and receipt number, out and off times, fuel burn, and fuel remaining. As we reached our parking spot, I wrote in the last items—block-in time and total flight time—as the captain set the brake. While doing all that, I forgot to call company radio to say we were on the ground. I also forgot to turn down the heat in back and roasted the jumpseaters riding there.

When we got back to Cincinnati after Tuesday's New York trip, I checked the computer to see if I'd been awarded any open time trips. Three extra trips would run me up to eighty-three hours for my last month at captain's wages and net me $2200 in overtime. My birthday present would be a 55% pay cut.

Although the seated pilot was supposed to wear his oxygen mask when the other pilot was out of his seat at high altitude, few did. Many pulled the mask out of its clip and held it ready to put it on in an instant. The first officer did that on our way to San Juan, and the hose pulled out of the overhead. The only way to stop oxygen from flowing was to shut off oxygen to all masks.

We decided to leave oxygen turned off. If something happened and we needed it, I'd pass my mask forward to the first officer and I'd use the nearest jumpseat mask. All I'd have to remember to do was turn the oxygen valve on before we passed out.

After changing out of uniforms, we walked to breakfast at a restaurant the first officer liked. On the way back to our new hotel—the Marriott in Condado—we passed a massage parlor. The captain, a notorious whoremonger, couldn't stand to pass it by. We were almost back to the hotel when he turned around. To check prices, he said.

Catering for the Mexico City flight was on our airplane one morning. We kept quiet and ate it on the way to Puerto Rico. We were late enough arriving to report fourteen minutes late that evening. The captain's attitude toward the contract was indifferent. I told him the only way we'd ever get long layovers back was to delay departures every time we got in late enough that contract rest required it. But I wasn't the captain, so we showed at the regular time.

A friend and his wife came over with a bottle of wine on my 60th birthday. They'd had dinner in Sequim and stopped by because they were in the neighborhood, they said. A few minutes later, another friend and his wife happened by, also with a bottle of wine. Slow to catch on to Barb's plan for my birthday, I thought two friends happening by was a happy coincidence. Then more people arrived, and we all sat around drinking beer and wine and coffee and talking about health issues, just as old people do.

While hunting that fall, I noticed with some surprise that my strength and stamina weren't what they'd been all my life. That was excuse enough to buy an ATV. I'd resisted those machines primarily because so many people abuse them, riding where they aren't supposed to, bypassing gates, and spoiling hunts for those who have hiked into the back country. I decided to regard the machine as a small Jeep rather than as a motorized horse. As long as I kept that frame of mind, I'd not become one of those ATV riders who makes everyone else mad.

Katrina turned 31. She was older than I'd been when she was born. Another sign that I wasn't a kid anymore was how tired I was after spending several days moving furniture, sanding floors, and applying new finish.

I drove to southeast Washington for a muzzle-loader elk season. Before falling asleep, I lay awake in the camper thinking about the awkward situation I'd both endured and thrived on for nearly four years. Something would have to change, and, as much as I shunned decision making and confrontation, I would have to make that change. What the most difficult decision of my life was coming down to was, who could I not say goodbye to?

One day I overheard Barb mention to her mother that she was going to string Christmas lights in my mounted elk's antlers. I told her she was not. She said it would be cute. I said it would be tacky. I was beginning to think of such petty arguments as nails in a coffin.

Nereida and I talked Thanksgiving evening via computer on the AOL chat feature. I got an email from her later saying I seemed very happy in my house with family around and that maybe we should end our relationship.

It would have made our lives easier if Nereida had been able to do what I could not, if she'd been able to walk away. But if Barb put Christmas lights on my elk, the marriage was over anyway.

I went to work the day after Thanksgiving. After being on vacation longer than I'd been on the Airbus, I went out to the airplane half an hour early and had a hell of a time trying to remember how to test everything.

A week later, I loaded the camper and went elk hunting east of the Cascades for a few days. After a day at home, I drove to the west end of the Olympic Peninsula to hunt deer.

I got vacation days for the 26th and 27th, but no decision on Christmas Eve and Christmas Day. If I didn't get those days off, I'd be sick. The indignity of the 55% pay cut was bad enough, and I was not going to sit in a hotel over the holiday with my seniority.

We were adjusting to my new income level. I'd been on reduced pay long enough to see that income met household expenses with almost nothing left over.

Early in January 2003, I went in for my FAA medical exam. My doctor suggested I take glucosamine for aging joints.

Not having my phone charger cost me nearly a thousand dollars. I'd left it at home, so I turned on my phone only when I wanted to make a call or check messages. Crew Scheduling tried to call me right after I'd gone to the hotel for a scheduled day off in Cincinnati. They wanted to know if I wanted to go right back to San Juan. The trip would have been good for nine hours at 150%. I bought another charger to keep in my flight bag.

We landed in San Juan one Wednesday exactly on time, but strong tailwinds should have gotten us in early, even after a de-icing delay in Cincinnati. The captain, whom I'll call Scrooge, had realized that headwind would make our return flight longer than scheduled, and, if flight time for the round trip went over schedule, we'd get paid extra for each extra minute. When that opportunity arose, Scrooge did everything he could to extend flight time.

On the way to San Juan, he flew at economy speed and refused shortcuts when ATC offered them. He refused the runway that put us next to our parking ramp and insisted on the runway that required ten minutes of taxi time. Because we blocked in exactly on schedule, nothing he'd done could be criticized. He could argue that insisting on the longer runway gave us a greater safety margin. He'd saved fuel by flying slowly, and he'd arrived on time.

I'd not have objected if he always flew that way, but he didn't. Picking up an extra few dollars for each extra minute seemed to be the primary motivating force in his life. He'd do nothing to make up for lost time and everything he could to lose time when he could back up his actions with company policy or safety considerations.

I didn't get to sleep easily. I saw no difference between what Scrooge was doing and stealing money from petty cash. What bothered me more was that his style of flying padded my paycheck, too.

On the return to Cincinnati against headwind, he didn't try to save time with shortcuts or flying faster. We flew the flight plan exactly and arrived late enough for a few minutes' extra pay.

After New York on Thursday, we flew to Los Angeles, a long trip with opportunity to add time. Scrooge called our block-out a minute earlier than it was, but I'd already logged it correctly. He called our block-in time a minute later than it was, but, again, I'd logged it correctly. Scrooge grumbled, but he didn't change the log.

On one trip with padding possibilities, he insisted on taxiing to a runway on the other side of the Cincinnati airport, an extra ten minutes or more. I'd never used that runway and didn't know anyone who had. His rationale was, that runway was a few feet longer than the one we'd otherwise have used and, therefore, safer.

When I talked about Scrooge's slow-flying for extra money, pilots were quick to name a couple of other captains who did the same thing. When flying with one of them for the first time, I worked in a comment at the outset about how I hated that sort of sleazy behavior, and, when I was on his crew, he never did it.

At home the last week in January, I felt another cold and sinus infection coming on and, as usual, prevented a sore throat by sleeping with cough drops in my mouth. Nasty weather made it easy to stay inside and defeat my cold.

Because a trainer had bought my San Juan weekend trip and the Tuesday following was an off day, I could have stayed home until Tuesday evening. But San Juan was on my schedule posted on the refrigerator, and, even if I wasn't completely healthy by Friday, all my ears and sinuses had to do was survive the descent into Cincinnati and another on the jumpseat to San Juan. I'd have four days in the sun to get well. I spent most of the week at home eating Sudafed and aspirin. In several days of inactivity, I even got tired of reading.

Nereida was at work, but she'd left beer and food in the refrigerator, a bottle of nasal spray on the table, and a card welcoming me home. I spent the afternoon watching news of the *Columbia* shuttle crash on TV.

I rode to Cincinnati Tuesday evening and flew back to San Juan Wednesday morning. When Scrooge said, just before takeoff, that the flight would be a moneymaker, I said, "Wouldn't it be easier just to find out where they keep petty cash and take a few dollars each week?"

He said he was just flying by the book. Yeah, I thought. His checkbook.

Coming out of San Juan, we were three minutes late because of a minor error on the load sheet. Scrooge told me to log it as on time. I told him he'd have to write that in the log because I wouldn't. He said he'd be glad to. That fraudulent log entry would have added time to a flight that was already going to pay extra. I told Scrooge that, if the trip went over scheduled time, I'd tell Crew Scheduling to take three minutes off my pay sheet.

Captain Scrooge didn't respond for a few seconds. Then he said to log the actual time and call the station to correct the on-time he'd given them over the headset. He muttered something about the inconsistency of someone who would step out on his wife but quibble over a few dollars. I conceded many character defects and said stealing from my employer was not one of them. I said I thought he was creating an opening for anyone who might want to get him fired.

Scrooge was a generous, likeable man, but my disdain for padding his and his crews' paychecks created a rift between us. My discomfort was compounded by contemplating differences, if any, between his padding flight time and my abusing sick leave.

We landed at Cincinnati in snow and fog. After sleeping a couple of hours in a chair, it was time to fly back to San Juan. Weather delays made our departure late. In spite of my discomfort at being part of another padded flight, the three of us spent most of the trip in enjoyable conversation about how we got into flying and dumb things we'd done in airplanes.

Our driver was a young man Scrooge had yelled at several days earlier for following too closely. He drove the same way everyone else on the island did, and I'd said as much. Scrooge said he didn't care, he didn't want to get killed on the way to the hotel. I suggested he might want to fasten his seatbelt.

The driver drove much more slowly than usual. He stayed off highways and took us on a long, roundabout route. Scrooge was talking and didn't seem to notice. At the hotel, I quietly told the driver that I enjoyed the scenic ride and that I knew why he'd done that. He grinned.

Because we'd arrived late, we'd depart late, and there was time for Nereida to pick me up when she got off work that evening. We went to the apartment and sit on the balcony in the cool breeze high above the beach and talked of small things in our lives until it was time for me to go.

The company complained that we used sick days when we couldn't get to work. We did that because we weren't allowed to take unscheduled vacation days, but Scrooge and some other pilots routinely picked up trips from open time for extra money and then called in sick.

There was good economic reason for keeping sick banks low. We'd been told our short-term disability insurance clock started at the time of illness or injury, but the policy didn't begin to pay until sick leave ran out. If we had a year of sick leave in the bank, we'd run out of sick days at the same time the short-term disability clock ran out, and all our insurance premiums would have been for nothing.

The sun had just come over the horizon as we were on final for Runway 4R at JFK, and its fiery reflection off Manhattan windows started at the south end of the island and worked its way north at the speed we flew. For an instant, the Empire State Building looked like a pillar of fire.

We had four jumpseaters on the return to Cincinnati. Three rode in back and a DC-8 first officer rode in the cockpit. Just before we started engines, he pointed at a circuit breaker on the overhead panel and asked if it was supposed to be out. Jumpseaters were reluctant to say anything, especially on an airplane they weren't familiar with, so I thanked him for mentioning it. I preferred a little embarrassment to something bad happening.

I slept four hours in Cincinnati before leaving for San Juan. Both pilots were from the training department, but we survived anyway. We got out of San Juan seven minutes late that evening because our dispatcher changed the fuel load and new paperwork arrived late. The captain told me to log it as on time. Then he asked if I was okay with that.

It wasn't going to put us over scheduled flight time, so there was no extra money involved. I said, "You're the boss, but I put the real time in *my* logbook."

The hot subject in the rumor mill that week was DHL International's purchase of Airborne Air Freight with intent to spin off ABX Air and form an alliance with it identical to its long-term agreement with DHL Airways. The problem was, we had an exclusive contract to carry nearly all DHL freight in the United States, and ABX Air had a similar agreement that gave it exclusive right to fly Airborne's freight, regardless of who owned Airborne.

I saw no immediate problem. We'd fly the stuff we always had, and they'd do the same. Only the name on the boxes they carried would change. Eventually, the pilot groups would probably have to merge, I thought. I didn't worry about that because I couldn't do anything about it and because I was too old for it to matter. Younger pilots drove themselves crazy with speculation.

Cincinnati was ten degrees above freezing when I went out to preflight the Airbus to San Juan early one Tuesday morning, but the airplane had arrived from a long flight with extra fuel. Cold fuel caused frost to form on the wings as it sat on the ramp. Frost on the bottom of the wings wasn't a problem, but I couldn't tell looking from the cargo door if the white stuff on top was frost or dew. I called Ramp Tower to get on the de-ice list, but, as warm as it was, there was no de-ice list. People came out to look at the airplane. After looking only at thick frost on the bottom of the wing, they agreed to de-ice us.

All we needed to satisfy safety concerns was to have the frost on top of the wing hosed off, but our manual allowed only two options—wings and tail or the entire airplane. We ordered wings and tail only and the boom truck operators sprayed the entire airplane anyway. Maybe they got paid by the gallon.

I left almost everything in the apartment in San Juan Friday because I'd be back in a few hours for the weekend. When we landed in Cincinnati, there was a new plan. As soon as the airplane was unloaded in San Juan Saturday morning, it would fly to Miami and return to San Juan on Monday for the normal non-stop to Cincinnati that evening. We couldn't legally do all that, having just flown the long trip in from San Juan. The captain was off and the first officer was a reserve. I was put on AVL for the weekend and a fresh crew was given our San Juan weekend trip.

I explained to the crew scheduler that that my toothbrush was in San Juan, and I asked him to put me on the flight release as a jumpseater. He reminded me that, on AVL, I could be called out to work on Sunday or Monday. I told them I hadn't had a disciplinary letter in my file in many years and could afford one.

The scheduler told me to remember to put myself down in the jumpseat book for my return Monday night. When I told him I already had and that I'd signed it off with his initials, he laughed. Before I went out to the airplane, I realized that, if Crew Scheduling called my cell phone and didn't reach me, they'd call my home. I went to the computer and logged out sick for Sunday and Monday.

An article in a Seattle newspaper speculated that DHL International might dissolve agreements with both DHL Airways and ABX Air and contract all flying out to lowest bidders. That was a scary prospect. It would put me out of work at an age at which I was too old to be hired by another company but without enough money to retire. Worse, it would put me out of Nereida's life, unless I made her my entire life. I read no more speculation on DHL's plans and soon forgot about that article.

For the first time in longer than I could remember, I did not sleep on the ride from Seattle to Cincinnati but read a book the entire time. That didn't matter, as I could sleep four hours on the jumpseat to San Juan. I'd sold the trip to my best customer in the training department.

I sat in a jumpseat in the entryway reading a book as the airplane was loaded in Cincinnati. One of the loaders told me I was wanted up front.

The captain explained that load planners had created a false zero-fuel weight by a process and for a reason neither of us understood, and it did not include jumpseaters. There was no real weight problem, but numbers said I could not ride. Even though weather-induced backups would delay us for at least an hour, SOC would not recalculate the load sheet. He said I wasn't on the jumpseat list for the flight.

The captain and I talked to the flight manager and Crew Scheduling by phone and by radio to no avail. He had no choice but to bump me. It was the first time in his career he'd done that.

I got off the airplane and rode a crew bus back to the Hub in heavy rain and ran upstairs to Crew Scheduling and asked to see the jumpseat book. I'd listed for the seat, but the scheduler

I'd talked to had forgotten to pass it on to Load Planning and to Dispatch.

I was furious. The scheduler on duty that night wouldn't give me the errant scheduler's phone number. I asked for his address so I could spend the weekend at his house instead of paying for a hotel.

The flight manager came in and said I'd have been bumped even if I'd been properly listed. SOC had done that to jumpseaters several times already that week.

As we understood it, System Operations Control staff were not employees of DHL Airways but worked for German-owned DHL International. FedEx and UPS, in an attempt to force revocation of DHL Airways' operating certificate, argued before Congress that DHLI had operational control of DHL Airways. To the extent a foreign entity controlled access to our jumpseats, their allegation seemed correct.

A Delta jumpseat to Orlando and a two-hour connection to American would get me to San Juan by mid-afternoon Saturday. Departure was delayed and we landed in Orlando too late for me to make my connecting flight. I waited for the next one in the evening, but it filled.

I called a nearby hotel and walked into the lobby just as free happy hour ended. I forgot I was in uniform and grabbed a couple of plastic glasses of beer and drank one as I checked in. When I dropped a dollar in a tip jar, the server was wiping down the counter and putting things away. He asked if I'd like another. I carried two glasses of beer to my room. I'd been awake thirty-four hours except for a nap on the flight to Orlando. The next morning, I got the last seat on the first flight out to San Juan.

I'd left several messages on Nereida's answering machine as plans changed. I hadn't heard from her, and there were no messages when I turned my phone on after we landed. When a man offered me a ride, I took it.

Nereida wasn't home but came in a few minutes later. She'd gone to the airport to pick me up but we'd missed each other. She was in a rare bad mood. Stress from uncertainties of our relationship was getting to be too much.

We talked about the practical considerations of a future together, and, though I didn't set a date, I made a commitment to leave my wife and my life. Thinking seriously and in detail of such things was both frightening and exhilarating. I felt like I was getting ready to leap off a cliff in the dark, not knowing what was below.

When I got back to Cincinnati, I started to apologize to the flight manager for my tantrum on Saturday morning, but he cut me off and said I'd not been out of line.

My Memorial Day weekend in San Juan was changed. After we unloaded in Puerto Rico Saturday morning, we'd fly the airplane to Greensboro, North Carolina, where it would be in maintenance until Tuesday. I emailed Nereida and called and left messages explaining the change in schedule.

Our driver in San Juan was waiting for us, as Crew Scheduling hadn't let him know we'd not be going to the hotel. I walked through the cargo building and glanced over the parking lot from the loading dock. Nereida was standing by her car, happy to see me if only for a few minutes. We said goodbye after our short visit and then we didn't take off for another two hours. Nobody in Cincinnati had told San Juan that the airplane wasn't staying, so there was no load manifest for the empty airplane and nobody in the offices who could generate one.

The mechanic called the load boss at home and he came out to the airport. The load boss called Cincinnati and someone told him they'd faxed the load sheet to us. The fax machine was out of paper.

We loaded paper and the machine began to spew out its backlog. By the time the fax got to ours, the empty airplane had heated in the sun and smoke detectors went off. We had to order an air conditioning truck to cool the airplane for an hour before we could fly. Retirement was beginning to look good.

Over a weekend that summer, our name changed from DHL Airways to Astar Air Cargo. It was difficult to make the case to Congress that we were separate from German-owned DHL when our name was also DHL. All of our airplanes but one DC-8 retained DHL's ketchup-and-mustard colors. The remaining DC-8 was painted white with blue and red trim and the Astar name.

DHL Airways, or Astar Air Cargo, had new owners, the previous major shareholder being too obviously not running the airline. Management outlined plans for our future. It all sounded pretty good, except none of us liked the computer-selected name. It is pronounced A (as in ABC)-star, but many pilots shortened the first A.

The company issued large stickers with the new name to cover the DHL on our manual covers. Some of us tried to get away with retaining the DHL device on our hats. We were proud to be DHL. Nobody wanted to be ass tar.

Barb and I put the camper on the truck and filled the utility trailer with gear for a weekend camping trip in eastern Washington. I'd planned to take the ATV but decided not to at the last minute. I didn't bother to reload the trailer to balance weight properly.

The first night we camped, I unhitched the trailer so I could maneuver the truck and camper into a level spot. The next morning, our truck blocked the road through the campground while I was hooking up the trailer. A man in a pickup had to stop and wait for me, so I was in a hurry.

When I jacked the trailer tongue down onto the hitch, it wasn't quite centered enough to settle onto the ball. If the heavy ATV had been in the back, I'd have been able to lift the hitch easily and move it. Instead, I gave it a shove and it slipped off the ball and dropped to the asphalt on top of my sandaled left foot.

The man jumped out of his truck and the two of us lifted the hitch and dropped it into place. All my toes worked, so I assumed I'd be okay. Pain became intense, though, so we canceled the trip and went home.

The doctor estimated it would be four weeks before I could walk normally. There was nothing to do but stay off my foot and keep it elevated. I figured I was going to get very tired of reading and of stairs in the following few weeks.

Nereida and I were coming up on five years in a relationship I hadn't been looking for, one I'd thought might last a few months at most. Nearly all of our time together had been hours and days in what was, for me, a vacation environment. Nereida had little exposure to my disorganized style of living and might find it as intolerable as my wives had. She did not know what I was like when I was busy with hunting, fishing, writing, and building projects, the things that occupied my normal life. On the other hand, she and I were alike—scatterbrained, impulsive, and happy. It was not a case of attraction between opposites.

Decision time became more and more difficult to push back. Five years seemed a good deadline. I thought I'd be able to leave my marriage and the county I'd lived in more than half of my life early in the coming year, but I was frightened by the biggest unknown facing me: I didn't know what effect guilt might have on me and a new life.

Aside from surviving emotionally, I had to consider whether I could survive financially. I knew several pilots who'd arrived home after a week at work to find nobody home, bank accounts cleaned out, and divorce papers on the table. One of our older pilots had fallen for a young flight attendant, left his wife to marry her, and then his bride went on medical disability, sued for divorce, and was awarded high alimony because she couldn't work. He'd have to work as a second officer until he died. I told him it would have been cheaper to shoot her. He said he'd considered it.

In a way, I was betting my life that Nereida was not scheming in a similar way. But none of those other guys thought they were being set up, either.

One thing I was certain of: My bourbon consumption had steadily increased in the preceding couple of years.

Just before Labor Day weekend, DHL International announced layoffs of drivers, cargo handlers, and office personnel to solve the problem of duplication caused by buying Airborne Express. DHL kept the Airborne ground operation and fired the DHL people who had built the company and who had personal contact with DHL's loyal customer base. DHL employees who had been with the company from its earliest days lost their jobs, and, if they wanted severance packages, they had to stay on long enough to train their replacements. Pilots were the only employee group in DHL's domestic operation with union protection.

Buying Airborne Express as a quick way to increase the size of the company was the Germans' first huge mistake, we thought. The Labor Day Massacre was the second. When DHL business customers learned why strangers were picking up and delivering packages, many were not happy. We heard stories that, when fired DHL people went to work for FedEx and UPS, many of those customers went with them. I was beginning to understand how Germany had managed to lose both world wars.

An article in USA Today told of how corporations were beginning to realize that their valuable people were not upper management but mid-level people who did not aspire to run the company, employees who did their jobs well and then some. It was too bad DHL's bean counters hadn't read that before they fired their best people.

I looked at my schedule and saw a way to begin my vacation a few days early. I'd lose nearly five hours of overtime, and it would mean dropping the last San Juan weekend before vacation. That would add two weeks to time away from my island home, but hunting season is hunting season.

I phoned my best customer in the training department—I'll call him Jerk—and left a message. Jerk called back to say he'd like the weekend trip. I asked if that was definite, as I needed to make plans based on his flying it. He promised he would buy it.

On Sunday, I began a week of daytime transcontinental trips I'd picked up out of open time. That series of trips would end in New York on a Friday morning with a day in the hotel before deadheading to Cincinnati. I went online to check ticket prices from New York to Seattle and found a cheap one-way on a Delta non-stop and grabbed it.

We flew from San Francisco to Los Angeles empty and picked up three race horses and their escort. The horse stall fit in the airplane just like a cargo container. The human escort had a medical kit including horse-sized hypodermic needles filled with tranquilizers. Although he didn't ride in the cockpit, it would have been an excellent way for a terrorist to get control of a large airplane. But the public doesn't see the insides of cargo airplanes, so the people running the security show don't care.

Thursday evening, we flew the last trip of the week to Los Angeles and then to New York. I'd spend a few hours in our hotel on Long Island before my Delta flight to Seattle. An email from Jerk said a family matter had come up and he couldn't fly my weekend trip after all. That would cost me a weekend of hunting and my non-refundable airline ticket.

The first time Jerk backed out after promising to buy a weekend trip from me, I was out more than a thousand dollars in unpaid sick leave. I called him after reading his email to tell him he should keep his promise to buy the trip and then call in sick. He said he had no sick leave in the bank. Too bad about my airline ticket, but he'd be happy to buy any of my San Juan weekends the next month.

Only once in my life have I slapped a grown man, but it was a good thing Jerk and I weren't talking face to face.

I considered throwing away my ticket and flying to San Juan, but I got on the computer and took unpaid sick leave and used my ticket as planned.

The last night before leaving my Colorado elk hunting camp, I had a dream about work. I was preflighting the airplane when the captain arrived and asked to see my ID. He was required to be sure everyone had their badges. I didn't have mine with me, and the captain I jumpseated with out of Seattle hadn't asked to see it. With no badge, I couldn't jumpseat home to get it.

While coffee brewed that morning, I turned on my computer to type hunting notes. A popup calendar reminded me to call that afternoon for a December jumpseat. Re-entry into the work world had begun.

My right shoulder had been tender ever since hunting season. A physical therapist thought it might be tendinitis or impingement on my rotator cuff. I didn't know what a rotator cuff was, and pain in the joint went away. The only lingering reminder was in a muscle near the biceps that felt strained or bruised.

Ever since selling my Nissan truck, I missed having a small, economical vehicle for commuting to Seattle and for short trips near home. I started checking ads for a suitable small car, hoping I'd find a Miata first. Instead, I got a stick-shift Toyota Echo good for forty miles per gallon on the highway.

We had a full Airbus crew riding with us to New York one Friday. When I got out to the airplane, the deadheading second officer asked if he could do anything to help. I didn't want help because it would derail my routine.

After landing and parking, the jumpseating crew emptied the closet and set luggage on the entryway floor. That was a normal courtesy, but doing anything beyond that was taboo. After we finished checklists, I left the cockpit to open the entry door, stepping over and around the assortment of crew bags to disarm the inflatable slide on the right side door. That was routine procedure even though we almost never opened that door. If a door was opened from inside without being disarmed, the slide would instantly inflate and deploy. I did not intend to become one of those who'd blown a slide.

Something seemed vaguely odd when I moved the lever to disarm the door and inserted the retaining pin. I was crossing through the obstacle course of bags to open the door on the left when one of the deadheading pilots told me the doors were already disarmed. What had felt odd was that I'd moved the lever to re-arm the door. The second officer who'd offered to help in Cincinnati said he'd disarmed the doors for me.

He was an older Airbus crewman with more time in the airplane than I had. He knew that nobody ever touched those doors except the second officer on the crew, and what I'd almost done was the reason why. I screamed in his face, "Don't *ever* fuck with my doors!" I don't remember what else I said.

The man avoided me for the rest of our time at DHL. I didn't for a moment consider apologizing for dressing him down in front of others. I thanked the pilot who had spoken up and saved me from blowing the slide.

The beginning of 2004 marked five years together for Nereida and me. I made plans to talk to a lawyer to find out what divorce would cost. Nereida seemed surprised as much as delighted. Maybe it was because in the beginning I'd told her never to believe a man who said he'd leave his wife for her, not even me.

I took the canoe and my dog to a lake for a day of duck hunting, something I seldom did and rarely successfully. It was good to be on the water. Fog and mist insulated me from the world. By the end of the afternoon, my shoulder hurt again.

At my annual medical appointment that week, my doctor told me to take triple the recommended amount of Aleve or Ibuprofen for shoulder pain, and, if that didn't work, he'd inject cortisone. I bought a big bottle of Naproxen.

When we pushed back in Cincinnati to fly to San Juan one morning, we got a Pneumatic light on the Master Warning Panel but no corresponding lights anywhere else and no obvious problems. I'd seen that in that airplane before and knew it was a gremlin. While we were on the radio with Maintenance Control and I was explaining that it was not a real problem, the light went out.

After we landed on our return to Cincinnati, the flight manager got on the radio and asked us to come to his office. We couldn't figure out what we'd done wrong, other than get out early three nights in a row. Maybe he wanted to tell us our stellar performance was making sluggards feel bad. Whatever it was, he'd had sense enough to wait until we were on the ground to call us so we wouldn't be distracted in the air.

The new vice-president in the new Astar Air Cargo had been monitoring company radio communications the night before. He'd been impressed with our get-on-with-it attitude, our realization that there was no real or legal reason not to fly with our weird little problem. He'd asked the flight manager to convey that to us.

We were pleased that a big-shot bothered with an attaboy over something so trivial. I thought that incident, plus shakeups in middle management, were good signs for our future. Cynics disagreed.

By mid-morning, snow began on Long Island. The company wanted us to leave the hotel half an hour early. When we got to the airport, a mix of light freezing rain, ice pellets, and snow was falling through fog, except that fog wasn't fog anymore. In new terminology, fog was mist. I never did learn what mist was supposed to be called.

The airplane was supposed to have been loaded early, but it was covered with snow and ice. Loaders spent fifteen minutes sweeping snow and chipping ice off the K-loader. Then it took three trucks more than an hour to blast ice and snow off the airplane with hot Type I fluid. Only one of the trucks had capability to pump Type IV anti-ice. Had precipitation not stopped, we'd have had to start de-icing all over again. As it was, block time to Cincinnati was twenty-six minutes over guarantee for the trip, extra money for once honestly earned.

The muscle in my arm was still sore, and something as innocuous as reaching up to scratch an ear caused paralyzing pain in my shoulder. I called my doctor's office to make an appointment.

When I checked email in Los Angeles, I learned I had an appointment to talk with a lawyer. That email moved impending divorce from abstract to reality, and it was scary. My first officer advised me not to tell my wife the real reason I was leaving. He said telling her I had a girlfriend would make her vicious and vindictive. I told him it was important to me that she not think it was her fault. He said I'd be better off saying I was gay.

My doctor ordered an MRI. With luck, a small incision to allow a surgeon to reach in and file off bone spurs would solve the problem. At worst, I'd need a new shoulder.

On Tuesday, I finally talked to a lawyer. I was apprehensive and nervous, but he put me at ease. What was a big deal to me was routine to him. I told him I'd not do anything before August because of vacation schedules and because I needed time to be sure I'd made adequate preparations for uprooting my life and destroying my marriage.

While we were taxiing in at Cincinnati, Ramp Tower called to say the second officer was "Code 90." I replied, "Oh, you mean a drug test? Okay." Why they insisted on using a code that everyone knew to inform us we'd been selected for a random drug test was beyond me.

The first officer asked me why I wasn't going to New York with them. That was news to me. When we went inside, I learned I'd been given a day off so a reserve second officer could get hours he needed to avoid going out of currency.

With the distraction of the impending drug test and the news I had a day off with pay, I disarmed the door we seldom opened and was talking to the jumpseater who'd ridden back there as I stepped across to disarm the door we always opened. I pulled the retaining pin and stowed it but didn't move the lever.

Aware of the danger of blowing a slide by opening an armed door, and also aware of the ease with which I was distracted, I'd developed a two-stage method of moving the door handle. If I just grabbed it and swung it, my brain wouldn't have time to register the warning beeps, so I routinely pulled the handle up enough to trip the alarm, paused a second, and then moved it the rest of the way. That procedure saved me from blowing the slide that day.

The captain I flew to New York with one night handled airplanes more roughly than any other pilot I ever flew with. His abrupt braking and turns would not have been acceptable in passenger airplanes, and he saw nothing wrong with slipping a huge swept-wing airplane to lose altitude, even though we'd had no training in that and had no idea of what the aerodynamic consequences might be. He was aware that his doing that made others uncomfortable, and he asked me if I minded. I minded very much and said so. I told him I was not a test pilot.

We were closed up and waiting to start engines and the airplane shuddered as though a giant terrier had given it a shake. I said, "What the hell was that?"

The captain said, "This?" and the airplane shuddered again. He had pedaled rapidly left and right a few times, and the fluttering rudder shook the entire airplane.

"Jesus," I said. "Haven't you been reading about Airbus rudders?" Failure of the vertical stabilizer in a newer version of the Airbus had caused a crash near JFK more than two years earlier.

"That's the plastic ones," he said. "Ours are steel."

I was beginning to wonder if I'd live long enough to retire.

I spent time at home finishing trim details inside the house that I'd put off for eleven years. I tried to mentally prepare for my wife's possible reactions to my impending announcement, anything from calm acceptance to smashed dishes and a restraining order.

My shoulder hurt more and more often. If I needed surgery, I wanted to wait until August, right after my backpacking trip and recurrent training so I'd have time to recover before hunting seasons. Medical leave might keep me from having to take unpaid time to settle a divorce and living arrangements.

I got a second cortisone injection. I told my doctor that I didn't want to have to get a shot every couple of months for the rest of my life. He said if that second dose worked for three years, that would be an acceptable interval. It didn't last three weeks.

When I next went to work, the crew lounge was abuzz with DHL's decision to abandon its brand new building in Cincinnati and move the sort hub to Airborne's privately owned airport in Wilmington, Ohio, just over an hour northeast by road. If I moved to the Cincinnati area to be near work, I'd have to be within ninety minutes of both Cincinnati and Wilmington to avoid having to move when DHL moved. I wanted to be close enough to both airports I could be on reserve at home. I thought I'd prefer to live on the south side of the river, as Kentucky seemed less civilized than Ohio.

I was gathering bags on my way out to preflight the Los Angeles airplane when my captain mentioned that an Airbus was going to San Juan instead of the scheduled DC-8. I found the reserve second officer and traded with him, assuring him pay was the same for both trips. Later, I realized the San Juan trip paid international override and higher per diem. I hoped the other guy wouldn't be upset if he figured that out, too.

The captain was an FFDO, a Federal Flight Deck Officer. Pilots of airplanes carrying mail were required to carry guns in the past, but, as firearms began to replace sex as our primary cultural taboo, the practice had gone away. After 9/11, Congress established a program to arm pilots as a last-ditch defense against hijackers. I favored the idea but not the method. Unless the pilot was on duty and in the cockpit, the gun had to be carried in a locked bag and the bag had to go aboard as checked baggage. Many of those recognizable bags disappeared before policy changed.

I didn't apply for the program primarily because I didn't approve of that method of carry and of the extra handling required to transfer the weapon from bag to person and back again. Guns go off by accident only when being handled, which is how a pilot shot a hole in his own passenger airliner a few years later. The other reason I didn't apply was, my shoulder wasn't in good enough shape for me to go through training.

I thought the chance of a repeat of the 9/11 hijackings was almost non-existent. They'd played that trick, and trying it again when the entire world was watching for it would not be successful. I thought cargo airplanes were even less at risk. Headlines are small when a freighter crashes.

FFDO's weren't supposed to talk about the program, but the captain was a talker and the first officer was a gun enthusiast and an FFDO applicant. They talked about the training and the firearm for the entire trip.

When we got into the van in New York Wednesday morning, two jetBlue flight attendants were already in it, sitting in the back row. I sat just in front of them and asked them to buckle up. They gave me questioning looks, and I explained I didn't want them to kill me on their way through the windshield. They fastened their belts and I thanked them. One asked what I'd have done if they'd refused. I told him I'd have gone back there and sat with them.

Of seven people in the van, all but Captain Scrooge, sitting behind the driver, had buckled up. The man behind me said we were all in trouble because the captain would kill the driver in a crash. I said, "I know, but you can't tell him anything."

I told the flight attendants of my fantasy of being the only one using a seatbelt in a fully loaded van that rolls over. I'm the only person uninjured, and I step out of the wreckage, gather my bags, and flag down a cab.

One of the flight attendants asked if I'd call for an ambulance. "Yes I would," I said. "As soon as I got to the hotel."

Storms west of New York caused long delays getting out of there. Usually when JFK was landing Runway 13L and departing 13R on the other side of the airport, we were able to get the left runway anyway and cut our taxi distance to almost nothing. Because of weather, we had to taxi all the way around the airport in line with everyone else. That took more than an hour.

At a point where the line we were in merged with another string of airplanes, Ground told a Pakistani 747 to follow an America West that was a couple of airplanes behind us. The Pakistani thought an American Eagle turboprop two airplanes ahead of us was the one he was to follow. When the Eagle moved up, the jetBlue between us and the small airplane began to move, too. So did the 747 on the merging taxiway.

The Pakistani got on the radio to complain of being cut off. Ground tried to explain the situation, and conversation got hot. The Pakistani captain didn't understand the difference between American Eagle and America West. I hoped he'd realize the error was his when the AWA Airbus came into his view. Otherwise, I figured he go home and join Al Qaeda.

The surgeon I'd been referred to said I had a torn rotator cuff. Surgery would put me off work for three to six months. I asked if I could go backpacking first. He said that was fine, that my shoulder would tell me if I shouldn't do something. We set a pre-op appointment for 3 August and surgery three days later, the day I was supposed to start recurrent training.

Knowing there was real damage in the joint made me reluctant to use my arm, and I had a long list of things to do before leaving for Wyoming.

Every year, my hiking partners and I swore we'd get our pack weight down, but we never succeeded. With packs around fifty pounds, we carried less than usual, but, as usual, we weren't in shape until the hike was over.

The day after we set up camp, I went fishing. The creek bank steepened as I worked my way upstream and became a craggy cliff that went almost vertically into the water. I waded on submerged rocks and found handholds on the cliff, moving my fly rod ahead a couple of feet and working my way to it. A rock that had been part of the mountain for millions of years broke off in my hand. To keep from falling, I grabbed the cliff with my right hand, and pain unlike any I'd ever felt shot through my shoulder. I tried to fish as I returned downstream, but even casting left-handed hurt.

I spent a couple of days wading through short-term disability insurance paperwork. Aches and pains I didn't know I had surfaced when I stopped taking pain pills prior to surgery. Barb and I got up before dawn to make an early ferry to Seattle.

Sensation began to return to my right arm before bedtime. Although opposed to taking drugs generally, I became a fan of Percocet and began to understand why the surgeon had said I'd be out for several months. I slept sitting up on the reclining couch for two weeks so I wouldn't roll over on my arm. I had only nine weeks to get well enough to shoot a rifle. The surgeon said I'd be healed enough by deer season, but in those first days, I thought I'd have to shoot left handed.

I began getting insurance checks from the first day I missed work. We'd been told disability checks would begin after sick leave was used up. Barb thought I should call someone. I said it wasn't up to me to do other people's jobs for them. I did enough of that at work. I opened a savings account for the early insurance checks in to make it easy to pay them back when they caught their error, if it was an error. Months later, I quietly asked others who'd been out on disability if their checks started on the first day regardless of sick leave. They had.

I got a lot of reading done and watched a lot of movies on TV. It was only a short time before I could type with both hands again, so I started a novel and a screenplay, working on them side by side simultaneously in my new, wide-screen computer.

Sitting still for days on end was not possible, which may have been why my shoulder improved faster than the therapist expected. Mowing the lawn, moving water hoses and sprinklers, and cleaning gutters all kept my shoulder moving, but I couldn't go to work until I had enough strength and mobility to climb out an airplane window and descend to the ground while hanging onto the handle of an inertial-reel cable.

I needed to know that Nereida would be happy in my world. The possibility that being with me on my turf would affect her like a splash of cold water worried me, but if she could live with me in the woods for a month in a camper the size of a large closet hunting deer and elk in rain and snow and enjoy it...
As soon as I was sure my shoulder would be well enough for hunting, I bought her a round-trip ticket to Seattle

Just before the middle of October 2004, I loaded the camper onto the truck and filled the cargo trailer with hunting gear and the ATV. I found Nereida standing in cold, wet air outside baggage claim at SeaTac dressed suitably for the tropics. Our first stop was at REI for clothes and boots. She'd had her gall bladder removed five days earlier.
The first day of her adventure must have felt like landing on Mars. Throughout those four weeks in the woods, she woke every morning eager to see what the day would bring. Everything we saw and did was a first for her, and she greeted it all with delight and childlike awe. Snow that fell on us was the first she'd seen. When we saw animals, she always saw them first. I often forgot she had to take it easy because of her recent surgery because she never complained. She didn't like wasting time sitting around anymore than I did.

My attorney assured me an uncontested divorce with property settlement agreed to in advance would take no more than three months. He advised selling our house. We'd clear enough on the sale to buy separate houses. I checked with Crew Scheduling to be sure I could take vacation immediately after being cleared to return to work at the end of December. Barb and I accepted an offer on the house we'd built that far exceeded the amount we'd hoped for.
I'd been looking at houses in Ohio and Kentucky on the Internet. I wanted one that, over the span of a few years, I could improve enough to make a profit when it came time to retire and sell. I emailed a real estate agent and made arrangements to spend a few days with Nereida in Wilmington in February looking for a place to live.

Buying the house in Ohio was complicated by foreclosure and the seller's bankruptcy, but we got permission to live in it free until the deal closed. When my vacation ended at the end of February, I had to take the recurrent training I'd missed in August. Nereida arrived at the end of March.

I had to work twice in April, but I didn't have to fly. I was called out in the middle of the night to drive the sixty miles to Cincinnati to replace the hot-standby reserve when he had to fly. I put on my uniform for the first time in more than eight months. When I signed in, I asked which airplane I was supposed to preflight. There was no spare Airbus. So why was I there? A blank on a clipboard had to be filled. I slept for a couple of hours until I was released and drove home. My other work that month was to fly support for a simulator session. I bid Reserve with preference to be called last. In May, I flew one trip.

I'd expected my divorce to become final by early April. First one attorney was on vacation, then the other. I emailed mine early in June: "I am getting married on June 22. It would be extremely convenient to be divorced before then." FedEx delivered the papers two days later.

Friends came from Puerto Rico to act as best man and matron of honor. Nereida and I were married by the mayor of Wilmington in his office on his lunch hour. We celebrated with dinner at home and invited our real estate agent and his wife to join the four of us. The house was filling with furniture, and we still didn't own it.

Near the end of June, I flew to New York and back. A few days later on a Sunday, I began a week-long, daytime schedule, flying to Austin and on to San Francisco for a weekend layover. By the end of July, I had logged only thirty hours since returning to work. I needed fifty hours every six months to stay current.

My plan to bid Reserve and stay home began to come apart. Junior Airbus second officers were bidding to fill first-officer vacancies as we acquired more 727s. When Nereida and I drove to Colorado in July, I got calls nearly every day asking if I wanted to fly a trip for 150%.

We became homeowners the last day of August. In September, DHL moved its entire Cincinnati operation to Wilmington. Airborne Express people considered us interlopers, and the merge was not smooth. DHL had just begun an advertising campaign with the theme that service was back in the shipping business. Airborne ground people loaded our airplanes only after Airborne airplanes were loaded, and they didn't hurry. Our flights got out several hours late for days.

I'd never heard of theft problems at DHL until we moved to Wilmington. When a few Airborne ground people were caught driving off with computers and prescription drugs stolen from shipments, company security began searching all vehicles leaving the secured air side, including buses transporting flight crews from the parking ramp.

DHL's domestic shipping business declined to the point it no longer needed two airlines. Younger pilots worried about their futures. I'd thought of staying on until I turned 70, both to build up my 401K and because Social Security checks would be significantly larger. If the gloom-and-doomers among us were right, I might not have that option.

I worked most of the last three weeks in September. My schedule included deadheading from Los Angeles to San Francisco on United. The TSA screener thought the first officer was working, but he saw tickets sticking out of the captain's and my shirt pockets and shunted us aside for more intrusive inspection. Our first officer disappeared down the concourse toward the gate.

The captain wanted to tell the security man about his error, but I talked him out of it. If we said anything, they'd have shut down the entire concourse, moved everybody out, and made us all go through security again.

I closed out 2006 flying more than I wanted to. Between flights, I usually drove home for an hour or two in the middle of the night for a meal and clean clothes. Bidding reserve meant getting called out often. Going to bed at night wondering if the phone was going to ring a couple of hours later got old. It would have been less stressful to bid a flying line and know what my schedule was, but I preferred being at home.

My father died in 2007. With my share of his estate, plus profit from selling the house in Sequim, plus my 401K, it occurred to me that I might not have to work forever. My father's death brought me one generation closer to the end of my own life. I had to ask myself how much of my remaining time I wanted to spend flying from hotel to hotel or wondering if the phone would ring in the middle of the night.

* * *

We'd been working three years without a contract. The union bought large ads in the Cincinnati papers. Large numbers of Astar pilots walked an informational picket line in Wilmington while Nereida and I were hunting in Colorado. Tension at work increased, and retirement looked better all the time.

My left shoulder began feeling about the same as the right one had before surgery. An MRI showed bone spurs and a torn tendon. I wished it was bad enough to require surgery, because right then seemed like a good time to be off work for a few months.

I came down with a severe cold and sinus infection a few days into December and had to take sick leave. I took one more day after I felt well enough to go back to work. I didn't want to retire with a lot of time in my sick bank.

Crew Scheduling often called on a day off to ask if I'd accept reserve that night. I usually did, unless they called after I'd poured my evening drink. I almost never got called out and got paid overtime for sleeping in my own bed.

Nereida and I drove to Cincinnati to talk to a Fidelity retirement advisor. We filled out questionnaires, and the man ran our numbers through his computers' various economic projections. He thought we'd not estimated high enough for groceries. I told him we planned to supplement our diet with deer and elk.

Yes, I could retire in the summer of 2008. Both of us could live long lives without fear of going broke, even if the economy went to hell as it had in 1929.

I knew I'd been extraordinarily lucky to fly big airplanes for a living after a late start and without a college degree. But once I realized I didn't have to do it forever, the idea of not working at all became pervasive.

I got home from a trip soon after midnight and was in bed an hour later. At three o'clock, the phone rang. I put my uniform back on and drove to the airport to sit hot reserve. I left my bags in the car, checked in, then slept in a recliner for two hours until my cell phone rang and I was released.

The phone didn't ring Wednesday night and I slept ten hours. In spite of rain and wind, I spent the day building a storage shed. Again, the phone didn't ring and I slept all night.

Near the end of March, I learned from a friend that his wife had died. The same day, I heard that another friend's husband had died. Such news occurred more frequently as I grew older. The sooner I retired, the better.

Building and painting a storage shed had not made my left shoulder happy. I sometimes woke in the night from pain of sleeping on it.

Crew Scheduling called one Sunday in April to ask if I'd accept a reserve assignment for Monday. Nothing flew on Monday, but a storm had put the Sunday sort so far behind schedule that crews would likely time out. If I took the reserve day, I might have to fly, might have to go to the airport for hot reserve, or might earn my 150% at home in bed.

I was called in Monday evening and was released as soon as I got to the airport. I earned nearly five hundred dollars for a ten-minute drive to the airport. Payback came the next night. I went to the airport expecting to doze for dollars and had to fly to New York.

While driving home from Cincinnati one day, Nereida and I stopped at an RV dealer's lot. I thought we might be spending a lot of time on the road before we figured out where we wanted to settle. It seemed a good idea to buy a big trailer that we'd be comfortable in for weeks at a time. If I'd known what fuel prices would become, I would have bought a little one.

Spring weather finally reached us. We bought a small boat and trailer. Later that spring, we bought a motor scooter from a neighbor. I became aware of an impulse to buy toys for retirement while I was still on a payroll.

We were eager to take our new trailer on its maiden voyage. We spent two weeks cruising back roads and secondary highways to spend a week in Maine visiting friends and looking over the area with retirement in mind.

My first flight in August was to New York. A second officer instructor I didn't know rode along for a SOLO observation, just what I didn't need on my first trip after many weeks off. He was a stickler for detail, a dedicated nitpicker. That didn't bother me unless he expected me to actually do all the useless things he suggested. I listened to everything he said, though, keeping in mind that there is always something new to learn, and a few of his comments on my deficiencies were valid.

I began spending time on the computer looking at land for sale in Wyoming. Colorado was crowded and expensive. Wyoming was neither. My ideal was to live within walking distance of a trout stream. We planned to go to look at Wyoming land in October after hunting pheasants in South Dakota.

Something in my left shoulder popped while I was mowing the lawn. Three Naproxens took the edge off, and it felt better the next day.

The premium for short-term disability insurance took a big jump for 2008. Too many captains went out with undefined back pain just before they turned 60 so they'd draw disability for a year based on captain's pay. I considered dropping the insurance. I wanted to put off shoulder surgery until after I'd retired so I wouldn't be helping raise insurance rates for the rest of the pilots again in 2009, but, if my shoulder couldn't wait until I retired, being uninsured would cost me a bundle. I renewed.

We had the early departure from New York, the one scheduled out at the peak of rush hour. Taxi time was an hour in good weather, twice that in bad. We spent the last twenty minutes of taxi time with our tail to the wind, the air conditioning packs pumping our own exhaust into the airplane. Just after takeoff, we got an alarm indicating smoke in the cargo bay. By the time we got our oxygen masks on, the light went out.

We thought of all the jet exhaust we'd sucked in and did not declare an emergency. I went back to check the cargo and saw no sign of smoke or fire. We didn't write anything in the log. Life was simpler that way.

We'd planned to leave for South Dakota on the last Monday in October 2007, but my having to work the Friday before didn't leave enough time to get the trailer ready. Naproxen, even in triple doses, couldn't cope with the pain in my shoulder. I called the orthopedist I'd seen a year earlier and made an appointment to see him Tuesday morning.

Cold wind worked in the pheasants' favor, and our group got very few. Because of strong headwind, Nereida and I decided not to drag the trailer to Wyoming. When we got home, I learned that one of our pilots had died after surgery at age 60.

I could no longer ignore my crippled shoulder. I scheduled surgery for after deer season. Being off work while recovering from surgery would be a trial run at life after retirement. My greatest challenge would be structuring time. I'd have to treat writing as a job, not as something to do when I wasn't doing other things.

I'd not been deer hunting that fall because the ground was dry and moving quietly was impossible. When rain softened fallen leaves, I put a tree stand in the woods and spent time in it with my crossbow and a book.

We were still working without a contract. Astar management complained that it couldn't staff all flights because we wouldn't accept overtime. Then it announced it was furloughing five pilots. DHL/Astar had never done that. We viewed the move as intimidation and nearly all of us signed up to contribute money to pay the furloughed pilots their full salary every month for a year.

Astar announced it was selling a 727 because so many sick calls over Christmas forced the company to a lower level of commitment to DHL. One of our pilots found the ad for that sale. It was dated 17 December.

It took time to get all the straps on my complicated arm sling adjusted comfortably after surgery in January. I slept sitting up a few minutes at a time the first night. For the first few days, I took the maximum allowable OxyContin and added whiskey in the evenings.

By week's end, I still couldn't lie down. I checked my diary for 2004 and discovered that I'd slept sitting up eighteen nights rather than the three or four I remembered. I stopped taking prescription pain killer as soon as I could and got by on Naproxen.

I took the sling off to let my arm move around in the shoulder joint. It seemed to be improving faster than I remembered from nearly four years earlier. Maybe I'd be ready to go back to work sooner than I'd thought. On the other hand, six months off would take me to sixty-five years and ten months, the age at which I could draw full Social Security. Unable to do physical things, I read and wrote, studied Spanish, and watched a lot of TV.

Union and management had a tentative agreement on a new contract. We'd have to wait a week for details.

Forever stamps were forty-one cents. I asked the clerk if there were twenty stamps per sheet. When he said that was correct, I asked for a hundred. He counted out five sheets. I told him I wanted a hundred sheets, what I figured was a lifetime supply. When I got home, I put them in the safe with my guns.

One evening, we watched *A River Runs Through It*. I was glad to see Nereida excited about scenery in the west. I was afraid she was becoming so attached to our house in the woods in Ohio that she might not want to move. I looked at another bunch of small Wyoming acreages on the Internet.

I ordered ten tons of gravel to improve the driveway and to make a level area to park trailers on. Physical work after weeks of inactivity felt good. When I went in for a final checkup, my surgeon was appalled that I'd been shoveling gravel. My shoulder felt fine. With the end of medical leave in view, I worked hard to finish projects.

The last day of April was my first day officially back at work, but I wasn't qualified to fly until after recurrent ground school and a simulator check. I survived two days of ground school without dying of boredom and lack of interest. I'd hoped it would be possible to never fly again, even though I was back to my plan of staying on the payroll until February. I wouldn't need fifty hours in my six-month look-back until November, and then I'd be on terminal vacation. Vacation would take me to the end of the year, and I'd take the next year's leave-shortened vacation in January and retire when it ran out. But I needed two legs in the airplane with a check airman to complete requalification.

I was getting used to having all my time free, and the prospect of being gone a week at a time or on call at night was depressing. I considered retiring as soon as I finished requalification, giving notice for July and taking all the year's vacation up to then. I plugged that new retirement date into Fidelity's computer program and it worked out all right. Then I wavered again and thought it best to stay with the plan and work into February with the goal of not setting foot in an airplane after my requalification trip.

But we were short of Airbus second officers, and I'd have to fly often. Again, I considered retiring at the end of June. I had enough vacation to cover all my time through that month. The chief pilot didn't think I'd have to finish requalification to do that.

I took a letter to the Airbus chief pilot on 23 May 2008:

> Dear Captain K———:
>
> It is my intention to retire, after nearly 22 years at DHL/ASTAR and after more than 30 years as a professional aviator, effective at the end of the day on 27 June 2008.
>
> I would like to take my remaining vacation between now and that date to the exclusion of any and all duty.
>
> My years at DHL/ASTAR have been beyond my dreams and expectations of how far I might go as a professional pilot when I decided, at age 32, that I was going to learn to fly and earn my living flying airplanes.
>
> Now, at age 65, it is tempting to continue in this excellent job, especially at this time of worldwide economic uncertainty. It is difficult to make the decision to retire from what is a huge aspect of any professional's life, but there is life beyond career, and it is time for me to step away and go fishing.
>
> Most sincerely,

I found one revision to a manual in my mail file. It gave me a strange feeling to drop it into a trash can. The chief pilot said the company insisted I be requalified before I could put in for vacation. I retrieved my manual revision from the trash.

Someone was supposed to tell me on Sunday when my requalification flight would be, but no one called until Tuesday. I was scheduled to fly to Miami Wednesday morning 28 May. I was put on reserve the next day in case my Miami trip didn't go. Friday, the last day of the bid period, I'd be on vacation. The crew planner said she would build a June schedule for me.

I told her I'd prefer 24-hour call and last out. She said it would be. I asked to have days off the last few days of the bid, just in case I couldn't get vacation, as we wanted to go to Sacramento the first part of July.

I had a feeling a cold was coming on. I should have taken a sick day, but I wanted to get my required flight over with. I searched my closet to find all parts of the uniform I hadn't worn since October.

A jackhammer in a nearby room woke me after only two hours of sleep. I was sitting on Miami Beach reading a book when a 727 captain came by and asked if I'd heard the news. DHL had announced it was going to abandon all its flying in the USA and, instead, contract shipping out to UPS.

We went into the hotel and used a computer in the lounge to find DHL's press release. I thought the plan to pay UPS to fly DHL cargo was akin to a hen hiring a fox to babysit.

While we were on the computer, I checked my schedule and discovered my reserve the next day had turned into a New York trip. By the time I got back to Wilmington from Miami, I'd have slept only four hours in the previous forty, so I called in fatigued for Thursday.

DHL's decision to shut down made me reconsider retiring. Our new contract, signed only weeks earlier, had a no-furlough clause that guaranteed we'd all be paid through March 2010. That was the tradeoff for dropping our suit against DHL for not honoring the contract that guaranteed us nearly all of DHL's domestic flying. If DHL shut down the next day, we'd all be paid for nearly two more years for doing nothing. I considered rescinding my resignation letter, but shutting down could take a long time. DHL could change its mind, or the shutdown could take the full two years our pay was guaranteed.

I had to weigh the prospect of free money against freedom from worry. I looked forward to going to bed at the same time and in the same bed every night after more than two decades of flying nights and living half the time in hotels. My job wasn't fun anymore.

The phone rang a little after midnight Wednesday morning. I had to go to the airport for hot reserve. I hadn't slept much because of constant thunder, and I hadn't used earplugs because I needed to hear the phone. I slept at the airport until released. I was on reserve again Thursday, but I had a headache and took an unpaid sick day and slept long and well Wednesday night with no fear of a late-night phone call.

The chief pilot left a voicemail on my phone. Because so many pilots were burning up sick leave before the company's demise, anyone calling in sick had to have a note from a doctor.

I called back and told him my sick days came out of my paycheck, and I was not going to get a note from a doctor as though I were a kindergartener.

I was surprised that DHL had the nerve to have a kiosk at Wilmington's annual Banana Split Festival. If DHL followed through with its plan to shut down domestic flying, that would be the end of eight thousand full- and part-time jobs in a town of only twelve thousand.

On a Sunday in the middle of June, I put on my uniform for what could be, I realized, the last time. I spent the afternoon on reserve chatting with other pilots, eating lunch, and watching golf on TV until I was released early in the evening. The scheduler who called my cell to release me congratulated me on my impending retirement. I told her it felt a little like a divorce.

Astar fired a class of new hires just days before they'd have finished training and received seniority numbers that would have included them in the no-furlough guarantee. Crew Scheduling called me to ask if I'd take a reserve shift on my day off. I said it was funny they needed people to take overtime when they'd just fired the new hires.

My last few days of work were days off. That flight to Miami and back at the end of May 2008 had been my last.

Epilog

Had I known the economy was going to crash a few months later, perhaps I'd have pulled my retirement letter and stayed on. DHL abandoned Wilmington and went back to Cincinnati. Astar parked its Boeing 727s in the Arizona desert, got rid of the Airbuses, and continued to operate a few trips with the remaining DC-8s. From a pilot group of five hundred, fewer than one hundred remained. The most senior captains remained captains. Captains lower on the ladder moved to the right seat and the back seat. Soon, Astar Air Cargo, the former DHL Airways, was gone. The article I'd read in the Seattle newspaper and forgotten had been right. Airplanes flying DHL colors in the United States are flown by contract pilots and several different charter companies.

If I'd stayed on, I'd have been furloughed within a few months when the Airbus went away. I'd have continued to draw my base salary for another year and more after that, but it would not have been worth working even those few months in the bitter atmosphere that intensified until the last airplane was parked.

I got in on the waning days of a glorious profession. It is ironic that, while airline deregulation in 1979 opened doors for people like me, it also enabled a race to the bottom in pay, working conditions, and career stability.

I'm surprised that I don't miss flying. My total time in all three seats is not particularly high, but it amounts to more than two years in the air. When people had asked what I intended to do when I retired, I said I'd do the same things I always did. I just wouldn't have to interrupt them to go to work.

When we began our life together in Wilmington, I told Nereida that Ohio was temporary. I wanted to fish in water I could see through, and my idea of hunting was not sitting in a tree waiting for a deer to come by.

I was still thinking of mountains in Montana and Wyoming. Late in summer a year after I retired, we hooked up the trailer and headed west to visit friends from my Air Force days. After spending a week on the Oregon coast eating fresh salmon, halibut, and Dungeness crab, we drove to Montana and a stretch of mountains I fell in love with when I passed through in 1973. We spent a couple of September days in a forest service campground looking at land and cabins. One frosty morning Nereida said, "I like Oregon better than Montana."

With my tunnel-visioned focus on the Rocky Mountains, I hadn't considered Oregon.

Nereida grew up within sight of the sea, and I like being near salt water, too. When I'm away from dry air, I forget how uncomfortable it is for me to breathe it. Montana reminded me.

"I like Oregon better, too," I said. We broke camp, hooked up the trailer again, and headed west.

Eric Rush
Hebo, Oregon

Acknowledgements

Thanks to Frank Harris, Paul Hornberger, John Price, and Jon Rush for detailed critique, to Robert Ball and Ken Lemon for feedback and suggestions, and to Cassidy Rush for leading me through the complexities of computerized color conversion.

And thanks to Cruz Nereida Delgado Nieves for not complaining about the hours and days and months I spent writing this when she'd have preferred that we'd been fishing.

www.ingramcontent.com/pod-product-compliance
Lightning Source LLC
Chambersburg PA
CBHW071853290426
44110CB00013B/1133